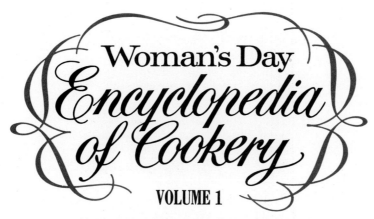

Woman's Day
Encyclopedia of Cookery

VOLUME 1

*in 12 volumes—over 2,000 pages—
with more than 1,500 illustrations in color,
1,000 entries and 8,500 recipes
1,200 menus, 50 specialty cook books
and a host of delightful features by distinguished food writers.*

Prepared and edited by the Editors of Woman's Day
Editor: EILEEN TIGHE
Managing Editor: EVELYN GRANT *Food Editor:* GLENNA MCGINNIS
Art Consultant: HAROLD SITTERLE *Photographic Editor:* BEN CALVO
Associates: OLIVIA RISBERG, CHARLOTTE SCRIPTURE,
CAROLYN STORM, JOHANNA BAFARO

SPECIAL PROJECT STAFF
Editor: NIKA STANDEN HAZELTON *Art Director:* LEONARD A. ROMAGNA
Associates: L. GERALDINE MARSTELLER, HELEN FEINGOLD,
SUSAN J. KNOX, INEZ M. KRECH

FAWCETT PUBLICATIONS, INC.   NEW YORK

PRINTED AND BOUND BY
FAWCETT-HAYNES PRINTING CORPORATION
ROCKVILLE, MARYLAND

Table of Contents

VOLUME 1

ABALONE TO BEAN SPROUTS

Definitions and 801 Recipes
How to buy, store, prepare, cook, and serve ·
Nutritive Food Values · Caloric Values

ACORN SQUASH.................... 6

ALLSPICE 11

ALMONDS........................... 11

AMBROSIA 17

AMERICAN COOKS ARE GOOD COOKS 18

AMERICAN COOK BOOK: Favorite recipes from our fifty states 22

ANCHOVIES........................ 80

ANGEL FOOD 80

ANTIPASTO 82

APÉRITIF 82

APPETIZER COOK BOOK 84

APPLE COOK BOOK 91

APRICOT COOK BOOK........ 104

ARTICHOKE...................... 110

ASPARAGUS...................... 112

HOW TO COOK SUPERBLY:
Aspics 115

AU GRATIN 119

AUSTRIAN COOKERY........ 120

THE SAVORY SCHNITZELS OF AUSTRIA 124

AVOCADO......................... 128

BABA................................ 131

BACON 132

BAKING 134

BAKED ALASKA 136

BANANA 138

BARBECUE COOKERY........ 144

BARLEY 147

BASIL.............................. 148

BASS............................... 148

BAVARIAN CREAM 150

BEACH PLUM.................... 150

BEAN COOK BOOK 151

BEAN SPROUTS................. 159

100 MENUS 160

To help you plan more varied meals
with the recipes in this volume

GENERAL INFORMATION..... 164
COMPLETE RECIPE INDEX.....165

Foreword

To the best of our knowledge, no work of this magnitude ever has been undertaken by any author, editor, or publisher in America. The editors of Woman's Day, with a special staff of experts, present to you this Encyclopedia of Cookery, a comprehensive and colorful library on all culinary matters. The twelve-volume encyclopedia contains in its 2,000 pages over 8,500 recipes from all over the world, 1,500 food illustrations in color, 1,200 menus, 50 special cook books and over 1,000 food definitions. In addition, there are full details about all foods, their nutritive and caloric values, how to buy, serve, prepare, and cook them. There is a history of food and cooking, articles on nutrition, diet, entertaining, menu planning, herbs and spices. Every topic of culinary interest is covered. Five years of intensive work have gone into its preparation, backed by twenty-five years of food and cookery experience in the publication of Woman's Day.

We think you will find this Encyclopedia of Cookery the most complete and authoritative work ever published on the subject. It is a library for everyone who cares about good food and the fine art of preparing it.

The Editors

ABALONE—This red or pink mollusk or shellfish is found in the Pacific Ocean off the coast of California. The beautiful, single, ear-shaped shell is about six to seven inches long and lined with mother-of-pearl which is used to make buttons.

The muscle of the shell is the edible part of the abalone and has a delicious clamlike flavor. It is a great delicacy.

Fresh, canned, and dried abalone is widely used in Oriental cooking.

Availability—In the United States, the fresh shellfish is limited to California. The law prohibits its shipment fresh to other parts of the country.

Caloric Values

☐ Fresh, 3½ ounces, raw = 98 calories
☐ Canned, 3½ ounces = 80 calories

Basic Preparation—Fresh abalone needs tenderizing before cooking. The meat should be cut into thin slices or strips and pounded with a mallet or rolling pin. Abalone must never be overcooked or it will become tough. Properly prepared, it makes an outstanding dish.

ABALONE CHOWDER

4 slices of bacon, diced

6 slices of abalone, pounded thin and diced
1 medium potato, peeled and diced
1 medium onion, peeled and minced
1½ cups hot water
3 cups milk or 2 cups milk and 1 cup light cream, heated
1 tablespoon butter
Salt and pepper

Cook bacon until golden in a 2-quart saucepan. Drain off all but 2 tablespoons of bacon fat from pan. Add abalone, potato, and onion. Sauté until golden brown. Add hot water and simmer until abalone and potato are tender. Add heated milk and butter and blend thoroughly. Season with salt and pepper to taste. Serve very hot. Makes 4 to 6 servings.

ABALONE SAUTÉ

Use abalone sliced thin and tenderized. Sauté in hot butter in skillet for about 1 minute, turning once. Season with salt and pepper to taste.

ACORN SQUASH

ACORN SQUASH—A fall and winter vegetable that belongs to the gourd family. It has a dark-green rind, yellow-orange flesh, and many seeds. Acorn squash can grow as large as eight inches long and five inches across. Its flavor is on the sweet side.

Acorn squash is a native American vegetable, and was unknown in Europe. The first settlers found the Indians enjoying squash; in fact, the word squash comes from the Massachusetts Indian word *asquash* which means literally "eaten green."

Availability—Late summer through winter, but it is at its plentiful best in the late fall.

Purchasing Guide—Should seem heavy for its size and have a hard dark-green shiny rind, free from cuts and bruises, with distinct ridges. May have some orange spots, but avoid those with large areas of orange; this usually indicates overmaturity.

☐ 3 pounds = 3 cups mashed

Storage—Cool, dry, well-ventilated place. If a large number is being stored, arrange squash so they do not touch and air can circulate between them. They can be stored for a few months, but they rapidly lose their quality.

☐ Refrigerator shelf: 4 to 6 months

☐ Refrigerator frozen-food compartment, prepared for freezing: 1 year

☐ Freezer, prepared for freezing: 2 years

Nutritive Food Values—Excellent source of vitamin A; fair source of vitamin C, riboflavin, and iron.

☐ 3½ ounces, raw = 44 calories

Basic Preparation—Before cooking, wash well to remove wax coating. Cut into halves or quarters, lengthwise between ribs, using a heavy butcher knife or cleaver. Scrape out seeds and fiber. Allow one half or one quarter for each serving.

☐ **To Bake**—Put halves, cut side down, in baking pan with ½ inch of boiling water. Bake in preheated hot oven (400° F.) for 40 to 50 minutes, or until tender. Turn halves cut side up; season with salt, pepper, and butter. Add a little brown sugar and/or a little minced onion, if desired. Or season with a pinch of nut-

SAUSAGE-STUFFED ACORN SQUASH
STEAMED ACORN SQUASH

meg, mace, or ginger. Continue baking until butter and sugar melt. To oven-steam, arrange quarters cut side up and cover pan.

☐ **To Mash**—Prepare and bake as directed above. When tender, cool slightly and scrape out pulp. Mash pulp, using a potato masher, electric mixer, or blender. Season to taste with salt, pepper, butter, and brown sugar if you wish, or add a little nutmeg, mace, or ginger to taste. Mashed cooked acorn squash may be seasoned and served like sweet potatoes. It may also be used in pie recipes calling for cooked mashed pumpkin.

Acorn squash may also be peeled and the pulp cubed and boiled. However, baking is the easier method since the rind is hard to cut away.

☐ **To Freeze, Baked**—Bake as described above, but for about 30 minutes only. Omit seasoning. Cool completely. Put halves or quarters in plastic bags, making sure pieces overlap to prevent air spaces, or freezer-wrap in foil. Seal tightly.

To use, defrost slightly, season, and bake until hot.

☐ **To Freeze, Mashed**—Prepare as for mashed squash but omit the seasoning. Cool quickly and pack in freezer containers, leaving 1-inch headspace. To use, defrost slightly, heat in top part of double boiler, and season to taste.

SAUSAGE-STUFFED ACORN SQUASH
    2 acorn squash
    1 pound bulk pork sausage
    1 small onion, grated
 1½ cups soft bread crumbs
    1 teaspoon salt
  ⅛ teaspoon pepper

Cut acorn squash into halves and remove seeds. Oven-steam squash, cut side down, in covered baking pan with ½ inch of boiling water in preheated hot oven (400°F.) until tender. Meanwhile, mash sausage with fork and fry until cooked but not brown. Drain off fat. Add onion, bread crumbs, and salt and pepper to sausage. Fill centers of squash halves with mixture. Reduce oven heat to moderate (375°F.) and bake uncovered for about 30 minutes longer. Makes 4 servings.

BAKED ACORN SQUASH SUPREME
    2 acorn squash
       Melted butter
  ½ cup heavy cream
  ½ cup maple syrup

Cut acorn squash into halves, remove seeds, and put squash, cut side up, in greased baking dish. Brush inside of each half with melted butter. Mix cream and maple syrup and fill each squash cavity about half full of the mixture. Bake, uncovered, in preheated moderate oven (350°F.) for about 1 hour. Makes 4 servings.

STEAMED ACORN SQUASH
Slice acorn squash about 1 inch thick.

Put into large skillet with small amount of water. Steam, covered, until tender. Drain if water has not all evaporated. Pour melted butter over squash and sprinkle with brown sugar. Heat a few minutes longer to glaze squash.

AGAPE—This Greek word means "love." It was used to describe the charity feasts of the ancient Christians, when the rich contributed liberally to feeding the poor in the churches. During more recent times, religious sects such as the Wesleyans and Moravians have tried to revive this custom on a much simplified and almost symbolical basis.

AGAR—A vegetable gelatin made from various kinds of algae or seaweed. The algae are collected, bleached, and dried. Then the gelatin substance is extracted with water and made into flakes, granules, powder, or strips which are brittle when dry.

Agar was used as a jellying agent in home-cooking before commercial gelatin was widely available. It is still used in the Orient in the preparation of soups and jellies, and at home as a thickening agent; in the commercial manufacture of jams, jellies, ice creams, and mayonnaise. It is also used in medicine. It is essential in microbiology, where it is used as a culture medium.

Before the Second World War, practically all agar came from Japan. Since then it has also been produced in the United States and other parts of the world.

AÏOLI or AÏLLOLI—This French word comes from *ail*, meaning "garlic," and defines a sauce of the consistency of mayonnaise, but with plenty of garlic in it. *Aïoli* is usually served with boiled fish; it is also good with cold meats, cooked vegetables, and salads. *Aïoli* is a specialty of Provence, a southern province of France bordering on the Mediterranean, which is famous for its olive oil and well-seasoned hearty foods made with oil.

AÏOLI
    4 large or 8 small garlic cloves
    1 egg yolk
  ¼ teaspoon salt
    1 cup olive oil
       Juice of 1 lemon

Peel garlic cloves. Mash in mortar or garlic press, or mince fine and then mash with tip of knife. Combine garlic with egg yolk and salt. Stir in, drop by drop, 3 tablespoons of olive oil. Stir in lemon juice. Stir in remaining oil, a little at a time, until sauce is thick. Makes about 1 cup.

AKVAVIT or AQUAVIT—The word comes from the Latin and means "water of life." *Akvavit* is its Scandinavian spelling. It is a colorless or light-yellow spirit. It is usually distilled from grains such as barley, or from potatoes, and is lightly flavored with caraway. The "water of life" is a favorite drink of the Scandinavians and northern Germans, who drink it in tiny glasses, followed by a beer chaser. In these countries, *akvavit* is always taken with food. The most famous *akvavit* comes from Aalborg in Denmark.

À LA—This French term means literally "in the manner of." It is usually followed by the name of the person who first created the dish (Waldorf Salad à la Oscar), or by the name of the person for whom it was created (Chicken à la King), or by the name of the place where the dish originated (Eggs à la Russe), or by one of the main ingredients in the dish (Macaroni à la Béchamel).

À LA CARTE—The literal translation of this French term is "in the manner of the bill of fare." *À la carte* is used to describe a meal in which each dish selected is paid for separately. The opposite term is *table d'hôte*, another French term, which means "the host's table." Here, one fixed price covers the cost of the whole meal.

À LA GRECQUE—This is a French culinary definition, meaning "in the Greek manner." The term describes vegetables cooked in a mixture of oil and vinegar, or lemon juice, with seasonings added. The vegetables are served cold or chilled. They make excellent appetizers or salads.

Artichokes, asparagus, celery hearts or stalks, cauliflowerets, cucumbers, mushroom caps, tiny white onions, whole spring onions, green and Lima beans, and zucchini squash can be cooked *à la grecque* with fine results. The vegetables are prepared for cooking in the usual manner and cut into bite-size pieces. Frozen vegetables can be used and need not be defrosted before cooking.

BASIC À LA GRECQUE RECIPE FOR VEGETABLES
    3 cups water
       Juice of 2 lemons or 2 tablespoons cider vinegar
  ½ cup olive oil
  ½ teaspoon salt
       Peppercorns
    1 celery stalk, minced
  ½ teaspoon crumbled dried thyme or 1 sprig fresh thyme
    1 bay leaf

Combine all ingredients in saucepan. Simmer, covered, for 5 minutes. Pour boiling mixture over vegetable that is to be cooked. Cook until vegetable is just tender. Cool in liquid. Drain and chill.

Makes about 3½ cups.

Note: Although *à la grecque* vegetables may be served separately or in a mixed salad, it is essential to cook each vegetable by itself, since cooking times differ. The *à la grecque* liquid may be used several times for vegetables with a related flavor.

À LA KING

À LA KING—A plain or rich white sauce that should contain any one or combinations of these vegetables: sliced mushrooms, chopped green peppers, chopped or sliced pimientos. The sauce names the dish: chicken à la king, ham à la king, etc. À la king sauce is most frequently used for chicken cooked and diced, but it is equally well suited for turkey, tuna, ham, hard-cooked eggs, shrimp, or lobster. À la king sauce is an excellent food stretcher and it transforms leftovers into appetizing dishes.

À la king dishes may be served on toast, in patty shells, on rice, noodles, or on other foods that need a sauce or a dressing.

HAM OR SHRIMP À LA KING
3 tablespoons chopped green pepper
1½ tablespoons chopped pimiento
¼ cup butter
½ cup drained canned sliced mushrooms
1½ tablespoons all-purpose flour
1½ cups light cream
½ teaspoon salt
Dash of paprika
2 cups cooked diced ham or cooked shelled deveined shrimps
2 egg yolks
2 tablespoons sherry (optional)

Sauté green pepper and pimiento in butter in a skillet over low heat for 5 minutes. Add mushrooms and sauté for 1 minute longer. Remove vegetables and reserve. Stir flour into pan liquid. Gradually stir in cream and cook until smooth and thick, stirring constantly. Stir reserved vegetables into cream sauce. Season with salt and paprika. Trim ham free of all fat. Add ham (or shrimps, chopped coarsely if very large) to skillet mixture. Cook over low heat for 2 minutes, stirring constantly. Beat egg yolks slightly; stir some of hot sauce into them. Blend well. Stir egg mixture into remaining hot sauce. Cook for 1 minute longer over low heat, stirring constantly. Remove from heat and stir in sherry, if desired. Serve on rice, noodles, or in heated patty shells. Makes 4 to 6 servings.

■ **Variation**—Prepare recipe as above but substitute 4 quartered hard-cooked eggs, or one 1-pound can drained and flaked red salmon for the diced cooked ham or shrimps.

À LA MODE

À LA MODE—In French, this means literally "in the fashion of." In cookery, à la mode has two completely different meanings. One is American, the other French. In American usage, à la mode describes cake, pie, pudding, or any other dessert topped with a scoop of ice cream, such as apple pie à la mode.

In French cooking, à la mode describes a beef pot roast larded with fat, braised with vegetables, and simmered in a sauce, such as *boeuf à la mode*.

BOEUF À LA MODE
One 4-pound beef round or other cut suitable for a pot roast
3 slices of bacon or salt pork
1 tablespoon butter
1 cup hot water
2 cups dry white wine or hot beef bouillon (wine is preferable)
Salt and pepper
1 bay leaf
1 parsley sprig
⅛ teaspoon crumbled dried thyme
⅛ teaspoon ground nutmeg
1 cracked veal knuckle (ask butcher for this in advance)
2 tablespoons brandy (optional)
4 carrots, scraped and cut into pieces
3 whole cloves
6 small white onions, peeled

Trim beef to remove all fat. Cut bacon or salt pork into long thin strips. Push bacon strips through meat with larding needle, or with a thin knitting needle. Heat butter in heavy Dutch oven or deep casserole. Brown meat in it on all sides. Add hot water, wine, and seasonings and top with veal knuckle. Simmer, covered, over very low heat for about 2 hours. Add brandy and carrots. Stick cloves into one onion. Add onions to meat. Return to low heat. Simmer, covered, for another 1½ hours, or until meat is tender. Remove veal knuckle and discard cloves and bay leaf. The sauce should be brown and rich. If too liquid, remove meat to hot platter and **keep** hot. Heat sauce to boiling point and cook for 2 to 5 minutes, or until sauce has desired consistency, stirring constantly. Slice meat and strain sauce over it, or serve sauce separately. Serve with boiled potatoes, noodles, or plain rice and a green salad. Serve it hot one day and cold the next. When cold, the sauce will have jellied. Makes about 6 servings.

ALBACORE—A fish which belongs to the tuna family. Albacore has the true white meat of all tuna and is used for the finest canned tuna and the most delicate dishes. Canned tuna labeled all white meat, solid pack, is albacore. Fresh alba-core, found in some fish markets in areas where tuna is caught, makes for excellent eating.

Availability—Albacore is available fresh, or canned in oil or water pack. It can be used in all recipes calling for tuna.

Storage
☐ Fresh, refrigerator shelf: 1 to 2 days
☐ Fresh, refrigerator frozen-food compartment, prepared for freezing: 2 to 3 weeks
☐ Fresh, freezer, prepared for freezing: 1 year
☐ Canned, kitchen shelf: 2½ years
☐ Canned, refrigerator shelf, opened but covered: 1 to 2 days

Nutritive Food Values—Excellent source of protein; small amounts of calcium, phosphorus, and iron.
☐ Fresh, 3½ ounces, raw = 177 calories
☐ Canned and packed in oil, ½ cup = 194 calories

FRESH ALBACORE SAUTÉ AMANDINE
Six ½-pound fresh albacore steaks, each 1 inch thick
Flour
¼ cup butter
Salt and pepper
1 cup slivered blanched almonds or commercially prepared chopped buttered almonds
3 tablespoons minced parsley
Lemon wedges

Coat fish with flour. Melt butter in skillet. Brown fish on one side over medium heat. Season with salt and pepper to taste. Carefully turn steaks with a pancake turner. Add almonds and parsley. Brown fish on other side. If necessary to prevent sticking, add a little more butter. Remove fish to hot dish. Pour pan juices over it. Garnish with lemon wedges. Makes 6 servings.

PICKLED ALBACORE
2 cans (7 ounces each) albacore
1 large red onion, thinly sliced
2 green peppers, sliced
2 oranges, halved and sliced
¼ cup olive oil
½ cup fresh lemon juice
1 cup fresh orange juice
2 bay leaves
½ teaspoon crumbled oregano
¼ teaspoon salt
Salad greens

Break albacore into large pieces. Cover with slices of onion, green pepper, and orange. Combine other ingredients and pour over fish. Refrigerate for several hours. Garnish with greens. Makes 8 servings as a main dish, 4 to 6 as a salad.

ALBACORE DIVAN
2 packages (10 ounces each) frozen broccoli, cooked
2 cans (7 ounces each) albacore
⅓ cup all-purpose flour
1 teaspoon salt
2 cups milk
⅓ cup grated Parmesan cheese
1 tablespoon fresh lemon juice
1 tablespoon fine dry bread crumbs

Albacore Divan

Pickled Albacore

Put broccoli in shallow baking dish. Drain oil from fish into saucepan. Stir in flour and salt. Add milk and cook until thickened, stirring. Remove from heat and add cheese and lemon juice. Break tuna into chunks and arrange over broccoli. Cover with cheese sauce. Sprinkle with bread crumbs. Bake in preheated moderate oven (375°F.) for about 20 minutes, until hot and bubbly. Makes 6 servings.

ALCOHOL—Only the alcohol used in beverages needs to concern us here, although there are other varieties used in industry. Alcohol in its pure form is a transparent colorless strong liquid, volatile and very inflammable. It is distilled from a great variety of fruits and grains that contain either natural sugar or substances that can be transformed into sugar. By the addition of natural or artificial yeast strains and mineral compounds, the sugar is changed by the process of fermentation into alcohol and other by-products which are used commercially. This is the alcohol commonly known as grain or wine alcohol. Its technical name is ethyl alcohol. It is found in beer, whiskies, wines, brandies, liqueurs, and rum. Alcohol must not be regarded as a single substance; failure to distinguish between the various alcohols can be fatal. Methyl or wood alcohol, which is very different from the grain or ethyl alcohol we drink, is the most frequently encountered poisonous alcohol. It should not be drunk or inhaled. The rule is: When in doubt about the origin of an alcohol or alcoholic drink, do not touch it.

AL DENTE—Literally, this Italian term means "to the tooth." It is used to describe foods cooked so that they are still firm to the bite and taste or, in other words, not overcooked. *Al dente* is used for pasta, rice, and vegetables.

ALE—Ale is a fermented malt beverage; beer is its brother. Ale, like beer, is brewed from malt, cereals, and hops, but the method of brewing ale is different from that of brewing beer. Ale is "top fermented," that is, during fermentation at a higher temperature, its yeast rises to the top. The result is a brew with a more pronounced hop flavor than that found in beer.

Porter and stout are two well-known varieties of ale, both sweeter and darker than the others. Porter has less hop flavor. Stout has a full hop flavor with a slightly burnt taste. Both are more popular in Great Britain than in America.

The word "ale" comes from the Saxon *eale*. Since Saxon days, ale has been a household beverage in all northern European countries, where grapes for wine won't grow. It was drunk by old and young instead of water, which was then not safe. It has been brewed both at home and commercially. Throughout the ages, ale has inspired much splendid verse and prose. Shakespeare, in *The Winter's Tale,* says: "For a quart of ale is a dish for a king." The undergraduates of Vassar, a woman's college in New York State, still acknowledge their debt to Matthew Vassar, founder of the college and a brewer, with:

And so for you, old V.C., our love
   shall never fail.
Full well we know that all we owe
To Matthew Vassar's ale!

Ale should be served cold, but not quite as cold as beer, at a temperature between 40° and 50°F. The glasses should be spotlessly clean and washed with a detergent so that not a trace of grease appears. Grease is the natural enemy of ale and beer, since it kills the foam.

Ale and beer are both used successfully in cooking. The recipes for ale and beer are interchangeable, but cheese and pork dishes taste better made with ale.

Caloric Value
☐ About 1 cup = 84 calories

KNACKWURST IN ALE
4 knackwurst
½ cup ale
1 tablespoon vinegar
½ teaspoon sugar

Simmer knackwurst in ale in covered saucepan over low heat for 15 minutes. Heat shallow heatproof serving dish and place knackwurst in it. Keep hot. Boil up pan liquid and reduce it to ¼ cup. Stir in vinegar and sugar. Pour over hot knackwurst. Serve with mashed potatoes and red cabbage or hot sauerkraut sprinkled with caraway seeds. Makes 4 servings.

WELSH RABBIT
1 teaspoon Worcestershire
½ teaspoon powdered mustard
   Dash of paprika
½ cup ale
1 pound natural sharp Cheddar cheese, shredded

Combine Worcestershire, mustard, and paprika in a skillet. Add ale and let stand over very low heat until ale is heated through. Stir in cheese and continue to stir until cheese has melted. Do not overheat. Serve immediately over hot toast on heated plates. Makes 4 to 6 servings.

ALEWIFE—This is an inexpensive edible fish belonging to the herring family. The origin of the name is obscure, although it may derive from the fact that alewife has a relatively big belly. The fish is a native of the Atlantic Ocean from Nova Scotia to the Carolinas, and

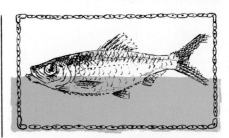

a southern species called Blueback is found as far south as Florida. The fish runs in the spring. Alewives grow to about ten inches in length and to about a half pound in weight. The fish is rather bony, but the flavor is pleasant and less oily than that of shad.

Most alewives are salted down for home consumption and export. Some of the fish is smoked, and the roe is sometimes canned. Fresh alewives are limited to markets in localities where the fish is caught. They can be cooked like any fresh herring. Salted alewives can be used in place of salt herring or mackerel. They should be freshened in cold water before cooking. Be sure to wipe the fish dry before using.

Caloric Values
☐ Fresh, 3½ ounces = 127 calories
☐ Canned, 3½ ounces, fish and liquid = 141 calories

ALEWIVES BAKED WITH LEMON
4 alewives, salted in brine
¼ cup butter or margarine, melted
   Juice of 3 lemons

Soak alewives in cold water for at least 3 hours. Drain and wipe dry. Carefully split fish open to keep whole. Place, skin side down, in well-greased shallow baking dish. Combine butter and lemon juice. Spoon half of mixture evenly over fish. Bake fish in preheated moderate oven (350°F.) for 7 minutes. Spoon remaining butter-lemon mixture evenly over fish and bake for 5 minutes longer. Serve very hot with plain boiled potato, garnished with parsley. Makes 4 servings.

ALLEMANDE—This is a classic French sauce, golden yellow in color, creamy in consistency, with excellent flavor. It is used with boiled or poached fish, meats, or vegetables. The main ingredient is *velouté* sauce (a white sauce made with chicken, veal, or fish stock instead of milk or cream), to which egg yolks, cream, and lemon juice are added. *Allemande* sauce is also known as *sauce blonde* or *sauce parisienne*. In spite of its name, which means "German," it has nothing to do with Germany or things German.

SAUCE ALLEMANDE
2 tablespoons butter
2 tablespoons flour
2 cups hot fish, veal, chicken, or clear vegetable stock
   Salt and pepper
¾ cup strong chicken stock, heated

2 egg yolks, slightly beaten
2 tablespoons heavy cream
1 tablespoon fresh lemon juice
1 tablespoon butter, softened

Melt 2 tablespoons butter in top part of double boiler. Stir in flour and blend thoroughly. Gradually stir in hot stock. Cook, covered, over simmering, not boiling, water for 30 to 45 minutes, stirring occasionally. Season with salt and pepper to taste. Strain through a fine sieve into a saucepan. Stir additional hot chicken stock into sauce. Blend thoroughly. Over medium heat, let sauce cook down to two thirds of its original volume, stirring constantly. Remove from heat. Beat egg yolks with cream. Gradually stir hot sauce into egg-yolk mixture. Return sauce to saucepan. Reheat over low heat, but do not boil. Just before serving stir in lemon juice and butter. Stir over low heat until butter is melted. Makes about 1⅔ cups sauce.

Note: ¼ cup thinly sliced sautéed mushrooms may be added to sauce.

ALLSPICE (Pimenta dioica; often called Pimenta officinalis)—Jamaica pepper is another name for the dried unripe fruit of a twenty- to forty-foot tree (*Pimenta dioica*) that is related to the myrtle family. The tree is native to the West Indies and is grown in all of the American tropics, but it is so common to Jamaica that the island practically has a monopoly on the spice. The berries are picked green and dried in the sun. This wrinkles them, turns them a reddish brown, and intensifies their aroma.

In spite of the name, allspice is *not* a combination of spices but one spice only; it is so called because its flavor resembles a combination of clove, cinnamon, and nutmeg.

Allspice can be bought both as dried whole berries or finely ground. It has a great many uses. It is frequently used in pickling and in the preparation of relishes and meats, especially pot roast; also in baking and in stewed and preserved fruits, mincemeat, and tomato-flavored dishes. It combines well with other spices.

SPICY SWISS STEAK

1½ teaspoons salt
½ teaspoon ground allspice
¼ teaspoon pepper
2 pounds beef round steak about 1 inch thick
⅓ cup all-purpose flour
3 tablespoons shortening or salad oil
1 medium onion, minced
3 cups peeled chopped tomatoes, fresh or canned

Rub salt, allspice, and pepper well into steak. Dredge meat with flour. Pound in flour with edge of a plate. Heat shortening in heavy casserole. Brown meat quickly in hot fat on both sides. Add onion and tomatoes. Cover and bake in preheated moderate oven (350°F.) for about 1½ hours, or until meat is tender. Check occasionally for moisture. If necessary add a little hot water, bouillon, or more tomato to prevent sticking. Makes about 4 servings.

SWEET POTATOES WITH ALLSPICE

1 can (1 pound, 7 ounces) syrup-packed sweet potatoes
¼ cup honey
1 teaspoon grated lemon rind
½ teaspoon ground allspice
2 tablespoons butter

Drain sweet potatoes and reserve liquid. Arrange pieces of sweet potato in greased shallow baking dish. Combine sweet potato liquid with honey, lemon rind, and allspice. Spoon mixture evenly over sweet potatoes. Dot with butter. Bake, uncovered, in preheated moderate oven (375°F.) for about 25 minutes, or until sweet potatoes are well glazed. Makes 4 servings.

SPICY ORANGE SLICES

2 large oranges
2 tablespoons flour
½ cup graham-cracker crumbs
1 tablespoon sugar
½ teaspoon ground allspice
3 tablespoons butter or margarine

Cut oranges into slices about ¼ inch thick; remove seeds. Mix flour, crumbs, sugar, and allspice. Dip oranges into mixture, being sure they are well coated. Brown on both sides in butter. Makes 4 dessert servings and about 8 servings as garnish.

QUICK ALLSPICE ORANGE-NUT BREAD

2 cups sifted all-purpose flour
1 cup sugar
1 teaspoon baking powder
¾ teaspoon allspice
½ teaspoon salt
½ teaspoon baking soda
1 egg
2 tablespoons grated orange rind
⅔ cup orange juice
3 tablespoons melted butter or margarine
1 cup chopped nuts

Into large bowl sift flour with sugar, baking powder, allspice, salt, and baking soda. Beat egg thoroughly and combine with orange rind, juice, and melted butter. Add liquid to flour mixture all at once. Stir only until well blended. Stir in

nuts. Bake in well-greased loaf pan (9 x 5 x 3 inches) in preheated moderate oven (350°F.) for about 50 minutes, or until loaf tests clean. Cool for 5 minutes before removing from pan. Cool completely before slicing. Makes 1 loaf.

ALLUMETTE—This French word for match is used to describe foods cut into thin matchlike strips. The term *allumette* is applied in particular to an *hors-d'oeuvre* made with thin strips of puff paste spread with a savory filling and covered with more puff paste before baking; to potatoes cut into thin strips (called shoestring potatoes in America); and to a tea cake, also made from a strip of puff paste, frosted before baking.

ALMOND—The word covers the tree and nut, the seed or kernel of *Prunus Amygdalus,* a subgenus which includes the peach tree. The almond closely resembles the peach in its blossom and young unripe fruit, although the almond tree grows larger.

The almond tree bears a leathery fruit which, upon maturing, splits open and exposes the nut in its shell. The pitted shell is light tan in color. The nut is covered with a medium-brown skin and is white inside.

Basically, there are two kinds of almonds, sweet and bitter, although there are many varieties of these. Sweet almonds are those we eat. Bitter almonds are a source of almond flavoring, but they must be processed first since they contain prussic acid, a poison. However, used in tiny quantities in cooking, such as three to five bitter almonds (European recipes sometimes call for them), they are not dangerous.

Almonds have been cultivated since antiquity in Mediterranean countries and the Orient. In the United States, they are grown commercially in California. It is said that they were brought here by early Spanish missionaries, since almonds have long been a favorite in Spain. Almond trees are often grown for the beauty of their flowers. The loveliness of tree and blossom has inspired artists and poets through the ages; especially charming are the Chinese interpretations. The ancient Phrygians, seeing the tree blossom early in the season before any others, believed it to be the father of all life. To the ancient Greeks, the almond was a symbol of fertility, and to the Moslems, the mark of heavenly hope.

Almonds are mentioned in the Bible, since the wood of the almond tree, the blossom, and the fruit were part of the Hebraic ritual. When Israel sent gifts to Joseph, they were "a little balm, and a little honey, spices, and myrrh, nuts, and almonds" (Genesis 43:11).

In cookery, almonds are one of the pleasures of life. With little trouble and at low cost, they add flavor and texture to food and make many bland commonplace dishes exciting. They are especially recommended for chicken, fish, seafood, curries, and as an ingredient of main-dish sauces, but they can be added to almost any food, and used as a garnish for main dishes, salads, and vegetables. Whole, chopped, slivered, and toasted almonds are an ingredient of candies, ice creams, and dessert sauces. Almonds are greatly used in baking; most Scandinavian, Spanish, Greek and Near Eastern cakes are based on almonds. Shelled almonds are used unblanched, that is, with inner brown skin still on; and blanched, that is, with the skin removed to reveal the white kernel. Blanched or unblanched, whole almonds may be salted or sugared for eating out of hand.

Almond oil is used in some parts of Europe for cooking and eating. The best known almond confection is marzipan, almond paste molded into fruits, animals, and other fancy shapes, and tinted realistically or imaginatively. Germany and Denmark both make famous marzipan.

Almonds have also been used for thousands of years in powders, creams, and lotions to enhance the beauty of women. They are said to soften and whiten the skin.

Availability—Sold the year round in various forms. Almonds are picked in the fall, and the heaviest marketing occurs in November.

Purchasing Guide

Unshelled—Look for nuts that are clean and free from scars, cracks, or holes, and well filled, so the kernel does not rattle. They are sold in bulk or in 1-pound plastic bags.

Shelled—Look for those that are plump and meaty, crisp and brittle. Limp shriveled nutmeats indicate staleness. Almonds are packaged in 5-pound boxes and 1- and 6-ounce plastic bags. You can also buy them in 6-ounce vacuum-sealed cans in these forms:

UNBLANCHED—Whole (also salted, roasted, buttered, and French-fried), Halved, Sliced, Coarsely Chopped, Finely Chopped, Meal, Diced

BLANCHED—Whole (also salted), Broken, Sliced, Slivered (also toasted), Small Pieces

☐ Unblanched, whole, 1 pound = 2⅔ cups

☐ Unblanched and blanched, ground, 1 pound = 2⅔ cups

☐ Unblanched, slivered, 1 pound = 5⅔ cups

☐ Unblanched and blanched, grated, 1 pound = 6⅔ cups

Almond-Filled Coffee Ring, Glazed Almond Cookies

☐ Blanched, whole, 5⅓ ounces = 1 cup

☐ Blanched, slivered, sliced, or coarsely chopped, 1 pound = 3¾ cups

Storage—Shelled uncooked nuts will store well for almost a year if kept in an airtight container in a cool dry place, such as the refrigerator. They may be stored in a freezer in sealed containers for even longer periods. For oven-roasted nuts, allow not more than three months refrigerator storage, and even less for those cooked in oil.

Nutritive Food Values—Almonds provide some protein, iron, calcium, phosphorus, and B vitamins. They are also high in fat.

☐ 3½ ounces = 598 calories

☐ 3½ ounces, roasted and salted = 627 calories

Basic Preparation

☐ **To Blanch**—Cover with boiling water. Let stand for 3 minutes, then test to see if skins slip off easily. Remove almonds from water one at a time, slip off skins, and let dry on paper towels for several hours.

☐ **To Sliver**—Cut into lengthwise strips with a very sharp knife while nuts are moist and warm.

☐ **To Chop**—Use a long, straightedged knife and wooden board, or a chopping bowl and chopper. Almonds may also be chopped in a blender. Place ½ cup at a time in the blender container, cover, and whirl for 30 seconds at high speed.

☐ **To Grind**—Use a special nut grinder, except for butters and pastes, when a food chopper or blender should be used. The easiest way to grind almonds is in the electric blender. Grind about ¼ cup at a time, at high speed. Do not overgrind or almonds will be pasty and oily, which is good for making almond paste, but not for general baking. For general baking purposes, almonds should be dry and fine, like meal.

ALMOND EXTRACT

Almond extract is prepared from the oil of bitter or sweet almonds. It is sold in 1¼- and 4-ounce bottles. Almond extract may be used to give almond flavor to cake or pastry, sauces, dessert puddings, gelatins, and other dishes.

ALMOND PASTE

Almond paste is a blend of ground almonds and sugar. It is available in specialty food stores in 8-ounce, 1-, 3-, and 5-pound cans. It should be kept in a cool place; stored in the refrigerator, it will keep indefinitely. Almond paste may be used to make marzipan, macaroons, and filling for Danish pastry or coffeecake.

BURNT ALMONDS

Mix 1 cup sugar and ⅓ cup water in skillet; bring to boil; cook until mixture spins a thread (candy thermometer registers 230° to 234°F.). Add 1 package (6 ounces) shelled unblanched almonds; cook for 2 minutes, or until syrup begins to sugar. Remove from heat; stir until mixture is dry and sugary. Continue cooking over low heat, stirring constantly, until sugar is melted and browned. Remove from heat; stir until nuts are well coated with syrup. Pour onto a buttered platter. With 2 forks, separate nuts quickly into single nuts. Put nuts separately on another buttered platter; let stand until cold. Makes 1½ cups.

Sauce Amandine

TOASTED ALMONDS

Spread blanched or unblanched almonds on ungreased shallow baking pan with sides. Bake in slow oven (325°F.) until lightly browned, stirring occasionally. Almonds may be halved or cut into lengthwise slivers before toasting. Do not overbrown. Cool and pack in airtight container.

SALTED ALMONDS

Spread blanched or unblanched almonds on ungreased shallow baking pan with sides. Dot with butter, using 1 teaspoon for each cup of nuts. Toast lightly in moderate oven (350°F.), stirring nuts frequently until golden brown. Remove from oven; sprinkle with salt. Cool and pack in airtight container.

ALMOND SOUP

1 cup blanched almonds, finely ground
3 cups chicken broth
1 small onion, stuck with 1 clove
½ bay leaf
2 tablespoons butter
2 tablespoons flour
½ cup hot milk
1 cup heavy cream
Slivered toasted almonds

Combine almonds, broth, onion, and bay leaf in saucepan. Simmer, covered, for 30 minutes. Discard onion and bay leaf. Keep soup hot. Melt butter in another saucepan. Stir in flour. Gradually stir in milk. Cook over low heat, stirring constantly, until smooth and thickened. Stir mixture into chicken-almond soup. Cook over low heat, stirring constantly, for 5 minutes. Remove from heat and stir in heavy cream. Heat through once more, but do not let boil. Serve sprinkled with slivered toasted almonds. Good hot or cold. Makes 4 to 5 servings.

TROUT WITH ALMONDS AND CREAM

4 small trout, fresh or frozen
Flour
½ cup butter
½ cup slivered blanched almonds
½ cup heavy cream
Salt and pepper

Wash trout and dry well. Coat lightly with flour. Heat butter in skillet. Sauté trout in butter until browned on both sides. Remove fish to hot platter and keep hot. Sauté almonds in skillet until golden brown. Add cream and stir thoroughly to loosen all particles; the sauce will be brown. Season with salt and pepper to taste. Simmer gently for 2 minutes. Pour sauce over fish. Makes 2 to 3 servings.
Note: This recipe may also be made with 1½ pounds fish fillets, fresh or frozen.

VEAL STEW WITH ALMONDS IN SOUR CREAM

3 pounds boneless veal shoulder, cut into 1½-inch cubes
Seasoned flour for dredging
½ cup shortening
3 medium onions, peeled and quartered
1 cup sliced celery
2 cups water

⅛ teaspoon crumbled dried thyme
12 small mushrooms, quartered, or ½ cup (one 4-ounce can) mushroom pieces, drained
1 cup slivered blanched almonds
¼ cup butter
1 cup dairy sour cream
¼ cup chopped parsley

Dredge veal with seasoned flour. Heat shortening in heavy pan and brown meat on all sides. Pour off pan drippings. Add onions, celery, water, and thyme to meat. Simmer, covered, over low heat for 1½ hours, stirring occasionally. Sauté mushrooms and almonds in hot butter until golden brown. Add to meat and simmer for 15 minutes longer. Stir in sour cream and reheat, but do not let boil. Sprinkle with parsley. Makes 6 to 8 servings.

CHICKEN-ALMOND MOUSSE

1 envelope unflavored gelatin
1¼ cups chicken broth
3 egg yolks
1 cup ground cooked chicken
½ cup ground blanched almonds
2 tablespoons chopped parsley
1½ teaspoons fresh lemon juice
½ teaspoon instant minced onion
½ teaspoon salt
¼ teaspoon white pepper
⅛ teaspoon hot pepper sauce
1 cup heavy cream, whipped stiff

Soften gelatin in ½ cup of the chicken broth. In top part of double boiler, slightly beat egg yolks. Stir in remaining broth. Cook over hot, not boiling, water until mixture thickens, stirring constantly. Remove from heat. Stir in softened gelatin. Blend until gelatin is dissolved. Add chicken, almonds, parsley, lemon juice, instant onion, salt, pepper, and pepper sauce. Chill until mixture begins to thicken to consistency of egg white. Fold in whipped cream. Brush a 1-quart salad mold with salad oil. Turn mixture into mold and chill until firm. Unmold and serve garnished with salad greens. Makes 4 servings.

SAUCE AMANDINE

Sauté over low heat ¼ cup slivered blanched almonds in ½ cup butter or margarine until light golden brown, stirring constantly. Stir in 1 tablespoon fresh lemon juice. Serve on chicken, sweetbreads, fish fillets, broccoli, green beans, asparagus, or other vegetables. Makes about ¾ cup.

ALMOND NOODLES

Cook and drain 1 pound broad noodles. Stir in ¾ cup sliced toasted blanched almonds. Put in serving dish and top with ¼ cup toasted buttered crumbs and an additional ¼ cup sliced toasted blanched almonds. Makes 4 to 6 servings.

RICE PILAF WITH ALMONDS

¼ cup butter or margarine
¼ cup minced onion
½ cup chopped blanched almonds
1 cup raw rice
2 cups hot beef bouillon or chicken broth
Salt and pepper to taste

Heat butter or margarine in heavy saucepan. Add onion and sauté until onion is transparent. Do not let brown. Add almonds and sauté for 1 to 2 minutes, or until barely golden. Add rice and sauté until rice is transparent, stirring constantly. Add hot bouillon all at once; mixture will sizzle. Cover tightly. Simmer over lowest possible heat for 15 to 20 minutes, or until rice is tender. Do not stir for first 10 minutes; then stir occasionally. Season. Makes 4 to 6 servings.

CELERY GRATIN WITH ALMONDS

3 tablespoons butter or margarine
3 cups thinly sliced raw celery
1 cup shredded blanched almonds
3 tablespoons flour
2 cups hot milk
Salt and pepper
¼ cup grated sharp Cheddar or Parmesan cheese

Melt butter in heavy skillet. Add celery and almonds. Sauté, covered, over low heat for 10 to 15 minutes, or until celery is tender. Blend in flour. Stir in hot milk gradually. Cook, stirring constantly, until sauce is smooth and thickened. Season with salt and pepper. Turn into greased 1-quart baking dish. Sprinkle with grated cheese. Bake in preheated hot oven (400°F.) until bubbly, or glaze briefly under hot broiler. Makes 4 to 6 servings.

ALMOND-CHICKEN SALAD

3 cups diced cooked chicken
½ cup golden raisins
⅓ cup toasted slivered blanched almonds
3 celery stalks, diced
1 bunch watercress, leaves only, chopped
¾ cup mayonnaise
¼ cup orange juice
Salt and pepper

Mix all ingredients and chill until ready to serve. Makes 4 servings.

JULY DAY SALAD

1 box (3 ounces) lemon-flavored gelatin
1 cup boiling water
1 cup mayonnaise
2 cups (1 pound) creamed cottage cheese
½ cup minced celery
1 large cucumber, peeled and diced
1 teaspoon instant minced onion
1 teaspoon salt
1 tablespoon cider vinegar
½ cup chopped blanched almonds
Salad greens

Dissolve gelatin in water and cool slightly. Stir in remaining ingredients, except greens, and pour into 1½-quart mold. Chill until firm. Unmold on greens. Makes 6 servings.

THOMAS JEFFERSON'S ALMOND CUSTARD

¼ cup blanched almonds
4 cups milk
6 eggs
6 tablespoons sugar
⅛ teaspoon salt

Grind almonds in electric blender or in nut grater. Combine almonds and milk and bring to a boil. Remove from heat. Beat eggs with sugar and salt. Beat almond-milk mixture gradually into eggs.

Turn into top part of double boiler. Cook over hot, not boiling, water until thickened, stirring constantly. Serve over cake or stewed fruit. Makes 4 to 6 servings.

ALMOND SOUFFLÉ
3 tablespoons butter
3 tablespoons all-purpose flour
1 cup milk
½ cup sugar
¼ teaspoon salt
1 teaspoon almond extract
½ cup chopped almonds
5 eggs, separated

Melt butter and stir in flour. Add milk and cook, stirring constantly, until smooth and thickened. Stir in sugar, salt, flavoring, and almonds. Remove from heat. Beat egg yolks and add to mixture. Beat egg whites until stiff. Fold into batter. Butter a 2-quart soufflé dish and sprinkle with sugar. Pour in mixture. Bake in preheated moderate oven (375°F.) for 30 minutes. Serve with cream, if desired. Makes 4 to 6 servings.

ALMOND BAVARIAN CREAM
2 envelopes unflavored gelatin
1½ cups milk
1 cup chopped blanched almonds
½ cup sugar
6 egg yolks, slightly beaten
¾ teaspoon vanilla extract
½ teaspoon almond extract
2 cups heavy cream, whipped

Soften gelatin in ½ cup of the milk. Combine remaining milk, almonds, sugar, and egg yolks in top part of double boiler. Cook over hot water until smooth and thickened, stirring constantly. Remove from heat. Stir in vanilla and almond extracts. Add softened gelatin; stir until completely dissolved. Chill until mixture begins to thicken to consistency of egg white. Fold in whipped cream. Lightly oil a 2-quart mold with salad oil. Turn mixture into it and chill until firm. Unmold and serve with crushed sweetened fruits or berries. Makes 10 to 12 servings.

ALMOND PASTE
1 pound blanched almonds
3 tablespoons fresh lemon juice
1 cup water
2 cups sugar

Force blanched almonds through fine blade of food chopper 4 times, or whirl in electric blender. Add lemon juice. Cook water and sugar until candy thermometer registers 240°F., or until a small amount of mixture dropped into cold water forms a soft ball. Add to ground almonds. Mix well. When cool enough to handle, knead until smooth. Cool. Pack in jar; cover, and store in refrigerator for at least 1 week to ripen. Makes about 2 pounds.

Note: If almond paste is too stiff to handle after storage, place in top part of double boiler and heat over hot, not boiling, water until sufficiently soft to

handle. Use in cookies, coffeecakes, or in other pastries and desserts.

ALMOND-FILLED COFFEE RING
1 package active dry yeast or 1 cake compressed yeast
2 tablespoons very warm water*
¼ cup sugar
½ teaspoon salt
½ cup milk
1 egg, beaten
2 cups sifted all-purpose flour (about)
¾ cup butter or margarine
Almond Filling
½ cup chopped candied cherries
Confectioners' Sugar Frosting
Whole candied cherries
Angelica

Sprinkle or crumble yeast into water. *Use very warm water (105°F. to 115°F.) for dry yeast; use lukewarm (80°F. to 90°F.) for compressed. Let stand a few minutes, then stir until dissolved. Stir in sugar, salt, milk, and egg. Add 1½ cups sifted flour and beat until smooth. Stir in enough more flour (about ½ cup) to make a very stiff dough. Turn out on well floured board and sprinkle with flour. Roll to ¼-inch thickness. Spread ½ cup softened butter on upper ⅔ of dough and fold lower third over middle third. Fold top third over that. Turn and roll again to ¼-inch thickness. Fold in thirds. Put on cookie sheet and chill about 30 minutes. Repeat rolling, folding, and chilling three times. Divide dough in half. Roll each into rectangle about 8 inches long. Brush with ¼ cup melted butter and spread each with Almond Filling. Sprinkle with chopped cherries. Roll up like jelly rolls. Form into rings. With scissors, cut through rings, almost to center, in slices about 1 inch thick. Turn each slice slightly. Put each ring on greased cookie sheet. Let rise in warm place until light (about 25 minutes). Bake in preheated moderate oven (350°F.) for about 30 minutes. Cool; frost and decorate with whole cherries and angelica. Makes two 9-inch coffee rings.

Almond Filling
Force 1 cup blanched almonds through fine blade of food chopper. Blend in ½ cup fine dry bread crumbs, ¾ cup sugar, and 2 tablespoons melted butter. Add 1 well-beaten egg and mix thoroughly.

Confectioners' Sugar Frosting
Combine ½ cup sifted confectioners' sugar with about 1 teaspoon milk or light cream, or enough to make a thick pouring consistency. Stir in a few drops vanilla flavoring.

ALMOND TORTE
1 cup sugar, sifted
6 eggs, separated
Grated rind and juice of 1 lemon
½ teaspoon almond extract
1 cup unblanched almonds, finely ground
½ cup toasted white bread crumbs
Lemon-Orange Filling

1 cup heavy cream, whipped
or confectioners' sugar, sifted

Beat sugar into egg yolks, a little at a time. Beat until very light and creamy. Add lemon rind and juice, almond extract, ground almonds, and bread crumbs. Blend well. Whip egg whites until stiff. Fold lightly into batter. Turn into two 8-inch layer-cake pans that have been greased and lined with wax paper. Preferably, use pans with removable rims. Bake in preheated moderate oven (350°F.) for about 40 minutes. Spread layers with Lemon-Orange Filling. Spread top and sides with whipped cream. Makes 6 to 8 servings.

Lemon-Orange Filling
2½ tablespoons fresh lemon juice
6 tablespoons fresh orange juice
Grated rind of 1 lemon
Grated rind of 1 orange
⅓ cup water
½ cup sugar
2 tablespoons flour
⅛ teaspoon salt
1 whole egg
1 egg yolk

Combine all ingredients in top part of double boiler. Cook over hot, not boiling, water until smooth and thick, stirring constantly. Cool thoroughly before using. Makes about 1½ cups.

ALMOND MACAROONS
½ pound almond paste
1 cup sugar
3 egg whites, unbeaten
⅓ cup confectioners' sugar
2 tablespoons cake flour
⅛ teaspoon salt

Cover cookie sheets with unglazed paper. Work almond paste (homemade or purchased) thoroughly with hands. Add sugar and egg whites, a small amount at a time, mixing thoroughly. Add remaining ingredients and mix well. Put teaspoons of mixture on prepared cookie sheets and flatten with fingers dipped into cold water. Cover and let stand for 2 or more hours. Bake in preheated slow oven (300°F.) for about 30 minutes. Lift unglazed paper from cookie sheet onto a damp cloth and remove macaroons. Makes about 2½ dozen.

NONSWEET ALMOND HEARTS
½ cup sifted confectioners' sugar
1 cup butter (must be butter)
2 egg yolks
1 teaspoon vanilla or almond extract, or rosewater, or fresh lemon extract
2½ cups sifted all-purpose flour
1½ cups finely ground blanched almonds (must be almonds)
Chopped nuts

Beat together sugar and butter. Stir in 1 egg yolk and extract. Add flour and almonds. Knead to a smooth dough. Chill for 2 to 3 hours. Roll out between sheets of wax paper to ¼-inch thickness. Cut with heart-shape cutter. Put on ungreased cookie sheet. Brush with 1 beaten egg yolk and sprinkle with chopped nuts. Bake in preheated moderate oven (350°F.) for 10 to 12 minutes, or until barely golden. Makes about 10 dozen 1½-inch hearts. A bland cookie that appeals to those not fond of sweets.

GLAZED ALMOND COOKIES

1 cup soft butter or margarine
1 cup sugar
½ teaspoon each of almond and vanilla extracts
2 eggs, separated
¾ cup chopped blanched almonds
2⅓ cups sifted cake flour
½ teaspoon salt
48 unblanched whole almonds

Cream butter and sugar until light. Beat in extracts and egg yolks. Add chopped nuts, flour, and salt; mix well. Roll into 1-inch balls, dip into unbeaten egg whites (this provides the glaze), and put 2 inches apart on greased cookie sheets. Put a whole almond in center of each ball, and push down to flatten cookie. Bake in preheated moderate oven (350°F.) for about 10 minutes. Makes about 4 dozen cookies, which keep well and can be successfully shipped.

FIGS STUFFED WITH ALMONDS

With a sharp pointed knife, cut a slit into dried figs. Insert a toasted blanched almond into each fig. Or use pitted dates instead of figs. A confection from the Mediterranean.

ALMOND BRITTLE

Caramelize ½ cup granulated sugar in heavy iron skillet. Turn heat high at first, then very low. Stir constantly, if possible with a long-handled wooden spoon. When sugar is melted and free from lumps (they will appear at first, but just keep stirring over low heat), add ¼ cup unblanched almonds. Pour candy at once onto greased marble slab, enamel kitchen table, or greased china platter. Cool candy; break into pieces and put through food chopper, using coarsest blade. If you do not own a chopper, put candy in clean kitchen towel or napkin and pound with kitchen mallet or wooden potato masher until candy is finely crushed. Use to sprinkle on cakes after frosting and on puddings and ice cream.
Note: Almond, pecan, or peanut brittle can be purchased and crushed, if desired.

ALSACE—This easternmost province of France is famous for its food and wines. Its two gastronomic masterpieces are *foie gras* (goose liver, usually made into pâtés) with truffles, one of the world's most prized delicacies, and *choucroute garnie*, a robust dish of sauerkraut, pork products, and boiled potatoes, cooked with white wine and juniper berries, which can be made at home. The two best known wines are the classic Riesling and the flowery Gewürztraminer, and the best known spirit is kirsch, a colorless brandy distilled from cherries. Strasbourg, one of Europe's most beautiful ancient cities and site of a splendid cathedral, is the chief town of Alsace.

CHOUCROUTE GARNIE

4 pounds sauerkraut
1 tablespoon lard
¾ pound bacon, diced
1 large onion, studded with 3 cloves
1 Polish sausage, cut into 2-inch pieces
1 pound smoked pork shoulder
¼ cup brandy (optional)
1 carrot, sliced
10 juniper berries and 6 peppercorns, tied in a cheesecloth bag
2 bay leaves
¼ teaspoon crumbled dried thyme
Salt to taste
2 cups dry Alsatian or other white wine
2 cups water
12 medium-size potatoes, peeled and boiled
12 frankfurters

Place sauerkraut in deep bowl. Loosen shreds. Fill bowl with cold water and let stand for 15 minutes. Drain and press out all water. Melt lard in Dutch oven. Add bacon and onion and cook until browned. Add sausage and pork shoulder and cook until meat is browned. Remove meats and reserve. Add sauerkraut to pan and cook, stirring constantly, until browned. Add brandy and cook for a few minutes longer. Add carrot, juniper berries and peppercorns, bay leaves, thyme, salt, wine, and water. Bring to a boil. Return pork shoulder to pan. Simmer, covered, over low heat for 3 hours. Return sausage to pan. Simmer, covered, for another 45 minutes. Add potatoes and frankfurters and continue simmering for 15 minutes more. Makes 6 to 8 servings.

ALSATIAN NOODLES

2 tablespoons butter
4 cups (8 ounces) medium noodles, cooked and drained
Salt and pepper
3 tablespoons grated cheese
¼ cup salad oil

Heat butter in saucepan. Add about two thirds of noodles. Season with salt and pepper. Cook over low heat for 5 minutes, stirring constantly. Add cheese and blend thoroughly. Turn into heated serving dish and keep hot. Chop remaining noodles very coarsely. Heat salad oil in skillet. Add chopped noodles and cook until browned, stirring occasionally. Toss with noodles in dish. Serve hot. Makes 4 servings.

ALTITUDE COOKING—High altitudes affect the cooking and baking of foods so special methods have had to be worked out to give homemakers successful recipes. Recipes which are foolproof at sea level and generally speaking, at altitudes up to 2,500 feet, can fail completely at higher altitudes because of the different atmospheric pressure. Foods that need baking or boiling or that are rich in sugar are most affected by high altitudes. Some foods, such as cake mixes, are made especially for high-altitude cooking.

When a homemaker moves to a new home at a higher altitude than her previous one, it is suggested that she contact the local utility company or the State Extension Service for information on special high-altitude recipes.

ALUM—The astringent effect of this chemical makes it useful in home-pickling to give crispness to cucumbers, melon rinds, onions, green beans, and other foods. Commercially, alum is used as an ingredient in some baking powders as well as in pickling. Alum can be bought in drugstores.

AMBROSIA—This Greek word goes back to Greek mythology and designated the substance which, with nectar, constituted the food and drink of the Greek gods, giving immortality to those who partook of it.

The word is also used to define anything very pleasing in the way of scent or taste. In cookery, ambrosia is a dessert of orange slices and/or other fruits, sprinkled with sugar and shredded coconut. Ambrosia is particularly popular as a dessert in the American south.

AMBROSIA DE LUXE

With a sharp knife section oranges, grapefruits, and tangerines, removing membranes and seeds. Arrange fruit in layers, sprinkling each with a little fine granulated, powdered, or confectioners' sugar and grated fresh or packaged coconut. Other fruit such as sliced bananas sprinkled with lime or lemon juice, pineapple tidbits, or canned mandarin oranges can be added. Chill before serving.

American Cooks Are Good Cooks

by Sophie Kerr

A lot of talk goes round now and then to the effect that American cooks are away behind cooks of other lands when it comes to producing a first-rate meal, and that American food in general lacks the elegant subtlety of foreign dishes. I don't know who started this nonsense, but nonsense it is, and it should be labeled so in large black letters. Actually, there is a great tradition in American cooking, and thousands of women have come to respect and perpetuate it.

To be sure, American cooking has had its ups and downs—but they were mostly ups. Let me invite you to a dinner at the home of my grandmother, some fifty years ago, on the Eastern Shore of Maryland. The hour is twelve-thirty. There is a white cloth on the long table, the china is white with gold bands, the goblets are simple three-mold style, the knives and forks are of shining steel with bone handles. At one end of the table is a big chicken pie, the top richly brown, the undercrust crisp on the bottom with a delicious jelly above, the chicken meat artfully enhanced in taste with black pepper, bay leaf, and mace, the gravy a creamy river of delight.

At the other end of the table is a dish of scalloped oysters—oysters fresh from the bay, salty and lean, immured in toasted crumbs of homemade bread, drenched in the oysters' own savory liquid, seasoned by a knowing hand, the whole dish baked just long enough to cook the oysters through and brown the top.

Around and about these two main dishes are potatoes whipped to airy snowiness, buttered green garden peas, tomatoes sliced with sweet onion, crisp celery in tall glasses, chowchow, spiced peaches as big as your fist, plates of hot, fresh-baked rolls. For dessert there is probably a cherry pudding made with

the fruit from an avenue of tall trees stretching from house to highway. There is sure to be hot black coffee in the white, gold-banded cups, and thick cream to go with it. A plain American dinner, friends, cooked by an American woman in an old-time, unhandy American kitchen at which moderns would gaze with amused horror.

In those halcyon days, women cooked *con amore,* and every housewife had her treasured recipes, which she wouldn't give away even to her dearest friends. Those were the days of bake sales for church and charity, when the knowing ones lined up early to get some of Mrs. So-and-So's pocketbook rolls, or Mrs. Whosis' white cake with almond frosting, or Mrs. Query's green-apple custard pie, and if the supply was gone when they got there, they screamed like Indians. Everyone who cooked well was intensely proud of it then. And since a good many of us can recall those days, they were not very long ago.

Early in the 1900's there appeared a new school of thought among American cooks. This was the era when careers for women were opening up in business and in the professions and arts, so certain groups, perhaps a little oversold on career stuff, proclaimed that it was menial to cook and that women now, for the first time, had their chance to come out of

the kitchen. These groups made a noise considerably larger than their numbers warranted; but they did effect a slight hush-hush about recipes and good eating in general and particular. They said it wasn't intellectual to be interested in food, and, of course, no woman likes to be publicly labeled as unintellectual. American cooking took something of a beating during this dark period; but it is cheering to remember that, in spite of all the shouting against them, there were plenty of sensible women who simply laid low and cooked better and better, confident that the tide would eventually turn.

Sure enough, along about the First World War the tide *did* turn, and it has been rising higher and higher ever since. Of course, it got a lot of skilled assistance. Architects set up breakfast nooks and food bars right in the kitchen; inventors worked wonders on kitchen stoves and cooking utensils and gadgets; food magazines sprang up and flourished and food departments in women's magazines grew more comprehensive and alluring.

More and more cook books were—and are—printed and, what is better, were sold and used; schools and colleges added classes in cooking and domestic economy; metropolitan dailies saw the trend and

promoted it by publishing market news, recipes, specialized household information; radio supplemented the press; and now television has entered the field in a big way. Canners, packers, the frozen-food industry, fruit and vegetable growers are all part of the big parade. I am told the sale of kitchen aprons is booming, so it is apparent that cooking has become smart, cooking has become fun! Young Mrs. America and her modern kitchen stove are working together very cozily.

I said that American cooking has a long tradition; actually it goes back to the Indians. We have four widely used dishes that still bear Indian names. Pone and hominy are from the Algonquian tribes, succotash is from the Narraganset, and pemmican from the Cree. The last was once widely used by early explorers and pioneer plainsmen; today it is called jerked beef or jerky. Pone, hominy, and succotash appear on our tables frequently, although not cooked over a campfire.

The use of our native corn thus comes naturally to us. And what a great part it plays in American cooking! From the first juicy ears of sweet corn, gleaming gold, sloshed in butter, and hot and sugary, right along through succotash, corn fritters, corn pudding, sweet corn with shrimps, with sweet potatoes, with

green peppers, sweet-corn soup with tiny hand-rubbed egg dumplings (a super soup), sweet corn with casserole chicken, this American vegetable is a constant joy to the eye and the palate. And consider other delectable corn dishes, such as hominy grits and samp, which are lickin' good just by themselves.

As for what can be done with corn-meal—well, I could write a book! Just for a high spot, there's Indian pudding, slow-baked to a quivery sweet jelly. From there we'll go on to spoon bread of infinite variety; custard corn bread; cornmeal dumplings with cabbage or kale or turnip greens; spider bread; johnnycake; hoecake in pioneer style, baked on a board before the hearth fire; cornmeal mush served hot with butter and cream, or cold and sliced and fried to crispy fingers to be eaten with or without syrup; cornmeal pancakes about the size of a silver dollar, hot little zesty wafers, crusty on the edges, waiting their libation of melted butter and maple syrup or pale rosy apple jelly! They make the much-touted *crêpes Suzette* look like the limp little liquor-soaked indigestibles they really are!

Right here I think I must insert the recipe for Custard Corn Bread that has been used in my kitchen for years. It calls for ¾ cup white cornmeal, ¼ cup

sifted all-purpose flour, 1 or 2 (according to your taste) tablespoons sugar, ½ teaspoon salt, 1 teaspoon baking powder, 1 cup plus 2 tablespoons milk, 1 egg, 2 tablespoons butter. Sift cornmeal, flour, sugar, salt, and baking powder. Stir in milk and well-beaten egg. Melt butter in 8-inch square pan. Pour in mixture. Just before closing the oven door, float a generous half cup of whole milk over the top of the batter. Do not stir in! Bake in preheated hot oven (400°F.) for at least half an hour. The result will be a tender spoon bread topped by a layer of perfect corn-flavored custard under a frail brown crust. As a breakfast dish, as a companion for bacon or ham or sausage or pork chops, in place of Yorkshire pudding with roast beef, this corn bread, to my taste, is superb! But then, I am one of those people who like all corn dishes.

Another product the American cook uses with the art its flavor demands comes from a native American tree, the sugar maple. Have you ever eaten baked grapefruit halves, the cores cut out, the holes filled with maple syrup? Or layer cake with filling and icing made with maple sugar? Or blueberry pancakes, flipped right off the griddle onto a hot plate, and with cream and maple sugar spooned over them? Or apples cored and stuffed with maple sugar, then slowly baked to fruit lusciousness? Oh, beautiful and generous sugar-maple tree—what your spring juices can do to a blasé appetite!

In all the tradition of American cooking there is one dish that, in many varieties, has come to general popularity; everyone likes it, everyone eats it, and every cook makes it. I mean, naturally, PIE! And of all American pies, apple pie is, by actual statistics, by far the most favored. The apple pie of England, which is only sourish applesauce with a crust over it; the little apple tartlet of France dolled up with custard and glaze —these are not to be mentioned in the same breath with an honest-to-goodness American apple pie, the fruit all ruddy richness, the sugar lightly but sufficiently provided, the crust light brown, beaded with carameled dots, and breaking gently ahead of the fork. What a peerless combination of brittle and soft, tasty and tangy and sweet! To gild the lily, you *can* put a generous dollop of vanilla ice cream on top of a piping-hot wedge of apple pie. Personally, I take my apple pie straight, and I cling to the plain style even under the temptation of apple custard, apple chiffon, and even apple meringue pie, which by any standard is extra edible.

There is something in the American character that responds with inventive excellence to pies. Think of oyster pie and clam pie with rich, tender crusts full of the fresh seafood savor. Pennsylvania-German housewives make their pies with special fillings—green tomatoes, green currants, black walnuts, raisins, onions—and pies with names like shoofly and crumb and schnitz. Farther south there is a splendid tendency to make pies of sweet potatoes, and in the Deep South lime pie, pecan pie, and shrimp pie flourish happily. The Middle West has always seemed to make the finest lemon meringue pie, and in New England pumpkin pie is at its supreme best, and that is supreme indeed.

There's a great deal more than supreme pumpkin pie in the cuisine of New England—baked beans, steamed brown bread, and clam chowder, for instance, all native to this part of the country. In Maryland, we have another special regional trilogy—baked shad, beaten biscuit, deviled crab. And all over America women bake wonderful high layer cakes and pour dark, glossy chocolate on their tops, or smother them in fresh coconut, or place fondants of fruits and sugars and nuts between their layers, with all sorts of individual and original flavors and decorations! Try to get layer cakes like these in any foreign bakery— or rather, I should say, don't waste your time trying. They are strictly American.

Also unique to America is strawberry shortcake, with a rich hot biscuit base, heavily buttered, supporting a roseate blanket of ripe red berries and thick cream, a delight to the eyes as well as the taste. And only in America are there blueberry muffins, made with just the least bit of batter, but with such quantities of berries that the muffin breaks open by the sheer weight of its juiciness! Serve them sometimes with roast beef or a broiled steak; you will find it's a surprising combination and perfectly wonderful.

American cooks are favored by the variety of meat, game, vegetables, and fruits this country supplies and by our great distribution system, which makes it possible to buy almost anything anywhere, in small towns or large, and at all four points of the compass. Everyone must have noticed that seasons have stretched enormously. Fresh fruits and vegetables, which once were available for a few weeks only, now are offered all the year round. And what the growers and railroads have so well established, the canners and freezers are ably supplementing. There is a challenge to taste and to try when so much is offered. The American woman who buys and cooks an odd vegetable she has never seen before is the legitimate descendant of her pioneer great-grandmother, who went into the woods and gathered fiddleheads and poke shoots and boiled them in a pot over the campfire for greens, or who learned from Indian lore how to mix corn and beans to make succotash.

One of the features of American cooking is this readiness to try new ingredients and to use old ingredients in new ways. The housewives who settled here from other lands brought their native recipes with them—the Scotch and Irish their good hot breads, the British their meat pies and steamed puddings, the French their sauces and sweets, the Italians their pastas, the Scandinavians their infinite smorgasbord, and so on. Gradually, these recipes have been swapped around, adapted to materials and ingredients at hand, and combined with what experience had already taught the cooks of this country would best suit the conditions of life here. It's a very fine thing for all concerned and has resulted in a noble repertoire of food.

Cooking is a lot quicker, a lot simpler, and a lot easier than it used to be. There is still extant a recipe for "A Rich Black Cake" that Martha Washington used at Mount Vernon, although we are not told she made it herself. The recipe begins with "Take twenty eggs" and goes on with a lavish "two pounds of butter worked to a cream." It had to bake for five and one-half hours! No doubt it was an awfully good cake, but today the cost of materials makes such a loaf prohibitive, save for the grandest party or the most eventful occasion. Yet it's nice to think of it as a sort of legacy from Martha to her historical descendant, the brisk young creature who in half an hour whipped up an icebox cake, mixed a salad, and broiled a half-dozen hamburgers, and is now calmly waiting to welcome her guests.

In this great land of ours, American Cookery is as diversified as the fifty states that make up the union.

Regional specialties abound as they are flavored by the ancestry of many lands: Scottish, Irish, French, Italian, German, Scandinavian, English, Russian, Oriental.

In this American Cook Book you will find the favorites and specialties of every state in the U.S.A.

Alabama

Scents of camellia and mimosa cling to the plateau of the Piedmont. Here Cotton is King and ships of Seven Seas yaw and splash in Mobile Bay. Sweet potatoes ripen in the sun of Coosa Valley; the Azalea Trail exudes heady perfume, and yellowhammers brighten the Cumberland. The twang of banjo and whir of cotton gin: familiar sounds of the Deep South.

OKRA SOUP

2 pounds lean, raw chuck beef, diced
¼ pound butter or margarine
12 large tomatoes, peeled, diced
1½ pounds fresh or frozen okra,
  cut into thin slices, crosswise
  Boiling water
2 cups cooked Lima beans
1 pound boiled, cured ham, diced
  Salt and pepper to taste
  Toasted croutons or bread cut
  into small squares

In deep kettle, brown meat in butter. Add tomatoes and okra. Cover with boiling water and simmer, covered, over medium heat for 1 hour. Then add 4 cups boiling water. Bring to boiling point. Lower heat and simmer, covered, stirring frequently. Skim soup as it boils. Cook until okra and tomatoes are soft. Add the cooked Lima beans and diced ham. Season with salt and pepper. Serve in plates with croutons floating on top. Makes 8 to 10 servings.

GULF-BAKED RED SNAPPER

1 red snapper (3 pounds)
1 garlic clove
1 teaspoon salt
¼ teaspoon pepper
5 tablespoons bacon fat, olive oil, melted
  butter, or margarine
1 tablespoon fresh lemon juice
2 onions, chopped
4 celery stalks, chopped

½ green pepper, chopped
2 tablespoons chopped parsley
½ teaspoon sugar
2 cups fresh or canned tomatoes
¼ teaspoon crumbled dried thyme
1 bay leaf
  Worcestershire

Put fish, cleaned, with head and tail removed, in buttered roasting pan. Crush or mince garlic. Add salt, pepper, melted fat, and lemon juice. Rub fish inside and out with this mixture. Let stand in cool place for 1 hour. Add all other ingredients. Place in preheated moderate oven (375°F.). Bake for 1 hour, or until fish flakes. Makes 6 servings.

FRIED CHICKEN
WITH PUFFS AND GRAVY

2 young broiling chickens (2½ to
  3 pounds each)
  Salt and pepper
  All-purpose flour (about 2 cups)
  Lard (about 2 cups)
1½ teaspoons baking powder
3½ cups milk

Quarter chickens. Season with salt and pepper and roll each piece in flour. Use 2 iron frying pans. Add lard to depth of 2 inches or more. Heat lard, add chickens, and cover or a few minutes. Then sauté, uncovered, until nicely browned. Remove chicken to absorbent paper and keep in warm place. Make biscuit dough using 1½ cups flour, ¼ cup lard, 1 teaspoon salt, the baking powder, and ½ cup milk. Pat out on board to ½-inch thickness and cut into 2-inch rounds. Drop biscuits into hot lard the chicken was cooked in. Brown biscuits on both sides, drain on paper, and keep hot. To make gravy, pour off lard. Return ¼ cup lard to one of the pans and blend in ¼ cup flour. Gradually stir in 3 cups milk. Cook, stirring constantly, over low heat until thickened. Season to taste. Serve chicken with biscuit puffs and gravy. Makes 4 servings.

BAKED CANDIED TOMATOES

2½ to 3 cups canned tomatoes with juice
1½ cups sugar
4 thin slices firm bread
6 tablespoons butter or margarine
  Ground cinnamon

Mix tomatoes with sugar and pour into a 1-quart loaf glass dish. Break bread into quarters and put it into the tomatoes. Slice butter thinly and dot on top of dish. Sprinkle with a little ground cinnamon. Bake in preheated slow oven (325°F.) for about 1½ to 2 hours or until tomatoes are the consistency of a thick pudding. Push bread down frequently with a spoon. Serve with meat or fowl. Makes 4 to 6 servings.

HOPPIN JOHN

2 cups blackeye peas or beans,
  washed and drained
½ pound sliced bacon

1 onion, minced
2 cups rice
1 tablespoon salt
¼ teaspoon pepper
1 hot red pepper

Bring peas and 3 quarts water to boil. Boil for 2 minutes. Cover pan and let stand for 1 hour. Cut up bacon and cook until brown; add onions and cook until golden. Pour bacon mixture into peas. Cover and simmer until peas are tender, about 1 hour. Stir in rice and seasonings. Cook, covered, without stirring until rice is tender. Makes 8 to 10 servings.

SOUTHERN CORN-SOUFFLÉ PUDDING

5 ears young field corn
¼ cup melted butter or margarine
1 cup milk
3 egg yolks
2 tablespoons sugar
¼ teaspoon salt
⅛ teaspoon pepper
3 well-beaten egg whites

Grate corn or split kernels with a corn scraper or sharp knife. Hold cobs over a bowl and scrape corn with back of knife. Add other ingredients except egg whites and beat well to blend. Fold in the well-beaten whites. Pour into well-greased 9-inch casserole or baking dish and put in shallow pan of water in preheated moderate oven (375°F.). Cook until the mixture just sets, 50 to 60 minutes. Serve at once. Do not cook too long. Makes 4 to 6 servings. This pudding is excellent with roast baby lamb or spring chicken, especially in the summer.

SWEET-POTATO PUDDING

3 cups grated raw sweet potatoes
½ cup light brown sugar
½ teaspoon salt
1 teaspoon ground nutmeg
½ cup light corn syrup
1 cup milk
2 eggs, beaten
½ cup chopped pecans
2 tablespoons butter, melted

Mix all ingredients in bowl. Blend well. Pour into buttered pan, 12 x 8 x 2 inches. Bake in preheated moderate oven (350°F.) for about 1 hour. Serve warm or cold with cream or ice cream. Makes 6 servings.

MAMMY'S SOUR-MILK BISCUITS

2 cups sifted all-purpose flour
1 teaspoon baking powder
½ teaspoon baking soda
1 teaspoon salt
¼ cup soft butter or margarine
1 cup thick sour milk (or less
  if not thick), or buttermilk

Sift dry ingredients into bowl. Cut in butter with pastry blender. Add enough sour milk to make a soft dough, mixing lightly with fork. Turn out on floured board and knead about 20 turns. Roll out to ½-inch thickness and cut with floured 2-inch cutter. Bake in preheated very hot oven (450°F.) for 10 to 12 minutes. Makes 12 to 14.

Alaska

The Klondike is cold and Sitka spruce shiver in empty loneliness. Otter, seal, caribou, grizzly and reindeer are ready for it. So are the native Aleut and the adventurous sourdough. The treeless tundra, glassy glacier and frozen fjord call ever to the wild. There is majesty in Mount McKinley and gold in them thar hills. But north of the untamed Yukon Territory, it's cold.

PIROK (Salmon Pie)

Pastry for 2-crust 8-inch square pie, unbaked
2 cups cooked rice
2 cups medium cream sauce
2 medium onions, thinly sliced
2 tablespoons butter
1 pound fresh salmon or 1 can (1 pound) salmon
2 hard-cooked eggs, finely chopped
½ cup grated Cheddar cheese
½ cup mayonnaise

Roll out half the pastry ⅛ inch thick and use to line an 8-inch square pan. Mix rice with ½ cup cream sauce. Sauté onions in butter until golden. Place half of rice mixture in pastry. Add pieces of salmon. Distribute onions and eggs over salmon, then cover with remaining rice. Roll out second half of dough and place over rice. Moisten edges and seal to lower crust. Make a few slits in top crust for escape of steam. Bake in preheated moderate oven (350°F.) for 1 hour if raw salmon is used, or for 15 minutes in very hot oven (450°F.) if canned salmon is used. Melt cheese in remaining cream sauce. Remove from heat and fold in mayonnaise. Cut Pirok into squares and serve with mayonnaise-cheese sauce. Makes 4 to 6 servings.

TRAPPER'S GAME STEW

2 pounds moose, elk, caribou, venison, or beef pot roast, cut into 1½-inch cubes
2 tablespoons bacon fat
Hot water
1 bay leaf
6 medium carrots, cut into 1-inch pieces
Salt and pepper
3 medium onions, coarsely chopped
6 medium potatoes, peeled and cut into 1-inch cubes
1 small green cabbage, quartered

Brown meat in hot bacon fat in Dutch oven or heavy saucepan. Add enough hot water to cover meat and simmer, covered, for 1 hour. Add bay leaf, carrots, salt, and pepper. Simmer, covered, for 30 minutes more. Add onions and potatoes. If necessary, add more hot water to keep ingredients covered. Simmer, covered, for 30 minutes longer. Add cabbage and cook, covered, for 15 minutes longer. Add seasonings to taste. Makes 4 to 6 servings.

MARINATED VENISON

4½ pounds venison, shoulder, neck, or breast
3 medium onions, sliced
2 carrots, sliced
3 celery stalks, chopped
2 garlic cloves, mashed
1½ teaspoons salt
15 peppercorns
8 juniper berries, crushed
2 tablespoons chopped parsley
2 bay leaves
¼ cup fresh lemon juice
3 cups beer
¾ cup salad oil

Remove skin, bones, and tendons from meat. Cut into 1½-inch cubes. Place remaining ingredients in stoneware or earthenware crock and mix well. Add meat and stir well. Cover. Let stand in refrigerator for 1 to 2 days, stirring meat several times. Place meat with marinade in a large kettle and bring to a boil. Cover, lower heat, and simmer for 1½ to 2 hours, or until meat is tender. Remove meat and strain cooking liquid, pressing vegetables through the strainer. If desired, sauce may be thickened with a little flour mixed with cold water. Makes 8 to 10 servings.

ALASKA DUCK SALAD

2 cups cubed duck meat
1½ cups cubed peeled apples
1½ cups canned or fresh orange sections
½ cup finely diced celery
¼ cup French dressing
Lettuce

The duck meat and apples (peeled and cored) should be cut into ½-inch cubes and the orange sections cut into halves, so that the fruit and meat are about the same size. Combine meat, fruit, and celery, and toss with French dressing. Chill. Serve on a bed of crisp lettuce. Makes 6 servings.

CHOPPED-CABBAGE PICKLE

5 pounds cabbage
6 medium onions
3 green peppers
½ cup salt
¾ cup mustard seeds
2 tablespoons celery seeds
4 cups sugar
Vinegar

Using a chopping bowl, chop cabbage, onions, and peppers very fine. Do not grind. Stir in salt and let stand for 24 hours. Drain well. Add mustard seeds, celery seeds, and sugar and mix well. Cover with vinegar. Pack in sterilized pint jars and cover. Keep in a cool place. Makes about 9 pints.

SPICED BLUEBERRIES

4 cups (1 quart) fresh blueberries
5 cups sugar
½ cup cider vinegar
½ teaspoon each of ground cinnamon, cloves, and allspice
1 cup liquid fruit pectin

Mix all ingredients except pectin in a saucepan. Bring to a boil and cook for 1 minute. Remove from heat and add fruit pectin. Stir well. Pack into sterilized jars. Seal. Makes about 4 pints.

RASPBERRY-JAM BREAD PUDDING

3 cups toasted bread cubes
4 eggs
4 cups milk, scalded
Sugar (about 1 cup)
¼ teaspoon salt
1 teaspoon vanilla extract
⅓ cup melted butter or margarine
¾ cup raspberry jam

Place bread cubes in a 2-quart casserole. Beat 2 eggs with 2 egg yolks, reserving 2 egg whites for the meringue. Gradually beat scalded milk into eggs. Beat in ½ cup sugar, salt, vanilla, and butter. Pour milk mixture over bread cubes. Bake in preheated moderate oven (350°F.) for 25 minutes. Spread jam evenly over top of pudding. Beat egg whites until stiff but not dry. Beat in sugar, 1 tablespoon at a time, until meringue is stiff and glossy. Pile meringue over jam, making sure to spread meringue to edge of dish. Bake for another 15 minutes. Makes 8 servings.

SOURDOUGH PANCAKES

2 packages active dry yeast or 2 cakes compressed yeast
1 quart water*
6 cups sifted all-purpose flour
2 teaspoons salt
1 teaspoon baking soda
3 tablespoons molasses
½ cup hot water
5 eggs, beaten

* Use very warm water (105°F. to 115°F.) for dry yeast; use lukewarm (80°F. to 90°F.) for compressed. Sprinkle dry yeast or crumble cake into water. Let stand for a few minutes; then stir until

dissolved. Stir in flour. Cover and let stand for 24 hours at room temperature. Add salt, soda, molasses, and hot water. Add eggs. Don't beat them in, but just mix them in. Let stand for 30 minutes. Cook on a lightly greased heated griddle in the usual manner. Makes about forty 5-inch pancakes.

Arizona

Sirocco winds scud through Canyon Diablo, bending the giant cactus and paloverde tree, sending the tumbleweed scurrying across the desert floor. Cactus wrens soar over the red-veined copper lodes. Painted Desert, Petrified Forest—where Hopi, Yaqui and Navajo dwell. Place of the canyons: Grand, Black, Glen—where prehistoric heavings have rent the land.

GRAPEFRUIT-HONEY NOG

1 egg, separated
1 cup chilled grapefruit juice
  Dash of salt
2 to 4 teaspoons honey
  Grated nutmeg

Beat egg white until stiff. Set aside. Beat egg yolk. Gradually add grapefruit juice, beating constantly. Add salt and honey. Add to egg white, mixing gently. Pour into chilled glass and sprinkle with nutmeg. Makes 1 serving.

■ **Variations**—Substitute half orange and half lemon juice for the grapefruit juice. Or substitute kumquat, tangerine, or grape juice with half lemon or lime juice.

MEATBALL SOUP

¾ pound ground beef
1 small garlic clove, minced
  Few parsley sprigs, chopped
½ teaspoon salt
⅛ teaspoon pepper
¼ cup uncooked rice
1 teaspoon chili powder
1 egg

6 cups beef bouillon
½ cup tomato sauce

Mix all ingredients except bouillon and tomato sauce. Shape into marble-size balls. Bring bouillon and tomato sauce to boil. Drop in meatballs. Simmer, covered, for 30 minutes. Makes 4 servings.

PICHOLA

2 pounds fresh pork, in one piece
2 medium onions, sliced
3 cups canned tomatoes
  Chili powder to taste
3 cups cooked and drained hominy

Fry pork until brown on all sides. Add onions, tomatoes, and chili powder to taste. Cover and cook over low heat until meat is tender, about 2 hours. Add hominy and cook for 30 minutes longer. Makes 6 to 8 servings.

JERKED VENISON OR BEEF

Cut fresh beef or venison into 1-inch-wide strips across the grain. Hang meat in the sun until meat has dried and is stiff and leathery. If the atmosphere is damp, the meat should be rubbed with salt before it is dried.

The strips can be chewed like chipped beef, or can be pounded and simmered until tender, like stew.

COWPUNCHER'S BEAN STEW

1 pound pinto beans
6 cups water
½ teaspoon ground cuminseed
1 to 2 garlic cloves
2 tablespoons salt
2 tablespoons bacon fat or lard
1 small red chili pepper, chopped fine (optional)

Cover beans with water. Add cuminseed and garlic. Simmer, covered, over very low heat for 1½ hours, adding more water if necessary. Add salt and bacon fat. Continue cooking, stirring occasionally, until beans are tender. Top with chopped red chili pepper, if desired. Makes 6 servings.

ARIZONA SWEET POTATOES

4 cups cubed peeled cooked sweet potatoes
1 cup chopped green pepper
1 cup chopped onions
½ cup shortening
  Salt and pepper

Mix potatoes with green pepper and onions. Sauté vegetables in hot shortening until brown and crisp. Add salt and pepper to taste. Makes 6 to 8 servings.

ARIZONA PECAN AND DATE PIE

3 tablespoons butter or margarine
⅓ cup sugar
3 eggs
¼ teaspoon salt
1 teaspoon vanilla extract
1 tablespoon all-purpose flour
1 cup dark corn syrup
12 dates, pitted and cut into pieces
¾ cup chopped pecans

Pastry for 1-crust 9-inch pie, unbaked

Cream butter with sugar. Beat in eggs, one at a time. Beat in salt and vanilla. Add flour and blend well. Add corn syrup. Fold in dates and pecans. Pour into pastry-lined 9-inch pie pan. Bake in preheated slow oven (325°F.) for 45 minutes, or until set. Makes 6 servings.

AVOCADO ICE CREAM

3 egg yolks
¾ cup milk
¾ cup sugar
  Dash of salt
1 cup heavy cream
2 ripe medium avocados, peeled
  Few drops green food coloring

Beat first 4 ingredients together in top part of small double boiler. Put over simmering water and cook, stirring, until thickened and mixture coats a metal spoon. Cool. Whip cream until thick. Add avocado to cream, one slice at a time, beating until blended. Add coloring. Fold into first mixture. Pour into freezing tray and freeze until firm. Serve plain or with a sauce made from 1 box thawed frozen raspberries, whirled in blender. Makes 4 servings.

POMEGRANATE ICE

1 quart pomegranate juice
3 tablespoons fresh lime juice
1 envelope unflavored gelatin
¼ cup cold water
¾ cup fresh lemon juice
2 cups sugar
4 cups water
  Red coloring (optional)

To obtain pomegranate juice, remove pomegranate seeds, making sure no yellow membrane remains. Place seeds in several thicknesses of cheesecloth. Crush seeds and drain off juice. Mix juice with lime juice. Sprinkle gelatin on cold water. Let stand for 5 minutes. Place over low heat until gelatin is dissolved. Add gelatin with remaining ingredients to the pomegranate juice. Stir until sugar is dissolved. Add red coloring, if desired. Pour into container of crank freezer and freeze until firm. Makes 2½ quarts.

SPICED CANTALOUPE

4 cantaloupes
2 teaspoons powdered alum
2 cups white vinegar
4 cups sugar
4 cinnamon sticks
1 tablespoon each of whole cloves and allspice

Peel melons; cut into halves and remove seeds and fiber. Cut into ½-inch cubes. Mix 3 quarts water with alum and add melon. Let stand overnight; drain. In preserving kettle mix vinegar, sugar, 1 cup water, and spices tied in cheesecloth bag. Add melon; cover and boil for 15 minutes. Pack melon into hot sterilized jars.

Pour in syrup to within ½ inch of top. Put on cap, screwing band tight. Put on rack in kettle. Add boiling water to 1 inch over jars. Bring to boil and boil for 10 minutes. Makes 5 pints.

Arkansas

Hot springs bubble in the Ozarks, where an Arkansas Traveler hears a canvasback or mallard honking for passage along the Mississippi flyway. Gum cypress, hickory and pine stretch out their leafy arms in the forests of the Ouachita, and a prospector digging mid Murfreesboro's sandstone highlands can keep any diamond he finds —but only up to five carats.

FRIED CATFISH, HOME STYLE

4 pounds catfish
  Salt and pepper
¼ cup bacon drippings or lard
  Juice of 1 lemon
¼ cup chopped parsley

Clean and skin catfish and pat dry. Sprinkle with salt and pepper. Sauté in hot bacon drippings or lard over moderate heat until browned on both sides. Drain fish on paper towels and place on hot serving dish. Sprinkle with lemon juice and parsley. Serve with turnip greens. Makes 4 servings.

BROILED TROUT
WITH WATERCRESS BUTTER

4 trout, about 1 pound each
2 tablespoons melted butter
  Salt, pepper, paprika
  Watercress Butter

Brush trout with butter, and season. Place on buttered sheet of foil in broiler pan. Put in broiler 4 inches away from high heat. Broil without turning for 6 to 8 minutes, or until done. Serve with Watercress Butter. Makes 4 servings.

Watercress Butter

¼ cup butter
½ teaspoon salt
⅛ teaspoon pepper
¼ teaspoon paprika
  Juice of ½ lemon
2 tablespoons cut watercress leaves

Melt butter over very low heat. Add remaining ingredients. Stir and serve. Makes 4 servings.

ROAST OPOSSUM WITH YAMS

To prepare opossum, clean but do not skin. Immerse in water just below the boiling point. When hair pulls out easily, remove from water. Scrape off hair while washing repeatedly with cool water. Remove small red glands in small of back and under each foreleg between the shoulder and rib. If the opossum appears to be full grown, it should be precooked in simmering salted water for about 1 hour. Then remove from water and wipe dry. Season inside with salt and pepper. Stuff lightly with buttered crumbs seasoned with diced cooked bacon and onions. Sew opening. Place in open roasting pan. Surround with peeled raw sweet potatoes. Roast in preheated moderate oven (350°F.) for 1½ hours, or until potatoes and meat are tender. Baste occasionally with melted butter mixed with a little Worcestershire, salt, and pepper. Makes 6 to 8 servings.

BRAISED QUAILS

6 quails
  Salt and pepper
  All-purpose flour
6 tablespoons butter or margarine
¾ cup water
8 medium-size fresh mushrooms, sliced
3 tablespoons chopped parsley
6 slices buttered toast

Wash quails, pat dry, and sprinkle inside and out with salt and pepper. Coat outside of quails with flour. Melt butter in a skillet and brown quails on all sides until golden brown. Add water and sliced mushrooms. Cover and simmer over low heat for 10 minutes. Add parsley, cover, and cook for 10 minutes longer, or until quails are tender. Serve on buttered toast with pan juice poured over quails. Makes 6 servings.

Note: The quail can also be served in trenchers made from 2-inch-thick slices of French bread. Scoop centers from slices of bread. Butter inside and out and toast lightly.

BARBECUED SPARERIBS

1 teaspoon dry mustard
1 teaspoon salt
1 teaspoon paprika
  Dash of hot pepper sauce
2 tablespoons Worcestershire
2 tablespoons honey
½ cup ketchup
1 cup vinegar
1 cup water
¼ cup butter or margarine
2 garlic cloves
2 onions, chopped
3 racks (6 pounds) spareribs, cut into serving pieces

Combine all ingredients except spareribs. Bring to a boil; cool. Pour over spareribs in a big bowl. Let stand for 2 to 3 hours, turning meat occasionally. Put ribs in roasting pan; roast in preheated slow oven (325°F.) for 1½ hours, turning and basting with marinade occasionally. Makes 6 servings.

CORN DODGERS

2 cups yellow cornmeal
1 teaspoon salt
2 teaspoons fat
2 cups boiling water

Combine cornmeal, salt, and fat. Add boiling water and beat thoroughly. Spread in a layer ½ to ¾ inch thick in two 9-inch pie plates. Bake in preheated hot oven (400°F.) for 30 minutes, or until crisp and brown, or bake in a skillet over an open fire as originally baked. Serve hot with butter, gravy, or stew. Makes 6 to 8 servings.

OZARK PUDDING

¾ cup sugar
2 eggs, beaten
2 tablespoons all-purpose flour
⅛ teaspoon salt
½ teaspoon baking powder
½ cup finely chopped peeled tart apples
½ cup chopped nuts

Beat sugar into eggs. Add remaining ingredients and mix well. Pour into greased 8-inch pie pan. Bake in preheated slow oven (325°F.) for about 30 minutes. Serve with cream or ice cream. Makes 4 to 5 servings.

PERSIMMON PUDDING

½ cup butter or margarine
1 cup firmly packed brown sugar
3 eggs
1½ cups sifted all-purpose flour
2 teaspoons baking powder
½ cup milk
1½ cups persimmon pulp
½ teaspoon ground cinnamon
¼ teaspoon ground cloves

Cream butter until light and fluffy. Gradually beat in brown sugar. Add eggs, one at a time, beating well after each addition. Sift flour with baking powder. Add flour alternately with milk, beginning and ending with flour. Fold in persimmon pulp and spices. Pour mixture into a greased 1½-quart pudding mold. Steam for 1½ hours. Makes 6 to 8 servings.

California

Redwood, orange blossom, green Yosemite, Rose Bowl, white Whitney, silver screen, Golden Gate—colors by the Pacific. City of Angels, Valley of Death, saintly towns of Diego, Barbara, Clara, and Francisco. Astronomers observe, skiers slalom, swallows return, abalone simmers, Mojave shimmers, trolleys clang, wines glow, and motorists drive through a giant sequoia.

FISHERMAN'S WHARF CIOPPINO

- 1 onion, chopped
- 1 green pepper, chopped
- ½ cup sliced green onion
- 4 garlic cloves, minced
- 3 tablespoons olive oil
- 2⅓ cups (one 1-pound, 3-oz. can) tomatoes
- 1⅓ cups tomato puree
  Pinch of dried thyme
- 1 bay leaf
- 1 teaspoon salt
- ¼ teaspoon pepper
- 2 cups dry white wine
- 12 small clams, in the shell
- 12 small oysters, in the shell
- 2 small lobsters or 4 lobster tails, quartered and cracked
- 1 large or 2 small hard-shell crabs, split, with legs disjointed
- 12 shelled and deveined shrimps

Cook onion, green pepper, green onion, and garlic in oil for 5 minutes. Add remaining ingredients except wine and fish. Bring to boil, cover, and simmer for 2 hours, stirring frequently. Add wine and cook for 10 minutes. Put scrubbed raw fish in large kettle. Pour sauce over all. Simmer, covered, for 20 minutes. Makes 4 generous servings.

CHINESE SWEET-AND-SOUR PORK

- ½ cup soy sauce
- ½ teaspoon ground ginger
- ¼ teaspoon each of salt and monosodium glutamate

- 1 garlic clove, minced or mashed
- 2 pounds lean pork butt, cut into thin strips, then into 1-inch pieces
  About ½ cup cornstarch
  Cooking oil for deep frying
- 1 cup pineapple juice
- ½ cup white vinegar
- ¼ cup ketchup
- ¾ cup firmly packed light brown sugar
- 1 tablespoon Worcestershire
  Dash of red pepper sauce
- 2 large green peppers, seeded and cut into 1-inch squares
- 2 tablespoons sliced green onions
- 2 large tomatoes, cut into small wedges
- 2 cups pineapple chunks, drained
- ¼ cup water
  Chinese parsley (optional)

Combine soy, ginger, salt, monosodium glutamate, and garlic. Pour over pork and allow to stand for 30 minutes; stir occasionally. Dredge pork pieces with 6 tablespoons cornstarch. Cook meat, a few pieces at a time, in hot deep fat (380°F. on frying thermometer) for 8 to 10 minutes, or until crisp and brown. Drain on absorbent paper; keep warm. In a skillet combine pineapple juice, vinegar, ketchup, brown sugar, Worcestershire, and pepper sauce. Bring to a boil. Add green pepper and onion and cook for 1 minute over high heat. Add tomato, pineapple, and cooked meat. Mix 2 tablespoons cornstarch and water, and add. Stir and cook for 1 minute, or until sauce is thickened and hot. Turn onto heated serving platter. Garnish with Chinese parsley if you wish. This recipe makes 6 generous main-dish servings. If the dish is to be served Chinese style, as one of several other main-course dishes, it will serve 8 or more.

TATSUTA-AGE (Japanese Fried Chicken)

- 2 raw chicken breasts, boned
- 1 tablespoon sake or sherry
- 1 tablespoon soy sauce
- 4 green peppers
  Oil for frying
  Cornstarch
- ½ teaspoon salt
- ⅛ teaspoon pepper
- ⅛ teaspoon monosodium glutamate

Slice chicken meat into thin pieces so that it can be eaten without cutting. Mix sake (or sherry) and soy sauce together and place chicken in this for about 30 minutes. Cut peppers into halves and take out seeds. Heat oil. Cover chicken with cornstarch. When oil is hot, fry chicken until tender. Drain on absorbent paper. Fry green peppers until just soft. Drain on absorbent paper. Sprinkle chicken and green peppers with salt, pepper, and monosodium glutamate. Arrange decoratively on serving platter. Makes 4 servings.

MEXICAN PUCHERO

- ¼ pound salt pork, diced
- 3 cups cubed boneless beef
- 1 garlic clove
- 1 medium onion, minced
- 1 cup chopped cabbage
- 1 teaspoon crumbled oregano
- ½ teaspoon ground coriander
- ½ teaspoon ground cuminseed
- 2½ cups canned tomatoes
- 2 tablespoons chopped parsley
- ¾ cup soaked garbanzos or chick-peas
- ⅓ cup rice
- 1 cup fresh cut kernel corn
  Salt and pepper

Brown salt pork. Add remaining ingredients, except last 2. Cover and simmer, stirring occasionally, for 1½ hours, or until meat is tender. Add corn and salt and pepper to taste. Cook for a few minutes longer to reheat. Drain broth and serve separately with the meat and vegetables. Makes 4 to 6 servings.

NAPA VALLEY LAMB CHOPS

- 4 shoulder lamb chops
  Meat tenderizer
- 1 garlic clove, chopped
- 3 tablespoons cooking oil
  Salt and pepper
- 1 medium onion, peeled and chopped
- 1 can (10½ ounces) condensed consomme
- ¾ cup white wine
- 4 carrots, sliced
- 4 white turnips, peeled and cut into quarters
- 4 new potatoes, peeled and halved

Cut edges of lamb chops to prevent curling. Sprinkle chops with meat tenderizer and let stand for 1 hour. Heat garlic in oil. Sauté lamb chops in oil until brown on both sides. Season meat with salt and pepper, and add onion, consommé, and wine. Cover and simmer over low heat for 30 minutes, or until meat is tender. Add vegetables, cover, and cook for 30 minutes longer, or until vegetables are tender. Add liquid to pan if necessary to keep meat and vegetables from sticking. Serve with pan juices which may or may not be thickened. Makes 4 servings.

VISALIA RIPE-OLIVE BREAD

- 3 eggs, well beaten
- 2 tablespoons sugar
- 1 teaspoon salt
- 3 tablespoons olive oil
- 2 cups chopped pitted ripe olives
- 3 cups sifted all-purpose flour
- 1 tablespoon baking powder
- ¾ cup milk

Beat eggs with sugar, salt, and oil. Stir in olives. Sift flour with baking powder and add alternately with milk to other ingredients. Stir gently until just blended. Pour mixture into a well-greased loaf pan (9 x 5 x 3 inches). Let stand for 30 minutes. Bake in preheated moderate oven (350°F.) for 1 to 1½ hours, or until bread tests done. Do not serve warm; bread improves on standing. Serve with sweet butter and cheese. Makes 1 loaf.

CAESAR SALAD

1 garlic clove, crushed
¾ cup olive oil
2 cups ¼-inch bread cubes, no crusts
2 large heads romaine lettuce
  Freshly ground black pepper
½ teaspoon salt
2 eggs, soft-cooked for 1 minute
3 tablespoons fresh lemon juice
½ cup grated Parmesan cheese

Mix garlic with oil and let stand overnight. Heat ¼ cup of the oil and sauté bread cubes until golden on all sides. Drain and set aside. Clean and trim romaine. Wash and break into bite-size pieces. Grind on plenty of black pepper. Add salt and remaining olive oil. Toss well to coat romaine. Place shelled eggs in center of salad. Add lemon juice and toss until salad greens are coated with a creamy dressing. Toss with Parmesan cheese and croutons. Serve at once. Makes 6 to 8 servings.

THOMPSON SEEDLESS GRAPES IN SOUR CREAM

1 pound tart seedless grapes
½ pint dairy sour cream
⅔ cup firmly packed dark brown sugar

Wash and stem grapes. Put in glass bowl. Top with sour cream and sprinkle with sugar. Chill for several hours before serving. Makes 4 servings.

Colorado

Big Horn sheep gambol where the columbine grows, and the deer and the antelope play in the Black Canyon of the Gunnison. Exhausted, dusty mining hamlets maintain their ghosts, and the caves of ancient cliff dwellers yawn and gape on the Mesa Verde. Great Sand Dunes and Garden of the Gods, above, Pike's Peak looms and cadets fly "into the wild blue yonder."

CAMPFIRE TROUT

6 brook trout, prepared for cooking
  All-purpose flour or cornmeal
12 bacon slices
  Salt

Wash trout and pat dry. Dip trout into flour or cornmeal to cover all surfaces. Cook bacon to desired crispness. Drain and reserve. Sauté trout quickly in hot bacon fat. Do not overcook. Taste for seasoning; if necessary, add salt to taste. Serve trout with crisp bacon and plenty of steaming campfire coffee. Makes 4 to 6 servings.

SMOTHERED STEAK

2 pounds shoulder steak
  Meat tenderizer
¼ cup all-purpose flour
1 teaspoon salt
1 teaspoon celery salt
¼ teaspoon pepper
2 tablespoons fat
2 onions, sliced
¼ cup chopped green pepper
2⅓ cups (one 1-pound, 3-ounce can) tomatoes
  Dash of hot pepper sauce

Use meat tenderizer according to manufacturer's directions. Mix flour with seasonings and use to dredge meat. Heat fat in skillet and brown meat on both sides. Cover steak with onion, green pepper, and tomatoes. Add a dash of hot pepper sauce. Roast in preheated slow oven (300°F.) for 2 hours, or until tender. Makes 4 to 6 servings.

GAME MULLIGAN

1 piece shoulder or rump (about 2 pounds)
¾ cup wine vinegar
¼ cup olive oil
3 or 4 juniper berries
1 yellow onion, sliced
8 to 10 whole cloves
6 to 8 peppercorns
¼ cup butter or margarine
1½ cups canned tomatoes
1 cup diced yellow turnips
¾ cup diced yellow onions
4 carrots, sliced
1 cup kernel corn
2 cups fresh sliced green beans
½ cup sliced celery

Wash meat and pat dry. Mix wine vinegar, oil, juniper berries, onion, cloves, and peppercorns. Marinate meat in mixture overnight or longer. Drain meat. Cube meat and brown on all sides in butter. Cover with cold water and bring to a boil. Reduce heat and simmer, covered, for 1½ to 2 hours, or until meat is tender. Add remaining ingredients and simmer, covered, until vegetables are tender. Makes 4 to 6 servings.

DENVER SANDWICHES

½ pound fresh ham, finely diced
2 onions, chopped
1 green pepper, chopped
  Butter

8 eggs
  Salt and pepper
8 slices of bread

Dice ham and fry with onion and pepper in 1 tablespoon butter until lightly browned. Add eggs and seasonings, stir gently. When lightly browned, turn, cut into 4 wedges, and serve between slices of buttered bread. Makes 4 sandwiches.

SQUAW CORN

½ pound bacon
1¾ cups (one 1-pound, 1-ounce can) cream-style corn
2 eggs, beaten
  Salt and pepper

Dice bacon and fry in a skillet until crisp. Pour off all but 2 tablespoons fat and add corn and eggs. Season. Cook over low heat, stirring, until eggs are creamy and thickened. Makes 4 servings.

PIKE'S PEAK—RAISED POTATO BISCUITS

1 medium potato
  Water
1 package active dry yeast
  or 1 cake compressed yeast
1½ cups milk
1 egg, beaten
½ teaspoon baking soda
1 teaspoon baking powder
1½ teaspoons salt
⅓ cup sugar
  Flour (about 6 cups)
  Melted lard (about ¾ cup)

Peel potato, slice, and cook in boiling water to cover until very tender. Do not drain. Mash with fork or force through sieve. Use very warm water (105°F. to 115°F.) for dry yeast; use lukewarm (80°F. to 90°F.) for compressed. Sprinkle dry yeast or crumble cake into ¼ cup water. Let stand a few minutes; then stir until dissolved. When potato mixture is lukewarm, add yeast. Add milk, egg, baking soda, baking powder, salt, sugar, and 2 cups flour. Beat well, cover, and let stand until bubbly. Stir in ½ cup melted lard and 4 more cups flour, beating well. Roll out on floured board to ½-inch thickness. Cut into rounds with floured 2½-inch cutter. Dip each into melted lard. Place on ungreased cookie sheets. Let stand for 30 minutes, or just until double in bulk. Do not let dough over-rise. Bake in preheated hot oven (425°F.) for 12 to 15 minutes. Makes about 4 dozen.

GINGERED MELON

Rocky Ford cantaloupe
Ground ginger
Wild honey
Pine nuts

Chill ripe cantaloupe, cut into halves, and scoop out seeds. Peel melons and cut into lengthwise slices, fanning out slices on plate. Allow half a melon per serving. Sprinkle lightly with ginger. Warm honey slightly and drizzle over top of melon slices. Garnish with a few pine nuts.

PAM'S APPLE PIE WITH CHEESE

Pastry for 2-crust, 9-inch pie, unbaked (pastry should be made with lard, or half lard and half shortening)
8 large Greenings or Rome Beauties
½ cup firmly packed light brown sugar
¼ cup honey
1 teaspoon ground cinnamon
2 teaspoons grated lemon rind
2 tablespoons butter
½ cup grated sharp Cheddar cheese

Roll out pastry and use half to line a 9-inch pie pan, allowing the pastry to hang 1 inch over edge of pie plate. Peel apples, core, and cut into slices ½ inch thick. Mix apples with sugar, honey, cinnamon, and lemon rind. Spoon mixture into pastry-lined pie pan, allowing the filling to heap high. Dot top with butter. Place top crust over apples. Press pastry firmly around apples, sealing edges with water and pressing them firmly together with tines of a fork. Prick or slash top to allow steam to escape. Bake in preheated moderate oven (375°F.) for about 1 hour, or until apples are easily pierced with a fork. Remove pie from oven and let cool until warm. Sprinkle cheese over top of pie and place pie under broiler until cheese is melted and bubbly. Serve at once. Makes 6 to 8 servings.

Connecticut

Gateway to New England, whose salt-boxes and church spires on village greens tell of colonial stalwarts who settled the lovely postcard towns: Litch-field, Guilford, Old Lyme. Mystic, where ancient mariners went down to the sea; New London, where submarines sink silently in the Sound. Yale fence, Housatonic's covered spans, and mellowing tobacco leaves.

NUTMEG STATE CRAB SOUP

2 tablespoons butter
2 tablespoons all-purpose flour
4 cups milk
Grated rind of 2 lemons
1 teaspoon Worcestershire
1 cup flaked crabmeat
2 hard-cooked eggs, sieved
1 cup heavy cream or evaporated milk
¼ cup sherry
Salt and pepper

Melt butter in top part of double boiler. Stir in flour. Gradually stir in milk, rind, and Worcestershire. Cook over boiling water until slightly thickened, stirring occasionally. Add crabmeat, eggs, cream, and sherry. Season to taste. Reheat and serve. Makes 1½ quarts.

PICKLED OYSTERS

5 whole cloves
10 peppercorns
½ cup cider vinegar
½ cup oyster liquid
4 cups fresh shelled oysters, drained

Add whole cloves and peppercorns to vinegar and oyster liquid. Bring mixture to the boiling point. Add oysters and simmer until oysters curl. Cool and then chill in refrigerator until ready to serve. Good for appetizers. Makes 6 to 8 servings.

BROILED CONNECTICUT RIVER SHAD

3- or 4-pound shad
Melted butter or margarine
Salt and pepper to taste
Parsley
¼ cup soft butter or margarine
1 tablespoon fresh lemon juice

Have shad cleaned and split. Put, skin side down, on an oiled and preheated plank or ovenproof platter. Brush with melted butter and sprinkle with salt and pepper. Broil for 15 to 20 minutes, depending upon size and thickness of fish. Remove to a serving tray and garnish with parsley. Cream butter, add lemon juice, and spread on fish. Serve at once. Makes 6 servings.

BOILED DINNER

4 pounds corned beef brisket
1 garlic clove, slivered
1 onion stuck with 3 cloves
8 whole carrots, scraped
Water
6 whole white onions, peeled
6 whole white turnips, peeled
1 medium head cabbage, quartered

Wash meat to remove brine. Let soak in cold water for 1 hour before cooking. Drain. With pointed sharp knife, cut little pockets in the meat and insert garlic slivers. Place meat in deep kettle. Add onion and 2 of the carrots. Add cold water to cover. Bring to a boil. Remove scum as it rises. Lower heat and cover. Simmer for 1 hour. Pour off liquid and add enough fresh boiling water to cover meat. Cover and continue cooking over

lowest possible heat for 4 to 5 hours, or until meat is tender. During the last hour, add remaining carrots, onions, and turnips. Add cabbage 15 minutes before serving time. Slice meat and arrange on hot platter. Surround with vegetables. Serve with boiled potatoes, mustard, and pickles. Makes 6 servings.

GREEN PEAS AND NEW POTATOES WITH CREAM

¼ pound salt pork
1 large onion, peeled and minced
10 new potatoes
3 cups cooked peas
1½ cups heavy cream

Slice pork and fry slices until crisp. Remove pork and reserve. Add onion to pork fat and sauté until golden brown. Scrub potatoes but do not peel. Place potatoes and pork slices in pan with onion. Cover and simmer, adding only a few spoons of water to keep potatoes from sticking, until potatoes are tender. Remove pork slices. Add peas and cream and simmer, stirring, until heated through and well blended. Makes 4 to 6 servings.

CORN OYSTERS

Combine 2½ cups grated fresh corn, 1 beaten egg, ½ cup milk, ½ teaspoon salt, 1 tablespoon sugar, and ¾ cup sifted all-purpose flour. Mix well. Heat 2 tablespoons butter in skillet. Drop batter into skillet by tablespoon. Brown on both sides. Makes 12 large "oysters."

RHUBARB PUDDING

4 cups of 1-inch pieces of young pink rhubarb
1 cup sugar
½ cup soft stale bread crumbs
6 tablespoons butter or margarine
Whipped cream sweetened with sugar and flavored with vanilla extract

Spread half of rhubarb pieces on the bottom of a shallow casserole. Sprinkle with half of sugar. Top with half of bread crumbs. Dot the top with half of butter. Repeat layering once more. Bake in preheated moderate oven (375°F.) for about 40 minutes, or until rhubarb is tender. Serve warm with well-chilled whipped cream. Makes 6 servings.

ELECTION CAKE

2 packages active dry yeast or 2 cakes compressed yeast
¼ cup water*
Granulated sugar
½ cup boiling water
½ cup firmly packed dark brown sugar
1¼ cups unsifted all-purpose flour
2¾ cups sifted cake flour
1¼ teaspoons salt
1 teaspoon each of ground nutmeg and mace
3 eggs
¾ cup shortening
½ teaspoon grated lemon rind
1 teaspoon vanilla extract
½ cup milk
½ cup currants or seedless raisins

½ cup each of diced candied pineapple and citron
¼ cup diced candied orange peel
Frosting

* Use very warm water (105°F. to 115° F.) for dry yeast; use lukewarm water (80°F. to 90°F.) for compressed. Sprinkle dry yeast or crumble cake into water. Let stand for a few minutes; then stir until dissolved. Add 1 teaspoon granulated sugar and let stand until frothy, 5 to 10 minutes. Pour boiling water over brown sugar. Cool to lukewarm; add yeast and all-purpose flour. Beat until smooth. Cover and let rise for 30 minutes. Sift 1 cup granulated sugar, cake flour, salt, and spices into large bowl. Add all remaining ingredients but fruit and beat for 3 minutes. Add yeast mixture and beat for 1 minute. Add fruit. Let rise in greased 9-inch tube pan until light, about 1 hour. Bake in preheated moderate oven (375°F.) for 50 to 60 minutes. Cool for 20 minutes in pan. Invert on rack and cool.

Frosting—Put 1 tablespoon each of light cream, pineapple juice, and butter in bowl; heat over hot water until melted. Add ¼ teaspoon each of grated orange and lemon rind and ½ cup sifted confectioners' sugar; beat until smooth. Add 2 tablespoons minced candied pineapple. Spoon over cake, letting it run down sides.

SNICKERDOODLES

6 tablespoons butter or margarine
1 cup sugar
1 egg
½ cup milk
2 cups sifted all-purpose flour
2 teaspoons baking powder
1 teaspoon ground nutmeg
Sugar and ground nutmeg

Cream butter until light and fluffy. Gradually beat in sugar. Beat in egg until well blended. Stir in milk. Sift flour with baking powder and nutmeg. Add all to batter at once and stir until well blended and smooth. Drop by tablespoon onto a greased cookie sheet. Sprinkle top of cookies with sugar mixed with additional ground nutmeg. Bake in preheated hot oven (400°F.) for 8 to 10 minutes, or until cookies are golden brown. Remove from pan while warm and cool on a rack. Makes about 4 dozen, depending on size.

Delaware

Corridor to Chesapeake Bay, capital of colonial New Sweden, first to ratify the Constitution, birthplace of nylon stockings. Delaware Bay gives it coast line, du Ponts give it economic and cultural transfusions. Proud of its fighting Blue Hen symbol, pleased with the old aura of New Castle and the clovered fields near Dover. Called by Thomas Jefferson "a jewel among states."

DEVILED CRAB CAKES

1 pound backfin crabmeat
Butter
2 tablespoons all-purpose flour
½ cup light cream
½ cup soft fresh bread crumbs (no crusts)
¼ cup minced green pepper
2 tablespoons chopped green onion
2 tablespoons prepared mustard
1 teaspoon Worcestershire
⅛ teaspoon hot pepper sauce
½ teaspoon salt
1 cup fine dry bread crumbs

Check crab for shells. Leave meat in large lumps. Melt 1 tablespoon butter. Stir in flour. Gradually stir in cream. Cook over low heat, stirring constantly, until smooth and thick. Remove from heat. Add soft bread crumbs, green pepper, onion, and seasonings. Add crabmeat and mix lightly. Place dry bread crumbs in a shallow dish. Put a large spoonful of crab mixture on the crumbs, sprinkle dry crumbs on top, and shape into a cake. Do not pack. Repeat, making 8 cakes in all. Heat 2 tablespoons butter in a large heavy skillet and sauté cakes lightly, adding more butter as needed. Carefully remove from skillet with broad spatula to individual hot plates. Makes 8 cakes (4 servings).

BAKED SHAD WITH OYSTER STUFFING

1 shad, 4 to 5 pounds
Salt and pepper
¼ cup butter or margarine
1 medium onion, minced
½ teaspoon crumbled dried thyme
¼ cup minced parsley
3 cups soft bread crumbs
½ pint shelled oysters
1 lemon, sliced

Wash shad in cold water. Pat dry with kitchen towel. Sprinkle inside and outside with salt and pepper. Heat butter. Sauté onion until soft. Add thyme, parsley, and bread crumbs. Mix thoroughly. Cut oysters into halves and add to mixture. Stuff shad with mixture; close opening with small poultry skewers, or sew. Place fish on well-oiled rack in roasting pan. Bake in preheated slow oven (325°F.) for 50 to 60 minutes. Arrange lemon slices on fish during last 30 minutes. Remove carefully to hot platter. Garnish with watercress or parsley if desired. Makes 6 servings.

MAGGI'S MAD HARE

2 young rabbits, cut into serving pieces
French dressing
Flour
Salt and pepper
½ cup cooking oil
1 garlic clove
1 cup water
½ large yellow onion
2 celery stalks
½ cup heavy cream

Wash rabbit and pat dry. Marinate pieces of meat, allowing ½ cup marinade for every pound of rabbit, for at least 24 hours. Drain. Dredge rabbit with flour. Season with salt and pepper. Heat oil in skillet with bruised garlic clove. Remove garlic. Brown rabbit pieces on all sides. Place browned pieces in large casserole. Add water, onion, and celery. Cover tightly and bake in preheated moderate oven (350°F.) for 1 hour, or until tender. Remove vegetables. Stir in heavy cream. Reheat slightly but do not boil. Serve rabbit with sauce. Makes 6 to 8 servings.

LEMON-FRIED CHICKEN

2 chickens (about 2½ pounds each), cut up
¼ cup fresh lemon juice
Cooking oil
¼ teaspoon garlic salt
½ teaspoon salt
¼ teaspoon crumbled dried thyme
¼ teaspoon crumbled dried marjoram
¼ teaspoon pepper
⅔ cup all-purpose flour
1 teaspoon grated lemon rind
1 teaspoon paprika

Wash chicken and pat dry. Place chickens in shallow dish. Mix lemon juice with ¼ cup oil, garlic salt, salt, thyme, marjoram, and pepper. Pour mixture over chicken

Roast Crown of Pork, Florida style

and marinate in refrigerator for 1 to 2 hours. Remove from marinade and drain. Roll chicken in flour mixed with lemon rind and paprika. Heat ½ cup oil in large skillet and brown chicken on all sides. Place browned pieces in a baking dish in a single layer. Bake, uncovered, in preheated moderate oven (350°F.) for 45 to 50 minutes, or until chicken is tender. Makes 4 to 6 servings.

BAKED EGGS

2 tablespoons butter
1 cup grated sharp cheese
4 eggs
4 dashes of hot pepper sauce
4 dashes of Worcestershire
¼ cup ketchup
⅓ cup light cream
   Buttered toast

Put butter into a baking dish that is at least 2 inches deep. Warm dish long enough to melt butter. Cool dish so eggs will not set but butter will remain liquid. Sprinkle one half of cheese over butter. Break eggs into 4 separate spaces, far enough apart so they will not run into each other. Put dashes of hot pepper sauce and Worcestershire in center of each egg yolk. Spoon ketchup over yolks. Pour in cream. Sprinkle remaining cheese over eggs. Bake in moderate oven (350°F.) until eggs are set. Serve each egg on a slice of buttered toast and spoon the pan sauces over it. Makes 4 servings.

DELAWARE SPOON BREAD

1 tablespoon shortening
1½ cups milk
½ cup white water- or stone-ground cornmeal
2 eggs
2 teaspoons baking powder
1 teaspoon salt

Turn oven to moderate (350°F.). Put a 1-quart casserole with shortening in oven. In a saucepan, scald 1 cup milk; stir in ground cornmeal. Cook until thick. Remove from stove and cool slightly. Beat in eggs, remaining milk, baking powder, and salt. Take casserole from oven and pour the melted shortening into mixture in saucepan. Now pour the whole preparation back into casserole dish. Bake at 350°F. for 1 hour. Makes 4 servings.

PEACH BAVARIAN CREAM

2 cups mashed ripe peeled pitted peaches
⅔ cup sugar
2 cups heavy cream
2 egg yolks
1½ envelopes unflavored gelatin
2 tablespoons cold water
⅛ teaspoon almond extract
   Whipped cream

Mix peaches with ⅓ cup sugar and stir until dissolved. Bring ½ cup cream to boiling point. Beat egg yolks and gradually beat in hot cream and remaining sugar. Sprinkle gelatin over cold water and let stand for 5 minutes. Add gelatin to hot cream mixture and stir until gelatin is dissolved. Cool and add to peach mixture. Chill until mixture starts to thicken. Whip 1 cup heavy cream until stiff. Fold cream into peach mixture. Pour mixture into 1-quart mold. Chill until firm. Unmold by dipping into lukewarm water for a few seconds. Whip remaining cream until soft and fluffy and fold in almond extract. Place Bavarian on a platter and spoon cream over it. Makes 6 to 8 servings.

FISH-HOUSE COOLER

2 cups orange juice
1 cup brandy
1 bottle (5th) sauterne

Chill ingredients. Pour over ice in punch bowl. Serve in frosted punch cups. Makes 12 servings.

Florida

Gleaming, whitewashed hotels crouch shadowless on the beaches of Miami, and alligators slither through the swamps of the Everglades. Natives wrench sponges from the ocean floor, and visitors peer through glass-bottomed boats to see inky denizens of the deep. Venerable St. Augustine, lyrical Suwannee and Okeechobee: siren calls to the Sunshine State.

SHRIMP PILAU ST. AUGUSTINE

¼ cup diced fat salt pork
1 large onion, finely cut
1 green pepper, finely cut
1 pound cooked shrimps
1 cup rice, cooked and hot
   Salt and pepper

Fry salt pork until well browned and crisp. Remove pork and cook onion and pepper in the fat. Add, with pork and shrimps, to rice. Season to taste and simmer for about 10 minutes. Makes 4 to 6 servings.

■ **Variation**—Sliced okra may be added. Brown okra in a little butter and add about 5 minutes before Pilau is done.

BROILED POMPANO

Split 4-pound pompano down back, wash, and pat dry. Season with salt, pepper, and cayenne. Dot with butter and sprinkle with lemon juice. Put fish, skin side down, on greased broiler rack, 4 inches below broiler heat. Broil for 15 minutes, or until fish flakes easily. Makes 4 servings.

ROAST CROWN OF PORK, FLORIDA STYLE

1 crown roast of pork, made from 12 to 14 ribs
2 tablespoons butter
3 tablespoons chopped onion
3 tablespoons chopped celery
4 oranges, sectioned
1 large grapefruit, sectioned
1½ cups cooked rice
2 cups toasted bread cubes
1 tablespoon crumbled leaf sage
1 teaspoon salt
¼ teaspoon pepper
1 teaspoon grated orange rind

Preheat oven to very hot (450°F.). Protect ends of rib bones with small pieces of aluminum foil. Place pork on a rack in a roasting pan. Place in the oven and immediately reduce oven temperature to moderate (350°F.). Roast for 40 minutes to a pound to an internal temperature of 185°F. Melt butter and sauté onion and celery until tender. Cut orange and grapefruit sections into halves. Add sections and remaining ingredients to onions and celery and toss to mix. One hour before roast is done, fill center with the stuffing. Baste twice during the last hour with drippings in the pan. Garnish with additional orange and grapefruit sections, and preserved crabapples, if desired. Makes 6 to 8 servings.

Note: The stuffing may also be used for duck or chicken.

HEARTS OF PALM IN CREAM

3 cups hearts of palm (fresh or canned)
¼ cup butter
1 tablespoon all-purpose flour
1½ cups light cream
1 teaspoon paprika
3 tablespoons cracker crumbs
   Butter

Place hearts of palm, well drained if canned, in a shallow baking dish. Melt butter and stir in flour. Gradually stir in cream. Cook over low heat, stirring constantly, until smooth and thickened. Stir in paprika. Pour sauce over hearts of palm. Sprinkle cracker crumbs over top of casserole. Dot top with bits of butter. Bake in preheated moderate oven (350°F.) for 20 minutes, or until top is lightly browned. Makes 4 to 6 servings.

GUAVA SALADS

Cut guava into halves. Peel. Remove seeds. Sprinkle cut surface with lemon juice to prevent darkening.

1. Marinate guava halves in lemon juice. Fill halves with grated fresh coconut and fresh orange sections. Serve with mayonnaise thinned with cream (cream dressing).

2. Stuff guava halves with fresh strawberries, dipped in confectioners' sugar, and pecan halves. Serve with cream dressing.

3. Stuff guava halves with chopped celery and cubes of cream cheese with a fruit dressing.

4. Fill guava halves with whipped cream cheese topped with fresh pitted cherries.

FLORIDA "GASPACHY" SALAD

1 cucumber
4 tomatoes
2 green peppers
1 pilot cracker
1 tablespoon minced onion
2 tablespoons dairy sour cream
½ teaspoon Worcestershire
½ teaspoon steak sauce
   Dash of salt
   Pepper and paprika to taste
¼ teaspoon powdered mustard
1 teaspoon sugar
   Lettuce

Peel cucumber and tomatoes and slice thin. Slice green peppers very thin. Soak cracker in a little cold water and squeeze dry. Put a layer of vegetables in bowl and sprinkle with cracker and onion. Mix sour cream and seasonings. Put some on cracker and onion. Repeat layers until all ingredients are used. Serve on lettuce. Makes 6 servings.

FRUIT SALAD BOWL

2 grapefruits
4 oranges
1 avocado
   Salad greens
   Juice of 1 lemon
¼ cup salad oil
1 can (6 ounces) frozen concentrated tangerine juice

Section grapefruits and oranges. Peel, pit, and slice avocado. Put in bowl with salad greens. Refrigerate while dressing is being made. Put lemon juice, oil, and tangerine juice in blender. Whirl until well mixed. Pour over salad greens and toss lightly. Makes 4 to 6 servings.

CREAM CHEESECAKE WITH COOKIE CRUST

   Cookie-dough Crust
5 packages (8 ounces each) cream cheese
1¾ cups sugar
3 tablespoons flour

¼ teaspoon salt
   Grated rind of 1 lemon
   Grated rind of ½ orange
5 eggs
2 egg yolks
1 cup heavy cream
   Toasted chopped blanched almonds

Make Crust. Have ingredients except ¾ cup cream at room temperature. Beat cheese until fluffy. Mix sugar, flour, and salt. Gradually blend into cheese, keeping mixture smooth. Add grated rinds. Add eggs and egg yolks, one at a time, beating well after each addition. Stir in ¼ cup cream. Turn into crust. Bake in preheated very hot oven (475°F.) for 15 minutes. Reduce heat to very slow (200° F.) and bake for 1 hour longer. Turn off heat and let stand in oven for 15 minutes. Remove from oven; cool. This cake will shrink some. Remove sides of pan. Top with ¾ cup cream, whipped, and the almonds. Makes 12 servings.

Cookie-dough Crust—Mix 1 cup sifted all-purpose flour and ¼ cup sugar. Add grated rind of 1 lemon, 1 egg yolk, and ½ cup soft butter; mix well. Chill. Roll ⅓ of dough to cover bottom of 9-inch springform cake pan. Bake in preheated hot oven (400°F.) for 8 minutes, or until lightly browned. Butter sides of pan. Put bottom, with crust, inside it. Cool. Roll out remaining dough into 2 strips 3½ inches wide and 14 inches long; press onto sides of pan.

Georgia

Brown thrashers singing in the pines; ping of marble hammers at Talking Rock, sweet scent of Cherokee rose, tropical flowers floating in Okefenokee Swamp, Scarlett O'Hara pirouetting on Peachtree Street. The Old Confederacy: where history comes alive at Chickamauga, Ft. Pulaski, Brunswick, Atlanta, and along Sherman's searing "March to the Sea."

CRAB CUSTARD

3 eggs, well beaten
⅓ cup melted butter
1½ teaspoons dry mustard
   Dash of cayenne
1 teaspoon Worcestershire
1 teaspoon salt
1 cup milk
1 cup light cream
2 tablespoons minced green pepper
1 pound crabmeat, flaked, with cartilage removed
½ cup cracker crumbs
   Butter

Combine all ingredients except cracker crumbs and butter and pour mixture into well-buttered 1½-quart baking dish. Sprinkle cracker crumbs over top. Dot top with pieces of butter. Bake in preheated slow oven (325°F.) until pie is set and top is golden brown, about 45 minutes to 1 hour. Makes 4 to 6 servings.

COUNTRY CAPTAIN

½ cup shortening
1 frying chicken (2½ to 3 pounds), cut up
   Salt and pepper
1½ teaspoons butter or bacon fat
1 small onion, thinly sliced
1 small green pepper, sliced
1 garlic clove
¼ cup chopped celery
2½ cups canned tomatoes
½ teaspoon salt
¼ teaspoon ground white pepper
½ teaspoon crumbled dried thyme
½ teaspoon curry powder
1 teaspoon chopped parsley

Melt shortening in a large skillet. Wash chicken and pat dry. Sprinkle with salt and pepper. Fry chicken in hot shortening until golden brown. Melt butter in a skillet and sauté onion, pepper, garlic, and celery until golden brown. Add tomatoes and cook for 10 minutes longer. Add remaining ingredients. Stir constantly and simmer for another 5 minutes. Place chicken pieces in pan with sauce, cover, and simmer for 45 minutes, or until chicken is tender. Serve with rice and sprinkle with slivered toasted blanched almonds and currants if desired. Makes 4 servings.

SWEET POTATO PONE

4 cups grated peeled raw sweet potatoes
1 egg, well beaten
¼ cup melted butter
1 cup milk
¾ cup dark corn syrup
½ cup all-purpose flour
½ teaspoon each of ground nutmeg and cinnamon
½ teaspoon salt

Mix sweet potatoes with egg, melted butter, and milk. Stir in corn syrup. Beat in remaining ingredients. Pour mixture into 1½-quart baking dish. Bake in preheated slow oven (325°F.) for 2½ hours. Stir occasionally during the first hour. Serve hot or cold. When cold, it can be sliced and served with milk or cream. Makes 6 servings.

TURNIP GREENS
WITH RAW VEGETABLE RELISH

3 pounds young turnip greens
¼ pound salt pork
3 cups boiling water
1 hot pepper pod

Strip turnip leaves from stems; discard stems. Wash leaves thoroughly. Drain. Brown salt pork on all sides in heavy kettle, add water, and boil, covered, for 10 minutes. Add greens and pepper pod. Cover and cook for 20 minutes. Drain; reserve pot liquor to serve in cups with main dish at dinner. Cut greens with scissors, slice pork, and mix, adding salt if necessary. Serve with Raw Vegetable Relish.

Raw Vegetable Relish

2 tomatoes
1 cucumber, peeled
1 green pepper
½ cup sliced celery
1 onion, minced
1 tablespoon salad oil
1 tablespoon vinegar
Salt and pepper

Dice tomatoes, cucumber, and pepper. Add remaining ingredients. Makes 4 servings.

RAISED BISCUITS

1 package active dry yeast
1½ cups lukewarm water
4½ cups unsifted all-purpose flour
2 teaspoons salt
1 tablespoon sugar
Butter or margarine (about ¾ cup)

Soften yeast in water; let stand for 5 minutes. Sift dry ingredients into large bowl. Cut in ½ cup soft butter. Add yeast and mix well. Roll about ¼ inch thick on floured board and brush with melted butter. Cut with floured 2-inch cutter and put on greased baking sheet, placing biscuits in pairs, one on top of another. Let rise in warm place (80 to 85°F.) for 1 hour. Bake in preheated hot oven (425°F.) for about 10 minutes. Makes about 3 dozen.
Note: For an attractive glaze, brush tops of unbaked biscuits with 1 egg yolk, beaten with 1 teaspoon water.

PEACH LEATHER

Peel freestone peaches and force through sieve or food mill. To each 4 cups pulp add 1⅔ cups sugar. Mix, bring to boil, and boil for 2 minutes at high heat, stirring constantly. Spread thin layer on cookie sheets. Cover loosely with cheesecloth. Dry in sun for 3 to 4 days, or until candy can be rolled like leather. Cut into strips and roll. Sprinkle with sugar and store in an airtight container.

PECAN PIE

Pastry for 1-crust 9-inch pie, unbaked
2 eggs
1 cup dark corn syrup
Pinch of salt

2 tablespoons melted butter
1 tablespoon all-purpose flour
1 teaspoon vanilla extract
½ cup sugar
1 cup pecan halves

Line 9-inch pie pan with pastry. Beat eggs. Add remaining ingredients. Fill pastry-lined pan. Bake in preheated slow oven (300°F.) for 1 hour, or until barely set. Cool. Top with whipped cream. Makes 6 to 8 servings.

PICKLED PEACHES

8 pounds firm ripe peaches
Whole cloves
2 quarts cider vinegar
8 cinnamon sticks
4 pounds (9 cups) sugar

Wash peaches and peel. Stud each with 2 whole cloves. Put vinegar, cinnamon, and sugar in kettle, bring to boil, and boil for 10 minutes, or until syrup is fairly thick. Add peaches and simmer gently until tender. Let stand in syrup overnight. Next day, lift out peaches and pack in hot sterilized jars. Boil syrup rapidly until thickened and pour over peaches in jars. Seal. Let stand for several weeks to develop flavor before using. Makes about 32 peaches.

Hawaii

Grass skirts, ukuleles, hula, and the ubiquitous pineapple: emblems of a Paradise of the Pacific, where Polynesian royalty reigned and volcanic Mauna Loa adds her periodic fireworks to luaus. Surfboards, outrigger canoes and fields of sugar cane mark Oahu, Maui, Molokai, Niihau, Kahoolawe—a tropic of vowels—whose Aloha means hail and farewell.

LOMI LOMI SALMON (Hawaiian Salad)

1 pound salt salmon
5 ripe tomatoes
1 large dried onion
Ice cubes

Soak salmon in water for 4 to 5 hours. Remove skin and bones and break or cut into pieces. Peel tomatoes and onion and chop. Squeeze all ingredients together through the fingers until all are in small pieces and well mixed. Add several ice cubes and chill thoroughly.

If salt salmon is not available, fresh salmon may be used if soaked overnight in a strong brine, instead of soaking in water.

PORK WITH PEAS

3 tablespoons soy sauce
2 tablespoons cornstarch
½ teaspoon salt
¼ teaspoon monosodium glutamate
1 tablespoon salad oil
1 pound pork, trimmed of fat and bone, cut into ½-inch cubes
1 package (10 ounces) frozen peas
1 teaspoon sugar
¾ cup water or chicken broth
½ cup fried blanched walnut meats

Mix 2 tablespoons soy sauce with 1 tablespoon cornstarch, salt, and monosodium glutamate. Marinate pork in it for 15 minutes. Heat oil and brown pork in it, turning occasionally to brown evenly. Add peas and sugar, cover, and simmer until peas are done, 4 to 5 minutes, separating peas with a fork as they begin to defrost. Mix remaining soy sauce and cornstarch. Add water and mix well. Pour over pork and peas and cook, stirring constantly, until clear and thickened. To blanch walnuts, boil for ½ minute, plunge into cold water, and scrub with a vegetable brush, getting off as much of the skin as possible. Heat enough oil to barely cover nuts and cook, stirring constantly, until golden brown. Sprinkle nuts on top of pork and peas and serve with rice.

CHICKEN LUAU

1 frying chicken (about 2½ pounds), cut up
2 tablespoons shortening
Salt and pepper
½ cup water
1½ pounds fresh spinach
1 cup coconut cream

Brown chicken pieces in shortening and sprinkle with salt and pepper. Add water, cover, and simmer until chicken is tender. Meanwhile, wash spinach and remove stems. Cut leaves into 1-inch pieces. Steam with a little water until spinach is tender. Drain spinach and chicken and combine. Add coconut cream and heat but do not boil. Makes 4 servings.

KOREAN STEAK
½ cup soy sauce
¼ cup salad oil
½ garlic clove, minced or crushed
3 green onions, thinly sliced
1 tablespoon sesame seed
½ teaspoon peppercorns, crushed
2 teaspoons sugar
1 teaspoon monosodium glutamate
3 pounds boneless tender steak,
  1 inch thick

Mix all ingredients except steak. Marinate steak in mixture for 3 to 4 hours. Remove steak and broil, 6 to 8 inches above charcoal heated to turn gray, to desired doneness. Makes 6 servings.

SWEET POTATO POI
Sweet potatoes
Salt and pepper
Coconut milk

Boil sweet potatoes in their jackets until tender. Peel and mash, beating until smooth. Season to taste with salt and pepper. Gradually beat in enough coconut milk to make the desired consistency —one-finger, two-finger, or three-finger poi. (The consistency of poi varies with the amount of liquid used and it is called one-finger, two-finger, or three-finger poi, depending upon how many fingers are needed to get it from the serving dish to the mouth without dribbling it on the chin.) Keep hot in top part of a double boiler. Serve in individual bowls.
Note: To make coconut milk, heat one 3½-ounce can flake coconut, or 1 cup fresh or frozen grated coconut, and 1 cup milk until it reaches the boiling point. Allow to cool at room temperature. Strain through 2 thicknesses of cheesecloth, squeezing out as much liquid as possible. Discard coconut, or save to use in other ways.

FRIED BANANAS
6 green-tipped bananas
  Salt and pepper
  Fresh lemon juice
1 egg
1 tablespoon water
½ cup dry bread crumbs

Cut bananas into halves crosswise and lengthwise. Sprinkle with salt, pepper, and lemon juice. Dip into egg beaten with water, then into bread crumbs. Fry in deep fat (325°F. on a frying thermometer) until golden brown. Drain on absorbent paper.

HAWAIIAN COCONUT CREAM
This is popular in the Islands for cooking meats, fish, and fowl, or it can be served as a sauce for a fruit dessert

Crack open coconuts. Drain the milk. Scrape out the white meat with a heavy metal spoon, stopping when the brown rind is reached. Place coconut on several thicknesses of cheesecloth and squeeze.

Discard the coconut pulp. Only the juice drained from the coconut is used in cooking.

Another method of obtaining coconut cream is to crack the coconut (roast in a 350°F. oven for 15 minutes to make it easier to crack) and remove the meat. Pare and grate the meat. Place coconut on several thicknesses of cheesecloth and squeeze. Proceed as above.

KONA COFFEE MOUSSE
1 envelope unflavored gelatin
¼ cup cold water
½ cup sugar
⅛ teaspoon salt
1½ cups strong coffee
1 cup dairy sour cream
2 tablespoons creme de cacao
  Chopped macadamia nuts
  Shaved unsweetened chocolate

Soften gelatin in the cold water. Heat sugar and salt with coffee. Add gelatin and stir over low heat until gelatin and sugar are dissolved. Chill until mixture has consistency of unbeaten egg white. Beat with rotary or electric mixer until fluffy. Fold in cream and crème de cacao. Spoon into 6 sherbet glasses and chill until firm. Sprinkle with nuts and chocolate. Makes 6 servings.

Idaho

Kamloop rainbow, world's largest trout, spawn in Pend Oreille lake and salmon jump in the cascades of the River of No Return. Waterfalls tumble in the Snake, Hell's Canyon runs deeper than Grand. Elk, cougar and antelope tempt hunters in the Sawtooth Mountains, fat pheasant and partridge abound in the Bitterroots. Idaho is so much more than potatoes.

BAKED SIRLOIN STEAK
4- to 5-pound sirloin steak, about 2½
  inches thick
  Salt and pepper
¼ cup butter
2 tablespoons all-purpose flour
½ teaspoon hot pepper sauce
4 onions, sliced thin
2 carrots, shredded
1 cup ketchup or tomato sauce
½ cup water

Heat a large iron skillet to sizzling hot. Sear steak quickly until brown on both sides. Remove steak to platter and season with salt and pepper. Add remaining ingredients to skillet; mix well. Cook for 5 minutes and pour off into small bowl. Return steak to skillet; top with sauce. Bake in preheated very hot oven (450° F.) for 20 to 30 minutes. Makes 6 servings.

IDAHO LAMB HASH
½ small onion, minced
1 tablespoon butter
1 tablespoon all-purpose flour
1 cup lamb, beef, or chicken stock
½ cup chopped celery
1 tablespoon chopped parsley
2 cups cubed cold roast lamb,
  cut into ½-inch cubes
1 cup cubed boiled potatoes,
  cut into ½-inch cubes
  Salt and pepper

Sauté onion in butter. Stir in flour and cook slowly over low heat for 3 minutes, until light golden brown. Gradually stir in stock. Add celery and parsley and simmer, covered, for 15 minutes. Make sure that lamb is free of gristle. Add lamb and potatoes. Season with salt and pepper. Heat to just below the boiling point. Serve with Pickled Idaho Prune Plums. Makes 4 servings.

SUGGESTIONS FOR IDAHO BAKED-POTATO GARNITURES
Serve split baked Idaho potatoes. Arrange a lazy Susan of accompaniments, selecting a half dozen or more of the following:

Dairy sour cream
Whipped butter
Chopped green onions or chives
Minced parsley
Caraway seeds
Chopped dill
Grated Gruyere cheese
Slivers of red onion
Seasoned salt and pepper
Minced red and green peppers
Sliced stuffed olives
Crumbled fried bacon or salt pork
Toasted sesame seeds

To bake potatoes, select firm, smooth ones with no blemishes and of a uniform size. Scrub well. Place in a shallow pan, on a potato baker, or directly on the oven shelf. Bake in preheated moderate oven (350°F.) for 1 hour and 10 minutes, or in a very hot oven (450°F.) for 40 minutes. When potatoes feel soft and are easily pierced, they are done. Potatoes can also be baked in a potato baker over low heat on top of the range for 1 hour. They can be wrapped in foil and baked at 350°F. for 1 hour. Foil-wrapped potatoes can be left in the oven while waiting for company without drying and shriveling. Cut a cross into the top of each potato and press the sides of the potato to allow steam to escape.

BAKED ONIONS

- 6 very large onions, peeled
- 3 tablespoons butter or margarine
- 1½ cups soft bread crumbs
- 1 cup shredded sharp Cheddar cheese
- ½ teaspoon salt
- ½ teaspoon ground ginger

Cover onions with boiling water and cook until onions are barely tender. Drain and cool. With a sharp knife cut out centers of onions leaving a shell about ½ inch thick. Chop onion removed from onion centers and sauté in hot butter. Add bread crumbs and sauté until onions are transparent and crumbs are lightly browned. Cool mixture and stir in cheese, salt, and ginger. Use mixture to tightly stuff onions. Place filled onions in shallow baking dish. Bake in preheated moderate oven (350°F.) for 30 to 40 minutes, or until onions are tender and easily pierced. Makes 6 servings.

IDAHO CORN OYSTERS

- 3 cups grated fresh corn
- 3 eggs, well beaten
- 1½ teaspoons baking powder
- ½ teaspoon salt
- ¼ teaspoon pepper
- 3 tablespoons light cream
- ⅓ cup all-purpose flour

Combine all ingredients and beat until smooth and well blended. Drop by tablespoon onto a hot buttered griddle and fry until golden brown on both sides. Makes 6 to 8 servings.

PICKLED IDAHO PRUNE PLUMS

- 4 pounds fresh prune plums
- 3 cups cider vinegar
- 4 cups sugar
- 2 cinnamon sticks
- 1 tablespoon whole cloves
- Piece of gingerroot
- 1 teaspoon whole allspice

Wash plums and prick each with fork. Combine vinegar and sugar in kettle and add spices, tied loosely in cheesecloth bag. Cook, covered, for 10 minutes. Reduce heat, add plums, and simmer gently for 10 minutes longer. Remove spice bag. Pack in hot sterilized jars, cover with boiling syrup, and seal. Makes about 4 pints.

CHERRY ICE CREAM

- 1 cup sugar
- 2 cups chopped pitted fresh sour cherries
- 2 cups light cream

Add sugar to cherries and let stand for 15 to 20 minutes. Add cream and freeze

in 2 ice-cube trays, stirring every 30 minutes until mixture is frozen through. Remove to bowl. Beat thoroughly with mixer. Put in containers, allowing room for expansion. Freeze until hard. Can be frozen in a crank-type ice-cream freezer. Makes about 1 quart.

Illinois

The prairie extends to the horizon in the Land of Lincoln. Chicago, "that toddling town," Sandburg's "City of the Big Shoulders," broods on the shores of Lake Michigan, toying with its trains, stacking its wheat, prodding its stockyards. One walks in the Emancipator's steps at Springfield, touches an atom-smasher at Champaign-Urbana, finds time at Elgin.

STOCKYARD INN BEEF-VEGETABLE SOUP

- 5 pounds beef shank with bone in
- Salt
- 2 quarts water
- 1 garlic clove, minced
- ⅓ cup pearl barley
- ½ cup chopped celery tops
- 2 cups chopped onion
- 3½ cups (one 1-pound, 12-ounce can) tomatoes
- ½ cup butter or margarine
- 1½ cups finely diced celery
- 1 cup each, diced carrots and potatoes
- 1 cup sliced green beans
- 1 cup finely cut green cabbage
- 2 cups fresh peas or 1 package (10 ounces) frozen peas
- 1 cup finely cut fresh spinach
- Salt and pepper

Have bones cut into several pieces. Put in kettle with 1 tablespoon salt and next 5 ingredients. Bring to boil, cover, and simmer for 3 hours, or until meat is tender. Skim soup. Remove bones and meat and set meat aside. Add tomatoes to soup. Melt butter in skillet. Add vegetables, except peas and spinach. Sauté for

7 minutes, stirring frequently. Add to soup, cover, and simmer for 20 minutes. Add peas, spinach, and the meat, cut into bite-size pieces. Cover and simmer for 10 minutes longer. Add salt and pepper to taste. Makes about 5 quarts.

TENDERLOIN STEAK WITH ROQUEFORT SPREAD

- 8 club or tenderloin steaks, cut 1½ inches thick
- Salt and pepper
- ½ cup crumbled Roquefort cheese
- ¼ cup heavy cream
- 1 teaspoon Worcestershire
- 1 teaspoon grated onion
- ½ teaspoon fresh lemon juice
- ⅛ teaspoon salt
- 2 drops hot pepper sauce

Cut fat edges of steaks to prevent curling during cooking. Broil steaks until desired doneness is reached. Sprinkle with salt and pepper. Blend remaining ingredients and spread mixture on steaks. Place steaks covered with cheese under broiler until cheese is melted and bubbly. Serve with grated fresh horseradish. Makes 8 servings.

QUAIL ON TOAST

Season dressed quail inside and out. Stuff with bread crumbs and minced onion, browned in butter. Allow about ¼ to ⅓ cup stuffing for each quail. Sew opening and roast in preheated moderate oven (350°F.) for 30 minutes, basting occasionally with melted butter. Serve on toast. Spoon pan gravy over top.

CUCUMBER MOUSSE

- 3 cucumbers
- 2 envelopes unflavored gelatin
- 3 packages (8-ounce) cream cheese or 1½ pints cottage cheese
- 2½ teaspoons salt
- Dash of pepper
- 2 tablespoons chopped chives
- ¼ teaspoon curry powder
- Green coloring
- Watercress

Peel cucumbers. Cut into halves lengthwise and scoop out seeds. Grate cucumbers until you have 2 cups. Put grated cucumbers in a strainer and let stand to drain thoroughly. Use cucumber liquid drained from cucumber, adding enough water to make 1 cup. Sprinkle gelatin over liquid and allow to soften for 5 minutes. Dissolve gelatin over low heat. Add dissolved gelatin to cucumbers with cream cheese which has been whipped until soft and creamy. Blend well. Add salt, pepper, chives, and curry powder. Add enough green coloring to tint a soft green. Pour mixture into 1-quart ring mold. Chill until firm. Unmold by dipping mold into lukewarm water for a few seconds. Place on serving platter with the center filled with watercress. Makes 4 to 6 servings.

TOMATO FROST

5 cups tomato juice
2 celery stalks
1 tablespoon chopped onion
1 teaspoon salt
3 tablespoons fresh lemon juice
1 teaspoon grated lemon rind
1 tablespoon sugar
 Dash of pepper
¼ teaspoon curry powder
¾ cup salad dressing or mayonnaise
 Sour cream

Heat 2 cups tomato juice with celery, onion, salt, lemon juice and rind, sugar, pepper, and curry powder. Bring to boil and simmer for 5 minutes. Strain mixture. Add salad dressing, beating with a rotary egg beater until very smooth. Stir in remaining tomato juice. Pour mixture into two ice-cube trays and freeze until firm. Scrape out portions to look like pink snow. Serve at once with teaspoon of sour cream on top. Makes 6 to 8 servings.

POTATO-FLOUR MUFFINS À LA MARSHALL FIELD'S

⅛ teaspoon salt
4 eggs, separated
1 tablespoon sugar
½ cup potato flour
1 teaspoon baking powder
2 tablespoons ice water

Add salt to egg whites and beat until stiff and dry. Beat yolks until thick; then beat in sugar. Fold yolks into whites. Add sifted flour and baking powder. Mix well and stir in water. Pour batter into greased muffin pans. Bake in preheated moderate oven (375°F.) for 15 to 20 minutes. Makes 12 muffins.

HICKORY-NUT CAKE

½ cup soft butter or margarine
1½ cups sugar
1 teaspoon vanilla extract
2 cups sifted cake flour
¼ teaspoon salt
2 teaspoons baking powder
¾ cup milk
1 cup chopped hickory nuts
4 egg whites
 Fluffy White Frosting (page 46)

Cream butter or margarine. Add sugar gradually, beating until light. Add vanilla. Sift flour, salt, and baking powder. Add alternately with milk to the first mixture, beating after each addition until smooth. Stir in nuts. Fold in stiffly beaten egg whites. Pour into two 9-inch round layer-cake pans, greased and lined on the bottom with wax paper. Bake in preheated moderate oven (350°F.) for about 25 minutes. Let stand on racks until almost cold. Turn out and peel off paper. Spread Frosting between layers and on top and sides of cake. Makes 8 to 10 servings.

STRAWBERRY CREAM

1 quart fresh strawberries
1 cup sugar
½ cup minute tapioca
¼ teaspoon salt
2 cups boiling water
1 cup heavy cream, whipped

Reserve 8 berries for garnish. Crush strawberries and mix with sugar. Let stand for 30 minutes. Mix tapioca with salt and water. Cook over low heat, stirring constantly, until tapioca is clear. Drain juice from berries and measure. Add water to make 2 cups. Stir juice into tapioca mixture and cook for a few minutes longer. Cool. Take half of tapioca mixture, add crushed berries, and divide among 8 sherbet glasses. Whip cream until stiff and fold in remaining tapioca mixture. Pile in sherbet glasses. Garnish with whole berries. Chill until ready to serve. Makes 8 servings.

Indiana

Picturesque covered bridges in the farm belt, steel's smoky fingers at Gary, sand dunes along Lake Michigan, yellow poplars on the Banks of the Wabash, stern-wheelers on the Ohio, Tippecanoe, Purdue and popcorn, limestone caverns, Lincoln's boyhood home, James Whitcomb Riley's too, South Bend's Fighting Irish. Here you race 500 miles or write to Santa Claus.

FRIED FRESHWATER FISH

You can use bass, walleyed pike, catfish, perch, trout, or bluegills. Dress fish and wipe with damp paper towel. Roll in yellow cornmeal seasoned with salt and paprika. Fry in hot shortening or clear bacon fat until brown on both sides, turning once with pancake turner. Serve immediately with wedges of lemon.

HOOSIER EGG CASSEROLE

8 hard-cooked eggs, coarsely chopped
2 cups diced celery
½ cup coarsely chopped pecans or walnuts
2 whole green onions, diced
½ green pepper, diced
¾ teaspoon salt
 Pepper to taste
1 cup mayonnaise
1 cup grated sharp Cheddar cheese
 Crushed potato chips

With 2 forks lightly toss together the first 8 ingredients. Pour into a buttered 2-quart casserole; sprinkle with cheese and top with crushed potato chips. Bake in preheated moderate oven (350°F.) for 30 minutes. Makes 6 servings.

CHICKEN WITH HARD CIDER

3½- to 4-pound chicken, disjointed
¾ cup butter
1 pound tart apples, peeled, cored, and thinly sliced
1 cup cashews, coarsely chopped
1 teaspoon sugar
⅔ cup hard cider

Sauté chicken lightly in ½ cup of the butter. Place apples in a buttered shallow baking dish; top with chicken and sprinkle with nuts and sugar. Add cider; dot with remaining butter. Cover. Bake in preheated moderate oven (375°F.) until tender, about 45 minutes. Makes 4 to 6 servings.

BAKED HOMINY GRITS WITH CHEESE

2 cups water
2 cups milk
1 teaspoon salt
1 cup hominy grits
2 eggs, slightly beaten
1 cup grated sharp Cheddar cheese
2 tablespoons butter

Combine water, milk, salt, and grits in a saucepan. Bring mixture to a boil. Lower heat and simmer until thickened, stirring occasionally. Allow 5 minutes for quick-cooking grits and 30 minutes for regular grits. Stir a little of the grits into eggs; return to saucepan and mix well with cheese. Pour into a buttered 1-quart casserole; dot with butter. Bake in preheated moderate oven (350°F.) for 40 minutes, or until lightly browned. Makes 4 to 6 servings.

HOOSIER FRIED TOMATOES, CREAMY GRAVY

Remove stem end of firm ripe or green tomatoes. Cut tomatoes into ½-inch slices. Dip slices into pancake flour or cornmeal; add salt and pepper. Fry in bacon fat until brown, turning once. Just before removing from skillet, sprinkle each slice with ½ to 1 teaspoon sugar. Keep in warm place. Make Creamy Gravy. Pour gravy around tomatoes and serve at once. **Creamy Gravy**—Stir flour and milk into drippings in skillet, using 3 tablespoons flour for each 3 tablespoons drippings and 1½ cups milk. Stir and cook until thickened. Season with salt and pepper.

WILTED LETTUCE OR SPINACH

4 slices bacon, diced
½ cup cider vinegar
½ cup water
1 teaspoon sugar
1 medium head iceberg lettuce or 6 cups
   young tender spinach leaves, washed
   and trimmed
½ cup onion rings
3 hard-cooked eggs, shelled and sliced

Fry bacon until crisp. Remove crisp bacon pieces. To the bacon fat, add vinegar, water, and sugar, and bring mixture to a boil. Place lettuce or spinach, torn into bite-size pieces, in a salad bowl. Top with onion rings and hard-cooked eggs. Pour hot vinegar mixture over salad and toss until well mixed. Sprinkle reserved bacon pieces over the top. Serve immediately. Makes 6 servings.

SCRIPTURE CAKE

*Look up the references
in the Old Testament*

Judges 5:25
   ½ cup butter or margarine
Jeremiah 6:20
   1 cup sugar
Isaiah 10:14
   3 eggs, separated
Exodus 16:31
   1 tablespoon honey
I Kings 4:22
   2 cups sifted all-purpose flour
Leviticus 2:13
   ½ teaspoon salt
I Corinthians 5:6
   2 teaspoons baking powder
I Kings 10:10
   ¾ teaspoon ground cinnamon
   ¼ teaspoon each of ground cloves,
      allspice, and nutmeg
Judges 4:19
   ⅓ cup milk
Genesis 43:11
   ½ cup chopped blanched almonds
I Samuel 30:12
   ½ cup chopped dried figs
I Samuel 30:12
   ½ cup chopped seeded raisins

Cream butter. Add sugar gradually, beating until light. Add egg yolks, one at a time, beating thoroughly after each addition. Beat in honey. Add sifted dry ingredients alternately with the milk and beat only until smooth. Stir in nuts and fruits. Fold in stiffly beaten egg whites and pour into a loaf pan (9 x 5 x 3 inches), lined on the bottom with wax paper. Bake in preheated moderate oven (350° F.) for 1 hour, or until done. Cool cake in the pan for 5 minutes. Turn cake out on a rack and peel off paper. Turn cake right side up to cool.

PERSIMMON GRAHAM-CRACKER DESSERT

Persimmons were one of the popular fruits of the early Hoosiers. The variety grown in Indiana is not to be confused with the Japanese persimmon, grown and marketed from California. The Hoosier plumlike yellow persim-mon probably came from Virginia; while green it is very astringent and puckers the mouth, but when ripe it is sweet and delicious in pies and puddings

2 cups graham cracker crumbs
1 cup confectioners' sugar
1 cup pureed ripe persimmon pulp
½ cup walnuts, coarsely chopped
¼ pound large marshmallows, cut into
   quarters

Mix all together. Cover and refrigerate overnight. Serve with whipped cream. Makes 4 to 6 servings.

Iowa

Truly America's Bread Basket, heartland of the nation's agriculture, where the corn is as wide as an elephant's hide and butter 'n' egg men live side by side. Des Moines recalls the French monks who came upon it almost three centuries ago; Pottawattamie speaks of the Siouan tribe that met them. "The Music Man's" town is here too, but disguised as Mason City.

IOWA CORN CHOWDER

½ cup chopped salt pork
1 onion, chopped
½ cup sliced celery
½ green pepper, diced
1½ cups diced potatoes
2 cups water
1 bay leaf
1 teaspoon salt
4 tablespoons all-purpose flour
2 cups milk
½ cup light cream
2 cups fresh corn cut from cob

Brown salt pork in heavy saucepan. Add onion; cook for 2 minutes. Add next 6 ingredients. Simmer until potatoes are tender. Mix flour with a little milk; add with remaining milk to potato mixture. Heat until thickened. Add cream and corn. Heat gently. Makes 4 to 6 servings.

SHORT RIBS WITH VEGETABLES

3 to 4 pounds beef short ribs
Salt and pepper
1 onion, sliced
1 cup water
8 small white onions, peeled
4 medium potatoes, halved and peeled
8 carrots, sliced
¾ pound whole green beans

Brown ribs slowly on all sides. Pour off fat and season ribs with salt and pepper. Add sliced onion and water. Cover and simmer for 2 hours, or until tender. Or bake, covered, in a large roasting pan in slow oven (300°F.). Add whole onions and potatoes. Cover and simmer for 30 minutes, basting several times with liquid in pan. Add carrots and beans. Sprinkle vegetables with salt and pepper. Cover and simmer until meat and vegetables are tender. Makes 4 servings.

RAW FRIED POTATOES

6 large potatoes
⅓ cup lard
Salt

Peel potatoes and cut into ⅛-inch slices. Soak in cold water until slices are crisp. Drain and dry on paper toweling. Heat lard until very hot. Add potatoes and fry slowly until crusty and brown. Turn occasionally with a pancake turner. Sprinkle with salt and serve immediately. Makes 6 servings.

TWO-BEAN SUCCOTASH WITH PORK CUBES

¼ pound salt pork, cubed
½ pound fresh green beans
2 cups fresh Lima beans
4 to 5 ears yellow corn
½ cup light cream
Salt and pepper

Slowly fry cubed pork until well browned and done. Cook cut green beans and Lima beans in small amount of boiling salted water for about 15 minutes. Add corn cut from ears and simmer for 5 minutes. Add cream, salt, and pepper. Heat gently. Serve topped with crisp pork. Makes 6 servings.

HAM SALAD

3 cups ground cooked ham
1 large dill pickle, chopped
2 hard-cooked eggs, shelled and chopped
½ cup minced celery
2 raw carrots, grated finely
1 cup light cream
¼ cup cider vinegar

Salt and pepper
1 teaspoon prepared mustard
2 eggs, well beaten
1 tablespoon butter

Mix ground ham with pickle, eggs, celery, and carrots. Chill. Mix together remaining ingredients and cook over low heat, stirring constantly, until smooth and thickened. Cool. Mix dressing with ham salad mixture and pile into a lettuce-lined salad bowl. Chill until ready to serve. Makes 6 servings.

CORN RELISH

18 ears yellow corn
1 small firm head green cabbage
4 yellow onions
3 red or green peppers
1 celery heart
2½ cups cider vinegar
1½ cups sugar
1 tablespoon each of mustard seed and celery seed
1 teaspoon ground turmeric
¼ teaspoon cayenne
4 teaspoons coarse salt

Cut kernels from corn. Put other vegetables through food chopper, using coarse blade. Heat vinegar, sugar, and seasonings; add vegetables. Bring to boiling point. Fill jars to ½ inch from top; adjust covers. Put in water bath, cover, and boil for 30 minutes. Makes about 10 pints.

APPLE-CIDER RAISIN PIE

1½ cups water
2 cups seeded raisins
1½ cups apple cider
¾ cup sugar
1 cup chopped tart apples
¾ teaspoon salt
1 teaspoon ground cinnamon
Grated rind and juice of ½ lemon
2 tablespoons butter
3 tablespoons cornstarch
Pastry for 2-crust 10-inch pie, unbaked

Mix 1 cup of the water with all ingredients except cornstarch and pastry. Bring to boil. Blend cornstarch with remaining ½ cup water. Stir into first mixture and cook, stirring, until thick. Pour into pastry-lined pan, adjust pricked top crust, and seal edges. Bake in preheated very hot oven (450°F.) for 10 minutes. Reduce heat to moderate (350°F.) and bake for 35 minutes longer. Cool.

IOWA FARM ICE CREAM

¼ teaspoon salt
6 eggs
1¼ cups sugar
2 cups heavy cream
2 tablespoons vanilla extract
2 cups milk

Beat salted eggs until thick and lemon colored; beat in sugar. Add cream, vanilla, and milk; pour into gallon can of ice-cream freezer. Freeze in ice and rock salt, using 8 parts ice to 1 part rock salt. Remove dasher and cover. Pack in ice and rock salt.

Kansas

Way station of the prairie schooners, jumping-off place for Lewis and Clark's expedition to the Northwest. Center of the Great Plains, it signifies "Home on the Range," a song it takes as its own. Deep Indian territory, its frontier forts still guard the land. Burial grounds of the Wyandots lie in the heart of busy Kansas City—a century-old promise kept.

LENTIL SOUP

1 pound dried lentils
5 beef-bouillon cubes
1 onion, chopped
1 garlic clove, minced
1 carrot, chopped
1 celery stalk, chopped
¼ teaspoon dry mustard
Salt and pepper

Wash lentils and soak overnight in 3 quarts water. Do not drain. Add bouillon cubes, vegetables, and mustard. Bring to a boil and simmer, covered, for 2 hours or until lentils are tender. If desired, whirl in blender or force lentils and vegetables through sieve or food mill. Season to taste with salt and pepper. Makes 2 quarts.
Note: Ham, corned-beef, or tongue broth can be used in place of part or all of water. In that case, omit bouillon cubes.

HAM WITH MUSTARD CRUST

2- pound slice of smoked ham, center cut
¼ cup prepared mustard
¼ cup all-purpose flour
2 tablespoons dark molasses
⅓ cup seedless raisins
15 whole cloves
1 cup milk
½ cup light cream
Raisin Gravy

Put ham in a shallow baking dish. Com-

bine mustard, flour, and molasses and mix well. Spread mixture over the ham. Sprinkle top of ham with raisins and cloves. Mix milk with cream and pour over ham. Bake in preheated moderate oven (350°F.) for 1 hour. Remove ham from baking dish and place on a platter. Serve with Raisin Gravy. Makes 6 to 8 servings.

Raisin Gravy

1 tablespoon butter
2 tablespoons chopped green pepper
1 tablespoon all-purpose flour
1 cup strained pan drippings
Raisins cooked with ham
Pepper and paprika

Melt butter and sauté green pepper until tender. Stir in flour. Gradually stir in pan drippings. Cook over low heat, stirring constantly, until smooth and thickened. Add raisins cooked with ham and season to taste with pepper and paprika. Pour sauce over ham and serve.

TOPEKA FRIED CHICKEN

Use 2 fryers weighing about 2½ to 3 pounds each. Pour boiling water over pieces and let stand for 15 minutes. Drain and dry between towels. Roll in flour seasoned with salt, pepper, paprika, and 1 teaspoon ground ginger. Heat shortening, composed of two thirds lard and one third butter, in a heavy skillet. Shortening should be ½ inch deep. When hot, add chicken pieces and brown on all sides. Reduce heat, cover, and cook slowly until chicken is tender. This will take about 45 minutes. Place chicken pieces on heated serving platter; garnish with parsley and brandied peaches. Makes 6 to 8 servings.

GREEN RICE

1 cup raw rice
1 cup chopped parsley
1 green pepper, minced
2 tablespoons butter
1 tablespoon grated onion
1 teaspoon salt

Cook rice until tender, adding parsley during the last 5 minutes of cooking. Drain well and keep hot. Sauté green pepper in butter until tender. Add green pepper, grated onion, and salt to rice. Reheat slightly until piping hot, if necessary. Makes 4 to 6 servings.

LIBERAL PANCAKES

2½ cups sifted all-purpose flour
½ teaspoon baking soda
½ teaspoon salt
1 teaspoon baking powder
2 tablespoons sugar
1 egg, well beaten
2½ cups buttermilk
2 tablespoons butter, melted

Sift first 5 ingredients. Add remaining ingredients and mix well. Drop double tablespoons of batter onto hot greased griddle. Turn when bubbles begin to break on the unbaked side and the edges turn brown. Brown on other side. Serve with whipped butter, syrup, jam, or fruit sauce. Makes about 14 medium pancakes.

CRACKED WHEAT BREAD
2 packages active dry yeast or
  2 cakes compressed yeast
½ cup water*
3½ cups milk, scalded
¼ cup firmly packed dark brown sugar
4 teaspoons salt
¼ cup butter or margarine
6 to 7 cups unsifted all-purpose flour
5 cups cracked wheat

*Use very warm water (105°F. to 115°F.) for dry yeast; use lukewarm (80°F. to 90°F.) for compressed. Sprinkle dry yeast or crumble cake into water. Let stand for a few minutes; then stir until dissolved. Pour hot milk over sugar, salt, and butter. Cool to lukewarm. Add 3 cups flour and beat well. Add cracked wheat and enough more flour to make a stiff dough. Turn out on floured pastry cloth or board. Knead until smooth and elastic, about 10 minutes. Put in greased bowl. Turn once, cover, and let rise until doubled in bulk. Punch down lightly and again let rise until almost doubled. Put on floured board and divide into 4 equal parts. Cover and let rest for 5 minutes. Roll each piece into a 9-inch square. Roll up as for a jelly roll. Seal the ends of the roll and place each roll into a loaf pan (9 x 5 x 3 inches), making sure ends of roll touch short ends of pan. Let rise until double in bulk. Bake in preheated moderate oven (375°F.) for about 45 minutes.

PUMPKIN-PRUNE CAKE
⅔ cup soft shortening
2½ cups sifted cake flour
4 teaspoons baking powder
1 teaspoon salt
1 teaspoon each of ground cloves and ginger
2 teaspoons ground cinnamon
1½ cups sugar
¾ cup milk
1 cup canned pumpkin
1 cup chopped cooked dried prunes
2 eggs

Put shortening in mixing bowl. Add sifted dry ingredients, ½ cup milk, pumpkin, and prunes. Beat for 2 minutes. Scrape bowl frequently during beating. Add eggs and remaining milk; beat for 2 minutes longer. Pour batter into two 8-inch square cake pans, greased and floured. Bake in preheated moderate oven (375°F.) for about 40 minutes. Let stand for 5 minutes; then turn out on racks to cool. Frost if desired. Makes two 8-inch squares.

WILD-PLUM JELLY
Wash plums that are not too ripe. Cover with cold water and cook until tender. Press through a coarse sieve. Place in jelly bag and allow to drip without squeezing. Bring 6 cups juice to a rolling boil for 10 minutes. Add 4 cups sugar and boil rapidly until drops of jelly come together and sheet off spoon, or until candy thermometer registers 220°F. Pour into hot sterilized glasses. Seal with ¼ inch of melted paraffin. Makes 6 to 8 glasses.

Kentucky

Lexington, where the grass is blue and thoroughbreds come forth each spring from Calumet and Greentree to make the Derby's "Run for the Roses" at Churchill Downs. Limestoned valleys that Daniel Boone and Simon Kenton traversed, blazing a trail through the Cumberland Gap. Mammoth Cave with its mysteries, Fort Knox with its gold, and Floyd Collins' Crystal Cave.

BLACK KETTLE SOUP
1 shin of veal, with bone cracked
3 quarts water
  Salt and pepper
2 tablespoons rice
2 cups each of corn, canned tomatoes, diced potatoes, sliced okra
  Browned flour
¼ cup currant jelly
1 tablespoon Worcestershire

Place shin of veal in a deep covered kettle. Cover with water, season, and let cook for about 1 hour. Skim. Add rice and vegetables. Bring to a boil. Lower heat and cover. Simmer for 1 hour, or until meat and vegetables are tender. Strain broth and return broth to kettle with bone. Purée vegetables and add to soup. Thicken soup with browned flour

mixed with water. Stir in currant jelly and Worcestershire. Reheat until piping hot and serve. Makes 12 to 16 servings.

KENTUCKY ROAST LAMB
1 leg of lamb, about 6 pounds
3 cups soft bread crumbs
⅓ cup chopped celery
¼ cup melted butter
¼ teaspoon pepper
½ teaspoon ground allspice
  Brown sugar
  Cayenne
  Salt
1 teaspoon grated nutmeg
  Jelly Sauce

Have butcher bone leg of lamb. Ask for the bones to make stock. Mix bread crumbs with celery, butter, pepper, and allspice. Use mixture to stuff leg of lamb. Skewer or sew opening to enclose the stuffing. Sprinkle outside of meat with brown sugar, cayenne, salt, and grated nutmeg. Roast on a rack in preheated slow oven (325°F.) for 2 to 3 hours, or until internal temperature on a meat thermometer registers 182°F. Cut into slices and serve with Jelly Sauce. Makes 8 servings with some leftovers.

Jelly Sauce
2 tablespoons lamb fat or other fat
2 tablespoons flour
1 cup lamb stock made from boiling the bones or pan drippings
¼ cup firmly packed brown sugar
  Juice of 2 lemons
⅛ teaspoon ground allspice
¼ teaspoon grated nutmeg
½ cup red currant jelly
  Salt and pepper

Melt fat and stir in flour. Gradually stir in stock and sugar. Cook over low heat, stirring constantly, until smooth and thickened. Add lemon juice, allspice, nutmeg, jelly, and salt and pepper to taste. Reheat slightly and serve with sliced lamb.

KENTUCKY BURGOO
1 fat fowl (about 5 pounds)
2 pounds each of beef, lamb, pork, and veal shanks
  Cold water
3 tablespoons salt
6 each of potatoes, onions, and carrots, peeled and diced
2 cups each of diced celery, sliced okra, whole kernel corn, Lima beans, chopped green cabbage
2 green peppers, diced
  Dash each of cayenne, hot pepper sauce, steak sauce, and Worcestershire

Cover all meat with cold water and bring to boil in a 20-quart stock pot. Cover, reduce heat, and simmer for 3 to 4 hours, or until meat falls from bones. Remove meat from bones; discard bones. Cool meat and dice; return to stock. Add remaining ingredients. Simmer until thick, stirring frequently during first part of cooking and almost constantly toward the end. Makes 25 servings.

LACE-EDGE CORN CAKES

½ teaspoon salt
½ teaspoon baking soda
1 cup water-ground white cornmeal
1 egg
1¼ cups buttermilk

Mix salt and baking soda thoroughly with meal. Mix egg well with buttermilk. Combine both mixtures and beat until smooth. Pour 1 tablespoon of batter onto a hot greased griddle. Bake until underside is brown (lift edge gently and peek). Then turn, but only once. Never pat or flatten the cakes with a turner. Stir batter well before dipping out next batch. Makes 4 servings.

TELEPHONE PUDDING

6 eggs, separated
Sugar
Salt
1½ teaspoons vanilla extract
2 cups medium cream
24 almond macaroons
1 cup blackberry or black raspberry jam

Beat egg yolks with 6 tablespoons sugar and ⅛ teaspoon salt until thick. Add vanilla. Scald cream and beat gradually into egg-yolk mixture. Line a baking dish (13 x 9 x 2 inches) with macaroons, cut into halves. Pour custard over them. Set dish in pan of hot water. Bake in preheated moderate oven (350°F.) for 25 minutes, or until custard sets. Do not overcook. Remove from oven; dot custard with jam. Beat egg whites with ¼ teaspoon salt until foamy. Beat in 6 tablespoons sugar, 1 spoonful at a time, beating until stiff. Spread meringue over custard. Bake in preheated slow oven (325°F.) for 18 minutes. Serve warm or cold. Makes 8 servings.

BLUEGRASS SORGHUM CAKE

½ cup butter or margarine
1 cup sugar
1 egg
2 cups sifted all-purpose flour
½ teaspoon salt
1 teaspoon baking powder
½ teaspoon baking soda
½ teaspoon each of ground cinnamon
    and nutmeg
¾ cup sour milk or buttermilk
½ cup sorghum syrup

Cream butter. Add sugar gradually, beating until light. Add egg and beat thoroughly. Sift ingredients and add alternately with liquids to creamed mixture. Beat until smooth. Pour batter into greased pan (8 x 8 x 2 inches). Bake in preheated slow oven (325°F.) for 45 minutes. Makes 6 to 8 servings.

GREEN-TOMATO KETCHUP

Slice three measures of choice green tomatoes and one measure onions in a large pan. Sprinkle handfuls of salt over

it. Let it rest for 30 minutes so that juice drains out of tomatoes. Drain well and sweeten to taste. Cover with boiling vinegar. Let tomatoes and onions get thoroughly hot but do not boil or cook. When thoroughly hot, fill jars and seal.

Louisiana

Stories of Jean Laffite, de Soto, and La Salle echo through the early history of the romantic bayou country. Spanish-French to the tip of its Delta fingers, it calls its great feast day Mardi Gras, its counties parishes and its gay city New Orleans. In Antoine's, the menu is exquisitely Creole. Levees restrain the mighty Mississippi in its 600-mile dash to the Gulf.

ANTOINE'S OYSTERS ROCKEFELLER

½ cup tightly packed parsley leaves
1 cup tightly packed spinach leaves
4 shallots or 1 small onion
1 tablespoon aniseed
1 cup water
¼ teaspoon hot pepper sauce
½ teaspoon salt
½ teaspoon ground thyme
1 tablespoon anchovy paste
½ cup butter or margarine
½ cup toasted bread crumbs
24 oysters
    Rock salt

Put parsley, spinach, and shallots through a food chopper. Simmer aniseed in water for 10 minutes. Strain out the seed. Add ground vegetables to anise-flavored liquid (this approximates the flavor of absinthe which was in the original formula). Simmer, covered, for 10 minutes. Season with hot pepper sauce, salt, thyme, and anchovy paste. Add butter and bread crumbs. If sauce is too thick to spread easily, thin it with a little of the oyster liquor. Open oysters with an oyster knife.

Place oysters on a bed of rock salt in a shallow baking dish. Bake in preheated moderate oven (350°F.) for about 6 minutes *or* broil them for 5 minutes only, until the edges curl. Spread each oyster with a spoon of the prepared sauce and return to broiler for 5 minutes longer. Makes 4 servings.

POMPANO EN PAPILLOTE

3 cups boiling salted water
1 lemon, sliced
1 bay leaf
¼ teaspoon crumbled dried thyme
6 pompano fillets
3 tablespoons butter
3 tablespoons all-purpose flour
2 tablespoons minced onion
1½ cups fish stock
1 cup cooked coarsely chopped shrimps
½ cup flaked crabmeat
6 mushrooms, sliced
¼ teaspoon salt
2 egg yolks

To boiling water add lemon, bay leaf, thyme, and fish fillets. Use a shallow pan so fillets can be cooked flat. Simmer until fish flakes. Carefully remove fillets with a wide spatula and reserve 1½ cups of the strained stock. Place pompano fillets on sheets of parchment paper large enough to enclose fillets completely. Melt butter and stir in flour. Add onion and slowly stir in fish stock. Cook over low heat, stirring constantly, until smooth and thickened. Add shrimps, crabmeat, mushrooms, and salt. Stir sauce slowly into beaten egg yolks. Spoon sauce over fillets. Fold parchment paper over fish to enclose completely. Place bags on a cookie sheet and bake in preheated hot oven (400°F.) for 10 minutes. Makes 6 servings.

FROGS' LEGS À LA CREOLE

16 large frog legs
    Boiling water
    Juice of ½ lemon
    Salt and pepper
2 eggs, well beaten
    Dry fine bread crumbs
    Deep fat for frying
    Onion Cream Sauce

Put frog legs in boiling water with lemon juice and salt and pepper. Scald for 4 minutes. Drain legs and pat dry. Dip legs into eggs and roll in bread crumbs. Fry in deep fat (370°F. on a frying thermometer) for 2 to 3 minutes, until legs are tender. Serve with Onion Cream Sauce. Makes 4 servings.

Onion Cream Sauce

2 tablespoons butter or margarine
2 tablespoons all-purpose flour
1½ cups light cream
½ teaspoon salt
2 tablespoons minced onion
1 tablespoon minced parsley
1 egg, well beaten

Treasures of Our Native American Table

**Fried Chicken with Puffs and Gravy
from Alabama
and a Lady Baltimore Cake
from Maryland**

Melt butter and stir in flour. Gradually stir in cream. Add salt, onion, and parsley. Cook over low heat, stirring constantly, until smooth and thickened. Beat some of sauce into egg. Add to remainder of sauce and cook for 2 minutes. Spoon sauce over frogs' legs.

CHICKEN-SHRIMP GUMBO FILÉ

1 fowl (about 4 pounds), cut into pieces
1 garlic clove
   Salt and pepper
¼ pound salt pork, diced
1 sweet red pepper, cut up
1 cup chopped onion
⅓ cup all-purpose flour
2⅓ cups (one 1-pound, 3-ounce can) tomatoes
1 package (10 ounces) frozen okra or 1 can (1 pound) cut okra, drained
1 pound uncooked shrimps, shelled and deveined
   Hot pepper sauce
2 teaspoons gumbo file powder
   Hot cooked rice

Cook fowl with 5 cups water, garlic, 1 tablespoon salt, and ¼ teaspoon pepper for 3 hours, or until tender. Cool and remove meat from bones. Cut into pieces. Strain broth and reserve. Add enough water to make 6 cups. Cool and skim off fat. Cook salt pork until well browned and done. Remove pork from kettle and pour off all but ¼ cup fat. Sauté red pepper and onion in fat for 5 minutes. Add flour and brown. Gradually stir in broth. Add pork and tomatoes. Cover and simmer for 30 minutes. Add chicken, okra, and shrimps. Simmer, covered, until shrimps turn pink. Season with salt, pepper, and hot pepper sauce. Gradually add gumbo filé powder and stir until completely blended. Put a scoop of rice in center of each soup bowl and fill bowl with gumbo filé. Makes 6 servings.

JAMBALAYA DE CANARD

1 duckling, about 4 pounds, including giblets
   Salt and pepper
1 cup long-grained rice
¾ cup chopped onion
½ cup chopped green pepper
1 garlic clove, minced
½ pound bulk sausage
1 bay leaf
½ teaspoon chili powder
½ teaspoon ground thyme
1 tablespoon chopped parsley
½ cup diced cooked ham
1 cup canned tomatoes

Wash duck. Trim all excess fat, and bone. Sprinkle duck with 2 teaspoons salt and ½ teaspoon pepper. Brown duck in a skillet for 30 to 40 minutes, turning occasionally. Cook duck bones and giblets, except liver, in enough water to cover, with ½ teaspoon salt, for about 40 minutes, or until giblets are tender. Add liver 10 minutes before cooking time is over. Drain and reserve 2 cups broth;

use remaining broth for soup or gravies. Chop giblets. After duck has been browned, drain off all excess fat from skillet and place duck pieces on absorbent paper to drain. Replace duck in skillet and add giblet stock. Cover and cook slowly for 1½ hours, or until duck is tender.

Soak rice in enough water to cover for 30 minutes, then drain. Add onion, green pepper, and garlic to sausage and cook over low heat until vegetables are tender and sausage is cooked. Drain excess fat. Add soaked rice and stir over low heat until rice is dry. Add 1½ teaspoons salt, ¼ teaspoon pepper, bay leaf, chili powder, thyme, and parsley. Remove duck from pan and mix rice mixture into gravy. Cover and cook for 10 minutes, or until rice is almost tender. Add giblets, ham, and tomatoes. Mix carefully, taking care not to mash rice. Place duck pieces on top of rice. Cover and cook for 10 minutes longer. Serve rice topped with a piece of duck. Makes 6 to 8 servings.

RED BEANS AND RICE

½ pound lean salt pork, diced
1 garlic clove, minced
   About 2½ cups (one 1-pound, 5-ounce can) red kidney beans, drained
3 cups cooked rice
   Minced parsley
   Salt and pepper

Fry salt pork until crisp and brown. Remove pork. Pour off about half of fat. Add garlic to fat in skillet and cook for 2 or 3 minutes. Add beans, rice, and parsley, and salt and pepper to taste. Heat. Serve topped with pork. Makes 4 servings.

PORCUPINES

2 cups shelled pecans
1 cup pitted dates
   Flaked coconut
1 cup firmly packed dark brown sugar
2 eggs

Grind pecans and dates finely. Mix with 2 cups coconut, sugar, and eggs. Shape mixture with the fingers into rolls 4 inches long and ½ inch thick. Roll in flaked coconut. Place rolls on lightly greased cookie sheet. Bake in preheated moderate oven (350°F.) for 10 to 12 minutes. Makes about 3 dozen.

CREOLE PRALINES

4 cups sugar
1 cup light cream or rich milk
1 teaspoon vanilla extract
2½ cups pecans or mixed nuts (pecans and black walnuts)
   Dash of salt

Boil 3 cups sugar with the cream in a large saucepan until it forms a soft ball (236°F. on a candy thermometer). Meanwhile melt remaining sugar in

heavy skillet, stirring until it reaches the brown-caramel stage. When both mixtures are ready, carefully add caramel to first mixture, stirring with a long spoon. Cook to soft-ball stage. Remove from heat and cool to lukewarm. Add vanilla, nuts, and salt and beat until stiff and creamy. Drop on a buttered cookie sheet. Let cool before removing from sheet. Makes about twenty 3-inch pralines.

Maine

The famed "Rock-ribbed Coast" is shattered by countless bays and inlets, Bar Harbor, Penobscot, Frenchman, at Eastport one is closest to the Spanish Main. Pine cone and balsam fir scent the cold air, and whoosh of ski blade and spin of angler's reel sound in this state whose face is pocked by more than 2,500 lakes and whose slopes are dressed in virginal white.

AROOSTOOK COUNTY POTATO SOUP

6 small onions, sliced thin
1 cup celery, sliced thin
5 tablespoons butter or margarine
4 cups milk
2½ cups potato, diced and peeled
1½ tablespoons all-purpose flour
   Salt and pepper
   Minced parsley

In top part of double boiler over direct heat, sauté onion and celery in 3 tablespoons butter until golden. Add the milk and cook over boiling water for 45 minutes, stirring occasionally. Cook potato in boiling salted water for 10 minutes; drain. Heat remaining 2 tablespoons butter and blend in flour. Gradually stir in first mixture and potato. Cook until thickened. Season to taste. Sprinkle with parsley. Makes about 1½ quarts.

MAINE SEAFOOD CHOWDER

- 6 slices salt pork, diced
- 1 onion, chopped
- 6 potatoes, peeled and diced
- 2 cups water
- 1 teaspoon salt
- 2 pounds cod or haddock, skinned, boned, and cut into pieces
- 1 pound sea scallops, cut into halves
- 2 boiled lobsters (about 1 pound each) shelled and cubed
- 4 cups hot milk
- 2 cups light cream
- ¼ cup butter or margarine

Cook salt pork until crisp. Add onion, potatoes, water, and salt. Simmer, covered, until almost tender. Add fish, scallops, lobsters, and hot milk. Simmer over very low heat for 10 minutes. Add cream and butter. Reheat but do not boil. Garnish with chopped parsley and sprinkle with paprika. Makes 6 servings.

SCALLOPED SCALLOPS

- 1 cup fine cracker crumbs
- ½ cup soft bread crumbs
- ½ cup melted butter or margarine
- 1 pint sea scallops
  Onion salt, pepper
- 1 cup heavy cream

Mix crumbs with butter. Arrange alternate layers of scallops, seasoned with onion salt and pepper, and crumbs in baking dish. Pour cream over mixture. Bake in moderate oven (350°F.) for 30 minutes. Makes 4 servings.

WISCASSET LOBSTER STEW

Cook 2-pound lobster in salted water for 15 minutes. Drain; remove meat from shell and cut into pieces. Heat broken shells in 3 tablespoons butter in large saucepan. Add 2 slices onion and sauté for 5 minutes. Add 2 cups milk, 2 cups light cream, and salt and pepper. Simmer for 5 minutes more. Strain into another saucepan. Add lobster and mashed coral. Reheat and add 2 tablespoons butter. Makes about 1 quart.

FRIED APPLES WITH BACON

- 1 pound sliced bacon
- 6 large tart apples
- ½ cup all-purpose flour
- ½ cup sugar
- 1 teaspoon ground nutmeg
- ¼ teaspoon ground cloves

Fry bacon slices until crisp. Remove slices and drain on absorbent paper. Drain all fat but ¼ cup from frying pan. Cut apples, cored but not peeled, into ½-inch thick round slices. Mix flour with sugar and spices. Roll apple slices in flour mixture. Fry apple slices in bacon fat until golden brown on both sides and apple is easily pierced and tender. Serve hot apple slices with crisp bacon slices. Makes 6 servings.

FIDDLEHEADS, MILKWEED, AND OTHER ROADSIDE GREENS

Pick the tender rolls of fern with 1 or 2 inches of stem. Wash, removing all brown scales and woolly covering. Cook in small amount of boiling salted water until tender, for 8 to 10 minutes. Serve with salt pork drippings or butter.

Fiddleheads are found early in spring and should be picked as soon as they appear.

Milkweed is best when picked in the spring. Pick only the young tender shoots. Wash, drain, and cook as you would cook spinach.

Cowslip, plantain, purslane, and pigweed are also picked when young and tender. Wash and cook as spinach is cooked.

BLUEBERRY BETTY

- 6 tablespoons butter or margarine
- 2 cups ½-inch white-bread cubes
- 2 cups blueberries
- 4 teaspoons fresh lemon juice
- ½ cup firmly packed dark brown sugar
  Whipped cream

Melt butter and mix with bread. Put ⅓ of bread in baking dish and top with 1 cup berries. Sprinkle with half the lemon juice and half the brown sugar. Repeat, ending with bread. Bake in preheated moderate oven (350°F.) for 20 minutes. Top with whipped cream. Makes 4 servings.

OLD-FASHIONED GINGERBREAD

- ½ cup butter or margarine
- ½ cup sugar
- 1 egg, beaten
- 1 cup dark molasses
- 3 cups sifted all-purpose flour
- 1½ teaspoons baking soda
- ½ teaspoon salt
- ½ teaspoon ground cloves
- 1 teaspoon ground ginger
- 1¼ cups boiling water

Cream butter until light and fluffy. Gradually beat in sugar. Add egg and molasses and beat until well blended. Sift flour with baking soda, salt, and spices. Add flour alternately with boiling water, beginning and ending with flour. Pour mixture into a well-greased pan (9 x 9 x 2 inches). Bake in preheated moderate oven (350°F.) for 40 to 50 minutes, or until top springs back when lightly touched. Makes nine 3-inch squares.

Maryland

At Fort McHenry waved the Banner that inspired Francis Scott Key to compose our National Anthem, and a half century later Lee fought McClellan at Antietam Creek. A proud military tradition continues at Annapolis, where midshipmen go down to the Chesapeake in trainers. In Baltimore stand the home of Edgar Allan Poe and Pimlico, where the Preakness is run.

FRIED SOFT-SHELL CRABS

Dip cleaned crabs into flour or bread crumbs, then into 1 egg diluted with 3 tablespoons water, then into dry bread or cracker crumbs. Fry them until golden brown in hot deep fat (375°F. on a frying thermometer) for about 5 minutes. They will rise to top of fat and should be turned once while frying. Or else, sauté crabs in hot butter for 5 minutes on each side. Drain on absorbent paper. Sprinkle well with salt and pepper. Serve with tartare sauce or drawn butter with almonds.

OYSTER FRICASSEE

- 1 cup butter
- 1½ quarts shucked oysters
- 2 tablespoons all-purpose flour
- 1 cup heavy cream
- 3 egg yolks, beaten
  Dash of mace
  Salt and white pepper

Melt butter; add oysters. Heat for 1 minute. Mix flour with a little cream. Add remaining cream, egg yolks, and seasonings. Cook until thickened, stirring gently. Serve at once on toast. May be cooked in a chafing dish. Makes 6 servings.

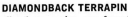
DIAMONDBACK TERRAPIN

Diamondback terrapins are found during late fall and early spring. Use only the females, 6½ to 7 inches in length. Boil a large kettle of water and drop in diamondback terrapins. Cover tightly and scald for 3 minutes. Remove from water; cut off toenails and remove skin. Replace terrapins in boiling water and cook for 45 to 60 minutes, or until tender. If fingers can press easily through the leg, the terrapin is done and should be removed from water at once or meat will be stringy. Reserve broth. Remove shell and remove intestines. Carefully remove liver and gall bladder. Wash eggs and set aside for use in broth. Slice liver into small pieces. Cut terrapin meat into small pieces. Heat stock until it is reduced by one third. Add terrapin meat and liver. Add 1½ cups sweet butter for every quart of meat. Heat, stirring very gently to prevent meat from stringing, until butter is melted. Season to taste with salt and cayenne pepper. Serve terrapin with eggs on top. Add sherry to taste at table.

MARYLAND FRIED CHICKEN

2 frying chickens (about 2½ pounds each), cut up
¾ cup all-purpose flour
1 teaspoon salt
¼ teaspoon pepper
½ cup butter or margarine
1 cup water
1½ cups light cream

Wash and dry chicken pieces. Shake in bag with flour, salt, and pepper. Heat butter in heavy skillet or chicken fryer. Put in chicken and brown quickly on all sides. Reduce heat, slowly add water, cover, and simmer gently until tender, about 30 minutes. Uncover and let chicken sauté slowly. Remove chicken to a hot platter. Blend 2 tablespoons flour into drippings in skillet. Gradually stir in cream and cook, stirring, until thickened. Season to taste and pour over chicken. If desired, garnish with corn oysters or small corn fritters, and broiled bacon. Makes 6 to 8 servings.

CHICKEN-AND-SWEETBREAD CROQUETTES

1 pair sweetbreads
Water
½ onion, minced
1 teaspoon pickling spice
Salt
3 cups ground cooked chicken, meat and skin
6 tablespoons butter or margarine
6 tablespoons all-purpose flour
1½ cups light cream
1 teaspoon onion juice
¼ teaspoon ground nutmeg
Dash of cayenne
1 tablespoon minced parsley

2 eggs
Seasoned bread crumbs
Fat for frying

Soak sweetbreads in ice water 15 minutes; drain. Cover with boiling water; add minced onion, pickling spice, and 1 teaspoon salt. Simmer 20 minutes. Drain; cover with ice water for 5 minutes. Mince fine, discarding membrane and tubes. Mix with ground chicken. Melt butter. Stir in flour. Gradually stir in cream. Add onion juice, nutmeg, cayenne, and 1 teaspoon salt. Cook, stirring constantly, over low heat until smooth and thick. Add parsley and mix enough white sauce with chicken and sweetbreads to make a mixture stiff enough to hold its shape. Spread in greased shallow pan and chill thoroughly. Shape into croquettes about 1 x 1 x 2½ inches. Dip each croquette into beaten egg, then roll in crumbs, covering completely. Let dry in a cool place or a refrigerator for 30 minutes or longer. Fry only a few at a time. Drop into hot deep fat (390°F. on fat thermometer) and fry until golden brown, for about 2 to 4 minutes. Makes 6 servings.

TOMATO DISH
(Fried Green Tomatoes)

Cut firm green tomatoes into ½-inch thick slices. Dip slices into flour mixed with salt and pepper, coating slices on all sides. Fry slices in hot butter until browned on only one side. Fill shallow baking dish half full of canned tomatoes; put tomato slices on top. Sprinkle with salt, pepper, and a little instant minced onion. Put 1 teaspoon dark brown sugar on each slice. Bake in preheated hot oven (400°F.) until dark brown, for about 15 to 20 minutes.

CREAM BISCUITS

4 cups sifted all-purpose flour
1 tablespoon cream of tartar
1½ teaspoons baking soda
¾ cup butter or margarine
2 cups heavy cream

Sift flour with cream of tartar and baking soda. Cut in butter until mixture resembles coarse cornmeal. Add cream and stir until a soft dough is formed. Knead on a lightly floured board until smooth. Roll out to ½-inch thickness and cut into 2-inch rounds. Place on a lightly greased cookie sheet and bake in preheated hot oven (400°F.) for 12 to 15 minutes, or until golden brown. Makes about 2½ dozen.

LADY BALTIMORE CAKE

⅔ cup soft butter or margarine
1½ cups sugar
1 teaspoon vanilla extract
½ teaspoon almond extract

2½ cups sifted cake flour
2½ teaspoons baking powder
⅔ cup milk
½ teaspoon salt
½ teaspoon cream of tartar
4 egg whites
Fluffy White Frosting
6 dried figs, chopped
½ cup each of chopped raisins and nuts

Cream butter. Add sugar gradually, beating until light. Add flavorings. Add sifted flour and baking powder alternately with milk, beating until smooth. Add salt and cream of tartar to egg whites. Beat until stiff, but not dry. Fold into first mixture. Pour into two 9-inch layer-cake pans, greased and lined on the bottom with wax paper. Bake in preheated moderate oven (375°F.) for 20 to 25 minutes. Cool. Make Fluffy White Frosting. To one third of frosting, add chopped dried figs, raisins, and nuts. Spread between layers. Use remaining frosting for top and sides of cake. Makes 8 to 10 servings.

Fluffy White Frosting

In top part of small double boiler, combine 2 egg whites, 1½ cups sugar, ⅛ teaspoon salt, ⅓ cup water, and 2 teaspoons light corn syrup. Put over boiling water and beat with rotary beater or electric mixer for 7 minutes, or until mixture will stand in stiff peaks. Fold in 1 teaspoon vanilla extract.

LORD BALTIMORE CAKE

½ cup soft butter or other shortening
1 cup sugar
1 teaspoon vanilla extract
3 egg yolks
2 cups sifted cake flour
2 teaspoons baking powder
½ teaspoon salt
⅔ cup milk
Fluffy White Frosting (above)
½ cup almond-macaroon crumbs
¼ cup chopped walnuts
¼ teaspoon almond extract
¼ cup chopped blanched almonds
12 quartered candied cherries
2 teaspoons fresh lemon juice
1 tablespoon sherry
Whole candied cherries
Angelica

Cream butter and sugar until light. Add vanilla. Add egg yolks, one at a time, beating well after each. Add sifted flour, baking powder, and salt alternately with milk, beating until smooth. Pour into two 8-inch layer-cake pans, lined on the bottom with wax paper. Bake in preheated moderate oven (375°F.) for 25 minutes. Make frosting. To one third of frosting stir in almond-macaroon crumbs, walnuts, almond extract, blanched almonds, cherries, lemon juice, and sherry. Spread between cooled layers. Use remaining frosting for top and sides of cake. Decorate top with whole candied cherries and strips of angelica.

Massachusetts

Paul Revere and the Old North Church, Salem's pillories, Minute Men of Lexington Green, Bunker Hill, Provincetown and Plymouth, Pilgrims' first landings—one stands amid history in the Old Colony. Gloucester ships combing Grand Bank for cod, Tanglewood's music and Harvard Yard; the dunes of Cape Cod, beans baked in Boston: past is prologue in this place.

CREAMED TURKEY AND OYSTERS

¾ cup water
3 cups shucked oysters
⅓ cup butter or margarine
½ cup all-purpose flour
1½ cups light cream
1½ teaspoons salt
¼ teaspoon pepper
   Sliced cold turkey

Add water to oysters and their liquor. Simmer for 2 minutes, or until edges of oysters curl. Drain and reserve liquid. Melt butter. Stir in flour. Gradually stir in 1½ cups reserved oyster broth and cream. Add salt and pepper. Cook over low heat, stirring constantly, until smooth and thick. Stir in oysters and reheat slightly. Add turkey slices and reheat slightly. Serve at once. Turkey can also be cut into chunks and mixture can be spooned into patty shells or over rice. Makes 6 servings.

CAPE COD TURKEY

2 pounds salt cod
¼ pound salt pork, sliced
6 medium potatoes
12 small beets
¼ cup butter
¼ cup all-purpose flour
2 cups milk
   Salt and pepper

3 hard-cooked eggs, sliced

Cut cod into individual portions. Cover with cold water and soak for 3 hours. Drain. Cover with fresh water and simmer, covered, for 20 minutes, or until cod flakes. Drain and keep warm. Fry salt-pork slices until crisp. Drain on absorbent paper. Cook potatoes and beets separately until tender. Drain and peel. Melt butter and stir in flour. Gradually stir in milk. Cook over low heat, stirring constantly, until smooth and thick. Season to taste with salt and pepper. Place fish on a platter and pour white sauce over fish. Garnish with crisp pork slices and hard-cooked egg slices and surround with potatoes and beets. Makes 6 servings.

SPOONED CODFISH CAKES

1 package (4 ounces) shredded salt codfish
4 cups cubed peeled raw potato
1 onion, minced
2 tablespoons all-purpose flour
   Salt and pepper

Freshen salt codfish by soaking in cold water. Drain. Place codfish, potato, and onion in a saucepan and cook in boiling water to cover until potato is tender. Drain. Mash well. Add flour, and salt and pepper to taste. Blend well. Cool, then chill. Drop by tablespoon into hot deep fat (350°F. on a frying thermometer) and fry until brown, for 2 to 3 minutes. Serve with ketchup or stewed tomatoes. Makes 4 servings.

HARVARD BEETS

2 teaspoons cornstarch
⅓ cup sugar
½ teaspoon salt
⅛ teaspoon pepper
⅔ cup vinegar
⅓ cup water or beet liquid
3 cups sliced cooked beets
1 tablespoon butter

Mix cornstarch with sugar, salt, and pepper. Stir in vinegar and water. Cook over low heat, stirring constantly, until mixture is smooth and thickened. Add beets and reheat. Stir in butter just before serving. Makes 6 servings.

BOSTON BAKED BEANS

2 cups dried pea beans, washed and drained
6 cups water
¼ pound lean salt pork
1 medium onion
1 teaspoon salt
½ cup light molasses
½ teaspoon dry mustard
1 tablespoon sugar

Cover beans with water. Bring to a boil and boil for 2 minutes. Cover pan and let stand for 1 hour; then cook until tender. Replace water to keep up level of liquid. Drain and reserve liquid. Put

beans in pot. Cut through pork rind every ½ inch, making cuts 1 inch deep. Bury onion and pork in beans, leaving rind exposed. Mix 1 cup bean liquid and remaining ingredients; pour over beans. Add enough liquid to cover beans. Cover pot and bake in preheated slow oven (300°F.) for 6 to 8 hours. Uncover pot last hour. Makes 6 servings.

BOSTON BROWN BREAD

2 tablespoons shortening
¼ cup sugar
1 egg
¾ cup dark molasses
2¼ cups whole-wheat flour
1 teaspoon salt
¾ cup yellow cornmeal
1½ teaspoons each of baking powder and baking soda
1¾ cups buttermilk
⅔ cup seedless raisins

Cream shortening and sugar. Beat in egg and molasses. Beat in remaining ingredients. Spoon into 2 well-greased 1-quart molds, filling molds a little more than half full. Cover with greased lids or foil. Set molds on rack in deep kettle and add boiling water to come halfway up sides of molds. Cover and steam for 2½ hours. Replace boiling water to keep up level of liquid. Makes 2 loaves.

BOSTON CREAM PIE

⅓ cup butter
1 cup sugar
2 eggs, beaten
2 cups sifted cake flour
2 teaspoons baking powder
½ teaspoon salt
⅔ cup milk
   Cream Filling
   Confectioners' sugar

Cream butter and sugar. Add eggs; mix well; then add sifted dry ingredients alternately with milk. Pour into two greased 8-inch layer-cake pans and bake in preheated moderate oven (375°F.) for 20 minutes. Turn out on cake racks to cool. Put together with Cream Filling. Sprinkle top with confectioners' sugar or shredded coconut; or cover with whipped cream. Makes 8 servings.

Cream Filling

⅓ cup sugar
2½ tablespoons all-purpose flour
⅛ teaspoon salt
1 cup milk
1 egg, beaten
½ teaspoon vanilla extract

Mix sugar, flour, and salt in saucepan. Add ¼ cup milk and stir until smooth. Pour in remaining milk and cook over low heat until thickened. Add mixture to egg; return to saucepan and cook for 2 minutes longer. Add vanilla, and cool.

BAKED INDIAN PUDDING

4 cups milk

5 tablespoons yellow cornmeal
2 tablespoons butter
½ cup firmly packed brown sugar
½ cup molasses
1 teaspoon salt
½ teaspoon each of ground ginger, cinnamon, nutmeg, and mace
2 eggs, beaten
1 cup light cream
Cream or vanilla ice cream

In top part of double boiler over direct heat, bring to boil 3 cups milk. Mix 1 cup cold milk with cornmeal and stir slowly into hot milk. Put over boiling water and cook for 20 minutes, stirring occasionally. Add butter, sugar, and molasses. Remove from heat and add salt and spices. Stir in eggs and pour into 1½-quart baking dish. Bake in preheated slow oven (300°F.) for 2 to 2½ hours, stirring occasionally during first hour. Then pour light cream over top and finish baking without stirring. Serve warm topped with cream. Makes 6 to 8 servings.

Michigan

Tulip festivals in Holland, ore boats locked in frozen Whitefish Bay, racing sloops at Mackinac Island, brant and plover nesting in the wild archipelago of Isle Royale—these tell the seasons in the Twin Peninsulas. Four Great Lakes wash these shores, canalboats ply the Soo, but the Wolverine State runs on cars coming off Detroit's assembly lines.

PIQUANT WHITEFISH STEW
1 pound fresh or thawed frozen whitefish fillets
1 tablespoon cooking oil
1 tablespoon cider vinegar
2 tablespoons minced onion
1 teaspoon salt
2 teaspoons Worcestershire

⅓ cup ketchup
¼ cup water
1 tablespoon drained capers
1 cup cooked peas

Cut fish into serving pieces. Bring oil, vinegar, onion, salt, Worcestershire, ketchup, and water to boil in top part of double boiler. Add capers and fish. Cover, and cook over boiling water for 25 minutes, or until fish is done, stirring gently several times. Add peas, heat, and serve. Makes 3 to 4 servings.

PASTIES
2 cups sifted all-purpose flour
½ teaspoon salt
½ teaspoon baking powder
1⅓ cups beef suet, ground twice
⅓ cup shortening
Cold water
Meat Filling
Butter

Sift flour with salt and baking powder. Add beef suet and shortening and cut fat into flour until particles are very fine. Add enough cold water to make a dough the consistency of pie crust. Chill. Roll out dough to ⅛-inch thickness on a lightly floured board. Cut out eight 7-inch rounds. Divide Meat Filling into 8 portions and cover half of each round with the mixture. Dot top of Filling with butter. Fold pastry over Meat Filling and seal by moistening edges. Lift with a spatula and put on a cookie sheet. Bake in preheated moderate oven (350°F.) for 1 hour, or until pastry is golden brown. Makes 8 pasties.

Meat Filling
Mix together 1 pound round steak cut into small cubes, 6 ounces lean pork, cut into small cubes; 3 cups finely diced peeled potatoes, ½ cup finely diced peeled yellow turnip, ½ cup sliced onions; 1 teaspoon salt and ¼ teaspoon pepper.

BOOYAW
1 pound pickled pork, cubed
5-pound chicken, rabbit, or any game, cubed
1 yellow turnip, peeled and cubed
2 large onions, peeled and sliced
6 carrots, cut into 1-inch pieces
6 large potatoes, peeled and cubed
2 celery stalks, chopped
Salt and pepper

Cover meats with water and cook, covered, until meats are tender. Add vegetables, cover, and cook for 20 to 30 minutes, or until vegetables are tender. Season to taste with salt and pepper. Makes 8 servings.

KALE WITH PORK
2 pounds kale
Water
1 pound metworst or piece of fresh pork
4 potatoes, diced
Salt and pepper

Cover kale with water; add meat. Cover, and cook for 1½ hours. Add potatoes and cook for 30 minutes longer. Drain, remove meat, slice; chop kale and wash potatoes; season to taste. Makes 4 servings.

MICHIGAN BAKED BEANS
1 pound dried Great Northern beans
6 cups water
2 teaspoons salt
½ teaspoon dry mustard
1 large onion, minced
⅓ cup firmly packed dark brown sugar
⅓ cup dark molasses
½ cup chili sauce
2⅓ cups (one 1-pound, 3-ounce can) tomatoes
8 slices of bacon

Cover beans with water, bring to boil, and boil for 2 minutes. Cover pan and let stand for 1 hour. Simmer until almost tender, about 1½ hours. Drain and reserve liquid. Add remaining ingredients except bacon; pour into shallow baking pan. Top with bacon slices, cut into halves. Bake in preheated slow oven (300°F.) for 2 hours, adding more bean liquid if necessary. Makes 6 servings.

FAT BALLS
¼ cup shortening
½ cup sugar
1 egg, well beaten
2½ cups potato cooking water
2 envelopes active dry yeast or 2 cakes compressed yeast
½ cup water*
6 to 7 cups sifted all-purpose flour
1 teaspoon salt
1 cup currants
1 cup raisins
Fat for frying
Brown sugar

Cream shortening with sugar. Add egg and potato water. *Use very warm water (105°F. to 115°F.) for dry yeast; use lukewarm (80°F. to 90°F.) for compressed. Sprinkle dry yeast or crumble cake into water. Let stand for a few minutes; then stir until dissolved. Add to mixture. Stir in flour with salt to make a rather stiff dough that can just about be beaten with a spoon. Add currants and raisins; beat well. Cover and let rise until double in bulk. With floured hands, stir and shape into small balls. Fry in hot deep fat (365°F. on a frying thermometer) until brown, about 2 to 4 minutes, turning once to brown both sides. Serve with brown sugar. Makes 5 to 6 dozen.

MICHIGAN SHORTCAKE
6 slices buttered bread, crusts trimmed
4 cups raspberries, strawberries, or blueberries
1 cup sugar
Whipped cream

Line bottom and sides of a 1-quart mold

with slices of buttered bread. Crush fruit with a potato masher and mix with sugar. Pour fruit into bread-lined pan. Top with additional buttered slices of bread. Place a weight on top of mold and chill for 24 hours. Turn out of mold and garnish with whipped cream and pieces of whole fruit. Makes 6 servings.

PICKLED CHERRIES
Pit sour cherries; put in large crock or bowl. Cover with cider vinegar. Let stand for 8 days; stir twice a day. Drain off vinegar. Mix cherries with equal amount of sugar. Let stand for 8 more days; stir twice a day. Fill sterilized jars; seal.

Minnesota
Longfellow's Minnehaha Falls and Minnetonka Lake, where the loons cry —heritage of the Sioux; Lake of the Woods, Rainy Lake and 10,000 more; ore fields of the vast Mesabi, legacy of nature. Elk herds run at Red Lake and fishermen mend their nets along Superior's shore. Winter is carnival time at St. Paul; at Rochester, a clinic offers its healing hand.

PICKLED FISH
Water
Salt and pepper
Celery tops, parsley
2 pounds small white fish
1 large onion
1 cup vinegar
1 onion, sliced
1 red pepper, cut into strips
1 tablespoon whole pickling spice

Boil 3 cups water; add 1 teaspoon salt, ¼ teaspoon pepper, celery tops, and a few parsley sprigs. Add fish and enough more boiling water to cover. Cover; simmer over low heat for 5 minutes. Remove fish to covered casserole, dis-

carding liquid. Sprinkle fish with salt and pepper. Mix remaining ingredients. Pour over fish. Cover, and refrigerate for a day or two, turning fish once or twice. Serve as an appetizer. Makes 8 servings.

NORWEGIAN FISH PUDDING
1 pound halibut or other delicate fish
3 egg whites
1 cup heavy cream or undiluted evaporated milk
1 teaspoon salt
½ teaspoon white pepper
  Cayenne, ground nutmeg, or celery salt
  Few drops of onion juice

Put fish through food chopper, using finest blade. Or whirl a small amount at a time in a blender. Put fish in a bowl set in a pan of ice water. Slowly stir in egg whites; beat with a wire whisk to keep mixture smooth. Stir in cream very slowly. Add salt and pepper. Season to taste with cayenne, ground nutmeg, or celery salt and the onion juice. Let stand for 1 hour. Pour mixture into a well-buttered 1½-quart mold or into individual timbale molds. Set in a pan of hot water 1 inch deep. Cover with foil. Bake in preheated moderate oven (350°F.) until firm. Makes 4 to 6 servings.

LIVER PUDDING
1½ cups raw rice
2 cups water
4 cups milk
1 onion, chopped
¼ cup butter
1 pound beef liver, chopped
1 egg, well beaten
1 tablespoon sugar
1 tablespoon salt
⅛ teaspoon pepper

Pour rice into water mixed with milk. Cook over high heat, stirring occasionally, until mixture is very thick. Sauté onion in butter until golden brown. To make chopping easier, dip liver into boiling water for 1 minute or freeze partially. Add liver, egg, onion, sugar, salt, and pepper to rice mixture. Put mixture into well-buttered 2-quart casserole and bake in preheated moderate oven (350°F.) for 1 hour. Makes 6 to 8 servings.

WILD RICE CASSEROLE
1 cup wild rice
¼ cup butter
3 tablespoons chopped onion
3 tablespoons chopped green pepper
½ cup slivered blanched almonds
3 cups hot chicken broth

Wash rice and drain well. Melt butter in skillet; add onion, green pepper, rice, and almonds. Sauté over low heat, stirring constantly, until rice begins to turn light yellow. Turn into a casserole; add hot chicken broth. Cover, and bake in preheated slow oven (325°F.) for 1½ hours, or until rice is tender and all

liquid is absorbed. Makes 4 servings.

RUTABAGA RING
3 tablespoons all-purpose flour
2 tablespoons light brown sugar
2½ tablespoons melted bacon fat
1 cup milk
4 egg yolks, beaten
2 cups mashed rutabagas
  Salt and pepper
5 egg whites
  Parsley

Stir flour and brown sugar into bacon fat. Gradually stir in milk and cook, stirring, over low heat until thickened and smooth. Remove from heat. Gradually stir hot sauce into egg yolks. Add rutabaga and seasonings; stir in about one fourth of stiffly beaten egg whites, then gently fold in the rest. Pour into well-buttered 1½-quart ring mold. Bake in preheated moderate oven (375°F.) for 30 to 35 minutes. Remove from oven, cover with a towel, and let rest for 5 minutes. Unmold on a heated serving dish. Garnish with parsley. Makes 4 to 6 servings.

SWEDISH RYE BREAD
1 package active dry yeast or
  1 cake compressed yeast
¼ cup lukewarm water*
2 cups milk or water
⅓ cup butter
¼ cup molasses
¼ cup brown sugar
2 teaspoons salt
2 cups rye flour
1 teaspoon caraway seeds or
  2 teaspoons pounded fennel or aniseeds
4 cups sifted all-purpose flour

*Sprinkle dry yeast or crumble cake yeast into warm water. Use very warm water (105°F. to 115°F.) for dry yeast; use lukewarm water (80°F. to 90°F.) for compressed. Let stand for a few minutes, then stir until dissolved. Scald milk; add butter, molasses, brown sugar, salt, and rye flour. Beat until smooth; when lukewarm, add caraway seeds and yeast. Add flour gradually to make a stiff dough. Knead until smooth and elastic to the touch, about 8 to 10 minutes. Cover, and let rise in a warm place until almost double in bulk. Toss on lightly floured board and divide into 2 equal parts. Form each into a flat round loaf. Cut out a small hole in the center. Place on buttered cookie sheet, prick with fork, cover, and let rise until light. Bake in preheated moderate oven (375°F.) for 35 minutes. Brush with warm water when half done and again when bread is taken from the oven.

PRUNE KOLACHE
1 package active dry yeast or
  1 cake compressed yeast
2 tablespoons water*
4 cups sifted all-purpose flour
¼ cup sugar

1 teaspoon salt
1 teaspoon grated lemon rind
¾ cup butter
3 egg yolks
1 cup heavy cream
  Prune Filling
  Confectioners' Sugar Icing

*Use very warm water (105°F. to 115°F.) for dry yeast; use lukewarm (80°F. to 90°F.) for compressed. Sprinkle dry yeast or crumble cake into water. Let stand for a few minutes; then stir until dissolved. Sift flour with sugar and salt. Add grated lemon rind and yeast; blend in butter. Beat egg yolks and add cream; combine with flour mixture. Blend well. Cover bowl tightly. Refrigerate overnight. Knead several times and roll on lightly floured board to ¼-inch thickness. Cut with 2-inch cutter and place rounds on ungreased cookie sheets. Cover, and let rise in warm place until double in bulk, for about 1 hour. Using fingertips, make a depression in the center of each kolache. Fill with Prune Filling. Bake in preheated moderate oven (375°F.) for about 10 minutes. While warm, spread with Confectioners' Sugar Icing. Makes 4 to 5 dozen.

Prune Filling

Soak 1½ cups prunes in water overnight. Simmer, covered, until tender; drain. Pit prunes and mash with fork. Add ¼ cup sugar and ½ teaspoon ground cinnamon.

Confectioners' Sugar Icing

Mix 1½ cups confectioners' sugar, 2 tablespoons boiling water, and 1 teaspoon lemon juice.

BISHOP WHIPPLE PUDDING

2 eggs
½ cup sugar
⅔ cup sifted all-purpose flour
1 teaspoon baking powder
1 cup coarsely chopped nuts
1 cup chopped pitted dates
  Brown Sugar Sauce

Beat eggs until thick and lemon-colored. Stir in sugar. Sift flour with baking powder. Add flour to egg mixture. Beat until well blended. Fold in nuts and dates. Spoon mixture into well-greased 9-inch layer-cake pan. Bake in preheated moderate oven (350°F.) for 20 to 30 minutes, or until top is golden brown. Serve warm with Brown Sugar Sauce. Makes 4 to 6 servings.

Brown Sugar Sauce

⅓ cup butter or margarine
½ cup heavy cream
2 cups firmly packed light brown sugar
¼ teaspoon salt
⅓ cup light corn syrup

Mix all ingredients in saucepan. Bring to boil and cook rapidly for 3 minutes (220°F. on a candy thermometer).

Mississippi

An antebellum mansion in a copse of Natchez magnolia trees recalls the Rebel host and a time of unfaded glory. Jackson, Vicksburg, Corinth—the names of battle ring out through Dixie Land. Look away, look away, to fields of cotton in the Yazoo delta and to stands of pecan trees. Rodeos for mackerel at Gulfport and shrimp boats trawling off Biloxi.

BILOXI SHRIMP STEW

2 yellow onions, sliced
1 cup diced celery
2 tablespoons shortening
1 tablespoon all-purpose flour
1 teaspoon salt
1 to 1½ tablespoons chili powder
1 cup water
2 cups canned tomatoes
2 cups shelled fresh peas
1 tablespoon cider vinegar
1 teaspoon sugar
2 cups cooked shelled deveined shrimps
⅓ cup sherry
6 cups hot cooked rice, seasoned to taste

Sauté onions and celery in hot shortening in a deep saucepan. Sprinkle flour and seasonings over vegetables. Stir to blend well. Gradually stir in water. Simmer, covered, stirring occasionally, for 15 minutes or until thickened. Add remaining ingredients except last two; and simmer for 10 minutes, or until peas are tender. Stir in sherry. Pack hot seasoned rice into lightly oiled 6-cup 9-inch ring mold. Unmold ring on a platter and fill center with hot shrimp mixture. It can also be served in soup bowls on top of cooked rice. Makes 6 servings.

STUFFED CRABS

12 hard-shell crabs
⅛ teaspoon cayenne
2 tablespoons chopped parsley

1 onion, quartered
1 cup soft bread crumbs
2 hard-cooked eggs, chopped finely
2 drops hot pepper sauce
1 teaspoon salt
1 teaspoon minced parsley
½ cup milk
½ cup light cream
¼ cup butter or margarine
  Dry bread crumbs and butter

Wash crabs and drain. Add cayenne, parsley, and onion to enough water to cover crabs. Bring water to a boil and add live crabs. Cover and cook over medium heat for 15 minutes. Drain crabs and cool slightly. Remove claws and pull meat in shell from back shell of crabs. Reserve shells and use later to fill. Clean shells thoroughly. Pick crabmeat from claws and main body. Add crabmeat to remaining ingredients. Use mixture to stuff back shells. Sprinkle tops with bread crumbs and dot with additional butter. Bake in preheated hot oven (400°F.) for 10 minutes, or until tops are golden brown. Makes 6 servings.

STUFFED HAM

1 uncooked smoked ham, whole and with skin (8 to 10 pounds)
  Water
  Stuffing
  Brown sugar

Put ham in a large kettle. Cover with water and simmer until ham is tender. Let ham cool in water. When cool, remove skin. With a sharp knife, cut deep incisions into meat all over the ham. Use Stuffing to stuff the cuts in ham. Rub ham with brown sugar. Bake in preheated moderate oven (375°F.) for 45 minutes to 1 hour, or until ham is brown. Makes 12 to 18 servings.

Stuffing

1 onion, chopped
4 cups soft bread crumbs
1 cup chopped celery
1 teaspoon each of crumbled dried thyme, marjoram, and sage
¼ cup minced parsley
¼ teaspoon cayenne

Mix onion with bread crumbs and celery. Add herbs and cayenne and mix well.

CANDIED SWEET POTATOES

12 small sweet potatoes
2 cups sugar
1 cup hot water
1 teaspoon ground cinnamon
1 tablespoon fresh lemon juice
¾ cup melted butter
1 teaspoon salt

Peel sweet potatoes and leave whole. Put potatoes in a shallow greased baking dish. Mix remaining ingredients and cook at a boil for 8 minutes. Pour hot syrup over potatoes and bake in preheated moderate oven (350°F.) for 1 hour, or until syrup is thick and potatoes are tender. Spoon syrup in dish over potatoes several times during cooking. Makes 6 servings.

Christmas at Sunnyside: Here is Washington Irving's dining room, all ready for the holiday feast of roast turkey and ham.

ANTEBELLUM SPICED NUT CORN BREAD

½ cup sifted all-purpose flour
2 teaspoons baking powder
¼ teaspoon salt
¼ cup sugar
½ teaspoon ground cinnamon
¼ teaspoon each of ground allspice and nutmeg
½ cup white cornmeal
½ cup finely chopped pecans
1 egg, beaten
½ cup milk
2 tablespoons melted butter

Sift first 7 ingredients. Add cornmeal and nuts; stir well. Add egg, milk, and 1 tablespoon melted butter. Blend to make a batter. Put 1 tablespoon butter in a 7-inch iron skillet. Heat skillet in preheated hot oven (400°F.), then brush heated butter on sides and bottom of pan. Add batter and return to oven at once. Bake for 30 minutes, or until corn bread tests done. Cut into 6 wedges and serve immediately. Makes 6 servings.

LEMON VELVET PUDDING

3 eggs, separated
⅓ cup fresh lemon juice
Grated rind of 1 large lemon
¼ teaspoon salt
1 cup sugar
⅓ cup cornstarch
1 cup water
1 tablespoon butter
1 cup heavy cream, whipped
1 dozen ladyfingers

Beat egg whites until stiff; beat yolks until thick. Add lemon juice and rind to yolks. Mix dry ingredients. Gradually stir in water. Stir into egg yolks and cook over low heat, stirring constantly, until thick and smooth. Remove from heat, add butter, and stir until melted. Fold in egg whites. Let stand until cool. Fold in whipped cream. Pour into glass bowl lined with ladyfingers. Makes 6 servings.

EGGNOG

6 eggs, separated
½ cup sugar
1 cup rye or bourbon whiskey
½ cup rum
4 cups heavy cream

Beat egg yolks until thick and lemon-colored. Gradually beat in sugar, whiskey, and rum. Beat egg whites until stiff but not dry and fold egg whites into whiskey mixture. Beat heavy cream until it holds soft peaks, and fold cream into whiskey mixture. Blend well and chill until ready to serve. Makes about 3 quarts of rich thick eggnog that can be eaten with a spoon.

Missouri

Huck and Tom, adrift in enduring boyhood, a Twain to mark the time-ignoring Mississippi. Lake of the Ozarks, complementing rocky glens, wide "Old Muddy," wandering, wandering. Place for Pony Express to begin, for Pulitzer to prize, for a man of Independence, for Kansas City and St. Loo too. Watermelons a-ripening, "Land of the big red apple." Show me, Missouri.

BULLHEAD OR CATFISH SOUP

3 pounds fish, cleaned, boned, and cut into pieces
2 quarts water
1 onion, sliced
½ cup chopped celery
Salt and pepper
1 bay leaf
2 tablespoons chopped parsley
½ teaspoon crumbled dried thyme
1 cup milk
2 tablespoons butter or other fat

Combine all ingredients in a large kettle. Bring mixture to a boil and lower heat. Cover, and simmer until fish falls to pieces. Serve hot. Makes 6 servings.

HOT PICKLED BEEF

2 cups cider vinegar
4 pounds boneless round steak
2 onions, sliced
1 lemon, sliced
1 teaspoon peppercorns
1 teaspoon juniper berries
2 bay leaves
2 tablespoons shortening
2 teaspoons salt
1 cup red wine

Pour vinegar over meat in glass or stainless-steel pan or bowl. Add onions, lemon slices, peppercorns, berries, and bay leaves. Cover and let stand in refrigerator for 48 hours, turning meat occasionally.

Remove from marinade. Wipe dry and brown slowly in hot shortening. Strain marinade and add 1 cup to meat. Add salt and wine, cover, and simmer slowly for 2 hours, or until tender. Thicken slightly with flour if desired. Pour juices over meat. Makes 8 servings.

WHEELSPOKE CASSEROLE

3 cups unsalted hot cooked rice
1 envelope onion soup mix
2 tablespoons butter
4 minute steaks
1 can (4 ounces) button mushrooms with liquid

Mix first 3 ingredients and put in shallow 1½-quart baking dish. Brown steaks lightly in greased skillet. Cut in strips 2 to 3 inches long and ½ inch wide. Arrange on rice, wheelspoke fashion. Pour mushrooms and liquid over top. Bake in slow oven (325°F.) about 30 minutes. Makes 4 to 6 servings.

SMOTHERED RABBIT AND ONIONS

Clean 1 rabbit and cut into small pieces. Season with salt and paprika. Dredge with flour. Melt 3 tablespoons butter in skillet. Sauté rabbit in butter until browned. Cover rabbit thickly with sliced onions. Sprinkle onions with salt. Pour in 1 cup dairy sour cream. Cover skillet and simmer for 1 hour. Or put in preheated slow oven (325°F.) and bake until tender. Makes 4 servings.

CORNISH GAME HENS WITH SAUERKRAUT

6 Cornish game hens
Salt and pepper
6 slices of bacon
2 parsley sprigs
1 small sprig of fresh thyme
¼ bay leaf
1 garlic clove
1 whole yellow onion
1 carrot, scraped
1 cup water
1½ pounds sauerkraut
2 teaspoons wine vinegar
2 teaspoons sugar
6 breakfast sausages

Rub Cornish game hens inside and out with salt and pepper. Place them in deep baking dish with slice of bacon tied over the breast of each. Tie herbs and garlic

in a square of cheesecloth and put them in the dish. Add onion, carrot, and water. Bake, uncovered, in preheated very hot oven (500°F.) for 10 minutes. Lower temperature to moderate (375°F.). Cover hens with sauerkraut mixed with wine vinegar and sugar. Bake, covered, for 30 minutes longer. Meanwhile half-fry sausages. Place sausages on top of sauerkraut after removing bag of herbs. Bake, uncovered, for 15 minutes longer. Makes 6 servings.

BAKED CORN

12 ears fresh corn
Salt and pepper
1 tablespoon sugar
2 tablespoons water
¼ cup heavy cream

With a sharp knife cut down center of the kernels of corn. With back of the knife press out pulp without removing any of hull. Add salt and pepper to taste. Stir in sugar and water. Pour mixture into lightly greased shallow baking dish. Bake in preheated moderate oven (350°F.) for 30 minutes. Remove from oven and stir cream into corn. Serve at once. Makes 6 servings.

BAKED DOUGHNUTS

1 box hot-roll mix
Sugar
1 egg, beaten
Melted butter or margarine
1 teaspoon grated lemon rind
½ teaspoon each of ground cinnamon and nutmeg
All-purpose flour

Prepare hot-roll mix as directed on label, adding only half the flour in package. Add ¼ cup sugar, egg, ¼ cup melted butter, and lemon rind. Beat until bubbly. Add spices to remaining flour from mix; stir into first mixture. Beat in ¼ to ½ cup sifted flour to make soft dough. Cover and let rest for 10 minutes. Turn out dough on a lightly floured board and knead until smooth. Put in greased bowl; turn dough over so entire ball of dough is greased. Cover and let rise until double in bulk. Roll to ½-inch thickness; brush with melted butter. Cut with floured 2½-inch doughnut cutter and put 2 inches apart on greased cookie sheets. Let rise until double in bulk. Bake in preheated moderate oven (375°F.) for about 10 minutes. Brush again with melted butter and roll in sugar. Makes about 2 dozen.

HONEY GINGERBREAD

½ cup soft butter or margarine
½ cup sugar
1 cup honey
1 egg
2½ cups sifted cake flour
1 teaspoon salt
1 teaspoon baking soda
½ teaspoon baking powder
1 teaspoon each of ground cinnamon and ginger
1 cup buttermilk

Cream butter and sugar; add honey; cream until light. Add egg and beat well. Sift dry ingredients together and add alternately with buttermilk, beating until smooth. Pour into greased pan (13 x 9 x 2 inches) lined on the bottom with wax paper. Bake in preheated oven (350°F.) for about 45 minutes, or until cake springs back when touched lightly. Turn out on rack and peel off paper. Cut into squares and serve warm or cold. Makes 12 to 15 servings.

FRUIT KETCHUP

3 pounds tart fruit (grapes, crabapples and red plums)
1 cup water
4 cups cider vinegar
2 cups sugar
1 teaspoon ground cinnamon
½ teaspoon ground cloves
¼ teaspoon ground allspice

Clean fruit, removing stems, cores, and pits. Add water to fruit and simmer, covered, for 30 minutes, or until fruit is tender. Press fruit through a sieve. Pour fruit pulp into a large kettle; add remaining ingredients. Cook over medium heat, stirring frequently, until smooth and very thick. Spoon mixture into hot sterilized glasses. Seal tightly. Cool and store. Makes three 8-ounce glasses.

Montana

When spring's Chinook winds kiss this "Land of Shining Mountains," Big Horns frolic, bitterroot begins to blush and wind-sculptured buttes shed mantles of snow. Copper and sapphires are treasures, but the Chinook is gold: in its wake pasture lands turn green, wheat ripens, tourists come. Only at Glacier Park does Chinook fail: there winter is eternal.

LAMB ON SKEWERS

2 pounds boneless shoulder of lamb
¾ cup French dressing

1 garlic clove, minced
Small mushroom caps
6 slices of bacon, cut into squares
Seasoned salt

Cut meat into 1-inch cubes. Put into bowl with French dressing and garlic. Refrigerate for at least 3 hours; turn meat occasionally. Arrange alternate pieces of lamb, mushroom, and bacon on skewers. Sprinkle with seasoned salt to taste. Broil until fork-tender over coals heated to turn gray. Turn occasionally to cook evenly. Serve with buttered brown or wild rice. Makes 4 to 6 servings.

Note: The broiling may be done in a range broiler.

BLIND RABBIT

1 pound ground beef
1 pound ground veal
1 pound ground pork
4 slices of white bread, soaked and squeezed dry
2 eggs, well beaten
Juice of 1 lemon
Salt and pepper to taste

Combine all ingredients and shape into a loaf. Put loaf in a greased large shallow baking pan. Bake in preheated moderate oven (350°F.) for 1 hour. Slice and serve hot. Makes 10 to 12 servings.

ROAST WILD DUCK

2 wild ducks
Salt and pepper
2 slices of onion
6 juniper berries (optional)
1 cup red wine
½ cup veal or beef broth
Rind of 1 orange, cut into matchlike strips

Wipe ducks with damp cloth; season with salt and pepper inside and out. Put a slice of onion and 3 juniper berries, if used, inside each duck. Place in a shallow roasting pan with wine, broth, and orange rind. Roast in preheated extremely hot oven (500°F.) for 15 to 20 minutes, basting frequently. Remove ducks from pan drippings. Boil drippings rapidly for 2 to 3 minutes and pour over ducks. Makes 4 servings.

CHUCK-WAGON BOILED BEANS

4 cups Great Northern dried beans, washed and drained
¼ cup dark molasses
1 tablespoon salt
1 hot red pepper pod
¼ cup bacon fat
2 onions, quartered
1 teaspoon liquid or powdered smoke

Cover beans with cold water; bring to a boil. Boil for 2 minutes, cover pan, and let stand for 1 hour. Do not drain. Add water, if needed, to cover. Add remaining ingredients. Cover pan and simmer until tender, adding more water if necessary to keep from sticking. Makes 10 servings.

SCALLOPED CARROTS

8 carrots, coarsely shredded
3 cups soft bread crumbs
  Salt and pepper
1 cup grated cheese
  Hot milk

Put carrots and bread crumbs in alternate layers in a shallow baking dish. Sprinkle each layer with salt and pepper. Sprinkle top with cheese. Add enough hot milk just to cover mixture to the top. Bake in preheated hot oven (400°F.) for 1 hour. Makes 4 servings.

CARROT PIE

  Pastry for 1-crust 9-inch pie, unbaked
1½ cups pureed cooked carrots
 ½ cup firmly packed light brown sugar
 1 tablespoon cornstarch
 ½ teaspoon salt
 ½ teaspoon each of ground cinnamon
    and ginger
 ¼ teaspoon each of ground allspice and
    nutmeg
1½ cups milk
 2 eggs, well beaten
 ½ teaspoon vanilla extract

Line a 9-inch pie pan with pastry, fluting a high edge. Combine all ingredients and beat with rotary egg beater until well blended. Pour mixture into pastry-lined pan. Bake in preheated moderate oven (350°F.) for 50 to 60 minutes, or until filling is set. Cool before cutting into wedges. Makes 6 to 8 servings.

CUSH

4 cups crumbled corn bread
½ cup melted butter or margarine
  Hot water
  Salt and pepper
  Butter

Mix corn bread with melted butter and enough hot water to give mixture the consistency of a crumbly stuffing. Add salt and pepper to taste. Fry mixture in shallow hot butter until crumbs are crisp. Good for breakfast. Makes 6 servings.

SOURDOUGH DOUGHNUTS

 2 eggs
 1 cup sugar
 1 cup sourdough starter
 ½ cup buttermilk
 1 tablespoon melted lard or cooking oil
4½ cups sifted all-purpose flour
 1 teaspoon baking powder
 ½ teaspoon baking soda
 ½ teaspoon salt
 ½ teaspoon ground nutmeg
  Fat for frying

Beat eggs and sugar together. Add starter, buttermilk, lard, and sifted dry ingredients. Mix well. Turn out dough and knead on a lightly floured board until smooth. Roll to ½-inch thickness and cut with 2¾-inch doughnut cutter. Put on greased cookie sheet and let rise for 30 minutes. Fry in hot deep fat (370°F. on a frying thermometer) until golden brown and done. Roll in sugar. Makes about 3 dozen.

Note: Starter may be purchased by mail order from The Gilded Cage, Anchorage Chapter, Alaska Crippled Children's Association, 225 East Street, Anchorage, Alaska.

Nebraska

Halfway to anywhere: midpoint between Atlantic and Pacific. Here sound the songs of Indians, barracks soldiers, homesteaders, and cowboys, in a spot where Angus and Herefords graze and cornfields stretch to the sky. Nourished by the broad, curving Platte River, this land so needed shade that one of its pioneers insured trees by creating Arbor Day to plant them.

DIFFERENT BEAN SOUP

1 cup dried white beans, washed,
  drained
¼ pound salt pork, cut into pieces
4 cups milk
  Salt and pepper
3 hard-cooked eggs, shelled and sliced

Put beans in 3 cups water. Bring to boil and cook for 2 minutes. Let soak for 1 hour. Add salt pork and enough water to cover. Cook until beans are tender. Do not add water during cooking, but allow beans to absorb the water as they cook. When beans are tender, press them with the liquid through a colander or whirl in a blender. Add milk, and salt and pepper to taste. Reheat until piping hot but do not boil. Pour soup into a tureen or bowls containing the hard-cooked eggs. Serve hot. Makes 4 to 6 servings.

BAKED TROUT

8 whole trout, cleaned
2 tablespoons water
  Juice of 1 lemon
  Salt and pepper
3 tablespoons chopped chives
1 tablespoon butter
3 tablespoons all-purpose flour
2 cups heavy cream
1 cup buttered soft bread crumbs

With a sharp knife bone the fish but do not remove the heads. (Bones may be left in if desired.) Put fish in a glass or earthenware baking dish in a single layer. Add water, lemon juice, and salt and pepper to taste. Sprinkle with chives. Bake in preheated moderate oven (375° F.) for 10 minutes. Melt butter and stir in flour. Gradually stir in cream. Add salt and pepper to taste. Cook over low heat, stirring constantly, until smooth and thick. Pour sauce over fish. Sprinkle top with bread crumbs. Continue baking for 10 to 15 minutes, or until top is lightly browned. Makes 8 servings.

RIB ROAST OF BEEF ON A SPIT

Bone 3 or 4 ribs of beef and roll or tie well. Have meat at room temperature. Put on spit and test for balance. Crush 3 garlic cloves in 2 tablespoons salt; add 1 teaspoon freshly ground pepper and 1 tablespoon ground ginger; rub well into meat. Insert meat thermometer. Bank grayed coals to back of grill. In front of coals put a pan, made of foil and larger than the roast, to catch the drippings. Roast for 2½ to 3 hours on constantly turning rotisserie according to your preference of doneness, gauged by thermometer (140°F. for rare, 160°F. for medium, 170°F. for well done). Remove and let stand for 20 minutes before serving. Put on heated serving platter. Makes 6 to 8 servings.

CORNED BEEF AND CABBAGE, NEBRASKA STYLE

Cover a brisket of corned beef with cold water. Heat slowly to the boiling point. Never allow to boil briskly. Simmer, covered, until fork easily penetrates thick part of brisket. Allow about 1 hour of gentle simmering for each pound of corned beef. Plunge brisket into a pan of cold water, fat side down. The size of pan is important: the meat should cover the bottom. Add just enough water to cover. Allow meat to remain in water for 15 to 20 minutes. The heat of the meat will bring up temperature of water so meat will be ready to serve. This treatment solidifies and bleaches fat and seals in juices. Place a quarter-head of cooked cabbage on each individual plate. Slice corned beef into thin diagonally cut slices. Arrange slices over cabbage and serve with parsley-buttered boiled new potatoes.

NEBRASKA CORN FRITTERS

1½ cups whole kernel corn, drained
 2 eggs
 ½ teaspoon salt
  Dash of pepper
 1 teaspoon sugar
 3 tablespoons all-purpose flour
  Butter or margarine

Mix ingredients together. Heat 2 tablespoons butter in a large skillet. Drop batter by double tablespoon to make small oval cakes. Cook over medium heat for 5 minutes, or until browned on both sides. Turn only once. Add more butter or margarine if necessary to keep corn fritters from sticking. Makes 4 servings.

WHITE CAKE WITH DOUBLE FROSTING
½ cup butter or margarine
2½ cups sifted all-purpose flour
2½ teaspoons baking powder
1¼ cups sugar
¾ cup milk
1 teaspoon vanilla extract
3 egg whites
  Caramel Frosting
  Fluffy Frosting

Combine butter, flour, baking powder, 1 cup sugar, milk, and vanilla. Beat for 2 minutes with electric beater at medium speed. Beat egg whites to a froth. Gradually beat in ¼ cup sugar and continue beating until stiff. Add to butter mixture and beat for 1 minute. Pour into greased and floured 9-inch square pan. Bake in preheated moderate oven (375°F.) for 25 to 30 minutes. Let stand in pan for 5 minutes. Unmold and cool on a rack. When cold, cover with Caramel Frosting and top with Fluffy Frosting.

Caramel Frosting
Heat and stir 2 tablespoons sugar in a heavy skillet until brown and melted. Add 6 tablespoons butter or margarine and ¾ cup brown sugar; heat until butter is melted and sugar dissolved. Add 6 tablespoons light cream, 1 tablespoon at a time; stir well after each addition. Boil for 1 minute. Remove from heat. Add 1½ cups confectioners' sugar and beat until mixture loses its gloss.

Fluffy Frosting
Stir 1 cup sugar, ⅓ cup water, and 2 tablespoons light corn syrup over low heat until sugar is dissolved. Bring to boil and boil for 2 to 3 minutes without stirring. Beat 1 egg white until stiff but not dry. Gradually beat hot syrup into egg whites. Beat until mixture is cool and of spreading consistency.

SAGE-HONEY SOUR-CREAM PIE
  8-inch piecrust, baked
  Sage Honey*
2 tablespoons all-purpose flour
1 teaspoon ground cinnamon
3 egg yolks, well beaten
1 cup dairy sour cream
1 cup chopped pitted dates or raisins
3 egg whites
3 tablespoons honey

Bake and cool piecrust shell. Mix ⅓ cup honey with flour and cinnamon. Stir mixture into egg yolks. Beat in sour cream and chopped dates. Cook mixture over low heat, stirring constantly, until smooth and thick. Cool and pour mixture into baked pie shell. Beat egg whites until stiff. Gradually beat in 3 tablespoons honey until stiff and glossy. Spread meringue on top of filling in pie, making sure the meringue is attached to the pie-crust edge. Bake in preheated slow oven (300°F.) for 10 to 15 minutes, or until top is lightly browned. Makes 6 to 8 servings.

*Any honey may be used.

Nevada

Brilliantly red in the setting sun are the tablelands, and gleaming white are the alkali flats, where yucca and sagebrush fight the starkness. Comstock Lode in the Sierra Nevada—the "Snow Clad"—frustrated the first fortune-seekers but still they come: those who seek atomic boom at Yucca Flat, or those who pursue rolling riches at Reno and Las Vegas.

CREAM OF CAULIFLOWER SOUP
1 large head cauliflower
  Juice of 1 lemon
2 tablespoons minced onion
2 celery stalks, minced
¼ cup butter or margarine
¼ cup flour
4 cups chicken broth or bouillon
2 cups light cream, scalded
  Dash of nutmeg
  Salt to taste
  Grated Parmesan cheese (optional)

Wash cauliflower and break in flowerets. Cook with lemon juice in small amount of boiling water until tender. Drain and whirl cauliflower in blender until puréed, or force through food mill. Sauté onion and celery in the butter 2 or 3 minutes. Blend in flour and stir in broth. Cook, stirring, until slightly thickened. Stir in cauliflower, cream, nutmeg, and salt. Garnish with cheese. Makes about 1¾ quarts, or 6 servings.

SHEEPHERDER'S STEW
1 pound salt pork
  Cornmeal
6 potatoes, peeled and sliced
3 onions, sliced
  Pepper
  All-purpose flour
1 can (14½ ounces) evaporated milk, undiluted

Slice salt pork, dip into cornmeal, and brown lightly in iron skillet. Pour fat into bowl; reserve. Return 3 slices pork to skillet; cover with a layer of potatoes and one of onions. Season with pepper and dredge lightly with flour. Repeat layers, ending with potatoes. Add evaporated milk. Cover and cook over low heat until potatoes are tender. Makes 4 servings.

BEEF POT ROAST WITH VEGETABLES
2 pounds beef for pot roast
1½ cups canned tomatoes
1½ cups water
  Salt and pepper to taste
1 onion, chopped
6 carrots, peeled and diced
2 cups diced potatoes
2 cups fresh or frozen peas

Brown meat on all sides in heavy kettle, adding a small amount of fat if necessary. Add tomatoes, water, and salt and pepper. Bring to boil, cover and simmer for 1 hour, or until meat is nearly tender. Add onion and carrots and simmer for 15 minutes. Add potatoes, and cook until vegetables are tender. Add peas and cook for a few minutes. If desired, thicken liquid with flour blended with a little cold water. Makes 6 servings.

HOT SPICED WHOLE TOMATOES
6 firm ripe tomatoes
¼ cup butter or margarine
1 onion, minced
¼ cup firmly packed light brown sugar
½ teaspoon ground ginger
¼ teaspoon each of ground allspice
  and cinnamon
½ teaspoon salt
2 tablespoons cider vinegar

Peel tomatoes, but do not remove stem ends. Melt butter in skillet; add onion and sauté for 2 to 3 minutes. Add sugar, spices, and salt; mix well. Arrange tomatoes, stem end down, in the sugar mixture. Cover and simmer for 5 minutes over low heat. Uncover and add vinegar. Cook, covered, over very low heat for 45 minutes, basting occasionally with sauce. Do not stir. Carefully remove to serve. Makes 6 servings.

GRILLED CORN MUSH
1 cup yellow cornmeal
¾ cup boiling water
1 teaspoon salt
2 teaspoons chili powder
½ teaspoon crumbled dried oregano
½ pound salt pork, diced
2 yellow onions, diced
1 garlic clove, minced
1 egg, slightly beaten

Sprinkle cornmeal slowly into boiling water in top part of double boiler. Add seasonings. Cook over boiling water for 45 minutes, stirring occasionally. Meanwhile fry salt pork until crisp, add onions and garlic, and sauté for 3 to 4 minutes. Cool; add egg. Combine salt-pork mixture with cornmeal. Mix thoroughly. Pour into oiled loaf pan (9 x 5 x 3 inches). Chill overnight. Unmold and slice into 1-inch slices. Brown in hot fat in outdoor grill over coals that have been heated to turn gray. Makes 4 servings.

VIRGINIA CITY SALAD

4 cups shredded green cabbage
1 cup pineapple tidbits, drained
½ cup miniature marshmallows
½ cup slivered blanched almonds
   Snow Dressing

Just before serving, combine all ingredients except dressing. Top with Snow Dressing. Makes 6 servings.

Snow Dressing

½ cup sugar
1 tablespoon all-purpose flour
½ teaspoon salt
3 tablespoons boiling water
¼ cup cider vinegar
   Juice of 3 lemons
4 egg whites, stiffly beaten

Mix sugar and flour and salt. Add water, cider vinegar, and lemon juice. Stir until well blended. Fold in beaten egg whites. Cook over low heat, stirring constantly, until smooth and thick. Chill and serve on top of salad.

HONEY APPLE PIE

   Pastry for 2-crust 9-inch pie, unbaked
6 large cooking apples
2 tablespoons minute tapioca
½ cup honey
½ teaspoon each of ground cinnamon
   and nutmeg
2 tablespoons butter

Line a 9-inch pie pan with pastry. Peel and core apples and cut into thin slices. Mix apples with tapioca, honey, and spices. Spoon mixture into pastry-lined pie pan. Dot top with butter. Cover with a second round of pastry; moisten edges with water and seal. Cut a few slits in top. Bake in preheated moderate oven (375°F.) 40 to 45 minutes, or until apples are easily pierced. Cool before cutting into wedges. Makes 6 to 8 servings.

New Hampshire

Rugged, pulse-stirring, genteel, the Great Stone Face, the crest of Mount Washington, the charm of proudly aging Portsmouth. Skiers test its slopes, hikers clamber high where wild winds lay bare the peaks. Wispy falls seep from granite crags made gay by white birches and evergreens. In this place Daniel Webster exclaimed, "God Almighty makes Men!"

OLD-TIME SALT-PORK SOUP WITH DUMPLINGS

¼ pound salt pork, diced
4 potatoes, peeled and diced
6 carrots, scraped and sliced
2 quarts water
1 cup sifted all-purpose flour
¼ teaspoon salt
1 teaspoon baking powder
2 teaspoons butter
½ cup milk

Fry pork until crisp and brown. Remove pieces and reserve. Add potatoes, carrots, and water to fat. Simmer, covered, until vegetables are tender. To make dumplings, mix dry ingredients. Cut in butter until mixture has consistency of cornmeal. Add milk and mix until dry ingredients are moistened. Drop batter by double tablespoonfuls into vegetables. Cover and simmer for 15 minutes. Add fried pork cubes and season; serve immediately. Makes about 2 quarts.

RED FLANNEL HASH

2 cups chopped cooked corned beef
2 cups chopped cooked beets
4 cups chopped cooked potatoes
1 large onion, chopped
   Salt and pepper to taste
2 teaspoons Worcestershire
   Light cream
¼ cup bacon or pork drippings

Combine beef with beets, potatoes, onion, seasonings, and enough cream to bind

mixture. Heat drippings in a large skillet. Spoon meat mixture into skillet and spread evenly into pan. Cook over low heat, without stirring, until the bottom is well crusted. Fold as you would an omelet; serve immediately. Serves 4 to 6.

FRIED TRIPE

¼ cup (about 2 ounces) salt pork
1½ pounds pickled honeycomb tripe
   Salt and pepper to taste
   All-purpose flour
¼ cup butter or margarine

Cut pork into small pieces. Fry in large skillet until brown and crisp. Remove pork and keep warm. Season tripe and dust with flour. Fry slowly in hot pork fat until tender and brown, turning frequently. Put on hot platter. Dot with butter; top with crisp salt pork. Serves 4.

HASHED TURNIPS

2 cups coarsely chopped cooked
   yellow turnips
1 teaspoon salt
¼ teaspoon white pepper
¼ cup water
¼ cup melted butter, or bacon
   or sausage drippings

Mix turnips with salt, pepper, and water. Heat butter until hot. Add turnip mixture and cook slowly until lightly browned. Makes 3 to 4 servings.

CINNAMON RAISIN BUNS

1 package active dry yeast
2 tablespoons warm water
1 cup milk, scalded
¼ cup butter
⅓ cup sugar
½ teaspoon salt
1 egg, beaten
3 to 3½ cups all-purpose flour
1 teaspoon cinnamon
¾ cup seedless raisins
   Cinnamon Frosting

Soften yeast in water. Pour milk over butter, sugar, and salt in bowl. Let stand until lukewarm; then stir in yeast. Stir in egg and half the flour sifted with cinnamon; beat smooth. Stir in raisins and enough more flour to make a soft dough. Cover; let rise in warm place until double. Punch down; shape in balls the size of a walnut; let rise on baking sheet until double. Bake in preheated hot oven (425°F.) for 25 minutes. Spread with Cinnamon Frosting made with 1 cup sifted confectioners' sugar, 1 tablespoon water, and ¼ teaspoon cinnamon. Makes 24.

MAPLE CUSTARD

3 eggs
½ cup 100-per-cent maple syrup
   Dash of salt
2 cups milk

Beat eggs with maple syrup and salt until foamy and well blended. Scald milk. Gradually beat milk into eggs. Pour mixture into 6 custard cups. Place cups in a pan of hot water in preheated moderate oven (350°F.) for about 40 minutes. Custard is done when tip of a silver knife inserted into custard comes out clean. Cool, then chill. Makes 6 servings.

NEW HAMPSHIRE TURNOVER APPLE PIE

5 cups thinly sliced peeled tart apples
Pastry for 1-crust 9-inch pie, unbaked
Sugar
Ground cinnamon
2 tablespoons butter

Fill 9-inch pie pan with apples. Roll out pastry. Fit over top of apples and trim edge. Bake in preheated hot oven (425°F.) for 25 minutes, or until apples are soft. Remove from oven and turn upside down on warm serving plate. Lift up pie pan. Scrape out apples remaining in crust and mix with apples left in pan; mash with spoon. Add ½ cup sugar, ⅛ teaspoon cinnamon, and 1 tablespoon butter. Spread apple mixture on crust; dot with remaining butter. Sprinkle with sugar and cinnamon. Put in warm place until butter is melted. Serve warm with ice cream or whipped cream. Serves 6.

BLUEBERRY UPSIDE-DOWN CAKE

2 tablespoons butter
1 cup firmly packed light brown sugar
2 cups fresh blueberries, rinsed and drained
3 egg yolks, beaten
1 cup sugar
5 tablespoons milk
1 cup sifted all-purpose flour
1 teaspoon baking powder
½ teaspoon salt
3 egg whites, beaten
Whipped cream

Melt butter in the bottom of a baking pan (9 x 9 x 2 inches). Sprinkle with brown sugar. Add blueberries. Beat egg yolks and stir in sugar. Beat in milk, flour, baking powder, and salt. Beat egg whites until stiff. Fold egg whites into cake batter. Pour batter over the blueberries. Bake in preheated moderate oven (350°F.) for 45 minutes, or until cake springs back when lightly touched. Loosen edges; turn out on a serving platter. Cut into squares; serve with sweetened whipped cream. Makes nine 3-inch squares.

NEWTON SUGAR SQUARES

1 cup soft butter
1¼ cups sugar
2 eggs
2 cups sifted all-purpose flour
¼ teaspoon soda
¼ teaspoon salt
1 teaspoon ginger
2 tablespoons buttermilk

Cream butter with 1 cup sugar; add eggs and beat well. Add sifted dry ingredients and buttermilk; mix well. Spread in greased 15 x 10 x 1-inch pan; sprinkle with remaining sugar. Bake in hot oven (400°F.) about 20 minutes. Cool; cut in 40 cookies about 2 inches square.

New Jersey

Palisades and Water Gap, gouged by eons, crossroads of Revolution, where Washington slept—and fought. Oak-trimmed mountains level toward the golden Atlantic strand ruled by Miss America. Frenetic beside its heartland roads, place of machines, place to live, serene in its Pine Barrens, whose wild orchids and pixie moss defy the passage of both time and men.

POACHED EGGS ALLA ROMANA

1 can (8 ounces) meatless spaghetti sauce
4 eggs
Salt and pepper to taste
4 slices of toast
Grated Romano cheese

Heat sauce in skillet. Carefully drop eggs, one at a time, into sauce. Season. Cover and poach for 5 minutes for medium-done eggs. Put 1 egg and some of sauce on each slice of toast. Sprinkle with cheese. Makes 4 servings.

ROAST LOIN OF PORK

4- to 5-pound pork loin
2 teaspoons salt
½ teaspoon pepper

Trim excess fat from meat. Rub with salt and pepper. Put on rack in shallow baking pan. Roast in preheated slow oven (325°F.) for 35 to 40 minutes to the pound, or until meat thermometer registers 185°F. Serve broiled peach halves or baked apples, if desired, on the platter with the meat. Makes 6 servings.

CORNISH GAME HENS WITH APPLES

2 Cornish game hens
Salt and pepper to taste
½ teaspoon celery salt
2 tablespoons butter
2 tablespoons olive oil
6 tart cooking apples, peeled, cored, and finely chopped
¼ cup heavy cream

Season birds inside and out with salt, pepper, and the celery salt. Brown on all sides in hot butter and oil in heavy skillet or Dutch oven. Remove birds and cook apples in remaining fat until softened. Arrange birds on the apples. Sprinkle with cream. Cover and cook over low heat or in preheated moderate oven (375°F.) for 30 minutes, or until tender, turning occasionally. Makes 2 servings.

BROILED FLOUNDER FILLETS WITH PUFFY CHEESE SAUCE

1½ pounds flounder fillets
Salt and pepper to taste
½ cup mayonnaise
Dash of cayenne
2 tablespoons chopped pickle
1 tablespoon chopped parsley
⅓ cup grated sharp Cheddar cheese
1 egg white
Pimientos

Wipe fish with damp cloth and put on greased broiler rack. Broil under medium heat 8 to 12 minutes. Sprinkle with salt and pepper. Mix mayonnaise, cayenne, pickle, parsley, and cheese. Beat egg white until stiff and fold into dressing. Spread on the fish; broil 5 minutes, or until sauce is puffed. Garnish with strips of pimiento. Makes 4 servings.

FRENCH-FRIED ASPARAGUS

Remove scales from fresh asparagus tips. Cook only until tender-crisp. Drain thoroughly. Dip each tip into lightly beaten egg, then into fine dry bread crumbs. Chill on tray covered with wax paper. Drop, a few at a time, into hot deep fat (380°F. on a frying thermometer) and fry for about 3 minutes. Drain on absorbent paper and serve at once. For variety, mix grated Parmesan cheese with the dipping crumbs, using half cheese and half crumbs.

LEEK SALAD

16 leeks
Salted water
French dressing

Trim leeks leaving about 1 inch of green on each leek. Slice leeks lengthwise leaving the bottoms attached. Wash leeks well and remove all sand. Tie leeks to keep them from separating during cooking. Cover with boiling salted water and cook for about 12 minutes, or until leeks are tender. Drain, remove string, and chill thoroughly. Place 4 leeks on a salad plate and spoon French dressing over each serving. Makes 4 servings.

SALTWATER TAFFY

1 cup sugar
2 tablespoons cornstarch
¾ cup light corn syrup
½ cup water
½ teaspoon salt
2 tablespoons butter
2 teaspoons vanilla extract

The All-American Coffee Hour—
A pot of coffee and a bit of cake

Mix sugar and cornstarch in saucepan. Stir in next 3 ingredients. Add butter and bring to a boil, stirring constantly until sugar is completely dissolved. Then cook without stirring until 260°F. registers on a candy thermometer, or until a small amount of syrup dropped into very cold water forms a hard ball. Remove from heat and stir in vanilla. Pour into well-greased 9-inch square pan and let stand until cool enough to handle. Then pull until white and satiny in appearance. Pull out in ½-inch strips and cut into 1-inch pieces with scissors. Wrap in wax paper. Makes ⅞ pound.

New Mexico

Sangre de Cristo, Llano Estacado, Alamogordo, Jornada del Muerto. Santa Fe, old when Plymouth was young, Taos pueblo, ancient when Santa Fe was born. Irrigation greens this enchanted square, but nature hewed the mesas and the canyons and fashioned the Caverns of Carlsbad. As an old Spanish saying goes: "Tomorrow is the flower of its yesterdays."

SOPA DE ALBONDIGAS (Meatball Soup)
    4 cups (two 1-pound cans) tomatoes
    2 cups beef bouillon
    1½ teaspoons chili powder
    2 teaspoons salt
    2½ cups boiling water
    1 pound ground beef
    ½ pound lean pork, ground
    1 slice of dry bread
    1 egg, beaten
    1 garlic clove, minced
    ¼ teaspoon each of crumbled dried
      mint, ground sage, and pepper
    1 medium onion, chopped
    2 tablespoons cooking oil

Force tomatoes through a sieve. Add bouillon, chili powder, 1 teaspoon salt, and the water. Bring to boil and boil until about one fourth of the liquid is evaporated. Combine meats. Dip bread into cold water, squeeze dry, and add to meat. Add remaining salt and other ingredients except onion and oil. Mix lightly but thoroughly. Brown onion in the oil; discard onion. Shape meat mixture into ¾-inch balls and brown in the hot oil. Add to soup mixture, cover and simmer for 1 hour. Makes 6 servings.

EGGS, RANCH STYLE
    1 can (8 ounces) tomato sauce
    2 onions, chopped
    2 green peppers, chopped
    ½ cup grated American cheese
      Dash of cayenne
    ½ teaspoon salt
    4 tortillas
    ⅓ cup olive oil
    4 fried eggs
    2 pork sausages, fried and sliced

Combine tomato sauce, onions, peppers, cheese, cayenne, and salt. Mix and refrigerate. Fry tortillas in olive oil; place a fried egg on top of each tortilla. Pour sauce over all; garnish with sausages. Sauce can be heated, if desired. Makes 4 servings.

TAMALE PIE
    1 onion, chopped
    1 garlic clove, minced
    ½ green pepper, chopped
    2 tablespoons olive oil
    1 pound round steak, ground
    3½ cups (one 1-pound, 12-ounce can)
      tomatoes
      Salt
    1 dozen ripe olives, pitted
    1 teaspoon ground coriander
    1 or 2 tablespoons chili powder
    1 cup yellow cornmeal
    1 cup cold water
    1 quart well-seasoned beef or chicken
      broth
      Butter

Sauté onion, garlic, and pepper in hot olive oil in a skillet. Add beef and sauté until meat loses red color, stirring with a fork to crumble meat. Add tomatoes, 1 teaspoon salt, olives, coriander, and chili powder. Cook slowly for 20 minutes. Meanwhile, mix cornmeal and cold water in top part of double boiler. Add hot broth slowly and cook over boiling water until thickened, stirring occasionally. Line an oiled 2-quart casserole with half the mush mixture. Add meat mixture and top with remaining mush. Let cool slightly and crisscross top with knife. Dot generously with butter. Bake in preheated moderate oven (350°F.) for 45 minutes. Makes 6 servings.

HOT BEAN POT
    About 5 cups (two 1-pound, 4-ounce
      cans) red kidney beans
    2 teaspoons dry mustard
    1 red hot pepper
      Dash of cayenne
      Piece of bay leaf
    2 garlic cloves, minced
    1 onion, diced
    ¼ cup bacon fat
    ½ cup sweet-pickle juice
    2 tablespoons vinegar
    ¼ cup strong coffee
    6 slices of bacon

Pour beans into 2-quart casserole. Mix mustard, seasonings, and onion with bacon fat, pickle juice, vinegar, and coffee; pour over beans. Bake in preheated moderate oven (350°F.) for 45 minutes. Garnish with cooked bacon slices. Makes 6 to 8 servings.

MEXICAN RE-FRIED BEANS
Cover 1 cup washed and dried California pink or pinto beans with 4 cups water. Bring to boil and boil for 2 minutes. Cover and let stand for 1 hour. Then cook until tender. Drain, reserving liquid. Heat 2 tablespoons bacon fat or lard, add beans, and cook over low heat for about 10 minutes, mashing beans with fork. Add bean liquid and cook until liquid has evaporated. Cook 1 minced small onion in 2 tablespoons bacon fat for 5 minutes; add ½ cup tomato purée. Add to beans and season to taste. Makes 4 servings.

FRIED BREAD
    2 cups sifted all-purpose flour
    1 teaspoon baking powder
    1 teaspoon salt
    1 tablespoon shortening
    ¾ cup water
      Deep fat for frying

Mix dry ingredients, work in shortening, add water, and mix well. Shape into 6 balls of equal size. Roll one ball of dough at a time to ⅛-inch thickness; cut each into 6 wedges. Fry in hot fat (375° F. on a frying thermometer) until puffy and brown. Makes 3 dozen.

FROZEN AVOCADO CREAM
    1 tablespoon cornstarch
      Sugar
    ¼ teaspoon salt
    4 cups milk
    2 eggs, beaten slightly
      Juice of 1 lemon
    2 avocados
    1 cup heavy cream
      Green food coloring

In top part of double boiler mix cornstarch, ¾ cup sugar, and salt. Stir in milk. Cook over hot water, stirring constantly, until thickened. Pour over eggs, mixing thoroughly. Let cool. Put lemon juice, ½ cup sugar, and avocado pulp in blender. Blend for a few seconds. Combine with custard; add cream. Add a few drops of green coloring. Pour into crank-type freezer and freeze until firm. Makes about 2 quarts.

5-DAY PICKLED FIGS
    1 pint white vinegar
    3½ pounds sugar
    ¼ teaspoon salt
    2 cinnamon sticks
    2 teaspoons whole cloves
    1 teaspoon allspice
    7 pounds fresh figs

Combine vinegar and sugar with salt and spices in saucepan. Boil for 5 minutes. Pour over figs in crock; cover. Let stand overnight. Next morning drain; heat syrup to boiling and pour over figs. Repeat for 3 more mornings. Cover and keep in cool dark place. Serve as a spicy condiment, or with cream for dessert. Makes about 6 pints.

New York

Lake Tear-of-the-Clouds, where rises the lordly Hudson; an Island called Manhattan, topped by towers of fashion and finance, of peace and creation. Adirondacks and Catskills, timbered and free; Niagara of thunder, Finger Lakes touched by ivied halls, an island long to Montauk. Seat of Empire, where no royalty reigns, for Miss Liberty welcomes all the world.

CHEDDAR-CHEESE SOUP

1 onion, sliced
1 cup diced celery
¼ cup butter
¼ cup all-purpose flour
½ teaspoon dry mustard
1 teaspoon Worcestershire
½ teaspoon garlic salt
½ teaspoon monosodium glutamate
2 bouillon cubes
2 cups water
1 carrot, diced
4 cups milk
8 ounces sharp Cheddar cheese, shredded
Salt and pepper

In large saucepan, cook onion and celery in butter for about 5 minutes. Blend in next 5 ingredients. Add bouillon cubes, water, and carrot. Bring to boil and simmer, covered, for 15 minutes. Add milk and heat almost to boiling. Add cheese; stir until cheese is melted. Season to taste. Makes about 6 cups.

HOLLANDSCHE BIEFSTUK (Dutch Steak)

2½ pounds round steak or sirloin, about 1½ inches thick
3 tablespoons vinegar
¾ teaspoon salt
1 teaspoon pepper
½ cup butter or margarine
¾ cup water
Hot boiled potatoes

Cut meat into 2-inch pieces and pound with rolling pin. Mix vinegar, salt, and pepper and rub into both sides of meat. Set aside in cool place for thirty minutes. Heat butter in skillet. Brown meat quickly for 1 minute on each side for rare steak, a little longer for well done. Remove to a hot platter. Pour the water into hot skillet and bring to boil. Pour over steak and potatoes. Makes 6 servings.

ROAST LONG ISLAND DUCKLING

Allow 1 large or two small ducklings for 4 servings. Wash and dry ducks. Rub well with cut onion, salt, and pepper. Sprinkle with crumbled rosemary inside and out. Put ½ orange in each cavity. Place ducks, breast side up, on a rack in open roasting pan. Roast in preheated slow oven (325°F.), allowing about 1¾ hours for small ducks and 2 to 2¼ hours for large duck. Drain drippings from pan every 30 minutes to get duckling crisp on all sides. Cut into halves or quarters for serving. Makes 4 servings.

WALDORF SALAD

Dice 4 unpeeled cored red eating apples. Sprinkle apples with lemon juice to prevent darkening. Mix with 1 cup diced celery, ½ cup chopped walnuts, and a little boiled dressing. Mayonnaise may be used if desired. Chill. Serve in lettuce cups. Makes 4 servings.

THOUSAND-ISLAND DRESSING

1 cup mayonnaise
Juice of ½ orange
Juice of ½ lemon
¼ cup chopped green onions
1 pimiento, chopped
2 teaspoons chopped parsley
¼ cup chili sauce
1 hard-cooked egg, chopped

Combine all ingredients and blend well. Chill thoroughly before serving. Makes about 2 cups.

SHERRY JELLY

2 envelopes unflavored gelatin
½ cup cold water
1 cup boiling water
⅔ cup sugar
Dash of salt
Juice of 1 orange
Juice of 1 lemon
2 cups sherry wine

Soften gelatin in cold water for 5 minutes. Add boiling water to gelatin and stir until dissolved. Add sugar and salt; stir and cool. Add remaining ingredients and mix well. Pour into a 5- or 6-cup mold. Chill until firm. Makes 6 servings.

BAKED APPLE TAPIOCA

⅓ cup minute tapioca
1¼ cups boiling water
½ cup sugar
½ teaspoon ground cinnamon
½ teaspoon salt
¼ cup lemon juice
4 cups sliced peeled tart apples

Add tapioca to boiling water. Stir in sugar. Cook over low heat, stirring constantly, until mixture is clear and thick. Stir in cinnamon, salt, and lemon juice. Put apples in greased shallow baking dish. Pour tapioca mixture over top. Bake in preheated moderate oven (350° F.) for 30 minutes, or until top is slightly browned and apples are tender. Serve hot or cold with cream, if desired. Makes 4 to 6 servings.

North Carolina

Hatteras and Fear, capes of dread on sands of joy. Westward the Great Smokies, crowned in haze, alive in ballads and fingertip arts. Rhododendrons and dogwood glorify the spring, tobacco leaves turn golden in curls of smoke. Here Roanoke Island lost a colony, Thomas Wolfe looked forever homeward, Kitty Hawk set earth-bound men to soaring in the clouds.

STEAMED OYSTERS

Wash oysters in shells and put in large kettle. Add ½ cup water, or enough to cover bottom of kettle. Cover and steam over low heat for 15 minutes, or until shells open. Serve in shells in soup plates, accompanying each serving with a small dish of melted butter to which a few drops of lemon juice have been added. Serve strained oyster liquor in cups.

ROCKFISH MUDDLE

5 pounds rockfish
1 pound salt pork, diced
3 large onions
3½ cups (one 1-pound, 12-ounce can) tomatoes
Salt, red and black pepper
½ pound unsalted plain crackers, crumbled
12 eggs, beaten
1 cup butter

Simmer fish in water to cover for 10 minutes. Drain; reserve broth. Remove bones from fish. Brown salt pork, add sliced onions, and sauté until golden. Pour off fat. Put fish, salt pork, onions, and broth into kettle. Add tomatoes. Cook, covered, over low heat for 30 minutes or longer. Season to taste. Stir vigorously while adding crackers, eggs, and butter. Simmer for 2 to 3 minutes longer. Makes 10 servings.

PINE-BARK STEW

2 pounds red-snapper fillets
½ cup chopped bacon
1 cup diced onion
7 cups (two 1-pound, 13-ounce cans) tomatoes
1 cup ketchup
2 cups diced potatoes
2 tablespoons Worcestershire
2 teaspoons salt
½ teaspoon pepper

Cut fish into 1-inch pieces. Fry bacon until crisp. Add onion; cook until golden. Add remaining ingredients. Cook for 30 minutes, stirring occasionally. Add fish and cook for 15 minutes longer. Makes 6 servings.

MISS MOLLIE'S BOILED POT

2 ham hocks
¼ teaspoon hot red pepper
2 onions, sliced
6 carrots, cut into chunks
6 potatoes, quartered
3 small heads cabbage
8 ears corn
Cornmeal Dumplings

Boil ham hocks in water to cover until tender. Add pepper, onions, carrots, and potatoes. Cook for 20 minutes. Cut cabbage into wedges, add to pot, and cook for 10 minutes. Add corn and Cornmeal Dumplings. Cover and simmer for 20 minutes. Makes 8 servings.

Cornmeal Dumplings

1 cup water-ground cornmeal
1 cup pancake flour
½ teaspoon salt
1 teaspoon sugar
Water

Mix ingredients, using only enough cold water so mixture can be molded in hand. Pat into flat round cakes about 2 inches in diameter, ½ inch thick. Drop into pot on top of ham hocks and vegetables. Cover and simmer for 20 minutes.

SWEET-POTATO BISCUITS

1 small sweet potato, baked
2 tablespoons shortening
1 cup sifted all-purpose flour
1 teaspoon baking powder
¼ teaspoon salt
2 to 3 tablespoons milk

Peel and dice sweet potato. Cut potato and shortening into flour sifted with baking powder and salt; add milk and stir until mixed. Turn onto floured board and knead gently. Roll to ½-inch thickness and cut. Bake on greased cookie sheet in preheated hot oven (400°F.) for about 12 minutes. Makes ten to twelve 2-inch biscuits.

CAROLINA FRUITCAKE

1 package each (4 ounces each) of candied orange and lemon peel
1 pound each of candied cherries, pineapple, and citron
2 boxes golden raisins
1 box seedless raisins
½ pound each of figs and dates, cut up
2 pounds (8 cups) shelled pecans
4 cups sifted all-purpose flour
1 teaspoon ground cinnamon
½ teaspoon each of ground nutmeg, cloves, and allspice

Reserve a little of the candied fruit and a few pecan halves to decorate tops of fruitcakes. Cut cherries into halves, pineapple and citron into pieces. Break nuts into halves. Mix fruit, flour, and spices thoroughly, so that each piece of fruit and nut is coated lightly with flour.

Batter

1 pound margarine
2½ cups sugar
12 eggs, beaten
1¼ cups sifted all-purpose flour
1 teaspoon salt

Cream margarine; add sugar gradually. Add eggs, mixing thoroughly. Stir in flour and salt until well blended. Pour batter over fruit-nut mixture. Mix with hands until fruit and nuts are well coated with batter.

Baking and Molding

Spread mixture in a greased roasting pan (17 x 11½ x 2¼ inches). Bake in preheated moderate oven (350°F.) for 30 minutes. Reduce heat to slow (325°F.) and continue baking for 1 hour. After 45 minutes of second baking, remove roaster from oven and quickly stir mixture, breaking up the top crust, scraping sides and bottom of pan. Continue baking 15 minutes. When done, the batter will lose its gloss and be brown and crumbly. In the meantime, grease pans you wish to use: loaf pans, muffin pans, coffee cans, etc. Spoon cake, while hot, into one pan at a time, making a layer about ¾-inch thick, pressing firmly, adding another layer, pressing, and so on until pan is full. Decorate while hot with crystallized

fruit and nuts. If possible, get extra help at this point to help pack mixture into pans. If batter gets too cold to mold properly, put roaster back in oven to heat for a few minutes. If packed firmly, cake may be sliced very thin. Makes four 9 x 15 x 3-inch loaves.

North Dakota

Its durum wheat makes macaroni but its bonanza is spring wheat. Canada and the United States join hands across the border in International Peace Garden, by the Turtle Mountains where the 13-striped flickertail squirrel scampers and wild birds sing. Man-made Garrison Lake holds sweet Missouri water; glacier-formed Devils Lake is laden with salt.

BAKED SPARERIBS

2 racks of fresh spareribs
2 tart apples, peeled, cored, and sliced
½ cup pitted prunes
1 cup water
Salt and pepper to taste

Leave spareribs in one piece. Cover 1 rack of spareribs with apples and prunes. Cover with second rack of spareribs. Skewer or sew ribs together. Put filled ribs in shallow baking pan. Add water. Sprinkle ribs with salt and pepper. Bake in preheated moderate oven (350°F.) for 1½ hours. Remove skewer or thread and cut ribs into pieces. Serve 1 pound of spareribs for each portion.

SQUAW DISH

½ pound piece of bacon
4 eggs, well beaten
2 cups canned whole kernel corn, drained
Salt and pepper

Cube bacon and fry until crisp. Remove excess fat. Beat eggs and combine with corn. Pour egg mixture over crisp bacon.

Scramble eggs lightly and season to taste with salt and pepper. Makes 4 servings.

BRAISED RABBIT

1½ cups cider vinegar
1 onion, sliced
1 tablespoon dry mustard
2 teaspoons salt
½ teaspoon pepper
2 rabbits, disjointed
1½ cups all-purpose flour
¼ teaspoon ground nutmeg
1 teaspoon sugar
Clear bacon fat

Mix vinegar, onion, mustard, salt, and pepper. Pour over pieces of rabbit in large bowl. Let stand for 1 hour, turning rabbit occasionally. Refrigerate for several hours. Drain. Mix 1 cup flour with nutmeg and sugar in paper bag. Add rabbit, a few pieces at a time. Shake well to coat rabbit with flour. Brown rabbit in hot bacon fat in large iron skillet. Remove rabbit; pour off all but ½ cup fat. Stir in ½ cup flour. Gradually stir in 3 cups boiling water. Cook over low heat, stirring constantly, until thickened. Arrange pieces of rabbit in gravy; cover and simmer on top of range or in preheated very slow oven (250°F.) until tender, 1½ to 2 hours. Makes 6 servings.

WILD-RICE STUFFING

Butter or margarine
2 cups wild rice
1 large onion, minced
1 cup finely diced celery
4 cups chicken broth
¼ teaspoon monosodium glutamate
1 cup chopped walnuts
1 can (3 ounces) chopped mushrooms, drained
½ teaspoon celery salt
½ teaspoon poultry seasoning
Salt to taste

Put ⅓ cup butter in saucepan with rice. Brown rice lightly; add onion and celery and cook 2 or 3 minutes. Stir in broth and monosodium glutamate. Cover; simmer 30 minutes. Sauté walnuts and mushrooms lightly in 1 tablespoon of butter. Add with remaining ingredients to first mixture. Makes about 7 cups.

WHOLE GLAZED SQUASH

1 butternut squash, about 3 to 4 pounds
¾ cup firmly packed dark brown sugar
¼ cup butter or margarine
1 tablespoon water

Bake squash in preheated moderate oven (350°F.) for 1 hour, or until squash is tender. Peel rind and leave squash whole. Mix brown sugar, butter, and water. Cook slowly for 3 to 4 minutes. Spoon thick syrup over all surfaces of the squash. Bake for 15 minutes longer, or until squash is glazed. Cut into serving pieces and serve with Canadian bacon or ham. Makes 4 to 6 servings.

TRAPPER'S SWEET BANNOCK

1 cup sifted all-purpose flour
1 teaspoon baking powder
2 tablespoons sugar
1 tablespoon nonfat dry-milk solids
½ teaspoon salt
2 tablespoons cooking oil
½ cup water
⅓ cup raisins

Mix dry ingredients. Add oil and water and mix well. Stir in raisins. Spread in well-greased skillet. Cover and cook slowly on back of grill over hot coals. Or bake in preheated moderate oven (350°F.) for 25 to 30 minutes. Makes 4 servings.

FINNISH BARLEY PUDDING

1⅓ cups barley, large or medium grain
4 cups water
6 cups boiling milk
1 teaspoon salt
½ teaspoon pepper
⅓ cup butter or margarine

Soak barley overnight in water. Cook in same water. As water is absorbed, add boiling milk and seasonings. Cook over very low heat, stirring frequently to prevent sticking, for 30 minutes. Pour into a buttered 3-quart baking dish. Dot with butter or margarine. Bake in preheated very slow oven (250°F.) until golden brown, about 2 hours. Makes 6 to 8 servings.

BAKED HONEY CUSTARD

4 cups milk
½ cup honey
8 eggs, well beaten
¼ teaspoon salt
1 teaspoon ground nutmeg

Scald milk and stir in honey. Gradually beat honey mixture into eggs. Stir in salt and nutmeg. Pour mixture into buttered custard cups and put cups in a pan of hot water. Bake in preheated slow oven (300°F.) for 40 to 50 minutes, or until a knife inserted comes out clean. Serve hot or cold. Makes 8 servings.

WILD CHOKEBERRY JAM

Clean and stem chokeberries. Wash. Add 1 cup water to 1 quart berries. Cook over low heat, stirring occasionally, until fruit is tender. Press pulp through a sieve. For every 4 cups pulp, add 4 cups sugar. Boil rapidly until jam sheets from a spoon (220°F. on a jelly thermometer). Fill clean dry hot sterilized jars and seal. About 4 cups pulp makes 3 to 3½ cups jam.

Ohio

Maker of glass, creator of pottery, forger of steel, molder of tires, edged by the meanderings of La Belle Rivière and the vastness of Lake Erie. Place of mound builders, welcomer of Johnny Appleseed, spawner of Presidents, home of McGuffey's Readers and Horace Mann. Market place, factories, fertile fields, Indians had the proper word for "great": Ohio.

LIEDERKRANZ APPETIZER CHEESE BALLS

3 ounces Liederkranz cheese
2 tablespoons cracker crumbs
1 egg yolk
¼ teaspoon Worcestershire
Dash of hot pepper sauce

Combine the above ingredients. Form into small 1-inch balls. Fry in hot deep fat (375°F. on a frying thermometer) for 1 to 2 minutes. Drain on absorbent paper. Serve immediately. Makes about 1 dozen.

KOENIGSBERGER KLOPS

1½ pounds ground beef
¼ pound ground veal
¼ pound ground lean pork
2 ounces ground beef suet
¼ cup finely chopped green onion
4 flat anchovy fillets, chopped
¾ cup stale bread, softened in milk and squeezed dry
2 eggs
1 teaspoon salt
¼ teaspoon pepper
Juice of ½ lemon
3 tablespoons butter or margarine
Caper Sauce

Put meat and suet through food chopper twice. Add remaining ingredients except butter and sauce. Form into small balls (*klops*) and brown in hot butter; this will take only 5 to 6 minutes. Prepare Caper Sauce, using same skillet. Add *klops*, heat thoroughly, and serve with buttered noodles. Makes 6 to 8 servings.

Caper Sauce

2 tablespoons butter
2 tablespoons all-purpose flour
1 cup beef bouillon
½ cup dry white wine
1 teaspoon sardine or anchovy paste
Juice of ½ lemon
½ teaspoon sugar
¼ cup chopped chives
2 tablespoons chopped parsley
⅓ cup drained capers

Add butter to drippings in skillet; stir in flour. Gradually stir in bouillon and wine. Cook over low heat, stirring constantly, until thickened and smooth. Add remaining ingredients. Simmer for another 5 minutes.

PORK, APPLESAUCE, AND KRAUT CASSEROLE

2 onions, sliced
¼ cup butter or margarine
2⅓ cups (one 1-pound, 3-ounce can) tomatoes
2 teaspoons sugar
Salt and pepper
Dash of oregano
1 cup soft bread crumbs
2 cups (one 1-pound can) applesauce
¼ cup horseradish
2 cups (one 1-pound can) sauerkraut
6 large lean pork chops
1 tablespoon fat

Brown onions lightly in butter. Add tomatoes, sugar, 1 teaspoon salt, ¼ teaspoon pepper, and remaining ingredients except last 2. Pour into large shallow baking dish. Brown chops on both sides in fat; sprinkle with salt and pepper. Put in baking dish with applesauce and kraut. Cover with foil and bake in preheated moderate oven (350°F.) for 1¾ hours. Makes 6 servings.

SUMMER-SQUASH CASSEROLE

3 tablespoons butter
⅓ cup green onions, chopped with green tops
¾ cup diced celery
3 cups sliced small yellow summer squash
1½ cups cherry tomatoes, halved, or 2 large tomatoes (cut large ones into eighths)
1 teaspoon salt
Pepper to taste
1 teaspoon chopped fresh sweet basil or ¼ teaspoon ground dried basil

Melt butter. Add onions and celery and cook until onion is transparent. Add squash and blend. Pour into a shallow casserole. Cover with a layer of cherry tomatoes. Mix salt, pepper, and basil and sprinkle over tomatoes. Cover and bake in preheated slow oven (300°F.) for 30 minutes. Makes 4 servings.

SQUASH PANCAKES

2½ pounds yellow summer squash
3 eggs, beaten
1 cup all-purpose flour
½ cup milk
2 teaspoons salt
¼ teaspoon white pepper
2 tablespoons grated onion
Vegetable oil for frying

Grate uncooked squash. Beat in remaining ingredients, except oil. Drop by tablespoon into a little hot oil in skillet. Brown on both sides and serve hot. Makes 4 to 6 servings.

BRANDIED APPLE FRITTERS

6 apples
¼ cup brandy
⅛ teaspoon ground cinnamon
1 egg, separated
2 teaspoons granulated sugar
½ cup milk
1 cup sifted all-purpose flour
½ teaspoon salt
1½ teaspoons baking powder
Confectioners' sugar

Pare apples; cut into ½-inch slices and cut out cores with a sharp knife. Pour brandy and cinnamon over apples in a bowl. Cover bowl tightly and marinate for several hours. To the beaten egg yolk add granulated sugar, milk, sifted dry ingredients, and the marinade; fold in stiffly beaten egg white. Dip apple slices into batter; lift out with a fork, letting excess batter drain off. Lower carefully into hot fat (370°F. on a frying thermometer); fry until delicately brown. Drain on absorbent paper. Sprinkle with sifted confectioners' sugar. Serve hot. Makes 8 servings.

BLACK-WALNUT MERINGUE

4 egg whites
1 teaspoon cream of tartar
1 cup sugar
1 teaspoon vanilla extract
8 soda crackers, crushed fine
½ cup chopped black walnuts
Ice cream
Berries

Beat egg whites until almost stiff. Sift cream of tartar over whites and blend. Gradually add sugar and continue beating until mixture is very stiff. Add vanilla. Fold in cracker crumbs and nuts. Pile lightly in buttered 9-inch pie pan. Bake in slow oven (275°F.) 45 to 60 minutes. (Top should look dry.) Cut in wedges and serve with ice cream and berries. Makes 6 servings.

BUCKEYE MAPLE-SYRUP CAKE

⅓ cup shortening
½ cup sugar
¾ cup maple syrup
2¼ cups sifted cake flour
3 teaspoons baking powder
¼ teaspoon salt
½ cup milk
3 egg whites
Maple Icing
¾ cup chopped butternuts or walnuts

Cream shortening; add sugar gradually, beating until light and fluffy. Stir in maple syrup. Add sifted dry ingredients alternately with milk. Beat egg whites until stiff but not dry. Fold into first mixture. Turn into greased 9-inch square pan, lined with wax paper. Bake in preheated moderate oven (350°F.) for 35 minutes. Turn out on rack; remove paper; cool. Spread top and sides of cake with Maple Icing. Sprinkle icing with chopped butternuts.

Maple Icing

2 cups maple syrup
Pinch of salt
2 egg whites

Boil maple syrup until it spins a thread (232°F. on a candy thermometer). Pour slowly over stiffly beaten salted egg whites, beating constantly with rotary beater or wire whisk. Continue beating until mixture stands up in soft peaks.

BISMARCKS

1 cup milk, scalded
¾ cup sugar
1 package active dry yeast or 1 cake compressed yeast
2 tablespoons lukewarm water*
3½ cups sifted all-purpose flour
2 egg yolks
1 egg
1 teaspoon salt
½ teaspoon vanilla extract
⅓ cup melted butter
Thick jam or pureed prunes
Egg white
Fat for frying

Cool milk to lukewarm; add 2 tablespoons of the sugar, the yeast dissolved in water (* use very warm water, 105°F. to 115°F., for dry yeast; use lukewarm water, 80°F. to 90°F., for compressed. Let stand for a few minutes, then stir until dissolved.) and 2 cups of the flour; beat well. Cover and let rise in a warm place until double in bulk, about 25 minutes. Beat egg yolks and egg until thick and lemon-colored; beat in remaining sugar, salt, vanilla, yeast mixture, remaining flour, and melted butter. The dough will be soft, but it can be kneaded in the bowl until smooth and satiny. Allow to rise in a warm place for 1 hour. Turn out on a lightly floured board and divide into 2 parts; cover and let rest for 10 minutes. Roll out to ½-inch thickness. Cut into 2½-inch rounds; on half of them place heaping teaspoons of jam. Brush edges with egg white. Top with remaining rounds, pressing edges firmly to seal. Arrange uncovered on board and allow to rise until very light, about 1 hour. Drop doughnuts into hot deep fat (375°F. on a frying thermometer); turn as they rise to surface and show a little color. When nicely browned, lift from fat with tongs; do not prick. Drain on absorbent paper. Sprinkle with sugar. Makes about 3 dozen.

Oklahoma

Indian forever, in beginnings, in name, in spirit, even if homesteaders came "sooner" than expected. Cattle browse its ranges, hardwoods top its Ozarks, and pines hide the Ouachita. Corn, if not "as high as an elephant's eye," is tall. Wide rivers quench soil's thirst, but humans are sustained in oil. Indian names, great open fields, gushing wells: plenty to share.

FISH BAKED IN A BLANKET

Clean a large whole fish weighing 4 to 5 pounds. Season fish inside and out with salt and pepper. Sprinkle with lemon juice and dot with butter. Make a thick paste of flour and water. Cover entire fish with paste; place on greased baking sheet. Bake in preheated very hot oven (450°F.) for 25 to 30 minutes. Remove from oven. Crack crust with mallet and remove fish carefully. Discard crust. Serve fish with lemon. Makes 6 servings.

SOONER-STATE BEANS WITH SPARERIBS

    1 pound dried pinto beans,
       washed and drained
    3 pounds fresh pork spareribs
       Salt, pepper, chili powder
    2 green peppers, cut into quarters
    2 onions, sliced
    3½ cups (one 1-pound, 12-ounce can)
       tomatoes

Cover beans with cold water, bring to boil, and boil for 2 minutes. Cover pan and let stand for 1 hour. Do not drain. Meanwhile, cut spareribs into serving pieces. Brown lightly in heavy skillet. Cover with water. Simmer, covered, until tender. Drain beans and pour into roasting pan. Arrange spareribs on top of beans. Add water in which spareribs were cooked. Season with salt, pepper, and chili powder. Put peppers and onions on top of pork; pour tomatoes over all. Cover and bake in preheated slow oven (325°F.) 1 hour. Serves 6.

PICNIC CHICKEN

    3 broilers, 2 to 2½ pounds each
    2 cups cider vinegar
    2 tablespoons salt
    ½ cup cooking oil
    ¼ teaspoon pepper

Have broilers split into halves. Mix the remaining ingredients and pour over the chicken. Let stand for 1 hour. Drain chicken, reserving marinade, and place chicken halves, skin side up, over charcoal or in a broiler about 8 inches from source of heat. Brush with marinade every 15 minutes during cooking. Broil for 20 to 25 minutes on each side, or until chicken is brown and tender. Makes 6 servings.

FRIED SQUAW BREAD

    3 cups sifted all-purpose flour
    1 teaspoon salt
    3 teaspoons baking powder
    1 tablespoon sugar
    1 tablespoon melted butter
    1½ cups water
       Fat for deep frying
       Confectioners' sugar
       Squaw Bread Syrup

Sift dry ingredients; add butter and water. Mix thoroughly. Drop by tablespoon into hot fat (375°F on a frying thermometer). Cook for 2 to 4 minutes, or until brown. Drain on paper towels. Sprinkle with confectioners' sugar. Serve hot with Squaw Bread Syrup. Makes 6 servings.

Squaw Bread Syrup

Put 1 cup light brown sugar, 2 cups light corn syrup, 2 tablespoons bacon fat, and 1 teaspoon maple flavoring in saucepan. Heat to boiling.

INDIAN SHUCK BREAD

       Inner husks from 1 dozen ears of corn
    2 cups yellow cornmeal
    ½ teaspoon salt
    1 teaspoon baking powder
       Boiling water

Remove silks from corn husks. Put husks in pan of cold water for a few minutes. Drain. Mix dry ingredients; slowly add 1½ cups boiling water. Mix thoroughly. Roll meal mixture into finger-shaped pieces. Wrap in corn husks and tie with string. Drop packs into boiling water. Boil for 10 minutes. Serve hot in husks. Makes 12.

CHILI SAUCE

    12 ripe medium tomatoes
    2 medium onions, chopped fine
    2 green peppers, chopped fine
    2 cups cider vinegar
    ¾ cup sugar
    2 teaspoons each of ground cinnamon,
       whole cloves, and salt
    ½ to 1 teaspoon cayenne

Dip tomatoes into boiling water. Core, remove skins, and cut into eighths. Add remaining ingredients. Cook at a slow bubble until sauce is thick and vegetables tender. Pour mixture into hot sterilized jars; seal, cool, and store. Makes about 2½ pints.

PEPPER BUTTER

    ⅓ cup soft butter or margarine
    1 tablespoon each of minced red
       and green pepper
    1 teaspoon grated onion
    1 tablespoon minced parsley
       Garlic salt
    ⅛ teaspoon cayenne
       Juice of ½ lemon

Cream butter. Add remaining ingredients. Mix well. Excellent for steaks, fish, and chops. Store in covered jar in refrigerator.

BUTTERMILK SHAKE

       Juice of 6 lemons
    1 cup sugar
    2 quarts chilled buttermilk
       Crushed ice

Mix lemon juice with sugar and stir until dissolved. Stir in buttermilk. Shake with plenty of cracked ice and serve immediately. Makes 8 servings.

Oregon

Trail's end for wagon trains, life's beginning for spawning salmon struggling past Bonneville. Crater Lake, unbelievably blue in volcano bed, Klamath and Multnomah, falls of tumbling grace, Willamette, valley of lushness. Soaking autumn "mist" to raise its forests, Mount Hood to stand in snow-tiaraed majesty and a sea-carved coast to take the breath away.

RAZOR-CLAM BISQUE

    24 razor clams
    1 cup water

1 small onion, minced
1 tablespoon minced parsley
2 whole cloves
2 whole allspice
  Dash of ground mace
4 cups milk
¼ cup all-purpose flour
¼ cup heavy cream, whipped

Scrub clams and put in a kettle. Add water, cover, and cook over medium heat until shells open and clams can be easily removed, about 10 minutes. Reserve broth. Chop clams and mix with onion, parsley, cloves, allspice, and mace. Add clam mixture to broth in which clams were cooked. Simmer for 30 minutes. Mix ½ cup milk with flour to make a smooth mixture; add mixture to remaining milk. Cook over low heat, stirring constantly, until smooth and thick. Strain clam broth into milk. Reheat slightly and serve topped with whipped cream. Makes 4 to 6 servings.

BARBECUED COLUMBIA RIVER SALMON

4 slices of bacon, halved
2-pound piece of fresh salmon
1 teaspoon salt
¼ teaspoon pepper
1 garlic clove, minced
½ cup chopped onion
½ cup chopped green pepper
2 tablespoons cooking oil
1½ cups canned tomatoes
1½ teaspoons Worcestershire
½ bay leaf, crumbled

Place bacon in bottom of baking dish. Sprinkle salmon with salt and pepper. Lay on top of bacon. Sauté garlic, onion, and green pepper together for 3 minutes in hot oil. Add remaining ingredients and simmer for 5 minutes. Pour over salmon. Bake in preheated hot oven (400°F.) for about 30 minutes, basting often. Makes 4 servings.

WESTERN STEAK BARBECUE

1-inch thick chuck steaks
  (about 4 pounds total)
  Unseasoned meat tenderizer
½ cup minced onion
½ cup bacon drippings
⅓ cup fresh lemon juice
1 tablespoon each of ketchup, Worcestershire, and prepared horseradish
½ teaspoon salt
¼ teaspoon pepper
1 large garlic clove, minced or mashed
2 bay leaves

Prepare steak with tenderizer according to package directions. Sauté onion in melted bacon drippings just until limp. Stir in remaining ingredients. Pour sauce over steak and marinate at room temperature for 30 minutes. Turn steak once. Barbecue steak over hot coals to the doneness you prefer (about 4 minutes each side for rare). Baste with remaining marinade. Cut into serving pieces. Makes 6 generous servings.

OREGON CELERY SALAD

4 cups cooked 2-inch pieces of celery
  Salad greens
¼ cup cider vinegar
½ cup salad oil
½ teaspoon paprika
1 teaspoon salt
2 tablespoons chopped green pepper
2 tablespoons chopped pimiento

Chill cooked celery and arrange on salad greens. Shake remaining ingredients together in a tightly closed jar until well blended. Pour dressing over celery and greens; serve at once. Makes 4 to 6 servings.

GOLDEN CHEESE SPOON BREAD

2 cups milk
¾ cup yellow cornmeal
1 teaspoon salt
  Butter
2 tablespoons finely minced green pepper
1 cup cooked fresh or canned whole-kernel corn
¼ pound sharp Cheddar cheese, shredded
4 eggs, separated

Heat milk in a saucepan until hot, not boiling. Gradually add cornmeal; stir constantly. Stir in salt and 2 tablespoons butter. When butter is melted, remove from heat and stir in green pepper, corn, and cheese. Gradually stir hot mixture into slightly beaten egg yolks. Beat egg whites until stiff but not dry, and fold in. Turn into a buttered baking dish (about 1½ quarts). Bake in preheated moderate oven (350°F.) for 45 minutes, or until golden brown. Serve immediately. Pass warm melted butter to pour over each serving. Makes 6 to 8 servings.

PEACH CREAM ALMOND PIE

3½ cups peeled and sliced fresh peaches
  About ⅔ cup sugar
¼ cup all-purpose flour
¼ teaspoon ground nutmeg
  Pastry for 1-crust 9-inch pie, unbaked
1 cup heavy cream
¼ cup sliced blanched almonds

Toss peaches gently with sugar, flour, and nutmeg. Turn into pastry-lined pan. Pour cream over peaches. Bake in preheated hot oven (400°F.) for 35 minutes. Remove pie from oven, sprinkle top with almonds. Return to oven and bake for 5 minutes more, or until cream is set and almonds are lightly browned. Cool. Makes 6 servings.

CRANBERRY-APPLE CRISP

2 cups fresh cranberries
1 pound cooking apples, peeled, cored, and coarsely chopped
1 cup granulated sugar
1½ cups quick-cooking rolled oats
1 cup firmly packed dark brown sugar
½ cup butter or margarine
¾ teaspoon salt
  Cream or vanilla ice cream

Combine cranberries, apples, and granulated sugar. Turn into buttered 9-inch pie

pan. With pastry blender or finger tips work together rolled oats, brown sugar, butter, and salt to make a crumbly mixture. Sprinkle over fruit. Bake in preheated moderate oven (350°F.) for 1 hour. Serve warm with cream. Makes 6 to 8 servings.

OREGON FILBERT SQUARES

1 cup butter or margarine
1 cup sugar
1 egg, separated
2 cups sifted all-purpose flour
¼ teaspoon ground cardamom
1 cup finely chopped filberts

Cream together butter and sugar. Beat in egg yolk. Sift together flour and cardamom and blend into creamed mixture. Spread dough evenly over bottom of jelly-roll pan (15 x 10 inches). Press with palms to make a smooth surface. Beat egg white slightly; brush over top of dough. Sprinkle nuts evenly over surface; press them into the dough. Bake in preheated very slow oven (275°F.) for 1 hour. While hot, cut into 1½-inch squares. Cool. Makes about 5 dozen.

Pennsylvania

Cradle of Liberty, bed of coal, City of Brotherly Love, Hearth of the Nation. Midpoint of the 13 colonies, Keystone of steel and coal. Laurel in the Poconos, hex signs and shoofly pie in Dutch country, misery at Valley Forge, triumph at Gettysburg, flaming power at Pittsburgh. Penn's woods of green, mountains named Blue, iron fist firm in a glove of velvet.

PEPPER POT SOUP

  Veal bone
1 pound boneless stewing veal, cut up
½ pound tripe, cubed

½ bay leaf
Salt
½ teaspoon crushed peppercorns
3 onions, diced
1½ quarts water
2 potatoes, peeled and diced
2 carrots, diced
¼ cup diced celery
½ medium green pepper, chopped
2 tablespoons butter
Pepper
Minced parsley

Put bone, veal, tripe, bay leaf, 2 teaspoons salt, peppercorns, and ⅓ of onion in large kettle. Add water. Bring to boil, cover, and simmer for 2 hours. Remove bone. Sauté remaining onion, potatoes, carrots, celery, and green pepper in butter for 10 minutes. Add to meat mixture and simmer for 30 minutes. Add salt and pepper to taste. Serve with parsley. Makes about 2 quarts.

RIVVEL SOUP

Add 2 cups fresh corn to 4 quarts chicken broth; bring to full boil. Mix ½ teaspoon salt, 2 cups all-purpose flour, and 1 well-beaten egg and work together with the fingers until crumbly. Rub through the hands into boiling broth. Simmer for 15 minutes. Rivvel means lumps, and the rivvels look like rice. Makes 4 quarts.

PICKLED EGGS AND RED BEETS

2 bunches small young beets
½ cup water
½ cup cider vinegar
¼ cup firmly packed light brown sugar
1 cinnamon stick
6 whole cloves
1 teaspoon pickling spice
¼ teaspoon salt
6 hard-cooked eggs, shelled

Boil beets until tender. Skin and put in a deep bowl. Bring water, vinegar, sugar, spices and salt to a boil. Pour over beets and let stand overnight. Place eggs in the mixture, making sure eggs are completely covered with liquid. Let stand in refrigerator for 2 or 3 days before serving.

SCRAPPLE OR PANNHAAS

6 cups pork broth
1¼ cups yellow cornmeal
2 cups finely chopped cooked pork
1 teaspoon salt
¼ teaspoon white pepper
½ teaspoon rubbed sage

Heat broth in which pork was cooked. When broth begins to boil, slowly sprinkle cornmeal into broth. Cook until mush is thick. Stir in meat, salt, pepper, and sage. Stir to blend well. Pour mixture into a loaf pan (9 x 5 x 3 inches). Cool, and then chill. Unmold and cut into ¼-inch slices. Fry slices in hot fat until golden brown on both sides. Makes 8 servings.

SCHNITZ UND GNEPP
(Dried Apples and Dumplings)

2 cups dried sweet apples
2-pound smoked ham butt, cubed
2 tablespoons brown sugar
2 cups sifted all-purpose flour
3 teaspoons baking powder
½ teaspoon salt
1 egg, beaten
2 tablespoons butter, melted
½ cup milk

Cover dried apples with water and soak overnight. Put ham in a large kettle and cover with water. Simmer until ham is just tender. Add apples, and water in which they were soaked, and brown sugar. Simmer for 1 hour. Drop double tablespoonfuls of the dumpling mixture on top of simmering ham and apples. Cover and simmer for 20 minutes, or until dumplings are cooked.

To prepare dumplings—Sift flour with baking powder and salt. Mix egg with melted butter and milk. Add liquid to flour all at once and stir until just blended. Drop by double tablespoons on top of simmering mixture. Makes 8 servings.

BERKS COUNTY POTATO FILLING

1 cup mashed potatoes
2 eggs, beaten
1 cup milk
4 slices of bread
1 small onion, diced
2 tablespoons butter
Salt and pepper to taste

Thoroughly mix mashed potatoes and eggs with a fork. Add milk and set aside. Cut bread into ½-inch cubes and brown with onion in the butter. Stir onions and bread into potato mixture and add seasonings. Turn into a greased casserole and bake in preheated moderate oven (375°F.) for 1 hour. Serve as a vegetable. Makes 6 servings.

SHOOFLY PIE

¾ cup dark molasses
¾ cup boiling water
½ teaspoon baking soda
¼ teaspoon salt
1½ cups sifted all-purpose flour
¼ cup butter or margarine
½ cup firmly packed brown sugar
Pastry for 1-crust 9-inch pie, unbaked

Mix first 4 ingredients. With hands, mix next 3 ingredients. Pour about one third of molasses mixture into pastry-lined pie pan. Sprinkle with one third of flour mixture. Continue alternating layers, ending with flour mixture. Bake in preheated moderate oven (375°F.) for 35 minutes. Serve warm or cold. Makes 8 servings.

SOUR-CREAM DOUGHNUTS

1½ cups dairy sour cream
1 egg, beaten
¼ cup sugar
1 teaspoon baking soda
About 4 cups sifted all-purpose flour

Combine sour cream and egg. Sift dry ingredients together and then combine with cream mixture. If necessary to roll easily, add more flour. On floured board, roll to ½-inch thickness. Cut into 2-inch squares and prick each square with a fork. Fry in hot deep fat (360°F. on a frying thermometer) until golden brown, about 2 minutes on each side. Drain on absorbent paper. Serve with confectioners' sugar, molasses, or syrup. Makes about 2½ dozen.

Rhode Island

Smallest of all, facing the sea, here Roger Williams, in Providence, set men free. Block Island, to foretell trouble from wind, Point Judith on land, Prudence and Patience, isles at bay. Newport proud on a cliff, its many-mansioned miles a disdainer of breakers, a sustainer of wealth. Narragansett yachts, catching offshore gusts for Bermuda.

FRIED CLAMS OR FANNIE DADDIES

3 eggs, separated
¾ cup milk
2 tablespoons melted butter
1½ cups all-purpose flour
1 teaspoon salt
1 to 2 tablespoons fresh lemon juice
3 cups shucked cherrystone or littleneck clams, drained

Beat egg yolks with milk and melted butter. Add flour sifted with salt. Beat until mixture is very smooth. Stir in lemon juice. Beat egg whites until stiff and fold into batter. Add clams. Stir to blend. Chill for at least 2 hours or overnight. Fry clams, a few at a time, in deep fat (360°F. on a frying thermometer) for 3 to 4 minutes, or until golden brown. Clams will sink to the bottom of fat; when they rise to the top, remove quickly with a slotted spoon. Drain on absorbent paper and serve immediately. Makes 6 servings.

CHICKEN SMOTHERED IN OYSTERS

2 frying chickens (about 2½ pounds
   each), quartered
   Salt and pepper to taste
½ cup butter or margarine
1 cup milk
4 cups (1 quart) shucked small
   oysters, drained
2 cups light cream

Wash chicken pieces and dry on paper towel. Season with salt and pepper. Heat butter or margarine in a skillet. Sauté chicken in it, turning occasionally, until pieces are brown on all sides. Place pieces in a baking dish. Pour milk over chicken. Cover dish and place in pre-heated moderate oven (375°F.) for 45 minutes. Baste pieces occasionally during cooking time. Add oysters and cream, and cover. Roast for 15 minutes longer. Remove chicken pieces to hot platter. Pour oysters and cream over chicken. Makes 8 servings.

BLOCK ISLAND BAKED SWORDFISH

1 slice of swordfish, 2 inches thick
   (about 2 pounds)
   Salt and pepper
   Juice of 1 lemon
1 onion, sliced
½ medium green pepper, minced
2 tablespoons butter or margarine
½ cup water
1 lemon, quartered
   Parsley

Wipe fish with damp cloth and put in greased shallow baking dish. Sprinkle with salt and pepper to taste. Sprinkle with lemon juice. Arrange onion slices on fish. Sprinkle with green pepper. Dot with butter and add the water. Bake in preheated hot oven (400°F.) for 30 minutes, or until fish flakes easily with fork. Several times during baking, baste with liquid in pan. Serve with lemon quarters and a garnish of parsley. Makes 4 to 6 servings.

GREEN-CORN CAKES

8 ears of sweet corn
3 eggs, beaten
⅔ cup all-purpose flour
½ teaspoon salt
¼ teaspoon pepper
¼ teaspoon baking soda
1 tablespoon sugar
1 cup buttermilk

Score and scrape corn from cobs. Combine remaining ingredients and mix with corn. Drop by double tablespoonfuls onto hot greased skillet. Brown both sides. Serve at once. Makes 4 to 6 servings.

SCALLOPED CORN

1 small green or red pepper, chopped
1 small onion, minced
3 tablespoons butter or margarine
2 tablespoons flour
½ teaspoon salt
¼ teaspoon paprika
¼ teaspoon dry mustard
   Dash of cayenne

½ cup milk
2 cups (one 1-pound can) cream-style
   corn
1 egg yolk
½ cup dry coarse bread crumbs
⅔ cup buttered soft bread crumbs

Cook pepper and onion in 2 tablespoons butter for 2 or 3 minutes. Blend in flour and seasonings. Stir in milk and corn and cook, stirring, until thickened. Remove from heat and stir in egg yolk. Brown dry crumbs in remaining butter. Stir into first mixture. Put in shallow 1-quart baking dish or 9-inch pie pan. Top with buttered crumbs. Bake in hot oven (400°F.) for 10 to 15 minutes. Makes 4 servings.

JOHNNYCAKE

1 tablespoon sugar
1 teaspoon salt
1 tablespoon butter
1 cup white water-ground cornmeal
1 cup boiling water
¼ cup milk
   Bacon fat, butter, or margarine

Combine first 4 ingredients in a bowl. Cover with actively boiling water and stir vigorously until well mixed. Add milk and mix well. Drop batter by tablespoon onto hot griddle, well greased with bacon fat. Pat to about ½-inch thickness with greased pancake turner. Cook over medium heat until browned on one side. Put a little melted fat on the uncooked top of each cake, turn, and brown. Serve very hot with butter. Makes 9 or 10 cakes.

To bake—Melt 2 tablespoons fat in 8-inch square pan and grease sides of pan; heat in oven. Spread batter in pan and bake in preheated very hot oven (450°F.) for 30 minutes, or until cake is firm.

PEACH SLUMP

6 cups sliced peeled ripe peaches
1 cup sugar
1½ teaspoons ground cinnamon
½ cup water
1 dozen or more uncooked baking-
   powder biscuits, about 1½-inch size

Combine first 4 ingredients in a heavy skillet. Bring to a simmer and top with biscuits. Cover and simmer for about 30 minutes. Serve with cream. Serves 6.

CORN FLAKE-COCONUT MACAROONS

2 egg whites
½ cup sugar
¼ teaspoon salt
2 cups corn flakes
½ cup flaked coconut

Beat egg whites until almost stiff. Gradually add sugar and continue beating until stiff. Beat in salt. Fold in corn flakes and coconut. Drop mixture by teaspoon onto well greased cookie sheet. Bake in slow oven (275°F.) 50 minutes, or until golden brown. Makes about 24.

South Carolina

At Charleston, it's said, "the Ashley and the Cooper meet to form the Atlantic," and stately gardens augment white-pillared homes. Upcountry, Caesar's Head can wear a cap of snow, but ice is a stranger to the Pee Dee and to Wee Tee Lake. Cotton, wood pulp and bright-leaf mean wealth, wild rice, sweet jasmine and mockingbird mean boon for the soul.

SHRIMP CANAPÉ PASTE

Cook, shell, and devein 1 pound fresh shrimps. Force through medium blade of food chopper or pound to a paste in a mortar. Cream ½ cup butter or margarine, add shrimps and salt, celery salt, and cayenne to taste. Mix until smooth and pack in a greased small loaf pan (about 6½ x 4 inches). Bake in pre-heated moderate oven (350°F.) for 30 minutes, or until mixture leaves sides of pan. Cool; chill before slicing. Makes 6 to 8 servings.

CHARLESTON SHE-CRAB SOUP

¼ cup butter
1 pound crabmeat
2 cups light cream
2 cups milk
   Ground mace, salt, and pepper to taste
¼ cup cracker crumbs
2 tablespoons sherry

Melt butter, add crabmeat, and sauté for 1 to 2 minutes. Stir in cream, milk, and seasonings. Thicken with cracker crumbs and let stand over lowest possible heat for a few minutes, or until heated through thoroughly. Do not boil. Add sherry just before serving soup. Makes 4 servings.

SHRIMP AND CORN PIE

To 2 cups of corn grated from cob (or one 17-ounce can cream-style corn) add 2 lightly beaten eggs, 1 tablespoon butter, ½ cup milk, and 1 cup of cooked shrimps. To this mixture add 1 teaspoon Worcestershire, and salt, pepper, and mace to taste. Bake in a buttered shallow baking dish in preheated moderate oven (350° F.) for 30 minutes, or until firm. Makes 4 servings.

SOUTH CAROLINA SCRAPPLE

1½ pounds lean pork with bones
 Water
1⅓ cups yellow cornmeal
2 teaspoons salt
½ teaspoon ground sage
 Bacon or sausage fat

Simmer pork in water to cover until meat falls from bones. Drain; reserve meat and broth. Chill broth and skim off fat. Boil broth to reduce to 1 quart or, if too little, add water to measure 1 quart. Gradually add cornmeal and cook, stirring constantly, until thick. Chop meat fine and add seasonings. Add to mush and pack in loaf pans. Chill, slice, and fry in hot fat. Makes 6 servings.

RED RICE

½ cup bulk sausage meat
1 cup chopped onion
½ cup chopped red sweet peppers
 About 2 cups (one 1-pound can)
 tomatoes
1 can (6 ounces) tomato paste
 Dash of hot pepper sauce
 Dash of pepper
½ teaspoon salt
1 cup uncooked rice
2 cups water

Fry sausage meat until brown, stirring with fork. Add onion and peppers; cook for 2 to 3 minutes. Add remaining ingredients; mix well. Cover and cook over low heat until rice is tender and liquid is absorbed. Makes 4 servings.

BENNE-SEED COOKIES

*Sesame seed is called benne in
South Carolina*

1 cup firmly packed light brown sugar
1 cup benne seed
⅓ cup melted shortening
1 egg, beaten
½ cup sifted all-purpose flour
⅛ teaspoon salt
1 tablespoon hot water

Combine and blend all ingredients. Drop from teaspoon onto greased cookie sheets. Bake in preheated slow oven (325°F.) for about 10 minutes. Remove to rack. When cool, store in airtight containers. Makes about 2 dozen.

PARTY PUDDING

4 eggs, separated
1 cup sugar
1 cup brandy
2 cups heavy cream, whipped
12 ladyfingers, split

Beat egg yolks until thick and lemon-colored. Gradually stir in sugar. Slowly beat in brandy. Cook mixture in top part of a double boiler over boiling water until smooth and thickened. Fold in stiffly beaten egg whites. Cool, and then fold in whipped cream. Pour mixture into a bowl lined with split lady-fingers. Chill for several hours or overnight. Mixture can also be poured into ladyfinger-lined sherbet glasses. Serve garnished with whipped cream, nuts, chopped candied fruits, etc., if desired. Makes 8 to 10 servings.

SYLLABUB

1 cup sweet sherry
1 cup Madeira
2 lemons
4 cups heavy cream
1 teaspoon ground mace
½ cup superfine sugar

Mix sherry with Madeira. Add juice from lemons. Peel outer rind from lemons and add peel to wine. Let stand for 30 minutes. Strain wine and add to heavy cream, along with mace and sugar. Beat ingredients with a rotary egg beater or electric mixer until very frothy. Spoon the froth into dessert dishes and serve. Makes 12 servings.

South Dakota

Bad Lands, multihued in early dawn, starkly white at noon, red-toned under setting sun. Black Hills, with gold at Lead, Passion Play at Spearfish, buffalo at Wind Cave. Mount Rushmore facing history: Washington, Jefferson, Lincoln, Roosevelt. Split by the wide Missouri, verdant to the east, "full of distance" to the west, with seldom a clouded sky to darken a day.

PAN-BARBECUED HAM

1 pound thinly sliced boiled ham
¼ cup butter or margarine
1 tablespoon sugar
1 tablespoon prepared mustard
½ cup cider vinegar
⅛ teaspoon pepper
 Toast or crackers

Sauté ham slices in hot butter. When lightly browned, remove ham and keep warm. Add next 4 ingredients to pan drippings. Stir to blend well. Bring to a boil, lower heat, and add ham. Cook for 5 minutes, spooning sauce over ham. Serve on toast. Makes 6 servings.

WILD GOOSE

Rub goose inside and out with the juice of 1 lemon, salt, and pepper. Stuff lightly, skewer, and truss. Place on its back on rack in a shallow roasting pan. Cover breast with bacon slices. Roast, uncovered, in preheated slow oven (325°F.) for 20 to 25 minutes per pound. Baste often with pan drippings. Remove to a heated serving platter and garnish with parsley. Serve with red cabbage or sauerkraut and potato dumplings. Makes 6 to 8 servings.

Stuffing

¼ cup butter
½ cup chopped onion
½ cup chopped celery
¼ cup chopped parsley
1 cup chopped tart apples
1 cup chopped dried apricots
3 cups soft bread crumbs
 Salt and pepper
½ teaspoon summer savory

Melt the butter in a large saucepan; add the onion and celery and cook until transparent, but not browned. Stir in remaining ingredients.

CABBAGE WITH BACON AND CHEESE SAUCE

½ pound bacon
¼ cup bacon fat
¼ cup all-purpose flour
2 cups milk
¼ pound Cheddar cheese, shredded
 Salt and pepper
1 medium head cabbage, cut into
 wedges
 Croutons

Cook bacon, drain, and keep warm. Prepare a white sauce with bacon fat, flour, and milk. When thickened, stir in cheese and add salt and pepper to taste. Cook cabbage in small amount of boiling salted water until tender, about 7 minutes. Drain and put on hot platter. Top with cheese sauce and garnish with bacon. Sprinkle with croutons. Makes 4 servings.

PARSNIP FRITTERS

Scrub parsnips and cook in boiling salted water until tender. Plunge into cold water and slip off skins. Mash. Season with butter, salt, pepper, and a dash of sugar. Flour hands. Shape into small flat cakes. Sauté in butter until delicately browned on each side.

CHEYENNE RIVER BEAN SALAD

3 cups leftover boiled beans
4 green onions, diced

½ green pepper, diced
½ cucumber, diced
½ cup salad dressing
1 teaspoon Worcestershire
Dash of cayenne
Shredded cabbage
2 slices of crisp bacon, crumbled

Mix all ingredients except cabbage and bacon. Refrigerate for 1 hour. Serve on shredded cabbage and garnish with crumbled bacon. Makes 4 servings.

BUTTERMILK BISCUITS

4 cups unsifted all-purpose flour
2 teaspoons salt
2 teaspoons baking powder
1 teaspoon baking soda
½ cup lard
1¼ cups buttermilk

Sift flour with next 3 ingredients. Cut in lard until mixture resembles coarse cornmeal. Add buttermilk and stir until dough cleans the bowl. Turn dough out on a lightly floured board and knead dough until smooth. Roll out to ½-inch thickness and cut into 2-inch rounds. Bake on ungreased cookie sheet in preheated hot oven (400°F.) for 10 to 12 minutes, or until biscuits are golden brown. Makes 2 dozen.

POLYNEES (Swedish Almond Tarts)

2 cups sifted all-purpose flour
½ teaspoon salt
1 tablespoon sugar
1 teaspoon baking powder
¾ cup butter or margarine
1 egg yolk
2 tablespoons brandy
Raspberry jam
Almond Filling

Sift flour, salt, sugar, and baking powder; cut in butter. Add egg yolk and brandy; blend well. Chill. Roll out dough ⅛ inch thick. Butter eight 4-inch fluted tart pans and line with dough. Roll remaining dough and cut into ½-inch strips. Place 2 teaspoons raspberry jam in each unbaked tart shell. Fill three fourths full with Almond Filling. Arrange 2 strips of pastry on top to form a cross. Bake in preheated slow oven (325°F.) for about 30 minutes. Makes 8.

Almond Filling

Beat 4 egg whites until stiff but not dry. Gradually beat in ½ cup sugar and 1 cup ground blanched almonds.

RHUBARB PIE

3 tablespoons all-purpose flour
1 to 1¼ cups sugar
¼ teaspoon salt
4 cups diced rhubarb
Grated rind of 1 orange
¼ cup fresh orange juice
Pastry for 9-inch pie with strips, unbaked
2 tablespoons butter or margarine

Mix flour, sugar, salt, and rhubarb. Add orange rind and juice. Turn into pastry-lined pie pan. Dot with butter. Cover with strips of pastry, lattice fashion.

Bake in preheated very hot oven (450°F.) for 20 minutes. Reduce heat to moderate (350°F.) and bake for about 20 minutes longer. Makes 6 to 8 servings.

Tennessee

Mountain folk say only the "journey proud" ever leave. Beloved Davy Crockett did, to his woe. Those who stay talk of Lookout's "Battle of the Clouds," of Nashville's Grand Old Opry, of Memphis levees, of marble, of smooth-strutting Walking Horses. Tennessee, the "Big Bend," whose waters aid TVA to make all the land green by day and bright by night.

TENNESSEE BAKED HAM

1 country ham (10 to 12 pounds)
4 cups yellow cornmeal
1 cup firmly packed dark brown sugar
1 tablespoon pepper
Water
Dry bread crumbs

Soak ham overnight in cold water. Drain, and wipe dry. Mix cornmeal with brown sugar and pepper. Add enough water to make a claylike paste. Put ham in a shallow baking pan. Cover ham with cornmeal paste, making shell about 1 inch thick. Roast in preheated moderate oven (350°F.) for 4 hours, or until meat thermometer registers 170°F. Add a little boiling water to the pan but do not baste. Remove from oven. Strip off paste and skin. Sprinkle ham with dry bread crumbs, replace in oven, and roast until brown. Makes about 24 servings.

HOG AND HOMINY

3 pounds pork neck bones
Salt and pepper to taste
1 onion, chopped
2 tablespoons lard
3 large cans (1 pound each) whole hominy
2 tomatoes

Season meat with salt and pepper. Brown

with onion in hot lard, using heavy kettle. Cover with hominy; top with sectioned tomatoes. Cover kettle and simmer over very low heat for 1 hour, adding a little water if necessary. Makes 4 servings.

BEAN POT ROAST

2 pounds beef round or rump, cut into 2-inch cubes
1 teaspoon salt
1 cup canned tomatoes
1 cup whole parboiled small white onions
8 small white peeled potatoes
Pepper

Put meat with salt into a bean pot with tight-fitting lid. Cover and put pot in preheated moderate oven (350°F.) for 1½ hours. Remove from oven and add vegetables and pepper to taste. Replace lid and continue cooking for 45 minutes longer, or until vegetables and meat are tender. Makes 6 to 8 servings.

TURNIP GREENS WITH HOG JOWL

1 pound mustard greens
½ pound salt pork, fresh hog jowl, or ham hock
1 pound young tender turnip tops

Wash and drain mustard greens. Put in pot with meat. Add just enough water to cover. Simmer, covered, until meat is tender. Wash and drain turnip tops. Put in a pot with enough water to cover and simmer until tender. Add turnip greens with juice to mustard greens and meat. Simmer, covered, for 10 minutes. Drain and reserve liquid. Slice meat and serve over greens. Juice drained from vegetables is called "pot likker" and is served separately in cups. Serve with corn bread. Makes 4 servings.

BUTTER BEANS WITH PECANS

2 cups cooked butter beans
1 beef bouillon cube
½ cup water
½ cup chopped pecans
1 medium onion, chopped
Dash of Worcestershire
½ cup grated mild American cheese
⅓ cup soft bread crumbs
2 tablespoons butter

Put butter beans in a small casserole. Add bouillon cube to water and stir until dissolved. Add water to beans with pecans, onion, Worcestershire, and grated cheese. Toss lightly to blend. Sprinkle top with bread crumbs. Dot with bits of butter. Bake in preheated moderate oven (350°F.) for 30 minutes. Makes 4 servings.

FRIED CREAM

3 egg yolks
½ cup all-purpose flour
2 tablespoons sugar
1 tablespoon cornstarch

A Robust Treat From Texas: Beefsteak and Oysters

¼ teaspoon salt
1 cup milk
½ teaspoon vanilla extract
1 whole egg
1 teaspoon cold water
Fine corn flake crumbs
Ground cinnamon
Fat for frying
Cinnamon sugar

Beat egg yolks until thick and lemon-colored. Sift flour with sugar, cornstarch, and salt. Add alternately to egg yolks with milk, mixing well after each addition. Cook in top part of a double boiler over boiling water. Stir until mixture becomes thick and smooth. Add vanilla. Pour into buttered 8-inch square pan, cool, and chill. Beat whole egg slightly with water. Cut custard into 4-inch strips, 1 inch wide. Carefully dip each strip into egg, then into crumbs lightly spiced with cinnamon. Refrigerate. Fry a few at a time in 2 inches of hot fat in a skillet. Serve hot, sprinkled with cinnamon sugar. Makes 4 servings.

STRAWBERRY CHESS TARTS
Tart pastry (recipe using 2 cups flour), unbaked
½ cup softened butter or margarine
Sugar (about 1⅓ cups)
Salt
2 tablespoons all-purpose flour
3 eggs, separated
1 quart strawberries

Roll out pastry ⅛-inch thick. Line 8 plain tart pans with pastry and flute edges. Cream butter with 1 cup sugar. Add ⅛ teaspoon salt, flour, and well-beaten egg yolks. Wash and cap berries; dry on paper towel. Add berries to sugar mixture and fill tart shells. Bake in pre-heated hot oven (400°F.) for 10 minutes. Reduce heat to slow (325°F.) and bake for 20 minutes longer. Beat egg whites with a dash of salt until foamy. Add remaining sugar gradually and beat until stiff and glossy. Top tarts with meringue; spread it to the edges. Reduce oven heat to 300°F. and bake for 15 minutes longer. Cool tarts before serving. Makes 8.

STRAWBERRY CIRCLE CAKE
⅓ cup butter
Sugar
1 egg
½ teaspoon vanilla extract
1¼ cups sifted cake flour
1 teaspoon baking powder
½ teaspoon salt
⅓ cup milk
3 cups hulled fresh strawberries
⅛ teaspoon red food coloring
1 tablespoon cornstarch
1 cup heavy cream, whipped and sweetened

Cream butter and ⅔ cup sugar. Beat in egg and vanilla. Add sifted dry ingredients alternately with milk, beating until smooth. Pour into 8-inch layer pan, lined on the bottom with wax paper. Bake in

moderate oven (350°F.) 25 to 30 minutes. Cool; turn out on plate. Heat berries, ¼ cup sugar, and coloring until juice begins to flow. Spoon out berries and put on cake. Blend cornstarch into juice and cook, stirring, until thickened. Cool slightly; pour over cake and chill until set. Decorate with whipped cream.

Texas

From Red River to Rio Grande, big in miles, long on memory. Remember the Alamo, Lone Star Flag and longhorns on the trek to Kansas. San Antonio, Houston, Big D, Fort Worth, great cities near the plains, in sight of roaming steer. Roses in Tyler, fruit in Magic Valley, rice beside the Gulf. First in oil, grain and winter vegetables; first in prideful spirit.

BEEFSTEAK AND OYSTERS
Broil a steak almost to desired degree of doneness. Cover with drained oysters. Season with salt and pepper and dot with butter. Bake in preheated moderate oven (375°F.) until oysters are plump (about 15 minutes) and begin to curl at the edges. Garnish with chopped parsley and lemon wedges.

BEEF PICADILLO
½ pound ground beef
½ pound ground pork
2½ cups water
1 tablespoon salt
¼ teaspoon pepper
4 medium tomatoes, peeled and diced
¾ cup seedless raisins
2½ garlic cloves, finely chopped
3 green onions, finely cut
1 can (6 ounces) tomato paste
3 raw potatoes, peeled and diced
2 jalapeno or hot peppers, chopped
¾ cup diced pimientos
Dash of ground oregano
¾ cup toasted blanched almonds

Cover meat with water. Add salt and

pepper and simmer, covered, for 30 minutes. Add remaining ingredients. Simmer, covered, until potatoes are done, about 20 minutes. Makes 6 servings.

TURKEY AND BEEF TENDERLOIN
Butter
2 tablespoons all-purpose flour
2 cups light cream
1 can (4 ounces) mushroom buttons
Salt, pepper, ground nutmeg
2 tablespoons dry white wine
6 slices of bread
6 slices of beef tenderloin, ¼ inch thick
6 slices of breast of roast turkey
Paprika

Melt 2 tablespoons butter; blend in flour. Gradually stir in cream. Cook over low heat until thickened, stirring constantly. Add drained mushrooms; season to taste with salt, pepper, and a dash of nutmeg. Stir in wine. Keep warm. Cut bread into rounds, butter, and sauté in well-buttered skillet until brown on both sides. Keep hot. Quickly sauté beef on both sides. Place slices of fried bread on individual plates. Top each with beef and turkey. Cover with mushroom sauce. Sprinkle with paprika. Makes 6 servings.

BARBECUED TURKEY
1 turkey, 10 to 15 pounds
½ cup melted butter or margarine
½ cup cooking oil
2 cups cider vinegar
1 cup ketchup
½ cup sugar
2 medium onions, grated
¼ cup Worcestershire
⅓ cup fresh lemon juice
2 tablespoons dry mustard
3 tablespoons chili powder
2 teaspoons pepper
2 teaspoons salt
2 garlic cloves, mashed

Defrost turkey if frozen by leaving at room temperature overnight. Remove giblets. Wash turkey; pat dry. To make sauce, simmer remaining ingredients for 10 minutes. Brush sides of turkey with barbecue sauce. Insert spit rod, running it through tail and diagonally through breastbone. Fasten turkey with spit forks. Wings and legs should be tied closely to body. Rotate spit to make sure turkey is properly balanced and will turn evenly. To know exactly when turkey is ready, insert a meat thermometer into thickest part of the thigh. Heat charcoal until coals turn gray. Push coals to rear of firebox. Push spit into holders. Make a drip pan of foil to catch drippings and place under turkey. Brush turkey with barbecue sauce every 15 to 20 minutes while it rotates. Add charcoal as needed to keep temperature high. When thermometer registers 185°F., or the thickest part of the drumstick feels tender (about 20 minutes per pound), remove turkey. Allow to cool for 20 minutes before carv-

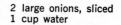

ing. Serve with any remaining barbecue sauce. Makes 10 to 15 servings.

TOASTED RICE

Spread 1 cup uncooked rice in shallow pan with sides. Bake in preheated hot oven (400°F.), stirring frequently, until golden. Cool. Place rice in a 1½-quart casserole. Add 1 teaspoon salt and 2½ cups boiling water. Cover and bake in moderate oven (350°F.) for 30 minutes. Makes 4 servings.

RANCH-HOUSE BEANS

4 cups dried pinto beans, washed and drained
8 cups water
½ pound salt pork
2 to 4 tablespoons chili powder, depending on taste
¼ to ½ teaspoon hot pepper sauce, depending on taste
Salt to taste

Bring beans and water to a boil. Remove from heat, cover, and let stand for 1 hour. Add salt pork and simmer, covered, for 1½ to 2 hours, or until beans are tender and water is almost absorbed. While beans are cooking, remove scum from top and stir occasionally. Remove salt pork and stir in enough chili powder, hot pepper sauce, and salt to give beans a spicy flavor. Beans can be prepared ahead of time and reheated. Makes 10 to 12 servings.

SPINACH AND ONION SALAD

2 pounds spinach leaves
2 Bermuda onions, sliced into rings
1 cup French dressing

Trim tough stems from leaves and tear spinach into bite-size pieces. Wash well. Mix spinach with onion rings. Just before serving, mix salad with French dressing. Makes 4 servings.

TEXAS AMBROSIA

4 navel oranges
2 red tart apples, peeled and sliced
Fresh lemon juice
¾ cup chopped pecans
1 cup crushed pineapple
1 small coconut, peeled and shredded
¾ cup cherries

Peel oranges, removing white membrane. Cut oranges into sections, removing all membranes. Sprinkle apples with lemon juice to prevent darkening. Toss oranges with apples, pecans, pineapple, coconut, and cherries. Chill, and serve dusted with confectioners' sugar, if desired. Makes 4 to 6 servings.

FLAN SOL Y SOMBRA
(Sun and Shadow Custard)

4 eggs
⅓ cup honey
½ teaspoon salt
1 teaspoon ground coriander
3 cups milk
1 teaspoon vanilla extract

2 tablespoons almond liqueur or rum
Ground nutmeg

Blend eggs, honey, and salt. Add remaining ingredients except nutmeg. Blend well. Butter a 1½-quart baking dish; pour in mixture and sprinkle nutmeg over top. Set dish in a pan of warm water and bake in preheated very slow oven (250°F.) for 2 hours, or until firm. Cool; chill. Makes 4 to 6 servings.

Utah

Great Salt Lake, six times as salty as an ocean; Bingham Canyon, sunk for copper; Bryce Canyon, nature's cathedral. Rainbow Bridge, Monument Valley. Great Desert: echoes of distant past. Clean wide streets; voices massed in choir, tabernacle without nails; tributes to Mormon resolve. Honeybee for toil and a sea gull to recall a miracle of salvation in 1848.

CRAYFISH SAUTÉ

18 crayfish
½ cup butter
1 onion, minced
2 or 3 parsley sprigs, chopped
½ cup dry white wine
Salt, pepper, and paprika

Clean fish. Melt butter in skillet. Add onion and fish. Cook over medium heat until shells turn red. Add remaining ingredients and cover. Reduce heat and cook for 5 to 10 minutes longer. Makes 4 servings.

GRANDMOTHER'S STEAK

4 pounds round steak, cut ½ inch thick
½ cup all-purpose flour
½ cup cracker crumbs
1 teaspoon salt
¼ teaspoon pepper
4 slices of bacon, diced
¼ cup butter or margarine
¼ cup lard

2 large onions, sliced
1 cup water

Cut steaks into 6 pieces. Mix flour, crumbs, and seasonings. Pound into steak on both sides. In large iron skillet, cook bacon until crisp. Remove bacon and reserve. Add butter, lard, and onions and sauté for 3 to 4 minutes. Add steak and fry until brown on both sides. Pour off fat; add bacon and water. Cover and simmer for about 1 hour, or until tender. Thicken gravy with a little flour and water paste, if desired. Makes 6 servings.

SAND-PAIL PICNIC DINNER

For the cooked part of the meal, provide for each person a leg and a thigh of chicken, 2 ears of corn, and a large baking potato. Season chicken with salt and pepper, dredge with flour, brown well in hot fat. Cool, and refrigerate. Shuck corn, remove silk, spread with soft butter, season with salt. Wrap each ear of corn in aluminum foil. Scrub baking potatoes; grease skins with vegetable fat. Wrap each potato in foil. Now wrap each piece of chicken in foil. Into a large galvanized pail, put 2 inches of moist sand. Wrap each bundle of chicken, corn, and potato in a second piece of foil, using butcher wrap. Put a layer of chicken bundles on top of sand; fill with 2 more inches of sand. Add potato bundles, another layer of sand. Put corn bundles on top, cover with sand. Set pail on deep bed of coals, adding more charcoal as needed to keep fire going for 1½ hours. Then, wearing absestos gloves, empty pail on the ground. Let each person fish for his bundle of chicken, corn, and potato. Discard outer layer of foil. Inner layer will be clean and free of sand.

If party group is large, more than 1 pail will be needed.

CELERY FRITTERS

1 cup sifted all-purpose flour
1 teaspoon baking powder
½ teaspoon salt
¼ teaspoon white pepper
¾ cup milk
2 eggs, slightly beaten
1½ cups minced celery
Deep fat for frying

Combine first 4 ingredients. Blend milk and eggs and add to flour mixture. Beat until smooth. Add celery. Drop by tablespoon into deep hot fat (365°F. on frying thermometer). Fry for about 3 minutes; turn once. Makes 4 servings.

MORMON VEGETABLE STEW

2 small eggplants
2 green peppers
2 onions

2 tablespoons butter
2 tablespoons all-purpose flour
Salt and pepper to taste
1 can (8 ounces) tomato puree
Grated cheese

Peel eggplant; cut into ½-inch slices, then into dices. Chop peppers and onions. Cook for 5 minutes in butter in skillet. Put vegetables in 2-quart baking dish, season, and sprinkle with flour. Pour tomato purée over top. Sprinkle generously with grated cheese. Bake in preheated moderate oven (350°F.) for 25 minutes. Makes 4 to 6 servings.

MORMON BISCUITS WITH CREAM GRAVY

2 cups sifted all-purpose flour
½ teaspoon baking soda
1 teaspoon baking powder
½ teaspoon salt
1 tablespoon sugar
¼ cup vegetable shortening
Sour milk or buttermilk
Cream Gravy

Sift dry ingredients; work in shortening to consistency of fine meal. Add milk to make soft dough. Roll on floured board to ½-inch thickness. Cut with 2-inch biscuit cutter. Bake on greased cookie sheet in preheated very hot oven (450°F.) for 10 to 15 minutes. Split biscuits; pour Cream Gravy over them. Makes 4 servings.

Cream Gravy

3 tablespoons clear bacon drippings
3 tablespoons all-purpose flour
3 cups milk
Salt and pepper

Combine drippings and flour in skillet. Heat and stir for a minute or two. Add milk; cook until slightly thickened, stirring constantly. Season well with salt and pepper.

APRICOT MOUSSE

1 cup heavy cream
Juice of ½ lemon
1 cup sweetened fresh or stewed dried apricots
Fresh apricot halves
Fresh loganberries

Whip cream until just stiff. Mix lemon juice and apricots. Fold into cream. Turn into trays and freeze with setting at coldest point, or turn into mold and freeze. Unmold, and garnish with apricot halves and loganberries. Makes 4 to 6 servings.

ALMOND SLICES

1½ cups almonds with skins (8 ounces)
2 cups sifted all-purpose flour
1 cup sugar
1 cup soft butter
1 teaspoon ground cinnamon
2 eggs

Grate nuts, using small rotary grater; do not grind. Put nuts, flour, and sugar in bowl. Blend in butter with fingers or pastry blender. Add remaining ingre-

dients and mix well with fingers. Shape into 2 long blocks, 2 inches across. Wrap in wax paper and chill overnight; or freeze. Cut into ⅛-inch slices, crosswise. Put on greased cookie sheets and bake in preheated moderate oven (375°F.) for about 10 minutes. Remove at once to racks to cool. Store in airtight container. Makes about 8 dozen.

Vermont

New England's most rock-bound, without an inch of coast. Green the Mountains, from whence sprang Ethan Allen, from whence maple sugar and organ pipes. Taconic hills, sliced for marble, alive with ski lodges. Champlain, blue to the west, the Connecticut, rolling to the south. Covered bridges by towns as sturdy and proud as the people who founded them.

EGGS DROPPED IN CREAM

½ cup light cream
6 eggs
Salt and pepper to taste
Toast

Pour cream into a skillet large enough to hold 6 eggs. Heat cream, and drop in eggs carefully. Sprinkle eggs with salt and pepper. Cook slowly over low heat until eggs are set. Serve on toast. Makes 3 to 6 servings.

ROAST TURKEY WITH SAVORY GIBLET-BUTTERNUT STUFFING

Wash turkey in cold running water. Pat inside and out with paper towel. Sprinkle inside lightly with salt. Stuff turkey. Tie legs together; draw skin of neck to back and fasten with skewer. Bend wing tips under. Place turkey, breast side up, on rack in shallow pan. Cover loosely with foil. Roast in preheated slow oven (325° F.) according to timetable below; baste

several times with drippings in pan. Remove from oven 30 minutes before serving and make gravy, if desired.

Purchased ready-to-cook weight	Roasting time
12 to 16 pounds	4½ to 5½ hours
16 to 20 pounds	5½ to 6½ hours
20 to 24 pounds	6½ to 7 hours

Allow 1 pound of turkey per serving.

Giblet-Butternut Stuffing

Wash giblets; cook neck, heart, and gizzard for about 2 hours in boiling salted water with a small onion and a few celery leaves. Add liver during last 15 minutes. Drain, and reserve stock. Chop heart, gizzard, and liver. Melt 1 cup butter or margarine, add 1 cup each of chopped onion, celery, and butternuts, and sauté for 5 minutes. Add 1 tablespoon poultry seasoning, 1½ teaspoons salt, ¾ teaspoon pepper, and chopped giblets. Mix with 4 quarts soft stale bread cubes. Stuff neck and cavity. Enough to stuff a 16- to 20-pound turkey.

MAPLE SUGAR ON SNOW

Boil maple syrup until it forms a soft ball when tested in cold water (238°F. on a candy thermometer). Pour by tablespoons onto a bed of fresh clean snow. Twist sugar from snow on fork or skewer. Serve with hot doughnuts, crisp sour pickles, and plenty of coffee.

MAPLE CREAM

1 envelope unflavored gelatin
2¼ cups milk
3 eggs, separated
¼ teaspoon salt
¾ cup maple syrup
1 teaspoon vanilla extract

Soften gelatin in milk in top part of double boiler. Place over hot water and heat to scalding. Beat salted egg yolks, stir in syrup, and add to milk. Cook over simmering water, stirring, until mixture begins to thicken. Remove from heat. Beat in stiffly beaten egg whites. Add vanilla. Pour into pudding dish and chill until very firm. Makes 6 servings.

BREAD-AND-BUTTER PICKLES

8 cups thinly sliced unpeeled cucumbers
2 cups thinly sliced onions
¼ cup salt
2 cups cider vinegar
2 teaspoons celery seed
2½ cups sugar
2 teaspoons ground turmeric
1 cinnamon stick
4 green peppers, chopped

Mix cucumbers with onions. Sprinkle with salt and allow to stand for 1 hour. Drain. Put into a large kettle and add remaining ingredients. Bring to a boil, lower heat, and simmer for 30 minutes. Stir occasionally. Pour mixture into hot sterilized jars. Seal and cool. Makes 3½ pints.

RASPBERRY SHRUB

Mix 5 quarts red raspberries and 1 quart very mild vinegar. Let stand for 24 hours, then strain. Add 1 cup sugar to 1 quart juice. Bring to boil. Fill clean hot jars or bottles to overflowing. Seal and process for 5 minutes in boiling water bath. To serve, dilute with 3 parts cold water and pour over crushed ice in tall glasses. A refreshing summer drink, to be made when there are lots of raspberries. Makes about 3 quarts.

Virginia

Old Dominion, Mother of Presidents, home of the famed; Jamestown, Williamsburg, Yorktown, Appomattox, on history's path. Washington, Jefferson, Wilson, even Sam Houston, claimed Virginia birth. "Carry Me Back" to Smithfield hams, to Shenandoah apples, to the Trail of the Lonesome Pine. See again old Blue Ridge, or bustling Hampton Roads in Navy blue.

ALMOND BOUILLON

Combine 1 can (10½ ounces) beef bouillon and 1 can (12½ ounces) chicken broth. Add 1 cup milk, 1 cup light cream, and ¼ pound (⅔ cup) salted almonds, ground. Cook mixture in top part of a double boiler for 30 minutes. Makes 4 to 6 servings.

MARTHA WASHINGTON'S CRAB SOUP

2 tablespoons butter
2 tablespoons all-purpose flour

Grated rind of 1 lemon
4 cups milk, scalded
1 teaspoon Worcestershire
½ pound flaked crabmeat
2 hard-cooked eggs, chopped
½ cup heavy cream
½ cup dry sherry
Salt and pepper

Melt butter; stir in flour and lemon rind. Stir in milk gradually. Cook over low heat until slightly thickened; stir constantly. Add Worcestershire, crabmeat, and eggs. Heat. Add cream and sherry just before serving. Season to taste. Reheat, and serve at once. Makes 8 servings.

NORFOLK SHAD WITHOUT BONES

4 to 5-pound shad
Peanut oil
Salt and pepper to taste
3 slices of bacon
6 green onions, sliced

Put a large piece of cheesecloth dipped in oil in an oiled roasting pan. Season fish inside and out and place on top of cheesecloth. Cut bacon slices into halves and arrange on top of fish. Add boiling water to depth of 1 inch. Place onions around fish. Cover pan and bake in preheated very slow oven (200°F.) for 8 hours, or at 250°F. for 6 hours until bones disintegrate. Lift out fish carefully. Makes 4 servings.

BAKED SMITHFIELD HAM

Cover a Smithfield ham with water and soak for 12 hours. Change water and simmer over low heat for 4 to 5 hours, or until tender. Cool in liquid. When cold, remove skin. Put in roasting pan and make crisscross cuts in fat. Stud with whole cloves and sprinkle with a little sherry, if desired. Sprinkle with a mixture of 2 tablespoons fine cracker crumbs, 2 tablespoons brown sugar, and a little pepper. Bake in preheated hot oven (425°F.) for 25 minutes, or until lightly browned and hot. Slice ham paper-thin.

BRUNSWICK STEW

1 chicken (about 4 pounds), cut up
4 cups water
4 slices of bacon
½ pound beef chuck, cut into ¾-inch cubes
1 small onion, minced
1¼ teaspoons salt
1 teaspoon paprika
1¾ to 2 cups (one 1-pound can) tomatoes
1 package (10 ounces) frozen Lima beans
1½ to 1¾ cups (one 12-ounce can) whole kernel corn
3 medium potatoes, diced
Seasoned salt, and pepper
All-purpose flour

Cover chicken with water, bring to boil, and cook, covered, for 1 hour, or until tender. Cool chicken, remove meat from bones, reserving broth, and cut into

bite-size pieces. Dice bacon and brown in kettle. Remove bacon and brown beef and onion in fat remaining in kettle. Add bacon, chicken broth, salt, paprika, and tomatoes. Bring to boil, cover, and simmer for 1½ hours. Add remaining vegetables and chicken and simmer for about 30 minutes longer. Season to taste and thicken slightly with a flour-and-water paste. Makes 6 servings.

VIRGINIA BATTER BREAD

1 cup white water-ground cornmeal
1 teaspoon salt
1 teaspoon baking powder
2 tablespoons butter
4 cups milk, scalded
4 eggs, separated

Combine dry ingredients. Add butter to milk. When melted, stir into cornmeal mixture. Blend thoroughly. Add well-beaten yolks. Fold in stiffly beaten whites. Pour batter into greased 2-quart casserole. Bake in preheated moderate oven (350°F.) for 45 to 50 minutes; stir twice before crust begins to set. Makes 4 to 6 servings.

SPREAD APPLE PIE

Season 4 cups applesauce with juice of ½ lemon and a dash of nutmeg. Beat 4 egg whites with a dash of salt until stiff. Fold into applesauce. Spread in baked 9-inch pie shell. Chill, and serve with sweetened whipped cream. Makes 6 servings.

PEANUT BRITTLE

½ cup dark corn syrup
¼ cup each of molasses and sugar
2 tablespoons butter or margarine
1 cup salted peanuts
⅛ teaspoon baking soda

Cook first 4 ingredients until blended. Stir in peanuts and boil until a small amount of mixture separates in hard threads when dropped into cold water (280°F. on a candy thermometer). Stir in soda and pour into buttered shallow pan. When firm, break into pieces. Makes about 9 ounces.

PEANUT CHEWS

½ cup honey
¾ cup maple syrup
¼ teaspoon baking soda
¼ teaspoon cream of tartar
1 cup roasted peanuts

Pour honey and maple syrup into saucepan and cook until a small amount of mixture forms a hard ball when dropped into very cold water (255°F. on a candy thermometer). Remove from heat, add soda and cream of tartar; mix well. Stir in nuts and pour into buttered 8 x 8 x 2-inch pan. Cool, and cut into squares. Makes sixty-four 1-inch squares.

Washington

Evergreen gem of the Northwest, whose Olympic Mountains scan Puget Sound as Rainier stands icily aloof. Seattle, doorstep to the Orient, Spokane, welcome mat to Inland Empire. Wenatchee and Yakima Valleys give apples a day for all, the Columbia yields salmon to top tall tales. Grand Coulee, "biggest job on earth," dwarfs even the Pyramids of ancient Egypt.

RED CAVIAR IN CREAM

½ cup dairy sour cream
1 package (3 ounces) cream cheese
2 slices of onion, chopped
   Dash of salt
   Pepper to taste
1 jar (6 ounces) red salmon caviar

Put all ingredients except caviar in blender. Whirl for a few seconds. Add caviar. Mix lightly and chill. Makes about 1½ cups. Spread on toast rounds and garnish with dill or chives for a first course. Or use as a dip for potato chips, scallions, and carrot and celery strips.

DUNGENESS CRAB LOUIS

1 head lettuce, shredded
3 green onions, diced
5 or 6 radishes, sliced
½ medium cucumber, diced
2 cups fresh crabmeat
   Salt and pepper
2 tomatoes, quartered
3 hard-cooked eggs, quartered
½ to 1 cup Thousand-Island dressing
   Paprika for garnish

Combine lettuce, onions, radishes, cucumber, and crabmeat; season to taste. Garnish salad with tomatoes and eggs. Add dressing to lettuce mixture or spoon on top of each individual serving. Sprinkle with paprika. Makes 4 generous servings.

BAKED SALMON

3- pound whole salmon
   Salt and pepper
   All-purpose flour
¼ cup butter or margarine
1 cup tomato puree
1 small onion, minced
1 garlic clove, minced
1 tablespoon Worcestershire
½ cup light cream
   Lemon wedges

Clean and scale fish. Wash fish and wipe dry. Sprinkle inside and out with salt and pepper. Dip fish into flour and coat well. Melt butter in a shallow baking pan. Place fish in butter and bake in preheated hot oven (400°F.) for 10 to 15 minutes. Add next 4 ingredients. Bake for 30 minutes longer, basting frequently with pan juices. Using a spatula, remove fish to a serving platter. Add cream to pan drippings. Stir well to loosen all particles. Put pan over low heat and thicken sauce with a little flour mixed into a smooth paste with water. Pour sauce over fish; garnish with lemon wedges. Makes 4 to 6 servings.

VENISON MINCEMEAT

2 cups finely chopped venison
   (use flank or neck)
2 cups chopped peeled tart apples
1 cup ground suet
1 pound each of raisins and currants
½ pound citron, chopped
1 cup candied mixed fruits
1 tablespoon each of ground cinnamon
   and nutmeg
1 teaspoon ground cloves
2 cups sugar
2 teaspoons salt
   Liquid to cover (broth, cider vinegar,
   or sweet cider)

Mix ingredients thoroughly. Bring to a boil; simmer for 15 minutes, stirring frequently. Seal in scalded pint jars. This will make about 7 pints and each pint will make 1 pie.

BAKED LIMA-BEAN-AND-PEAR CASSEROLE

1 pound dried Lima beans,
   washed and drained
6 cups water
   Salt and pepper to taste
½ cup melted butter or margarine
1 cup firmly packed light brown sugar
2½ cups (one 1-pound, 13-ounce can)
   pear halves, cubed

Put beans in kettle, add water, and bring to a boil. Boil for 2 minutes; cover pan and let stand for 1 hour. Then simmer until tender; add more hot water if necessary. Drain, and season. Mix butter and brown sugar and a little syrup from pears. In a large casserole, alternate layers of beans and pears. Spread each layer with butter-sugar mixture. Top layer should be pears. Spread with remaining sugar mixture. Cover and bake

in preheated slow oven (325°F.) for about 2 hours. Makes 6 servings.

SCHLEE

6 slices of bacon
½ cup mild vinegar
1 tablespoon sugar
2 cups mashed potatoes
1 to 2 quarts shredded lettuce

Dice bacon and fry slowly until crisp and brown. Pour off part of fat and add vinegar and sugar. In large pot, cover mashed potatoes with lettuce. Pour hot bacon and vinegar mixture over all. Cover, and let lettuce wilt a bit. Then stir, and serve immediately. Makes 4 servings.

PRUNE BUTTER

Wash and pit prunes and put them in a kettle which has a tight-fitting lid. Add 1 cup water, more or less (just cover the prunes). Cover kettle and cook over low heat until prunes are soft. Put through a sieve or food mill. Put in preheated slow oven (300°F.) and cook for four or five hours until reduced by half; stir carefully every hour or two. Add 1 cup sugar to 1 quart pulp, and flavor to taste. The usual flavoring is ½ teaspoon ground cinnamon and ¼ teaspoon ground cloves for 1 quart pulp, but less can be used. Stir well while bringing this to a boil; put into hot sterilized jars and seal. Instead of ground cinnamon and cloves, which are added after prunes are cooked, a cinnamon stick and some whole cloves, tied in a muslin bag, can be added after prune pulp is sieved.

APLETS

2 cups tart well-flavored applesauce
½ teaspoon ground cinnamon
¼ teaspoon each of ground nutmeg
   and cloves
2 cups sugar
2 envelopes unflavored gelatin
½ cup cold water
1½ cups chopped nuts
   Confectioners' sugar

Use tart canned applesauce or use Jonathan or Winesap apples to make applesauce. Strain applesauce to make very smooth, or purée in a blender. Add spices and sugar to applesauce. Stir until sugar is dissolved. Soak gelatin in water for 5 minutes. Dissolve gelatin over low heat. Add dissolved gelatin to apple mixture. Stir in nuts. Pour mixture into buttered pan (8 x 8 x 2 inches). Chill until firm. Cut into small squares and roll squares in confectioners' sugar. Makes sixty-four 1-inch squares.

West Virginia

Bituminous to the core, favored by nature on its surface. Border lines wrinkled as a prune, fixed to neighbors by twin panhandles. Harpers Ferry, by the mingled Potomac and Shenandoah, recalls zealot John Brown; beautiful Kanawha lures industry, Greenbrier at White Sulphur Springs calls elite. In the hills a motto: "Mountaineers are always free."

BARBECUED PORK RIBS

6 pounds fresh pork ribs
4 onions, chopped
2 cups water
2 beef bouillon cubes
½ cup dark brown sugar
1 cup ketchup
½ cup cider vinegar
1 can (1 pound) tomato puree
1 tablespoon each of garlic salt, celery salt, and chili powder
½ teaspoon each of ground allspice, cloves, ginger, and mustard
½ cup drained sweet-pickle relish

Brown ribs in heavy kettle. Add remaining ingredients. Cover; simmer for 2 hours, or until tender. Makes 8 servings.

POT ROAST WITH APPLE CIDER

3½- to 4-pound eye round of beef
1 onion, sliced
6 whole cloves
Piece of gingerroot
Small piece of cinnamon stick
1½ teaspoons salt
2 cups apple cider
2 tablespoons shortening

Put beef with onion, seasonings, and cider in a large bowl in refrigerator. Let marinate overnight. Wipe meat; brown slowly in fat. Add marinade, cover, and simmer over low heat for about 2½ hours, or until meat is tender. Serve with pan juices. Makes 6 to 8 servings.

BAKED MUSHROOMS

6 slices of toast, buttered
Melted butter or margarine
24 medium-size fresh mushrooms
Salt and pepper to taste

Put buttered toast on a greased shallow baking pan. Stem mushrooms, wash, and drain. Use only the caps. Dip into melted butter. Put 4 mushrooms on each slice of toast. Sprinkle with salt and pepper. Bake in preheated hot oven (400°F.) for 15 to 20 minutes, or until mushrooms are tender. Makes 4 to 6 servings.

FRENCH-FRIED ONION RINGS

4 large Bermuda onions
All-purpose flour
4 eggs, well beaten
2 cups milk
Cracker meal
Deep fat or oil

Peel onion and cut into ⅛-inch thick slices. Separate into rings; dip rings into flour. Beat eggs with milk. Dip flour-coated rings into egg and milk; then dip into cracker meal. Fry onion rings in deep fat (360°F. on a frying thermometer) for 2 to 3 minutes, or until onion rings are golden brown. Drain on absorbent paper. Serve while hot with broiled steak. Makes 4 servings.

GOLDEN APPLE SALAD

3 cups cubed unpeeled Grimes golden apples
Fresh lemon juice
1 cup chopped pitted dates
½ cup shelled hickory nuts
¾ cup heavy cream
¾ cup mayonnaise
3 tablespoons fresh orange juice
⅓ cup orange marmalade
½ teaspoon salt

Sprinkle apples with lemon juice to keep them from darkening. Mix with dates and nuts. Whip cream and fold in mayonnaise and remaining ingredients. Chill separately. Combine salad with dressing just before serving. Makes 6 servings.

WILD HUCKLEBERRY PIE

1 quart huckleberries
3 tablespoons quick-cooking tapioca
1 cup sugar
¼ teaspoon salt
Juice of 1 lemon
Pastry for 2-crust 9-inch pie, unbaked
1 tablespoon butter

Stem and wash berries; drain. Mix with tapioca, sugar, and salt. Add lemon juice. Roll out pastry. Use half to line pie pan; trim edges. Pour in huckleberries. Dot with butter. Use remaining pastry to cover pie. Moisten edges of pastry and flute to seal. Cut vents in top. Bake in preheated very hot oven (450°F.) for 10 minutes. Reduce heat to moderate (350° F.) and bake for 30 to 35 minutes longer. Sprinkle with additional sugar and serve

with sweetened whipped cream, if desired. Makes 6 servings.

CHERRY PIE

2½ tablespoons quick-cooking tapioca
1 cup sugar
⅛ teaspoon salt
2 cans (1 pound each) water-packed pitted red sour cherries, drained
½ cup cherry juice
6 drops red food coloring
¼ teaspoon almond extract
Pastry for 2-crust 9-inch pie, unbaked
1 tablespoon butter

Combine tapioca, sugar, salt, cherries, cherry juice, food coloring, and almond extract. Mix well and let stand while preparing pastry. Line 9-inch pie pan with pastry and trim edges. Pour filling into shell and dot with butter. Moisten edge of bottom crust. Roll out remaining pastry and cut several slits or a design near the center. Adjust crust on filling. Open slits to let steam escape during baking. Trim top crust ½ inch larger than pan. Fold this edge under bottom crust and press together with fork or fingers. Bake in hot oven (425°F.) 50 minutes, or until syrup boils with heavy bubbles and top is golden brown. Serve slightly warm or cold.
Note: This pie is especially good served warm with ice cream or whipped cream.

MOLASSES COOKIES

½ cup melted butter
1 cup heated dark molasses
⅓ cup firmly packed dark brown sugar
¾ teaspoon each of ground cinnamon and cloves
½ teaspoon ground ginger
¼ teaspoon each of ground nutmeg and allspice
¾ teaspoon baking soda
3¾ cups sifted cake flour
Pinch of salt

Blend butter and molasses. Combine dry ingredients and add. Roll in wax paper and store in refrigerator for 1 week before baking. Roll very thin on well-floured board; cut. Bake on greased cookie sheets in preheated moderate oven (375°F.) for 6 to 10 minutes. Makes about 4 dozen.

APPLE BETTY

Mix 2 cups small bread cubes with 2 tablespoons margarine, ¼ teaspoon ground cinnamon, dash of salt, and ⅓ cup brown sugar. Arrange layers of crumb mixture and 2 cups chopped tart apples in individual baking dishes. Bake in preheated moderate oven (375°F.) for 30 minutes. Cool slightly and spread with Topping. Makes 4 to 6 servings.

Topping

Add 1 tablespoon evaporated milk and some grated lemon rind to ⅔ cup confectioners' sugar. Mix until smooth.

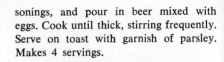

Wisconsin

Progressive testing ground, land of ideas and action. Dairyland of America, leader in milk, maker of half a nation's cheese. Milwaukee, brewing beside Lake Michigan; Green Bay, whose Packers are huge. Dotted with lakes, 4,000 on maps alone, led by Geneva, blue as Galilee, Mendota where the capitol stands, and Winnebago, site of Oshkosh, by gosh.

CHEESE APPETIZERS

½ cup butter
1 cup grated Cheddar cheese
1 cup all-purpose flour
  Dash each salt and cayenne

Cream butter and cheese well. Gradually add sifted dry ingredients, mixing well. Roll out on lightly floured board to ¼-inch thickness. Cut in rounds with 1¼-inch cutter. Bake in preheated moderate oven (350°F.) for 10 to 15 minutes. Serve warm or cold. Makes about 2½ dozen.

WALLEYED PIKE

2 pounds sliced filleted pike
  Salt and pepper to taste
2 eggs, well beaten
  Yellow cornmeal
  Fat or vegetable oil for frying

Cut fish into small slices. Sprinkle slices with salt and pepper. Dip slices into eggs. Then roll slices in cornmeal and coat well. Fry slices in deep fat (370°F. on a frying thermometer) for 3 to 4 minutes, or until fish is golden brown on all sides. Drain on absorbent paper and serve immediately. Makes 4 to 6 servings.

PAN-FRIED SMELTS

2 pounds smelts
⅓ cup evaporated milk, undiluted
⅓ cup all-purpose flour
⅓ cup yellow cornmeal
2 teaspoons salt
⅛ teaspoon pepper
  Fat for frying

¼ cup butter or margarine
  Juice of ½ lemon
1 tablespoon drained capers
1 tablespoon minced parsley

Wipe fish with paper towel. Dip into evaporated milk, then roll in combined flour, cornmeal, and seasonings. Heat enough fat to cover the bottom of a skillet. Pan-fry fish for about 5 minutes on each side, or until well browned and done. Meanwhile, melt butter; add lemon juice, capers, and parsley. Pour over hot fish. Makes 4 servings.

CRANBERRY-GLAZED HAM

1 smoked ham (8 to 10 pounds)
24 long-stemmed whole cloves
1 can (1 pound) jellied cranberry sauce
½ cup firmly packed dark brown sugar

Bake ham according to processor's directions. About 30 minutes before ham is done, score fat with sharp knife and stud with cloves. Pour off fat from pan and put ham back in pan. Crush cranberry sauce with a fork and mix with brown sugar. Spread over ham. Bake for 30 minutes longer, basting occasionally. Spoon sauce from bottom of pan over ham just before serving. Makes 12 to 18 servings.

VEAL PARSLEY PIE WITH DUMPLINGS

2 pounds cubed veal stew meat
2 onions, chopped
½ cup chopped parsley
1 teaspoon salt
¼ teaspoon pepper
  Dumplings

Put meat, onions, and parsley in a Dutch oven. Add salt and pepper. Add enough water just to cover. Cover and simmer for 1 to 1½ hours, or until meat is tender. Drop dumplings by tablespoon on top of simmering meat. Cover tightly and simmer for 10 minutes. Serve at once. Makes 4 servings.

Dumplings

2 cups sifted all-purpose flour
2 teaspoons baking powder
1 teaspoon salt
1 cup milk

Sift flour with baking powder and salt. Add milk and beat well until dough is smooth. Drop on top of simmering stew.

WISCONSIN CHEESE RABBIT

2 tablespoons butter
1 pound sharp Cheddar cheese, shredded
½ teaspoon dry mustard
  Dash of cayenne
½ teaspoon salt
1 teaspoon Worcestershire
½ cup beer
2 eggs, slightly beaten
8 slices of toast
  Parsley

Melt butter in top pan of chafing dish over direct heat. Add cheese and heat, stirring occasionally until cheese is melted. Put over boiling water, add sea-

sonings, and pour in beer mixed with eggs. Cook until thick, stirring frequently. Serve on toast with garnish of parsley. Makes 4 servings.

TWO-CHEESE LOGS

2 cups finely chopped pecans
1 small garlic clove, minced
4 packages (3 ounces each) cream cheese
4 ounces blue cheese
½ teaspoon Worcestershire
½ teaspoon salt
¼ teaspoon hot pepper sauce
2 tablespoons paprika

Blend all ingredients except paprika. Shape into 2 rolls about 7 x 1½ inches. Sprinkle paprika on foil. Roll the cheese logs in the paprika, coating evenly. Wrap in foil. Chill. Slice to serve on crackers. Makes 2 logs.

WASPS' NESTS

1 cup granulated sugar
½ cup water
5⅔ cups (1 pound) unblanched almonds, slivered
5 egg whites
⅛ teaspoon salt
1 teaspoon vanilla extract
3½ cups sifted (1 pound) confectioners' sugar
4 ounces (4 squares) unsweetened chocolate, melted

Cook granulated sugar and water until syrup spins a thread (234°F. on a candy thermometer). Add nuts slowly and continue stirring until all syrup is absorbed. Beat egg whites until frothy; add salt and vanilla; continue beating until whites are very stiff; gradually beat in confectioners' sugar. Fold in nuts and chocolate. Drop from teaspoon on well-buttered cookie sheets. Bake in preheated slow oven (300°F.) for 20 to 25 minutes. Makes 10 dozen.

CHERRY PIE, CHANTILLY

1 cup unsifted all-purpose flour
  Dash of salt
1 tablespoon sugar
½ cup soft butter or margarine
1 egg yolk
  Dairy sour cream
1 can cherry pie filling
  Sweetened whipped cream, flavored with almond extract
  Grated orange rind

Sift dry ingredients into bowl and cut in butter. Add egg yolk and enough sour cream to make a smooth pastry dough. Wrap in wax paper and chill overnight. Then roll to ⅛-inch thickness and fit into 8-inch pie pan. Trim edges and flute. Prick well with fork. Bake in preheated very hot oven (450°F.) for about 10 minutes. Cool, and fill with pie filling. Top with whipped cream and sprinkle with orange rind. Chill until ready to serve. Makes 6 servings.

Wyoming

No lyrics capture Yellowstone, home of geysers—Faithful and erratic—where bears hungrily eye tourists, but know their place. Nor are words enough for Grand Teton and Jackson Lake, awesome in beauty. Bronco riders at Cheyenne and Laramie are poetry in motion, and everywhere—Powder, Medicine Bow, Big Horn—the frontier is always close in nostalgia.

BOILED LEG OF MUTTON WITH CAPER SAUCE

1 leg of mutton, shank end removed
¼ cup shortening
2 onions, cut in quarters
1 bay leaf
½ teaspoon peppercorns
2 teaspoons salt
6 cups boiling water
¼ cup all-purpose flour
1 teaspoon cider vinegar
⅓ cup light cream
½ cup drained capers

Brown meat in hot fat in large heavy Dutch oven. Pour off excess shortening. Add onions, bay leaf, peppercorns, and 2 teaspoons salt. Add boiling water. Cover and bring to a boil. Reduce heat and simmer until tender, about 3 hours. Remove meat to large platter and keep warm. Skim off fat from liquid. In small saucepan, mix flour with ¼ cup of the fat. Gradually stir in 3 cups of the liquid, stir over low heat, and cook until thickened. Add vinegar, cream, and capers. Reheat but do not boil. Serve at once. Makes 10 servings.

JUNGLE STEW

1 cup dried beans, washed and drained
6 slices of bacon, cubed
2 onions, sliced
4 medium potatoes, peeled and cubed
2 cups canned tomatoes
2 cups water
Salt and pepper to taste

Cook beans in salted water until half done (about 1 hour). Drain. Fry bacon with onions until onions are golden brown and bacon is crisp. Add beans and remaining ingredients. Cover and cook until beans and vegetables are tender. Add more water if necessary to keep stew from sticking. Makes 4 to 6 servings.

TART MUTTON

2 tart apples
2 cups cubed cold mutton
2 cups cooked rice
3 tablespoons butter or margarine

Slice apples but do not peel. Use apples to line a greased 1½-quart casserole. Mix mutton with rice and pack mixture into apple-lined pan. Dot top with butter and bake in preheated moderate oven (350°F.) for 30 minutes, or until top is golden brown and apples are tender. Makes 4 servings.

BEAN SALAD

3 cups cooked dried beans
1 cup sliced celery
¼ cup chopped sweet pickles
1 small ripe tomato, chopped
2 tablespoons minced onion
¾ cup salad oil
¼ cup cider vinegar
1 teaspoon salt
1 teaspoon sugar
½ teaspoon paprika
1 teaspoon Worcestershire
¼ teaspoon ground cloves
Greens
Vegetable garnishes

Mix beans with celery, pickles, tomato, and onion. Place remaining ingredients except greens in a jar with a tight-fitting lid and shake until well blended. Pour salad dressing over bean mixture. Marinate for 1 hour. Serve salad on bite-size pieces of salad greens. Garnish with chopped cucumber, chopped green pepper, chopped scallions, slices of hard-cooked eggs, and strips of cooked beets. Makes 6 servings.

HONEY-CREAM SALAD DRESSING

1 cup dairy sour cream
½ cup native honey
Few grains of salt
Juice of 1 lemon

Whip cream and add remaining ingredients. Mix well. Chill before serving. Will keep for several days in the refrigerator. Serve on fruit salad or as a dressing for sweet slaw. Makes about 1½ cups.

QUICK ONION-CHEESE BREAD

½ cup minced onion
1 teaspoon chili powder
1 tablespoon cooking oil
1 egg, beaten
½ cup milk
1½ cups biscuit mix
1 cup grated Cheddar cheese
2 tablespoons butter

Sauté onion and chili powder in oil for 2 to 3 minutes. Add onion and oil to mixture of egg and milk. Combine with biscuit mix; stir just until dry ingredients are moistened. Add half the cheese. Spread in a greased pan (8 x 8 x 2 inches). Sprinkle remaining cheese over top. Dot with butter. Bake in preheated hot oven (400°F.) for 20 minutes. Serve hot. Makes 8 servings.

APPLE-BUTTER PIE

Pastry for 1-crust 9-inch pie, unbaked
½ cup sugar
3 tablespoons all-purpose flour
½ cup apple butter
2 tablespoons melted butter
2 eggs, well beaten
1½ cups milk
1 cup light cream
½ teaspoon ground nutmeg

Use pastry to line a 9-inch pie pan, fluting a high edge. Mix sugar with flour. Gradually stir in apple butter and melted butter. Beat eggs with milk and cream. Beat into apple-butter mixture. Pour into pastry-lined pie pan. Sprinkle top with nutmeg. Bake in preheated moderate oven (350°F.) for 50 to 60 minutes, or until a knife inserted comes out clean. Cool on a rack. Makes 6 to 8 servings.

CHEYENNE CHOCOLATE CAKE

¾ cup cocoa (Dutch-process preferred)
1¾ cups sugar
4 eggs
½ cup milk
½ cup butter or margarine
2 cups sifted all-purpose flour
1 teaspoon baking powder
1 teaspoon baking soda
½ teaspoon salt
1 cup dairy sour cream
1 teaspoon vanilla extract
Glossy Chocolate Frosting

Cook cocoa, ¾ cup of the sugar, 1 egg yolk, and milk over low heat until thick. Stir constantly to prevent sticking. Cool. Cream butter until soft. Gradually add remaining sugar, beating until well blended. Add 1 whole egg and 2 egg yolks. Mix well. Stir in sifted dry ingredients alternately with sour cream. Add vanilla and cocoa mixture. Fold in egg whites which have been beaten until stiff, but not dry. Pour into three 8-inch layer-cake pans, greased and lined with wax paper. Bake in preheated moderate oven (350°F.) for 30 to 35 minutes. Turn out on racks and peel off paper. Cool and thinly frost top and sides of cake layers with Glossy Chocolate Frosting.

Glossy Chocolate Frosting

Melt 6 ounces (6 squares) unsweetened chocolate. Add 1½ cups sifted confectioners' sugar and 5 tablespoons hot water. Beat well; add 1½ cups more sugar. Gradually beat in 6 egg yolks. When smooth and blended, beat in ½ cup soft butter or margarine. Makes enough frosting for tops and sides of three 8-inch layers.

Anchovy and Potato Casserole

ANCHOVY—This small fish belongs to the herring family. An anchovy is five to six inches long, narrow in shape, with a mouth that stretches almost to the gills. The best anchovies come from the Mediterranean, and they have been used as appetizers or as ingredients to flavor foods from the days of the ancient Romans.

Anchovies are used almost entirely in a preserved form, salted or pickled or packed in oil, and in fillets. Anchovy fillets come either flat or rolled around a caper. Anchovies are also made into a paste and into an extract. Used judiciously, and with a light hand, they add zest to a sauce or a dull dish. (For 1 cup sauce, use about ⅛ of a mashed anchovy or ⅛ teaspoon anchovy paste.) If anchovies are too salty, soak in cold water or milk for about 15 minutes, drain, and pat dry.

Always keep a can or two of anchovies or a tube of anchovy paste at hand to make canapés for unexpected guests and to pep up leftover foods.

ANCHOVY CANAPÉS

Spread crackers or toast rounds with butter. Top with slice of hard-cooked egg. Top this with a rolled anchovy fillet containing a caper in the middle.

ANCHOVY AND POTATO CASSEROLE

Buttered crumbs
6 medium raw potatoes, peeled
12 flat anchovy fillets, drained
1 onion, minced
2 cups light cream
¼ cup butter or margarine
Pimiento
Parsley

Sprinkle bottom and sides of greased casserole generously with buttered crumbs. Cut potatoes into paper-thin slices. Chop 10 anchovies. Place alternate layers of potato slices and anchovies in casserole, sprinkling each layer with minced onion; top layer should be potatoes. Pour cream over mixture and dot with butter. Bake in preheated moderate oven (350°F.) for 35 to 40 minutes, or until potatoes are tender and top delicately browned. Garnish with remaining anchovies, pimiento, and parsley. Makes 4 to 6 servings.

ANGEL FOOD—A high, delicate, fluffy white cake which contains no fat and uses only the whites of eggs. Air, beaten into these, provides the leavening agent. Angel food is usually baked in a tube pan. It is one of the most glorious of American cakes. Few other cakes have inspired as much research to produce perfection. Women used to be judged as bakers on the quality of their angel food.

It is considered a true party cake and lends itself to many elegant desserts and variations. It can be decorated and frosted with fruits, icings, or whipped cream. It can be scooped out and filled with ice cream, custard, whipped cream, or fruit for a delicious dessert.

Caloric Value

☐ Plain, 3-inch slice = 150 calories

BASIC ANGEL FOOD CAKE

1 cup sifted cake flour
1½ cups sugar
1½ cups egg whites (10 to 12 medium-size eggs)
¼ teaspoon salt
1½ teaspoons cream of tartar
1½ teaspoons vanilla extract
½ teaspoon almond extract

Sift flour and ¾ cup of the sugar together 3 times. Beat egg whites with salt and cream of tartar in large bowl at high speed of mixer until light and fluffy. Sprinkle remaining sugar over egg whites, 2 tablespoons at a time, beating thoroughly after each addition. Continue beating until stiff peaks form. Fold in extracts. Sift dry ingredients, 2 tablespoons at a time, over beaten egg whites. Fold in gently but thoroughly with a wire whip or rubber spatula. Pour batter into ungreased tube pan (10 x 4 inches). Make sure that there is not a trace of any fat or grease in pan, or cake won't rise. Cut gently through batter to remove large air bubbles. Bake in preheated moderate oven (350°F.) for 40 to 50 minutes, or until crust is golden brown and cracks are very dry. Invert pan immediately and place on funnel or bottle. Cool cake in upside-down pan for at least 1 hour. Cut cake out of pan with a sharp knife. Using two forks, separate cake into pieces or slice with a sawing motion using a knife with serrated edge. Makes 10 to 12 servings.

ANGELICA (Archangelica officinalis)—
The name of this aromatic herb means

"heavenly" in Latin. Angelica is a tall stout perennial with widespread leaves and greenish-white or bluish flowers shaped like umbrellas. The plant is a native of northern Europe, but it is also found in Switzerland and the Pyrenees. Angelica was once considered a powerful protector against witches and fearsome creatures. In Elizabethan England it was used as an antidote for the plague.

All of its parts are aromatic. The dried roots and fruits flavor cakes, candies, beverages such as bitters, and liqueurs like Benedictine. The stems and leaf stalks are candied in sugar and used for decorating desserts because of their bright-green color and pleasant flavor. The oil is used for flavorings, perfumery, and in medicine.

It is not as readily available as other glacéed or candied fruits, but food specialty stores carry it. Since it has a tendency to dry out, it should be kept tightly wrapped in wax paper or aluminum foil.

ANGELICA AS A GARNISH

■ Garnish a ham for Christmas with a poinsettia made of stem and leaves cut from angelica, petals cut from pimiento.
■ Trim a Bavarian cream dessert with tiny cubes of angelica and whole candied cherries.
■ Decorate frosting on *petits fours* with bits of angelica, candied pineapple, silver dragées, and candied cherries.
■ Frost a coffeecake with a white confectioners' sugar icing and sprinkle with tiny pieces of angelica and chopped nuts.

ANISE (Pimpinella Anisum)—This culinary herb belongs to the parsley family. It grows to a height of about two feet, and has feathery leaves and tiny grayish-brown fruits which are dried for use. The plants and fruits have a distinctive licorice flavor. The dried fruits are called aniseed.

Anise is of Mediterranean origin and is one of the earliest aromatic plants to

be mentioned in history. The Hebrews, Greeks, and Romans valued anise for its reputed medicinal properties and the Emperor Charlemagne, who in the 8th century was interested in experimental farming, caused anise to be grown in his gardens in Germany. It has been popular ever since.

Anise is one of the best-liked flavorings in European cuisine. In Italy it is used in liqueurs; Germans and Scandinavians flavor their breads with aniseed. It goes into stews and seafood cocktails, and it enhances carrot, cauliflower, and beet dishes. Aniseed is also much used in baking and candy-making, particularly in licorice confections. The aniseed is sold as whole seeds.

To release the full flavor of the seeds in cooking, place them between two sheets of wax paper and crush them with a rolling pin.

SUGGESTED USES FOR ANISEED

■ **Appetizers, seafood-cocktail sauces**—Sprinkle top with ½ teaspoon crushed aniseed, or more to taste.
■ **Stews, pot roasts, baked pork chops, Chinese meat-and-vegetable combinations**—Cook ½ teaspoon whole aniseed, or more to taste, with other ingredients.
■ **Cream sauce**—Add ¼ teaspoon whole aniseed for each cup of sauce.
■ **Mild cheeses**—Blend whole aniseed to taste into cottage, cream cheese, grated Muenster, and other mild cheeses.
■ **In baking**—Substitute ½ to 1 teaspoon crushed aniseed for other flavorings. Or sprinkle crushed aniseed on top of cookies before baking. Or use ¼ to ½ teaspoon of the whole aniseeds in fruit pies instead of cinnamon or nutmeg.

CHINESE ROAST GOOSE

1 goose (8 to 10 pounds), oven-ready
⅔ cup soy sauce
¼ cup instant minced onion
¼ cup finely chopped celery
1 tablespoon sugar
½ teaspoon ground cinnamon
½ teaspoon garlic powder
¼ teaspoon crushed aniseed
4 cups water
¼ cup honey
¼ cup cider vinegar
1 tablespoon soy sauce
7 teaspoons salt
2 teaspoons cornstarch
2 tablespoons water

Wash goose and wipe dry, both inside and outside. Combine the next 7 ingredients with 2 cups of the water. Bring to boiling point. Tie goose's neck tightly with a string so sauce will not seep out while cooking. Pour hot sauce into body cavity, saving 2 tablespoons for later use. Sew vent tightly with strong thread to prevent sauce from bubbling out. Rub outside skin of goose with reserved 2 tablespoons sauce. Place goose on a rack, breast side up, in a roasting pan. Cook in preheated slow oven (325°F.) for 30 minutes. Then heat remaining water with honey, vinegar, the 1 tablespoon soy sauce, and salt. Brush over skin of bird. Continue cooking for 3 to 3¼ hours, basting goose with sauce at 30-minute intervals. Remove from oven, cut thread to open body cavity, and drain sauce into a saucepan. Blend cornstarch with water and add to sauce. Stir and cook for 1 to 2 minutes, or until sauce is slightly thick. Serve sauce separately. Makes 8 to 10 servings.

Note: Duck may be cooked in the same way. Reduce the amount of sauce in proportion to weight of duck.

SPRINGERLE

- 4 eggs
- 2 cups sugar
- 2 teaspoons crushed aniseed
- 3 to 3½ cups sifted all-purpose flour
- ½ teaspoon baking powder
  Whole aniseed (about 3 to 4 tablespoons)

Beat eggs until light. Gradually stir in sugar, beating well after each addition. Stir in aniseed. Sift flour with baking powder. Add about 3 cups of flour to mixture to make a stiff dough. If dough is too soft, add more flour, a little at a time. Dough should be stiff enough to roll out to ⅓-inch thickness. Flour springerle molds or roll. Press hard upon dough to get a good picture. Cut cookies apart. (These cookies are usually stamped with quaint wooden molds or rollers to make a picture. If you do not have a mold, cut the dough into ¾-inch by 2½-inch bars.) Grease cookie sheets and sprinkle each sheet with 1 tablespoon whole aniseed. Place cookies, picture side up, on cookie sheets. Let stand overnight in cool place to dry out. Bake in preheated slow oven (300°F.) for about 15 minutes, or until lower part of cookie is pale yellow. Makes about 5 dozen cookies.

ANNATTO—A yellowish-red vegetable dye made from the pulp around the seeds of a small tropical tree, *Bixa orellana*. The tree is a native of the Caribbean and grows also in Central and South America. Annatto is widely used in coloring cheese, especially Cheddar, and, to a lesser extent, butter.

ANTELOPE—The name of this ruminant mammal comes from the Greek and means "a horned animal." It is related to the ox but is smaller and lighter and more gracefully built. There are zoologically no true antelopes in the United States, although a distinct group native to Oregon is known to Americans as antelope. For cooking, antelope is classified as game. The meat is on the lean side and is usually larded before cooking. Antelope meat may be roasted, broiled, or braised.

ROAST SADDLE OF ANTELOPE

Wipe a saddle of antelope and lard it liberally with salt pork. Sprinkle with salt and pepper, rub with flour, and start in a hot oven at 450°F. for 25 minutes. Reduce heat to 300°F. and cook for 1½ hours longer, or until the meat thermometer reaches 135°F. to 150°F. for rare meat.

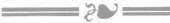

ANTIPASTO—An Italian word meaning literally "before the meal," *antipasto* is one or several foods served in small quantities as a first course. It is essential that the foods be attractively arranged. Antipasto is the Italian equivalent of French *hors-d'oeuvre* and American appetizers.

Antipasto can be very simple, such as slices of *prosciutto* rolled around melon wedges, or elaborate, as in fine restaurants, where dozens of foods are displayed in small dishes for the guest to choose from. For home use, *antipasto* can be arranged either on a big platter or on individual plates.

ANTIPASTO VARIATO

Preferably, use a large round platter. In center of the plate, place the contents of a can of solid pack tuna fish, drained. Coat fish with mayonnaise and sprinkle with drained capers. Arrange around tuna, in alternating rows radiating from the center, any of these: thin slices of hard salami, finger-length rolls of *prosciutto* or boiled ham, drained fillets of flat or rolled anchovies, artichoke hearts in oil (drained), pimientos cut into strips, radishes, thinly sliced fennel or celery hearts, hard-cooked eggs cut into quarters lengthwise, each topped with an anchovy fillet, and green and black olives. Serve olive oil and wine vinegar on the side.

CECI ALL' OLIO
(Chick-Peas in Olive Oil)

Use canned or home-cooked chick-peas, well drained. Sauté them in a little hot olive oil and sprinkle with a little garlic powder. Season to taste with salt and pepper. Serve from a relish dish.

MAIONESE DI SCAMPI E CAVOL FIORI
(Shrimp and Cauliflower Salad)

On a serving plate, arrange alternate layers of cooked, shelled, and deveined shrimps and cooked, drained, cold cauliflowerets. Cover with mayonnaise that has been thinned with a little lemon juice. Sprinkle with chopped parsley.

CAPONATINA

- 2 medium eggplants
- ¾ cup olive oil
- 2 onions, sliced
- ¼ cup tomato sauce
- 2 celery stalks, diced
- ¼ cup drained capers
- 6 green olives, pitted and cut into pieces
- 1 tablespoon pine nuts
- ¼ cup vinegar, preferably wine vinegar
- 2 tablespoons sugar

- ½ teaspoon salt
- ¼ teaspoon pepper

Peel and dice eggplant and fry in ½ cup of the olive oil until golden brown. Remove eggplant from skillet and reserve. Add remaining oil and onions and cook until onions are soft and golden. Add tomato sauce and celery. Cook until celery is tender, stirring occasionally. If necessary, add a little hot water to prevent sticking. Add capers, olives, pine nuts, and reserved eggplant. Heat vinegar and dissolve sugar in it. Add salt and pepper. Pour liquid over eggplant mixture. Simmer, covered, over very low heat for 20 minutes, stirring frequently. Cool before serving. This will keep for weeks in a covered jar in refrigerator. The recipe may easily be doubled and tripled. Makes 6 servings.

PICKLED GREEN PEPPERS

Put 3 or 4 large sweet green bell peppers under broiler and turn often until they blister. The tough skin can be peeled off easily with a sharp knife when peppers are held under running water. Or bake in moderate oven (375°F.) for 30 to 40 minutes and peel under running water. The first method is quicker. Cut peeled peppers into halves and remove cores and seeds. Then cut into strips about ½ inch wide. Place in a dish and pour over them a marinade made of 3 to 4 tablespoons fresh lemon or lime juice or wine vinegar, 3 to 4 tablespoons olive oil, and salt and freshly ground black pepper to taste. Cover and refrigerate for at least 2 hours before serving. These peppers will keep for 1 month, covered, in the refrigerator. Makes 6 to 8 servings.

TOMATO AND MUSHROOM SALAD

- 4 sliced chilled tomatoes
  Salt and pepper to taste
- 2 tablespoons olive oil
- ½ teaspoon fresh or dry crumbled basil or oregano
- 8 large mushrooms, sliced
- 1 to 2 teaspoons fresh lemon juice

Arrange tomatoes in overlapping rows on serving dish. Sprinkle with salt and pepper, 1 tablespoon of the olive oil, and basil or oregano. Arrange mushroom slices on tomatoes. Sprinkle with remaining tablespoon of olive oil and lemon juice. Makes 4 to 5 servings.

APÉRITIF by *James A. Beard*—*Apéritif* is a French word describing an alcoholic beverage taken before a meal to stimulate the appetite. In France and Italy an *apéritif* is usually a wine or a drink with a wine base, but elsewhere the word is often broadened to include such spirits as aquavit, or *akvavit,* to use the Scandinavian spelling of this Northern European favorite.

Most Europeans drink wine-based *apéritifs* at room temperature. Sometimes they dilute them with sparkling water. A popular American custom among those who prefer chilled *apéritifs* is to cool the wine in the refrigerator so that it need not be diluted with ice when served. *Apéritif* wines should never be shaken. If they must be iced quickly, they should be stirred over ice as one does a martini. The result is an *apéritif* frappé.

The French and Italian *apéritifs* are best known and usually ordered by their trade names. They can be described in four general classifications depending upon the predominant flavor or ingredient:

1. The Vermouth group
2. The Quinquina or quinine group
3. The Bitters group
4. The Absinthe group

Probably the most popular of the *apéritif* vermouths is Cinzano. This is actually a trade name that is becoming a generic word by usage; it is popularly used to include sweet vermouths made by a number of manufacturers. Europeans drink sweet vermouth straight without chilling it. Iced Cinzano is the American version.

Dry vermouth (an essential in the martini cocktail) is rarely served straight as an *apéritif*, but it is one of the ingredients of the Vermouth Cassis. This is a frappé composed of dry vermouth, *Crème de Cassis,* a strip of lemon peel, and a splash of sparkling water.

Among the quinquina *apéritifs,* the best known in the United States is Dubonnet. There is a subtle difference in the Dubonnet made in this country and that produced in Europe, and each has its own following. The blond variety of Dubonnet is an American specialty not found in France. St. Raphael is another well known quinquina drink, made from white wine, that is now produced in the United States. Both *apéritifs* are popularly drunk chilled or on-the-rocks, with a strip of lemon peel.

There are many other lesser known quinquinas. Some are heavily aromatized. Some are overly sweet by American standards. Among the most popular in Europe is a delicious light-bodied Bordeaux wine, Lillet, which is usually served chilled, on-the-rocks, or with a splash of sparkling water. Amer Picon is an *apéritif* liqueur generally consumed straight. Kina-Roc is similar to Dubonnet. Suze and Gentiane are highly flavored with gentian. Byrrh (not to be confused with beer) is a sweet *apéritif* with a red-wine base.

The family of *apéritif* bitters is perhaps best exemplified by Campari. This is usually drunk straight or with soda. Fernet Branca has a very low alcoholic content, and is usually combined with vermouth, orange juice, or lemonade, or

drunk straight to soothe a ruffled stomach.

Probably the most famous of all *apéritifs* is absinthe, a green liqueur with an aromatic licorice flavor. Absinthe made by the original formula contained the herb artemisia, or wormwood, and it is now banned in most countries because of its pernicious effects. Pernod is a popular French substitute, and there are also Spanish and Greek versions. Anisette is similar in flavor to absinthe but is somewhat sweeter. Several of the substitutes for absinthe are known by trade names, such as Oxygenée. *Apéritifs* in the absinthe family are customarily mixed with water and, even in Europe, ice is sometimes added.

Although *akvavit,* the high-proof national drink of Scandinavian countries, is generally taken with food, it is also regarded as a preprandial drink and is always served ice cold. The principal flavor is that of the caraway seed. Like *akvavit,* vodka as an appetizer is drunk straight and cold. It has no dominant flavor, tasting only of alcohol. Zubrowka, which is vodka flavored with aromatic grass, has a slightly bitter flavor. While vodka is generally regarded as a Russian drink, it is made throughout Northern Europe and also in the United States.

APICIUS—The author of the one and only Latin cookbook of antiquity, *The Roman Cookery Book,* that has come down to us. The book is extremely important, and also very entertaining, in telling us about the foods of the ancient Romans and how they were prepared, thus opening a window on the daily life of the ancient world. Apicius lived during the reign of Tiberius (B.C. 42-37 A.D.), at a time of the most incredible culinary extravagances, such as stews made entirely from songbirds' tongues. Apicius apparently also ran a cooking school. He committed suicide because he got into debt for spending too much money on food. Apparently he felt that the equivalent of several hundred thousand dollars which he had left would not be enough for him to live on. He was very highly regarded by his contemporaries.

À POINT—A French term meaning literally "to the point." In cooking, it refers to the perfect state of readiness of food as it is brought to the table.

Apéritif: Champagne Cassis

appetizers

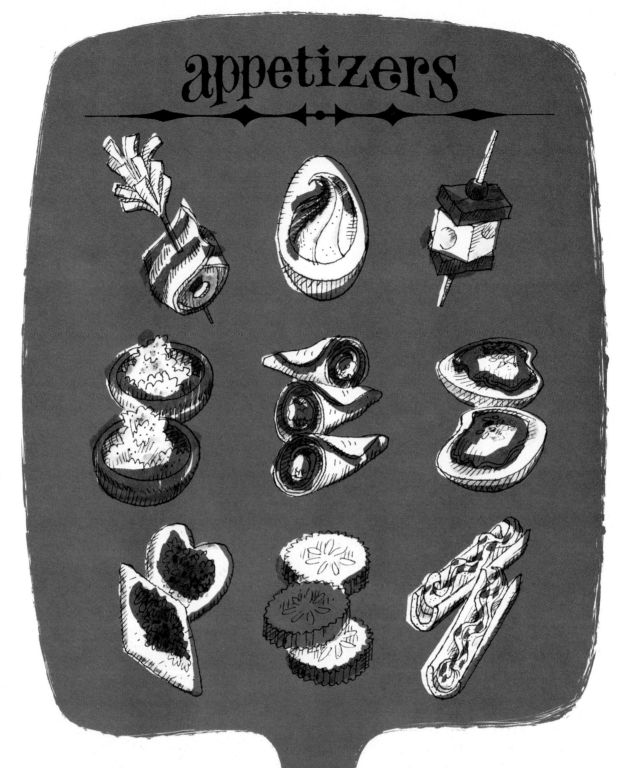

appetizers are small portions
a beverage before a meal or as the first
canapés, cocktails, dips, nibbles,
spreads, all of which somewhat
of hot or cold foods served with
course of a meal. The term includes
hors-d'oeuvre, relishes, and
overlap and are interchangeable.

APPETIZER

APPETIZER—A small portion of food served before, or as the first course of, a meal. Appetizers should be attractive in shape, color, and garnish, and have interesting flavor and texture combinations. Above all, they should not be too filling, since they are meant to stimulate, not to dull, the appetite for the meal that is to follow. Serve them always in small portions.

Apparently, appetizers have a basic appeal to human nature since every national cuisine features them. The Scandinavians have their *smörgåsbord* and open-faced sandwiches, the Slavs their *zakuska,* the Italians their *antipasto,* and the French their *hors-d'oeuvre.*

Appetizers provide the creative cook a first-class opportunity to produce food that is pretty. They can vary from simple canapés spread with a canapé butter and garnished with a sprig of parsley to elaborate hot creations. The garnishes should all be edible.

CANAPÉ

A French word meaning literally "a couch." In cookery, canapés are small hot or cold appetizers served on bread, crackers, or a pastry base so that they can be picked up with the fingers. Unlike hors-d'oeuvre which are served alone, canapés must have this base.

Canapés should be dainty and pleasing to look at. They must be served crisp and fresh, and they should be prepared just before serving. Canapés may be very simple, consisting of a cracker spread with a canapé butter and decorated with a little meat, fish, egg, or cheese, or a sprig of parsley or watercress, or a slice of pimiento, pickle, radish, olive, or lemon.

For canapés, use firm-textured bread or bread one day old. If not available, quickly partially freeze bread before cutting. White, rye, whole wheat, pumpernickel, and any breads trimmed free of crust are suitable for canapés, provided that bread and filling complement each other. Delicate crabmeat, for instance, is best served on white bread, a tangy cheese on dark bread. The breads can be cut into any fancy shapes with cookie cutters, or more simply into rounds, squares, diamonds, or fingers. Melba toast and plain or fancy crackers also make excellent bases for canapés. Allow about 4 to 6 canapés for each person.

COCKTAILS

Cocktails are appetizers that are served at the table with a sauce or dressing, and they are not to be confused with the potable alcoholic or nonalcoholic kinds. Seafood and fruit as well as vegetables are the ingredients most frequently used.

Shrimp cocktail, with a tangy sauce, is probably the favorite cocktail, especially before a steak dinner. Cocktails are always cold; most of them should be well chilled.

DIPS OR DUNKS

These savory mixtures are soft enough to be scooped up with crackers, potato chips, or vegetables without the aid of a spoon or knife. They are the quickest and easiest of appetizers. Dips are better suited to small groups than to large ones. They are typically American and not known in European entertaining.

Dips can be hot or cold. They should be firm enough so that they will not drip on clothes and carpets. Napkins should be available when dips are served.

Among the foods to be dipped are crackers, potato chips, narrow toast strips, corn chips, cooked shrimps, cocktail frankfurters, iced cucumber strips, mushrooms, Belgian endive blades, iced green-pepper strips, cauliflowerets, carrot sticks, radishes, celery sticks, and pretzels. All should be crisp and firm.

Dips may be very attractively served in big scooped-out apples, scooped-out eggplant, avocado, or red or green cabbages, or in a scooped-out pineapple.

HORS-D'OEUVRE

These words mean literally "outside the work." Hors-d'oeuvre are cold or hot appetizers that, unlike canapés, do not have bread or crackers as the base for other foods. Hors-d'oeuvre are usually eaten at the table, with a knife and fork, before the main part of the meal.

The hors-d'oeuvre should not repeat the ingredients of the main dish, or be too similar to it. If you're serving fish, avoid seafood hors-d'oeuvre; if you're having pork, do not serve bacon hors-d'oeuvre.

Hors-d'oeuvre can be served singly, or they can be varied. It is essential that they should be attractively arranged. It is easier to arrange hors-d'oeuvre prettily in several small dishes than on one large one. The small dishes can be grouped on a tray or a lazy susan. Hors-d'oeuvre can also be arranged on individual plates. Parsley sprigs, watercress, radish slices, thin lemon twists, and pickles are good garnishes. The food should look pleasing, but should not be tortured into fancy shapes.

An immense variety of foods is suited for hors-d'oeuvre, provided the selections are served in small quantities. Among these are aspics, salads, caviar, pâtés, eggs, small skewered foods, mayonnaise-dressed eggs, fish, or meats, chicken livers, artichokes, asparagus, vegetables *à la grecque,* and salads that are not sweet.

NIBBLES OR TIDBITS

These colloquial expressions are often used to name appetizers that can be picked up with the fingers or with a cocktail fork or toothpick. Almonds and other nuts, some of the relishes, bits of cheese, are often referred to in this way.

An attractive way of serving nibbles is to stud a pineapple, grapefruit, or red cabbage with tidbits on toothpicks.

RELISHES

Relishes include cold and crisp vegetables and other foods such as cottage cheese and preserves. They are usually served from a platter, and often on a bed of crushed ice to preserve crispness. Certain relishes, such as celery, carrots, scallions, pickles, and olives, may be left on the table during dinner.

In days past, relishes used to be more popular than now, especially with farm families. Old-timers relate the glory of a midwestern farm table set with a score of homemade relishes. Relishes are still the pride of Pennsylvania Dutch cooking. There they are colloquially called "the seven sweets and seven sours," although literal-minded souls should not always expect to find fourteen relishes on the table.

SPREADS

These are mixtures firmer than dips, and to be spread, as the name suggests, on crackers, bread, or toast with a knife or spoon.

COLD CANAPÉS

CANAPÉ BUTTERS

These savory butters add flavor to canapés and some of them may be used without additional spreads. Tightly covered, they keep well in the refrigerator. If the canapé butter is too hard to spread on the base, cream for desired consistency.

Cream ¼ cup butter with any of the following:

Anchovy Butter—Use 1 to 2 teaspoons anchovy paste or mashed anchovy fillets and ½ teaspoon fresh lemon juice. Good with a slice of hard-cooked egg.

Caper Butter—Use 1 tablespoon finely minced drained capers.

Chili Butter—Use 1 to 2 tablespoons chili sauce.

Chive Butter—Use 1 tablespoon finely minced chives or green onion tops and 1 teaspoon fresh lemon juice.

Chutney Butter—Use 1 tablespoon chutney. Good with ham and meats.

Curry Butter—Use ¼ to ½ teaspoon

curry powder. Good with fish.

Egg Butter—Use 2 mashed hard-cooked eggs, a dash of hot pepper sauce, and salt and pepper to taste. Good with vegetables.

Garlic Butter—Use 1 small garlic clove, mashed.

Horseradish Butter—Use 1 to 2 tablespoons drained bottled horseradish. Good with meats and cheese.

Onion Butter—Use 1 teaspoon mashed onion or onion juice.

Parmesan Butter—Use 2 tablespoons grated Parmesan or Romano cheese. Good with eggs and meat.

Parsley Butter—Use 2 tablespoons finely minced parsley.

Pâté Butter—Use 2 tablespoons mashed liverwurst or any canned pâté. Good by itself. Or decorate with watercress or radish slice.

Pickle Butter—Use 1 to 2 tablespoons minced pickle. Good with meats.

Sardine Butter—Use 2 tablespoons mashed sardines and ½ teaspoon each of fresh lemon juice and minced onion.

Shrimp Butter—Use 2 tablespoons ground or mashed cooked shrimp and ½ teaspoon fresh lemon juice. Serve with an additional shrimp or a slice of hard-cooked egg.

Tarragon Butter—Use ½ teaspoon finely chopped dried or fresh tarragon and a few drops of tarragon vinegar (optional). Good with fish or chicken.

Watercress Butter—Use 2 tablespoons finely chopped watercress and 1 teaspoon fresh lemon juice. Serve as is, with a few additional sprigs of watercress.

These recipes make ¼ to ⅓ cup.

CHEESE CANAPÉS

Blue Cheese Spread—Cream equal parts of blue cheese and sweet butter. Spread on crisp crackers.

Camembert Cheese Spread—Cream equal parts of Camembert and sweet butter. Spread on toast rounds. Sprinkle with chopped walnuts.

Cottage-Cheese Spread—Top toast rounds with cottage cheese mixed with chopped tongue or ham or crisp bacon. Garnish with slice of stuffed olive.

Simple Cheese Spread—Cream together 1 cup shredded cheese (Swiss, Cheddar, cheese food, etc.), and ½ cup butter. Spread on rye or other dark bread and place under broiler until slightly browned. Or serve as is, topped with a radish slice. Makes about ¾ cup.

Tiny Cheese Sandwiches—Spread crust-trimmed cracked-wheat bread with mayonnaise. Make sandwiches with bread and slices of cheese, sprinkled with pepper. Cut each sandwich into 4 squares. Dip ends of tiny pickled onions in paprika.

Fasten onions on sandwiches with toothpicks.

DANISH BEEF CANAPÉS

Butter thin slices of tiny rye-bread rounds. Top with thin slices of cold rare roast beef and paper-thin onions, fried crisp and dark brown.

FRANKFURTER ROUNDS

Cut end from unsplit frankfurter roll. With fork, hollow out enough center to hold a frankfurter. Spread hollow generously with mustard. Insert cooked frankfurter. Wrap in wax paper and chill. Cut into slices; dot each slice with a bit of pickle relish.

PEANUT-ONION CANAPÉS

Spread rounds of toast with peanut butter. Put a tiny white onion ring on each, a dot of ketchup in the middle.

SARDINE ROUNDS

Spread rounds of white bread with sardines mashed with lemon juice and mayonnaise. Garnish with cucumber slice, pimiento, and parsley.

SALAMI-EGG CANAPÉS

Cut sandwich rolls into thin crosswise slices. Butter. Cover each piece with slice of salami. Spread egg salad to within ½ inch of edge. Put 1 teaspoon caviar in center. Border egg with minced green onion. Cut into 6 wedges.

HOT CANAPÉS

BAHAMIAN TOMATO CANAPÉS

3 or 4 small ripe tomatoes
12 to 16 bread rounds
Butter
Bahamian or other sharp mustard
¾ cup mayonnaise (about)

Slice tomatoes about ¼ inch thick. Cut bread rounds as nearly as possible to match size of tomato slices; sauté bread in butter until golden. Put tomato slice on each round and spread lightly with mustard. Spread generously with mayonnaise. Broil until mayonnaise puffs up and browns. Makes 12 to 16.

CRAB CANAPÉS

2 cups crabmeat
¼ cup mayonnaise (approximately)
¼ teaspoon Worcestershire
1 large cucumber
Salt and pepper
24 small bread rounds, sautéed
Parsley, drained capers, and pimiento

Remove cartilage carefully and shred crabmeat fine. Mix with enough mayonnaise to hold it together. Season with Worcestershire. Peel cucumber and chop very fine. Season lightly with salt and pepper. Spread a thin layer of cucumber on each bread round. Cover with a mound of crabmeat, well smoothed.

Place under the broiler to brown lightly. Decorate with parsley sprigs, drained capers, pimiento strips. Makes about 24.

TOMATO CAVIAR

3½ cups (one 1-pound, 12-ounce can) tomatoes
1 package (3 ounces) cream cheese
1 tablespoon cream (about)
1 tablespoon onion juice
24 bread rounds, sautéed
¼ cup mayonnaise (about)
1 small jar red caviar

Drain tomatoes for at least 2 hours; reserve juice for other purposes. Blend cheese with enough cream to make it spreadable; mix in onion juice. Spread each sautéed bread round with cheese. Mash tomatoes and spread a little over cheese on each round. Cover with mayonnaise. Put a few dots of red caviar in the center of each round. Makes 2 dozen.

HOT CHUTNEY AND BACON FINGERS

20 to 24 toast fingers
10 to 12 slices of bacon
1 cup well drained chutney, chopped fine

Cut toast fingers the width of a bacon slice and half the length. Cut bacon slices in half crosswise; fry over low heat until half done, but not brown. Spread chutney on toast fingers and top each with half slice of bacon. Broil 5 inches from heat until bacon is crisp. Serve hot. Makes 20 to 24.

SAVORY CANAPÉS

2 hard-cooked eggs
2 tablespoons minced pimiento
¼ teaspoon dry mustard
1 tablespoon grated Parmesan cheese
¼ teaspoon salt
1 tablespoon minced parsley
¼ cup butter or margarine
Ketchup to moisten
12 to 14 small toast rounds

Shell eggs; chop fine. Mix with next 7 ingredients, using just enough ketchup to moisten and hold the rest together. Spread on toast rounds. Place in preheated very hot oven (450°F.) for 5 minutes. Makes 12 to 14.

COCKTAILS

CRABMEAT OR SHRIMP RÉMOULADE

1 pound cooked flaked crabmeat, or cooked, shelled, and deveined shrimps
6 lettuce cups
1 cup mayonnaise
1 tablespoon minced sweet pickle
1 tablespoon drained capers
1 tablespoon prepared mustard
1 tablespoon minced parsley
1 teaspoon minced onion
⅛ teaspoon each of salt and pepper

Place crabmeat or shrimps in lettuce cups. Combine all other ingredients and blend well. Spoon over seafood. Chill before serving. Makes 6 servings.

SHRIMP COCKTAIL SAUCE WITH MUSTARD

2 tablespoons cider vinegar
6 tablespoons olive oil
3 tablespoons prepared mustard, such as Dijon mustard
1 small garlic clove, minced
3 anchovy fillets, minced
½ teaspoon salt
1 tablespoon minced chives or scallion tops
1 tablespoon minced parsley
1 hard-cooked egg, mashed

Combine all ingredients and blend well. Chill, and serve with cooked, shelled, deveined shrimps. Makes about ¾ cup.

DICED-CUCUMBER COCKTAIL

2 large cucumbers
¼ cup ketchup
¼ cup chili sauce
1 teaspoon Worcestershire
  Juice of ½ lemon
1 teaspoon prepared white horseradish
  Dash of hot pepper sauce or cayenne
4 lettuce leaves

Chill cucumbers. Combine remaining ingredients, except lettuce, to make sauce; chill. Just before serving, peel cucumbers. Make lengthwise parallel grooves with tines of fork. Dice into ¼-inch pieces. Place on lettuce leaves in cocktail glasses. Top with sauce. Makes 4 servings.

FRESH PEACH COCKTAIL

2½ cups diced peeled ripe fresh peaches
1 tablespoon fresh lemon juice
2 tablespoons sugar
  Chilled ginger ale
  Fresh mint

Combine peaches, lemon juice, and sugar. Fill sherbet glasses; add 1 to 2 tablespoons ginger ale to each glass. Garnish with sprig of mint. Makes 4 servings.

WATERMELON COCKTAIL

Make watermelon balls with melon-ball scoop, or cut into 1-inch cubes, removing seeds. Sprinkle melon with lemon juice and superfine sugar, using ½ tablespoon lemon juice and 1 tablespoon superfine sugar for each portion. Cover and chill. Serve in cocktail glasses; garnish with fresh mint.

DIPS

CREAM-CHEESE AND CLAM DIP

1 package (8 ounces) cream cheese
1 can (10½ ounces) minced clams
½ small onion, grated
1 teaspoon Worcestershire
  Dash of garlic salt
1 teaspoon celery salt

Let cheese soften at room temperature. Drain clams, reserving liquid. Add cheese, remaining ingredients, and 2 tablespoons reserved clam liquid. Blend thoroughly; chill. Serve with pretzel sticks or Melba toast. Makes about 1½ cups.

TWO-CHEESE DIP

1 package (8 ounces) blue cheese
1 package (8 ounces) cream cheese
½ cup undiluted evaporated milk
  Dash of garlic salt
¾ teaspoon celery seed
  Pimiento or green pepper, chopped

Combine cheeses, milk, and seasonings; beat together until fluffy. Chill in refrigerator. To serve, pile dip in serving dishes and garnish with pimiento or green pepper. Makes 3 cups.

CHILI DIP

1 cup dairy sour cream
1 tablespoon chopped fresh basil or
  1 teaspoon crumbled dried basil
1 teaspoon paprika
½ teaspoon chili powder
  Salt to taste

Mix all ingredients well and chill. Serve with raw vegetable sticks. Makes 1 cup.

EAST INDIAN DIP

½ cup orange marmalade
3 tablespoons cider vinegar
2 tablespoons granulated sugar
1 tablespoon brown sugar
½ teaspoon salt
¼ teaspoon curry powder
¼ teaspoon ground ginger
1½ teaspoons Worcestershire
⅓ cup dairy sour cream

Combine all ingredients except sour cream in saucepan. Bring to boil. Simmer, stirring constantly, until sauce is blended. Let cool. Mix with sour cream. This keeps very well in refrigerator, thickening somewhat as it stands. Makes about 1 cup.

RÉMOULADE DIP FOR SCALLOPS OR SHRIMPS

2 cups mayonnaise
1 garlic clove, crushed
1 tablespoon prepared mustard
1 tablespoon chopped drained capers
1 tablespoon minced parsley
2 teaspoons minced chives

Blend all ingredients; chill. Serve in a bowl on a large plate, surrounded by cooked and chilled scallops or shrimps, speared with toothpicks. Makes about 2 cups.

RAW VEGETABLE TRAY OR BOWL

Choose any vegetables you like to eat raw, in good variety. Carrot sticks, green and red sweet-pepper sticks, cauliflower broken into flowerets, celery stalks, leaves of Belgian endive, radish roses, and tiny plum or cherry tomatoes are all beautiful and delicious. They should be served crisply cold and prettily arranged on a tray or in a bowl of crushed ice, accompanied by a dish of seasoned salt, a dish of plain salt, and a dip.

MUSTARD DIP FOR RAW VEGETABLES

¼ cup mayonnaise
3 tablespoons heavy cream
2 tablespoons prepared mustard
1 teaspoon Worcestershire

2 teaspoons fresh lemon juice
  Salt and pepper
  Dash of hot pepper sauce

Combine all ingredients and chill before serving. Makes about ¾ cup.

HORS-D'OEUVRE

HERRING AND APPLES IN SOUR CREAM

1 jar (16 ounces) herring fillets
1 cup dairy sour cream
2 tablespoons fresh lemon juice
1 medium onion, finely chopped
1 teaspoon salt
½ teaspoon pepper
2 medium unpeeled apples, cored and diced

Drain herring and cut into bite-size pieces if necessary. Whip sour cream until it stands in soft peaks. Blend sour cream with herring and all other ingredients. Toss to blend well. Chill before serving. Serve on lettuce leaves. Makes 6 to 8 servings.

SALMON-STUFFED EGGS

10 hard-cooked eggs
½ cup cooked or canned drained and boned salmon
1 anchovy fillet
½ cup butter or margarine
1 teaspoon Worcestershire

Shell eggs and cut into halves lengthwise. Take out yolks. Rub salmon, anchovy, and egg yolks through a sieve, or whirl in a blender. Cream butter. Add salmon mixture, Worcestershire, and seasonings to taste. Mix well. Stuff whites with mixture. Makes 20.

CHEESE TARTLETS

2 tablespoons butter
2 tablespoons flour
1 cup light cream
1 cup grated Swiss or Parmesan cheese
  Dash of cayenne
24 tiny tart shells, about 1½ inches across, baked

Melt butter. Blend in flour smoothly. Add cream and stir until thickened. Remove from heat. Add cheese and stir until melted. Add cayenne. Fill baked tart shells. Place under broiler 2 to 3 inches from heat until cheese is brown. Serve piping hot and bubbling brown. Makes 24.

RUMAKI

8 chicken livers
8 water chestnuts
8 slices of bacon
  Onion powder
½ cup soy sauce
¼ cup mirin (sweet sake) or sherry
4 red chilies, ground
1 garlic clove, mashed
1 slice of green gingerroot, minced
½ teaspoon ground turmeric

Cut chicken livers, water chestnuts, and bacon slices into halves. Sprinkle each piece of chicken liver with onion powder and fold it around a slice of water chest-

nut. Wrap bundle in a half slice of bacon. Impale with toothpick, being sure the pick goes through center of water chestnut. Mix soy sauce, mirin, and seasonings. Put bundles in mixture to marinate for at least 1 hour. Drain. Broil until bacon is crisp, turning to brown all sides. This recipe comes from the Orient. Makes 16.

ENDIVE TEMPURA

Mix together lightly 1 cup flour, 1 cup water, and 1 egg. The batter should be lumpy, like muffin batter. Add salt, if desired. Dip washed and dried leaves from 2 heads Belgian endive into batter and fry in hot deep fat (360°F. on a frying thermometer) until batter is golden brown, about 2 to 3 minutes. Drain and serve at once. Use soy sauce as a dip. Makes 3 to 4 servings.

MUSHROOM BEIGNETS

½ cup water
¼ cup butter or margarine
Dash of salt
½ cup sifted all-purpose flour
2 eggs
Mushroom Filling

Put water, butter, and salt in a small saucepan and bring to a boil. Add flour all at once. Stir hard, cooking until mixture leaves sides of pan and forms a ball. Beat in eggs, one at a time. Beat until mixture is thick and shiny. Using 2 teaspoons, shape little rounds of mixture (about 1 teaspoon each) and place 2 inches apart on ungreased baking sheet. Bake in preheated very hot oven (450° F.) for 15 minutes; lower heat to moderate (350°F.) and bake for 20 minutes longer. Cool. Slit puff shells on one side and fill with Mushroom Filling. Makes about 4 dozen.

Mushroom Filling

½ pound fresh mushrooms
1 tablespoon butter
1 tablespoon flour
½ cup heavy cream
¼ teaspoon curry powder
Salt and pepper

Stem mushrooms. (Use stems in sauce or soup at another time.) Chop mushrooms fine. Sauté mushrooms in butter for about 5 minutes. Sprinkle flour evenly over the mushrooms and stir until smooth. Gradually stir in heavy cream. Stir over low heat until thickened. Add curry powder, and salt and pepper to taste. Makes enough filling for about 4 dozen beignets.

CUBED COLD CUTS WITH TIERED FRUIT SALAD

Buy thick slices of olive loaf, liverwurst, bologna, salami, or other cold cuts; cut into cubes. Arrange slices of fresh pineapple on chicory or other salad greens and top each with pieces of fresh fruit (banana, plum, pear, nectarine, strawberries, etc.). Garnish with sprigs of mint, if desired. Serve with Whipped-Cream Dressing: Combine equal parts of mayonnaise and whipped heavy cream. Insert cubed cold cuts on toothpicks in a whole Edam cheese or a grapefruit.

CORNUCOPIAS OF COLD CUTS WITH TWO-CHEESE MOLDS AND MIXED FRUIT

Soften 1 envelope unflavored gelatin in ¼ cup water. Dissolve over hot water. Beat well: 1 pound creamed cottage cheese, ¼ cup crumbled blue cheese, ¼ teaspoon salt, ⅛ teaspoon paprika, dash of cayenne, and ½ cup milk or cream. Beat in dissolved gelatin. Put into 4 individual molds or one large mold. Refrigerate for several hours. Unmold and garnish with pimiento strips. Arrange on a bed of lettuce and watercress with cooked salami, pressed ham, or other cold cuts, rolled into cornucopias. Serve with chilled mixed fruit. Makes 4 servings.

NIBBLES

ALMONDS

Salted, deviled, or fried almonds make excellent nibbles.

CHEESE BOARD

Offer a board with several varieties of cheese to please all tastes; for example, a cheese board might contain a mild Cheddar, Swiss, Edam, Muenster, or any cheese which can be cubed and speared on toothpicks. Serve with simple crackers and cubes of fresh fruit.

STUFFED CELERY

Fill trimmed celery stalks with highly seasoned cottage cheese; serve. Or two filled stalks can be pressed together, chilled, and cut into ½-inch slices.

CUCUMBER SLICES

Slice cucumbers ¼ inch thick and spread with cottage cheese seasoned with a little anchovy paste.

GARLIC RIPE OLIVES

1 can (8½ ounces) large ripe olives
⅔ cup salad oil
⅓ cup cider vinegar
1 small garlic clove, minced

Drain olives. To olives, add mixture of remaining ingredients. Cover and chill. Save marinating liquid and use it for salad dressings.

OLIVES IN CHEESE

1 package (3 ounces) cream cheese
½ teaspoon Worcestershire
Cream
16 small stuffed olives, drained and dried
¼ pound salted almonds, chopped

Mix cheese and Worcestershire together with enough cream to make a thick smooth paste. Coat olives with mixture; roll in almonds. Chill. Makes 16.

CLAM BITES

1 egg, separated
1 can (10½ ounces) minced clams
1 teaspoon melted butter
½ cup all-purpose flour
Salt and pepper

Beat egg yolk until light. Drain clams, reserving liquid. Stir into egg yolk the butter, flour, ¼ teaspoon salt, and ¼ cup clam liquid. Add milk, if necessary, to make ¼ cup. Fold in stiffly beaten egg white. Add clams and let stand for at least 1 hour at room temperature. Drop by teaspoons into hot deep fat (375°F. on a frying thermometer) and fry until golden brown, 5 to 6 minutes. Drain on absorbent paper. Sprinkle with salt and pepper and serve hot on toothpicks. Fry these at the last minute before serving. Makes about 2 dozen.

MARINATED MUSHROOMS

1 pound small mushrooms
2 tablespoons olive oil
½ cup French dressing
1 garlic clove, halved

Lightly brown mushrooms in olive oil. Cover with French dressing; add garlic. Marinate for a few hours or overnight in refrigerator. Serve on toothpicks. Makes 4 to 6 servings.

OLIVES, CALIFORNIA STYLE

1 can (8½ ounces) ripe olives or
1 jar (10 ounces) green olives
3 lemon slices
2 garlic cloves, halved
½ cup olive oil

Drain brine from olives. Put in jar with remaining ingredients and cover tightly. Invert jar 2 or 3 times so olives will be coated with oil. Let stand for several hours. Chill slightly before serving.

POTATOES MAYONNAISE

3 medium potatoes
2 tablespoons dairy sour cream
½ cup mayonnaise
Dash of curry
Salt and pepper to taste

Boil potatoes in jackets. Do not overcook, as they must not be mushy. Cool potatoes. Peel and cut into small cubes. Mix remaining ingredients. Carefully coat cubes with mixture. Serve with toothpicks. Makes 3 to 4 dozen.

RELISHES

TOMATO APPETIZER

3 medium tomatoes, peeled and chopped
1 small green pepper, minced
⅓ cup diced celery
1 small onion, minced
1½ teaspoons salt
2 tablespoons cider vinegar

2 tablespoons sugar
½ cup cold water
⅛ teaspoon pepper

Mix all ingredients and chill for several hours. Makes 4 servings.

BEET AND CUCUMBER RELISH

2 cups cooked beets, coarsely shredded
    and drained
¼ cup beet cooking liquid
¼ cup cider vinegar
1 cup diced peeled cucumber
1 small onion, grated
3 tablespoons sugar
¼ teaspoon salt
    Dash of pepper
1 tablespoon chopped parsley or fresh
    dill

Thoroughly mix all ingredients except parsley. Cover, and store in refrigerator for several hours. Add parsley or dill just before serving. Makes 3½ cups.

REFRIGERATOR SUMMER RELISH

4 cups peeled chopped ripe tomatoes,
    drained
1½ cups finely chopped celery
1 cup finely chopped onion
1 unpeeled apple, chopped
2 tablespoons prepared white
    horseradish
2 tablespoons salt
2 tablespoons mustard seed
⅓ cup firmly packed brown sugar
½ teaspoon ground cinnamon
¼ teaspoon each of ground cloves and
    mace
    Dash of cayenne
1½ cups cider vinegar

Mix all ingredients thoroughly. Cover, and store in refrigerator. If relish is too juicy, drain off some liquid. This will keep for several weeks. Makes 1½ quarts.

PENNSYLVANIA DUTCH CHOWCHOW

2 cups each of:
    Sliced unpeeled cucumbers
    Chopped sweet peppers
    Chopped white cabbage
    Sliced yellow onions
    Chopped unpeeled green tomatoes
    Lima beans
    Cut green beans
    Sliced carrots
    Chopped celery
2 tablespoons celery seed
4 teaspoons mustard seed
4 cups cider vinegar
2 cups water
4 cups sugar
¼ cup ground turmeric

Soak cucumbers, peppers, cabbage, onions, and tomatoes in salted water overnight. Use ¼ cup salt for each quart of water. Cook Lima beans, green beans, carrots, and celery until barely tender. Drain *all* vegetables well. Mix soaked and cooked vegetables with remaining ingredients. Bring to boil, lower heat, and simmer gently for 10 minutes. Place while hot in hot sterilized jars and seal at once. Makes 8 to 10 pints.

CUCUMBER-ONION RELISH

3 large cucumbers
1½ teaspoons salt
1 onion, minced
½ teaspoon pepper
1 cup white vinegar
½ pimiento, chopped

Peel cucumbers, cut into halves lengthwise, and scoop out seeds with teaspoon. Discard seeds. Put cucumbers through food chopper, using coarse blade. Combine with salt. Let drain for 1 hour in colander. Add remaining ingredients. Cover and store in refrigerator. This will keep for several weeks. Stir every 2 or 3 days. Makes about 3 cups.

PICKLED COOKED MUSHROOMS

Steam or boil 2 pounds mushrooms in salted water for 15 to 20 minutes, or until tender; drain and put in large jar. Add ½ lemon, sliced, 1 bay leaf, and 1 onion, sliced, if desired. While mushrooms are still hot, pour over them the following marinade:

½ cup mixed pickling spice
2 cups white or wine vinegar
1 teaspoon salt, or more to taste
1 teaspoon sugar
1½ cups oil (use part olive oil, if possible)
1 garlic clove, halved

Mix pickling spice with vinegar. Add salt and sugar, bring to boil, and strain over mushrooms. Cool. Add oil and garlic. Keep in refrigerator. Shake jar well 2 or 3 times a day. Add more salt, if necessary, after 24 hours. Do not use for 2 or 3 days. These mushrooms will keep for 1 month in covered jar in refrigerator. Makes 8 servings.

SPREADS

WALNUT SPREAD

½ cup shelled walnuts
2 garlic cloves, crushed
2 slices of bread, crusts removed
1½ teaspoons cider vinegar
1 teaspoon olive oil
    Salt

Pound walnuts in a mortar or whirl in a blender. Add garlic and mix well. Soak bread in water. Squeeze out water and mix bread well with nuts and garlic, until you have formed a paste. Add vinegar and oil slowly, mixing well; season with salt. Serve with toast or crackers. Makes about ½ cup.

LIPTAUER CHEESE

2 packages (3 ounces each) cream
    cheese
½ cup sweet butter
2 tablespoons chopped drained capers
1 teaspoon salt
1 teaspoon anchovy paste
½ teaspoon minced onion

1 teaspoon dry mustard
1½ teaspoons paprika
    Dairy sour cream
    Whole drained capers
    Paprika

Cream cheese and butter together. Add other ingredients except last two. Mix well, using just enough sour cream to make mixture smooth and spreadable. Chill thoroughly. Serve in a mound decorated with whole capers and paprika. Surround with crisp crackers. Makes about 1 cup.

PORK PÂTÉ

1 pound raw pork liver
1 pound raw lean pork
1 tablespoon flour
1 egg
1 onion, minced
2 tablespoons minced parsley
¼ teaspoon crumbled dried thyme
¼ teaspoon rubbed dried sage
1 teaspoon salt
    Pepper
    Dash each of ground nutmeg, mace,
    and cloves
½ pound fat salt pork, sliced very thin
¼ cup (2 ounces) brandy
1 bay leaf

Grind liver and pork fine. Work flour into mixture well. Add egg, onion, parsley, herbs, seasonings, and spices; mix well. Line bottom and sides of pâté mold or deep casserole with slices of salt pork. Pour in half of pâté mixture. Put over it a layer of salt-pork slices. Fill with remaining pâté. Pour brandy over pâté. Cover top completely with salt-pork slices. Put bay leaf on top and put on cover. Seal edges of cover with a thick flour-and-water paste to prevent steam from escaping. Place in pan of hot water and bake in preheated slow oven (300° F.) for 3½ hours. Remove from oven and let sealed pot stand until cold. Then crack off seal and chill. Serve with toast points. Makes 8 to 10 servings.

EGGPLANT CAVIAR

1 eggplant
1 large yellow onion
1 garlic clove
2 large tomatoes
½ cup olive oil
1 teaspoon salt
    Pepper to taste
½ teaspoon sugar

Wash eggplant and bake in moderate oven (375° F.) until outside is black and inside soft, about 45 minutes. Run cold water over it. Peel carefully and dice. Peel onion, garlic, and tomatoes; chop well. Mix with eggplant. Add remaining ingredients; mix thoroughly. Chill well before serving with crackers or toast. Makes 6 to 8 servings.

*The apple, Pyrus Malus, to give it its proper botanical name,
grows on a round-crowned tree that rarely gets taller than 40 feet and
that may live to a hundred years. It is the most important
and most widely cultivated tree of the temperate zones,
and it has been grown for over 3,000 years in its native
region of eastern Europe and western Asia.*

Fresh Apple Chart

Note: *In chart, "cooking" indicates general cooking, and when apples are particularly good for pie or sauce, this is mentioned. "Eating" means the apples are especially suitable for eating out-of-hand, in salads or appetizers, any way they are served uncooked. Recipes follow the same terminology.*

YELLOW TRANSPARENT
Season—July-August
Characteristics—Greenish white to greenish yellow; white flesh; juicy, tart
Uses—Eating, cooking: sauce and pie

GRAVENSTEIN
Season—July-September
Characteristics—Yellow or green with red stripes; yellowish flesh; juicy, slightly tart
Uses—Eating, cooking

STARR
Season—August-September
Characteristics—Green or red flesh tinged with yellow; very juicy, tart
Uses—Eating, cooking

WEALTHY
Season—August-December
Characteristics—Bright red, striped; white flesh, sometimes stained with red; juicy
Uses—Eating, cooking

TWENTY OUNCE
Season—September-November
Characteristics—Greenish to yellow skin with red stripes; white flesh, sometimes tinged with yellow; juicy, slightly tart
Use—Cooking

McINTOSH
Season—October-February
Characteristics—Bright deep red, striped with carmine; white flesh; juicy, slightly tart becoming mild and nearly sweet when ripe
Uses—Eating, cooking: sauce, pie, and baking

GRIMES GOLDEN
Season—October-January
Characteristics—Deep yellow skin with small dark specks; yellow flesh; moderately juicy, sweet
Uses—Eating, salad

YORK IMPERIAL
Season—October-March
Characteristics—Red over yellow ground; usually lopsided; yellowish flesh; slightly tart, then flat at end of season
Uses—Cooking: pie and baking

JONATHAN
Season—September-February
Characteristics—Bright red skin; flesh is white or slightly yellow, sometimes tinged with red; juicy and slightly tart
Uses—Eating, cooking: pie

RHODE ISLAND GREENING
Season—October-February
Characteristics—Green or yellowish; yellowish flesh; juicy, slightly tart
Uses—Cooking: pie and baking

NORTHERN SPY
Season—October-March
Characteristics—Bright red, stripes over yellow; yellowish flesh; very juicy
Uses—Eating, cooking: pie, sauce, and baking

DELICIOUS, RED
Season—September-April
Characteristics—Bright red, solid or striped, 5 points at blossom end; yellowish-white flesh; juicy, very mildly tart
Use—Eating

DELICIOUS, GOLDEN
Season—October-April
Characteristics—Yellow or golden skin; yellowish-white flesh; juicy and sweet
Uses—Eating, salad

STAYMAN
Season—November-April
Characteristics—Dull red-striped; white flesh tinged with yellow; juicy and slightly tart
Uses—Eating, all cooking

BALDWIN
Season—November-April
Characteristics—Red, mottled with bright red; yellowish flesh; juicy, mildly tart
Uses—Eating, salad, cooking

WINESAP
Season—January-May
Characteristics—Bright deep red; flesh tinged with yellow; very juicy, slightly tart
Uses—Eating, cooking: pie

NEWTON PIPPIN (Albemarle)
Season—January-May
Characteristics—Greenish yellow to yellow; flesh is tinged with yellow; juicy, mildly tart
Uses—All cooking

ROME BEAUTY
Season—November-May
Characteristics—Yellow mingled with red; flesh is white with slight yellow or greenish tinge; juicy, mildly tart.
Uses—Baking, cooking

CRABAPPLE
Season—Fall
Characteristics—In its widest sense, a small wild apple, but varieties are cultivated for acidity and tartness in cooking and showy fruit for decoration
Uses—Jellies, preserves, decoration in fruit bowl

Sautéed Apples, Onions, and Raisins

Party Apple Salad

Apple Pie ▲

Chunky Applesauce ▼

Apple Appetizer ▲

Apple-Cranberry Shortcake ▼

Apple-Meringue Cake

Baked Apple ▲

Jellied Waldorf Salad ▼

APPLE—The fruit of any tree of the genus *Malus*. Apples come in many varieties. The ancient Romans knew twenty-two of them. At a banquet given by the Grand Duke Cosmo III of Tuscany in the year 1670, fifty-six different kinds of apples were served. Today, there are a staggering 6,500 or more horticultural forms.

Since the days of the Garden of Eden, apples have played their part in legend, science, art, and history. Apples were raised in the gardens of the Phoenicians. In Greek mythology, one of Hercules' labors was to obtain the golden apples of the Hesperides which were extremely well guarded because they bestowed immortality on those who had them.

Newton is said to have discovered the law of gravity when an apple fell on his head. Countless painters have used apples in their still lifes: Cézanne, Crivelli, and Courbet, to name just three. And finally, apples figure in the social history of our country. The first settlers included apple seeds in their precious supplies and Peregrine White, the first white child ever born in New England, planted apple trees there. American apples were exported to London before the American Revolution. Later, John Chapman traveled the Ohio wilderness, preaching and planting apple seeds, thus earning the affectionate nickname of Johnny Appleseed.

Who can describe an apple? In shape it can be round like a McIntosh or egg-shaped like the Delicious. In size, it can vary from a two-inch crabapple to a six-inch Rome Beauty. The flesh may be white as a Wealthy, yellow as a Golden Delicious, crisp as a Northern Spy, mellow as a Baldwin, sweet as a Grimes Golden, or tart as a new Winesap. The skin is thin and glossy and ranges in color from bright or russet red to yellow to green. Apples fit into every course in every meal and are munched between meals too; they're found in a lunch box and in a fancy torte. No wonder they are one of our favorite fruits and have even crept into our everyday speech: "the apple of his eye," "an apple for the teacher," "an apple a day keeps the doctor away."

FRESH APPLES

Availability—See chart, page 92.

Purchasing Guide—Fresh apples are sold by weight, sometimes by unit or original container. All apples are graded by U.S. standards for fresh fruit and vegetables. These grades include Fancy or Extra No. 1, U.S. No. 1, U.S. No. 2, U.S. No. 1 Cookers, U.S. Combinations; they designate the maturity, appearance, quality, waste, and use of the apple. The number count stamped on the shipping box indicates the size of the apple: the lower the number, the larger the apple.

☐ 1 pound = 2 to 3 apples

☐ ⅔ pound = 2 cups, sliced
☐ 1 pound = 2 cups sauce

The United States has developed a large number of varieties of excellent apples suited to many different uses. Whichever kind you choose, select firm well-shaped fruit with good color. Avoid blemishes and soft spots.

Storage—Place small quantities in plastic bags in refrigerator to prevent shriveling and transfer of odors. Store large quantities in a cool dark airy place. Long or improper storage results in mealy apples with brown cores. Sort occasionally to remove those with signs of spoilage.

☐ Refrigerator shelf: 1 to 2 weeks, depending on variety of apple
☐ Refrigerator frozen-food compartment, prepared for freezing: 2 months
☐ Freezer, prepared for freezing: 1 year

Nutritive Food Values—Fresh apples are a good supplement to the diet, since they contain carbohydrates and vitamins A and C. Apples contain cellulose to maintain body regularity and, when eaten raw, help clean the teeth.

☐ 1 medium, fresh = 75 calories
☐ Applesauce, unsweetened, ½ cup = 50 calories
   sweetened, ½ cup = 92 calories
☐ Apple juice, 1 cup = 126 calories
☐ Apple butter, 3½ ounces = 186 calories

Basic Preparation

☐ **To Serve, Raw**—Wash well. If cut apples must stand, dip into or sprinkle with lemon, orange, or other fruit juice to prevent darkening.
☐ **To Cook**—To maintain shape, add sugar at start of cooking. For sauces, add sugar after cooking. See recipes for basic cooking methods.
☐ **To Freeze, Whole**—Consult with County Home Agent for best variety to freeze. Freeze only tree-ripened perfect firm-fleshed apples.
☐ **To Freeze, Slices in Syrup**—Peel, core, and slice apples. Soak slices in a salt-water solution, ½ cup salt to 1 gallon water. Drain. Spoon apple slices into freezer containers, allowing 1-inch headspace. Cover with a syrup of 3 cups sugar to 1 quart water. To avoid discoloration of fruit, add ½ teaspoon ascorbic acid to the above amount of syrup. Or use a citric-acid compound (available in grocery store dietetic departments) in amounts recommended on package. Place crumpled wax paper under lid to keep fruit submerged in syrup.
☐ **To Freeze, Dry Pack**—Peel, core, and slice apples. Soak slices for 5 minutes (no longer or they will toughen) in a solution of 1 teaspoon sodium bisulfite and 1 gallon water mixed in a glass, enamel, or stainless-steel container. Drain and sprinkle with sugar, allowing 1

pound sugar to 10 to 12 cups apple slices. Let stand to dissolve sugar. Stir and pack as above.
☐ **To Freeze, Applesauce**—Cook applesauce the usual way. Sweeten to taste. Cool. Package with 1-inch headspace.
☐ **To Freeze, Baked Apples**—Chill. Pack in containers, separating apples with freezer paper.
☐ **To Freeze, Apple Juice**—Wash fruit and put through the coarsest blade of a food chopper. Do not heat. Squeeze juice out through 3 to 4 thicknesses of cheesecloth or muslin. Heat juice in the top part of a double boiler or over direct heat to 190°F. Chill juice quickly. Fill freezer containers, allowing 1-inch headspace.

CANNED APPLES

Availability—All year round, also in combination with other fruits, as jelly, butter, baby food, and dietetic pack; sliced and whole, applesauce and unfermented juice.

Storage—Store cans and bottles at room temperature. Rotate use of cans.

☐ Refrigerator shelf, opened and covered: 4 to 5 days
☐ Kitchen shelf, unopened: 1 year

Nutritive Food Values—See Fresh Apples, at left.

FROZEN APPLES

Commercially frozen apples are used primarily by institutions and bakeries. Some consumer-size slices and sauce are also available, and frozen ready-to-bake apple pies, apple cobblers, turnovers, and strudels are plentiful.

DRIED APPLES

Mature apples are peeled, cored, sliced, treated with sulfur dioxide, and dehydrated. They are marketed in 8-ounce packages which yield 4 cups when cooked. Once opened, the slices should be kept tightly covered, as mold forms rapidly from moisture. Available also in bulk or packed into dried-fruit mixtures.

Storage—Kitchen Shelf: 2 to 5 months.

Caloric Value

☐ 3½ ounces, dried, cooked without sugar added = 78 calories

FRESH APPLES
• • • • • • •
BASIC RECIPES
See chart, page 92, for variety of fresh apple best suited to the recipe

BAKED APPLES

8 Rome Beauty cooking apples
1 cup sugar
¼ teaspoon ground cinnamon or nutmeg
1 cup water

Wash and core apples. Starting at stem end, peel apples about ⅓ way down. Arrange in shallow baking pan. Mix sugar and spice; add water and boil for 5 minutes. Pour this syrup over apples and bake in preheated moderate oven (350°F.) for 45 to 60 minutes, basting frequently with syrup from pan.

■ **To glaze**—Sprinkle with ¼ cup sugar. Broil carefully under low heat, basting with syrup in pan until glazed and lightly browned. Serve warm or cold. Makes 8 servings.

BAKED APPLE DUMPLINGS

Pastry (2 cups flour recipe), unbaked
6 medium-tart cooking apples
1½ cups sugar
2 cups water
¼ cup butter or margarine
1¾ teaspoons ground cinnamon

Roll pastry to a little less than ⅛-inch thickness and cut into six 7-inch squares. Peel and core apples. Bring to boil 1 cup sugar, the water, 3 tablespoons butter, and ¼ teaspoon cinnamon. Put an apple on each square of pastry. Mix remaining sugar and cinnamon; fill apple cavities. Dot with remaining butter. Bring opposite points of pastry up over apple. Overlap, moisten, and seal. Lift carefully and put a few inches apart in baking dish. Pour hot syrup around dumplings. Bake in preheated hot oven (425°F.) for 40 minutes, or until crust is well browned and apples are cooked through. Serve warm with cream or whipped cream. Makes 6 servings.

APPLE PIE

Pastry for 2-crust 9-inch pie, unbaked
¾ to 1 cup sugar
1 teaspoon ground cinnamon or nutmeg
6 to 7 cups peeled and sliced tart cooking apples
1½ tablespoons butter

Line 9-inch pie pan with pastry. Mix sugar and cinnamon. Add to apples and mix well. Heap in lined pan. Dot with butter. Adjust top crust and cut slits for steam to escape. Seal edges and flute. Bake in preheated hot oven (425°F.) for 50 minutes, or until crust is well browned and apples are cooked through. If necessary to keep edge from excessive browning, cover with strip of foil. Serve pie warm or cold, topped with cream, whipped cream, or ice cream, if desired. Makes 6 to 8 servings.

APPLE-SOUR-CREAM SAUCE

Chop 1 cored but unpeeled red apple.

Add ¼ cup prepared white horseradish, ¾ teaspoon salt, ¼ teaspoon white pepper, and ¾ cup dairy sour cream. Serve cold on frankfurters, ham, or other smoked meats. Makes 1¼ cups.

APPLESAUCE 1 (Chunky)

Wash, peel, quarter, and core 6 cooking apples (about 2 pounds). Cook until soft in covered saucepan, using just enough water to keep them from scorching. Stir occasionally during cooking. Break up quarters a little and sweeten to taste with granulated sugar or brown sugar. Vary by adding lemon juice, ground cinnamon, ground nutmeg, ground cloves, raisins, or nuts. Makes 4 servings.

APPLESAUCE 2 (Smooth)

Wash and quarter 6 cooking apples (about 2 pounds). Do not peel or core. Cook until soft in covered saucepan, using just enough water to keep them from scorching. Stir occasionally during cooking. Force through a sieve or food mill and sweeten to taste. Vary as in Applesauce 1. Makes 4 servings.

APPLE BUTTER

- 4 pounds well-flavored apples, stemmed and quartered
- 2 cups cider or water
  Sugar
- 3 teaspoons ground cinnamon
- 1½ teaspoons ground cloves
- ½ teaspoon ground allspice

Cook apples in cider or water until soft. Strain pulp. To each cup of pulp add ½ cup sugar. Stir in remaining ingredients. Cook over low heat, stirring constantly, until mixture sheets from spoon. Pour into hot sterilized jars. Store in cool dry place. Makes about 10 six-ounce glasses.

APPLE JELLY

Remove stems and blossom ends from tart apples or crabapples. Quarter and add enough water to just cover. Simmer until soft. Strain through a jelly bag. Allow 1 cup sugar to each cup juice. Cook 4 cups juice at a time. Simmer juice and sugar until sheeting stage (220°-222°F.) has been reached. Pour hot jelly into dry hot sterilized jars. Seal with paraffin. Store in cool dry place. Four cups juice makes about 4 six-ounce glasses, depending on the pectin in the fruit, which is variable, and the length of time juice is cooked to reach the jelly stage.

APPETIZERS

APPLE APPETIZER

- 1 cup (8 ounces) creamed cottage cheese
- 1 small can (2¼ ounces) deviled ham
- 1 teaspoon grated onion
- 2 tablespoons chopped black olives
- 1 tablespoon minced pimiento
- 2 teaspoons dry sherry
- 3 unpeeled red eating apples, cut into wedges and sprinkled with lemon juice

Combine all ingredients, except apples, and mix well. Pile in small bowl and surround with apple wedges. Use apple wedges to dip into mixture. Makes about 1½ cups.

APPLE SNACKS

1. Cut a cored eating apple into ¼-inch slices. Dip into lemon or pineapple juice; spread with peanut butter.

2. Dip wedges of red-skinned apples, unpeeled, into lemon juice and sprinkle lightly with curry powder or ground ginger.

MEAT DISHES AND ACCOMPANIMENTS

APPLE-HAM CASSEROLE

- ¼ teaspoon ground cloves
- ½ teaspoon dry mustard
- 1 cup soft bread crumbs
- 3½ cups ground cooked smoked ham
- 1 tablespoon minced onion
- 1 egg, beaten
- ½ cup milk
  Salt to taste
- 3 eating apples, peeled, cored, and sliced
- ¼ cup honey
- 2 tablespoons butter

Mix first 8 ingredients. Pack in shallow baking dish. Arrange apples on mixture. Sprinkle with honey and dot with butter. Bake in preheated moderate oven (375°F.) for about 40 minutes. Makes 4 to 6 servings.

HAMBURGERS WITH APPLE RINGS

- 1½ pounds beef chuck, ground
- 1 small onion, chopped
- 2 tablespoons minced parsley
- 1½ teaspoons salt
- ⅛ teaspoon pepper
- 3 or 4 tart apples, peeled and cored
- 3 tablespoons butter or margarine

Mix lightly beef, onion, parsley, salt, and pepper. Shape into 8 patties. Broil to desired doneness. Keep warm. Cut eight ¾-inch apple rings. Sauté rings in butter in skillet. Cover and cook for 3 to 4 minutes. Put one ring on each patty and broil until just brown. Makes 4 servings.

APPLE-SMOTHERED PORK CHOPS

- 6 center-cut loin pork chops, about ¾ inch thick
- ¾ teaspoon salt
- ¼ teaspoon ground sage
- 3 tart apples
- 3 tablespoons molasses
- 3 tablespoons all-purpose flour
- 2 cups hot water
- 1 tablespoon cider vinegar
- ⅓ cup yellow raisins

Sprinkle chops with ¼ teaspoon salt and sage. Brown chops slowly in hot skillet. Reserve fat drippings in skillet. Put chops in large shallow baking dish. Peel and core apples and cut into ¼-inch slices; arrange on chops. Pour molasses over top. Stir flour into fat in skillet; cook until brown, stirring. Gradually stir in water and cook until mixture boils. Add vinegar, ½ teaspoon salt, and raisins. Pour sauce over chops and apples. Cover and bake in preheated moderate oven (350°F.) for about 1 hour. Makes 6 servings.

APPLE-FRANKFURTER CASSEROLE

- 2½ cups sliced peeled eating apples
- 3 large sweet potatoes, boiled, peeled, and sliced
- 1 pound frankfurters, split lengthwise and halved
- ¼ cup firmly packed light brown sugar
- ⅛ teaspoon ground cinnamon
- ¼ teaspoon salt
- 1 teaspoon fresh lemon juice
- ½ cup buttered soft bread crumbs

In shallow casserole alternate layers of apple, sweet potato, and frankfurter, until half are used. Mix next 3 ingredients and sprinkle half on contents of casserole. Add remaining apples, potatoes, and franks. Sprinkle with remaining sugar mixture and lemon juice. Top with crumbs. Cover and bake in preheated moderate oven (375°F.) for 45 minutes. Uncover and bake for 10 minutes. Makes 6 servings.

APPLE-LAMB CURRY

- 1 pound boneless stewing lamb
- 1 onion, minced
- 1 garlic clove, minced
- 3 tablespoons fat or cooking oil
- 1 tablespoon curry powder
- 1 teaspoon paprika
- ½ teaspoon ground ginger
- ¼ teaspoon chili powder
- ¼ teaspoon sugar
- 1 can (6 ounces) tomato paste
  Boiling water
- 2 cups chopped peeled tart apples
  Hot cooked rice

Cut lamb into 1-inch cubes. Sauté onion and garlic in fat until golden brown. Add curry powder, paprika, ginger, chili powder, and sugar. Blend well. Add lamb and brown on all sides. Add tomato paste and enough boiling water to cover. Stir well. Cover; simmer for 30 minutes over low heat. Add apples; cook for 15 minutes longer. Serve with rice. Makes 4 servings.

CURRIED APPLES

Cut 2 large cored unpeeled tart red apples into ½-inch slices. Blend 2 tablespoons molasses, 1 teaspoon curry powder, 3 tablespoons soft butter or margarine, and ⅛ teaspoon salt. Spread on one side of apple rings. Put on broiler pan, butter side up, and broil for 5 to 7 minutes. Mix ¼ cup each of toasted coconut and chopped almonds. Sprinkle apple slices with mixture. Serve hot with roast lamb, poultry, or ham. Makes 4 servings.

STUFFINGS

SAVORY APPLE STUFFING

- ½ cup chopped celery and leaves
- 1 yellow onion, chopped
- 2 tablespoons minced parsley
- ¼ cup butter or margarine
- 4 cups diced peeled tart apples
- ¼ cup firmly packed light brown sugar
- 1 teaspoon salt
- ½ teaspoon each of ground sage, marjoram, and thyme
- ¼ teaspoon pepper
- 2 cups toasted bread crumbs

The
All-American
Apple
can be found
everywhere...
baked, stewed,
in a pie
or just
tempting you
from the tree!

Baked Apple Dumplings

Rosy-Glazed Baked Apples

Deep-Dish Apple Pie

Poached Apples

Applesauce

Apple Kuchen

Sauté celery, onion, and parsley in butter for 5 minutes. Add apples, sugar, and seasonings. Cook for 5 minutes longer. Add bread crumbs and mix well. Especially good with pork or duck. Makes about 4 cups.

APPLE-PRUNE-RAISIN STUFFING

2 cups chopped peeled tart apples
½ cup chopped cooked prunes
½ cup seedless raisins
5 cups toasted bread cubes
¼ cup melted butter or margarine
¼ cup firmly packed light brown sugar
  Grated rind of 1 lemon
½ teaspoon paprika
½ teaspoon ground cinnamon
1 teaspoon salt
¾ cup apple juice or cider

Mix all ingredients. Use as stuffing for chicken, duck, or pork shoulder. Makes about 8 cups.

VEGETABLES

SAUTÉED APPLES, ONIONS, AND RAISINS

Heat ¼ cup bacon or sausage fat in skillet. Add 4 peeled and quartered medium yellow onions and 4 unpeeled cored red apples, cut into eighths. Sauté for about 5 minutes. Cover for 5 minutes; then add ⅓ cup yellow raisins and cook slowly, uncovered, until apples and onions are tender, stirring occasionally. Serve hot with sausage, roast pork, or pork chops. Makes 4 servings.

SPICY APPLES AND RED CABBAGE

2 yellow onions, minced
¼ cup butter or margarine
1 cup seedless raisins
3½ to 4 pounds red cabbage, cored and shredded
2 large apples, peeled, cored, and chopped
1 teaspoon mixed pickling spice
2 teaspoons salt
¼ teaspoon pepper
3 tablespoons sugar
¼ cup cider vinegar

Sauté onion in butter in large kettle until lightly browned. Add raisins, cabbage, and apple. Tie pickling spice in wet piece of cheesecloth. Add to cabbage mixture. Season with salt and pepper. Cover and cook over low heat for about 45 minutes. Mix sugar and vinegar; stir into cabbage. Simmer for 5 minutes. Remove spice bag. Makes 6 to 8 servings.

SALADS

PARTY APPLE SALAD

4 large eating apples
  Orange, pineapple, lemon, or grapefruit juice
1 cup diced celery
1 large banana, diced
⅔ cup coarsely chopped pecans
  Mayonnaise
  Prepared mustard
  Endive or other salad greens

Core apples, leaving bottoms whole. Hollow out, leaving a ½-inch shell. Sprinkle cavities and apple pulp with fruit juice. Chop pulp; add celery, banana, and nuts.

Moisten with mayonnaise and add mustard to taste. Mix well and fill apples, piling mixture up in center. Chill. Serve on greens. Makes 4 servings.

APPLE BAVARIAN SLAW

1 Spanish onion
2 red apples
4 cups shredded red cabbage
½ cup crosscut dill-pickle slices
  French dressing

Slice onion; separate into rings. Core apples but do not peel; cut into thin slices. Combine onion, apple, cabbage, and pickle. Chill. Just before serving, toss with French dressing. Makes 6 servings.

JELLIED WALDORF SALAD

3 medium-size red apples
  Fresh lemon juice
1 box (3 ounces) lemon-flavor gelatin dessert
1 cup hot water
⅛ teaspoon salt
½ cup mayonnaise
1 cup diced celery
½ cup chopped walnuts
½ cup heavy cream, whipped
  Salad greens
  Ripe olives

Core apples, but do not peel. Cut 1 into thin, even slices, and dice remaining 2. Sprinkle sliced and diced apple with a small amount of lemon juice. Arrange slices peel-side down, around bottom of a 5-cup ring mold. Refrigerate all apples. Dissolve gelatin in the water. Chill until slightly thickened. Add salt, and blend in mayonnaise. Fold in diced apple, and remaining ingredients, except greens and olives. Turn carefully into prepared mold, and chill until firm. Unmold on greens, and garnish with olives. Makes 6 servings.

BREADS

APPLE KUCHEN

1 package active dry yeast or 1 cake compressed yeast
¼ cup water*
¾ cup milk
  Butter or margarine
¼ cup sugar
1 teaspoon salt
2 eggs, slightly beaten
2¾ cups sifted all-purpose flour (about)
5 cooking apples
2 tablespoons melted butter or margarine
¼ cup sugar
½ teaspoon ground cinnamon
2 tablespoons raisins

*Use very warm water (105°F. to 115°F.) for dry yeast; use lukewarm (80°F. to 90°F.) for compressed. Sprinkle dry yeast or crumble cake into water. Let stand for a few minutes; then stir until dissolved. Scald milk; add ¼ cup butter, sugar, and salt, stirring until butter melts. Cool to lukewarm; stir in yeast and eggs. Beat in 1½ cups of the flour; cover and let rise in warm place until doubled in bulk, about 40 minutes. Stir in enough of the remaining flour to make an easy-to-handle dough. Knead

lightly on a floured board. Cover and chill for 30 minutes. Roll out and fit into a greased baking dish, 9 x 12 x 13 inches.

Peel, quarter, and core apples; cut into eighths. Press closely together into dough. Brush apples and dough with melted butter. Combine sugar, cinnamon, and raisins. Sprinkle over apples. Cover and let rise in warm place until dough springs back when touched lightly with finger. Bake in preheated moderate oven (350° F.) for 30 minutes, or until apples are tender. Makes 8 to 10 servings.

APPLE PANCAKE

3 or 4 tart apples
  Melted butter or margarine (about ⅔ cup)
  Sugar (about ⅔ cup)
⅛ teaspoon ground nutmeg
¼ teaspoon ground cinnamon
2 eggs
½ cup milk
½ cup sifted all-purpose flour
¼ teaspoon salt

Peel and core apples. Slice thin and sauté in ⅓ cup butter for 5 minutes. Mix ⅓ cup sugar and spices and add to apples. Cover and cook for 10 minutes. Cool. Mix eggs, milk, flour, and salt. Beat with rotary beater for 2 minutes. Heat 1 tablespoon butter in 10-inch ovenproof skillet. Pour batter into pan. Bake in preheated very hot oven (450°F.) for 15 minutes. As soon as batter puffs up in center, puncture with fork, repeating as often as necessary. Lower heat to moderate (350°F.) and bake for 10 minutes. Remove from oven; spoon 2 tablespoons melted butter over surface. Sprinkle with 2 tablespoons sugar. Spread apple mixture over half the surface; fold in. Spoon 2 tablespoons melted butter over top; sprinkle with 2 tablespoons sugar. Makes 6 servings.

AUTUMN APPLE BREAD

¼ cup shortening
⅔ cup sugar
2 eggs, beaten
2 cups sifted all-purpose flour
1 teaspoon baking powder
1 teaspoon baking soda
1 teaspoon salt
2 cups coarsely grated peeled raw apples
1 tablespoon grated lemon rind
⅔ cup chopped walnuts

Cream shortening and sugar until light and fluffy; beat in eggs. Sift next 4 ingredients. Add alternately with apple to egg mixture. Stir in lemon rind and nuts. Bake in greased and floured loaf pan (9 x 5 x 3 inches) in preheated moderate oven (350°F.) for 50 to 60 minutes. Cool before slicing. Makes 1 loaf.

PIES

APPLE CREAM PIE

5 large cooking apples, peeled and cut into eighths
½ cup sugar
½ cup water
  Pastry for 1-crust 9-inch pie, unbaked
1 egg
½ cup heavy cream

Put apples in saucepan with sugar and water. Bring to boil, cover, and simmer for 10 to 20 minutes, or until apples are tender. Drain, reserving syrup. Cool apples slightly and put in 9-inch pie pan lined with pastry: Beat egg and cream together and stir in reserved syrup. Pour over apples. Bake in preheated moderate oven (350°F.) for 30 minutes, or until firm. Cool. Makes 6 to 8 servings.

DEEP-DISH APPLE PIE

3 tablespoons quick-cooking tapioca
¾ cup granulated sugar
⅓ cup firmly packed dark brown sugar
¼ teaspoon salt
1 teaspoon ground cinnamon
½ teaspoon ground nutmeg
5 cups peeled cored sliced tart apples
Pastry (1 cup flour recipe), unbaked
Whipped cream, flavored with nutmeg
(optional)

Mix all ingredients except pastry and whipped cream. Pour into buttered deep 8-inch square baking dish. Roll out pastry ⅛ inch thick to fit top of dish. Cut several slits near the center and arrange pastry over apples. Bake in preheated hot oven (425°F.) for about 35 minutes. Serve with whipped cream, if desired. Makes 6 servings.

DESSERTS

POACHED APPLES

¾ cup sugar
1½ cups water
1 slice of lemon
6 cooking apples (about 2 pounds)
Ground nutmeg

Cook sugar, water, and lemon for 5 minutes. Remove lemon. Peel, core, and slice apples; cook a few at a time until tender, adding a little more water when necessary. Pour syrup over cooked apples. Serve warm or chilled as a dessert, sprinkled with ground nutmeg. Makes 4 to 6 servings.

APPLE BROWN BETTY

4 cups small bread cubes
½ cup melted butter or margarine
¾ teaspoon ground cinnamon
⅛ teaspoon salt
¾ cup firmly packed dark brown sugar
4 cups chopped peeled tart apples
1 cup medium cream
¼ teaspoon ground nutmeg

Mix first 5 ingredients and arrange in alternate layers with apples in 1½-quart baking dish. Bake in preheated moderate oven (375°F.) for 1 hour, or until apples are tender and top is brown. Serve warm with cream, flavored with nutmeg. Makes 4 to 6 servings.

APPLE-CRANBERRY SHORTCAKE

4 cups thinly sliced peeled eating apples
1 cup fresh cranberries
¼ cup water
⅔ cup firmly packed brown sugar
½ teaspoon ground cinnamon
Dash of salt
Shortcake mixture using 3 cups biscuit mix
Whipped cream (optional)

Put apples, cranberries, water, sugar, cinnamon, and salt in saucepan. Bring to boil; cover and simmer until apples are tender. Bake shortcake in two 8-inch layers. Put hot apple mixture between layers and on top of hot shortcake. Cut into wedges and serve with whipped cream, if desired. Makes 6 servings.

APPLE CRISP

2 pounds cooking apples, peeled and sliced (5½ cups)
¼ cup water
½ cup granulated sugar
½ cup firmly packed light brown sugar
½ teaspoon each of ground nutmeg and cinnamon
¼ teaspoon salt
¾ cup flour
½ cup butter or margarine

Put apples in shallow 2-quart casserole; add water. Combine sugars, nutmeg, cinnamon, salt, and flour. Cut in butter with pastry blender. Spoon evenly over apples. Cover and bake in preheated moderate oven (350°F.) for 30 minutes. Uncover and bake for 30 minutes longer. Makes 6 servings.

APPLE FRITTERS

3 large cooking apples
½ cup granulated sugar
2 tablespoons brandy
1 teaspoon each of grated lemon and orange rinds
1½ cups sifted all-purpose flour
¼ teaspoon salt
2 eggs, well beaten
1 teaspoon olive oil
⅓ cup beer
Fat for frying
Confectioners' sugar

Core and peel apples; cut into ½-inch rings. (Reserve ends for use in salad.) Mix ¼ cup granulated sugar, brandy, and grated rinds. Pour over apples and let stand for 2 hours. Mix remaining granulated sugar and other ingredients, except last 2. Let stand for 1 hour. Dip drained apples, one ring at a time, into the mixture. Fry in hot deep fat (375°F. on a frying thermometer) until brown on both sides. Drain on absorbent paper and sprinkle with confectioners' sugar. Serve warm. Makes 1 dozen.

APPLE MERINGUE CAKE

⅓ cup butter or margarine
Sugar (about 1 cup)
2 egg yolks
¾ cup unsifted all-purpose flour
⅓ cup chopped blanched almonds
Grated rind and juice of ½ lemon
5 egg whites
4 to 6 medium apples, peeled, cored, and halved
⅓ cup raspberry jam
Dash of salt

Cream butter; add 3 tablespoons sugar gradually, beating until light and fluffy. Add egg yolks and mix well. Add flour, almonds, and grated rind; mix just until flour is evenly distributed. Press on bottom of 9-inch pie pan and brush with 1 slightly beaten egg white. Bake in preheated moderate oven (350°F.) for 15

minutes, or until crust is browned. Combine apples, ⅓ cup sugar, and lemon juice in large skillet; cover and cook over medium heat until tender. Spread jam on crust in pie pan and arrange drained apples on top. Beat 4 remaining egg whites with salt until stiff, but not dry. Continue beating, adding ½ cup sugar, 1 tablespoon at a time (sugar granules must be completely dissolved). Continue beating and feel the meringue between the fingers until all gritty sugar particles dissolve. Pile lightly on apples. Bake in a preheated moderate oven (350°F.) for about 18 minutes, or until meringue is lightly browned. Makes 6 servings.

APPLE PANDOWDY

3 cups sliced apples
⅓ cup firmly packed dark brown sugar
¼ teaspoon each of ground cinnamon and nutmeg
¼ cup butter or margarine
⅓ cup granulated sugar
1 egg
¾ cup sifted all-purpose flour
¾ teaspoon baking powder
¼ teaspoon salt
⅓ cup milk
Cream

Put apples in 1-quart baking dish. Sprinkle with brown sugar and spices. Bake in a preheated moderate oven (375°F.) for 30 minutes, or until apples are soft. Cream butter; gradually add granulated sugar and beat until fluffy. Add egg and beat well. Add sifted dry ingredients alternately with milk, beating until smooth. Spread on cooked apples. Bake for 30 minutes. Serve warm with cream. Makes 4 servings.

APPLE STRUDEL

Dough
1 egg, slightly beaten
½ teaspoon salt
Cooking oil
1 cup unsifted all-purpose flour
1 tablespoon warm water
Melted butter or margarine
Sugar

Filling
¼ cup seedless raisins
2 tablespoons water
6 to 8 apples, peeled and sliced
1 cup sugar
¾ cup fine dry bread crumbs
⅓ cup butter or margarine
½ cup chopped blanched almonds
1 tablespoon ground cinnamon

Mix egg, salt, 2 tablespoons oil, and the flour. Add warm water and mix to form a soft dough. Knead on lightly floured board for 10 to 15 minutes, or until dough is *very* smooth and *very* elastic. Brush top with more oil and cover with a warm bowl. Let stand for 30 minutes. Meantime prepare ingredients for filling. Soak raisins in water. Peel and core apples and slice thin; sprinkle with ½ cup of the sugar. Brown crumbs in butter; later combine with raisins and liquid, almonds, cinnamon, and remaining sugar.

When strudel dough is ready, roll out as thin as possible on a large lightly floured cloth about 36 inches square. Melt ½ cup butter and brush entire top of dough. With palms up, slip hands underneath dough and stretch it carefully to paper thinness, working from the center out. If edges remain thick, cut them off. Dough should almost cover the cloth. Brush again with more melted butter to keep pliable.

Pile apples in a row about 2 inches from one end of dough. Spread raisin mixture over remaining dough. Lift edges of cloth nearest the apples; continue to roll dough over and over with help of cloth. Put roll on ungreased cookie sheet. Make into **U** shape if roll is too long for sheet. Bake in preheated hot oven (400°F.) for 30 minutes. During baking, brush 2 or 3 times with melted butter. About 5 minutes before strudel is done, sprinkle thickly with sugar. Makes 8 servings.

BAKED APPLE TAPIOCA

    3 large tart cooking apples
      Juice of 1 lemon
    3 cups water
    1 cup firmly packed light brown sugar
    ½ cup quick-cooking tapioca
    ½ teaspoon salt
    ¼ teaspoon ground mace
    2 tablespoons butter, melted
      Cream

Peel and slice apples and put in shallow baking dish. Mix lemon juice and water and pour over apples. Cover, and bake in preheated moderate oven (375°F.) for about 45 minutes. Mix sugar, tapioca, salt, and mace. Stir into apples. Dot with butter. Cover, and bake for 10 minutes; stir. Bake, covered, for 5 minutes longer. Serve at once with cream. Makes 6 servings.

BAKED APPLES WITH WINE

Core 6 large baking apples and peel a 1-inch strip from stem end. Put in shallow baking dish. In each cavity put 2 tablespoons honey, 1 tablespoon seedless raisins, and 2 split blanched almonds. Put 1 cup water in dish and bake, uncovered, in preheated moderate oven (350°F.) for 30 minutes. Remove from oven and baste with syrup in bottom of dish. Pour 1 tablespoon muscatel over each apple. Bake for 20 minutes, or until done, basting frequently with the syrup. Makes 6 servings.

OLD WORLD APPLE CAKE

Filling
    3 pounds cooking apples
    ⅓ cup sugar
    ½ cup water
    2 slices of lemon

Pastry
    2 cups sifted all-purpose flour
      Sugar (about 1⅓ cups)
    1½ teaspoons baking powder
      Butter or margarine, softened (about ⅔ cup)
    2 egg yolks

Peel and slice apples. Cook with sugar, water, and lemon until tender but not mushy. Drain and cool. Remove lemon slices.

Mix flour, 1¼ cups sugar, and baking powder. Cut in ½ cup butter with pastry blender, or work in with fingers until mixture is crumbly. Mix in egg yolks. Reserve 1 cup flour mixture for top. Pat remainder on bottom and sides of greased 9-inch springform pan. Fill with apples; sprinkle with reserved topping; dot with 2 tablespoons butter; sprinkle with 1 tablespoon sugar. Bake in preheated moderate oven (350°F.) for 1 hour. Serve warm or cold. Makes 6 to 8 servings.

ROSY GLAZED BAKED APPLES

Select large apples suitable for baking. Core and peel top half. Put in baking pan with about 1 inch of water. Cover, and bake in preheated hot oven (425°F.) for 30 minutes, or until apples are tender. Watch that apples do not get overdone. Uncover. If there is too much liquid in pan, remove some. Sprinkle each apple with 2 tablespoons sugar. Add a little grenadine to juice in pan. Continue baking until glazed, basting frequently with juice in pan. Sprinkle again with 2 tablespoons sugar a few minutes before serving. Allow 1 large apple per serving.

MISCELLANEOUS

APPLE SANDWICHES

Shred an apple into a bowl of softened cream cheese, add a few cut dates, and a dash of salt. Mix well and spread between slices of buttered bread. Remove crusts and cut into fingers.

HALLOWEEN APPLES ON A STICK

    12 small red eating apples
    12 wooden skewers
    3 cups sugar
    ¾ cup light corn syrup
    1 cup water
      Few drops oil of cloves
      Red food coloring or 12 red cinnamon candies

Wash apples in hot water and dry. Insert a skewer in blossom end of each apple. In a saucepan mix sugar, corn syrup, and water. Cook over direct heat, stirring, until sugar dissolves. Add oil of cloves and a little coloring. Continue cooking, without stirring, until a small amount of mixture forms a hard piece that cracks when dropped into cold water (290°F. on a candy thermometer). Set pan over boiling water. Dip each apple into syrup, remove, and whirl apple until syrup covers it smoothly. Stand apples, skewer side up, on tray or plate to cool and harden.

CANNED APPLES

APPLESAUCE FRENCHIES

Mix 2 cups (one 1-pound jar) applesauce, 1 tablespoon butter, and ½ tea-

spoon each of ground cinnamon and nutmeg; heat. Beat 2 eggs with 1 cup milk and dash of salt. Dip 8 slices of white bread into the mixture; brown on both sides in hot butter or margarine. Serve applesauce between 2 slices of toast and on top. Makes 4 servings.

SCALLOPED APPLES, PORK CHOPS, AND SWEET POTATOES

    2½ cups (one 1-pound, 4-ounce can) sliced apples, drained
    4 cooked peeled small sweet potatoes
    ⅓ cup seedless raisins
    ⅓ cup firmly packed light brown sugar
      Dash of ground nutmeg
    3 tablespoons currant jelly
    3 tablespoons prepared mustard
    4 center-cut rib pork chops, ¾-inch thick
      Salt and pepper

Divide apple slices and put half at each end of shallow baking dish. Cut sweet potatoes into thick slices and put in center of dish. Sprinkle with raisins, then with brown sugar and nutmeg. Mix jelly and mustard, beating until smooth. Trim excess fat from chops. Place chops over sweet potatoes and apples. Top with jelly-mustard mixture. Sprinkle with salt and pepper. Bake in preheated moderate oven (350°F.) for 1½ hours, or until chops are tender. Makes 4 servings.

WEST INDIES APPLE CHUTNEY

    2½ cups (one 1-pound, 4-ounce can) sliced apples, undrained
    ½ cup dark raisins
    ¾ cup molasses
    ½ cup cider vinegar
    ½ teaspoon salt
    1 teaspoon each of ground ginger and dry mustard
    1 tablespoon curry powder

Mix all ingredients in saucepan. Bring to boil, stirring to blend ingredients. Simmer, uncovered, over low heat for 15 minutes, stirring occasionally. Makes 3 cups.

APPLE OATMEAL COOKIES

    ½ cup butter or margarine
    ⅔ cup sugar
    2 eggs
    1 cup sifted all-purpose flour
    1 teaspoon baking powder
    1 teaspoon ground cinnamon
    ½ teaspoon each of ground nutmeg and salt
    1 cup quick-cooking rolled oats
    1 cup chopped well-drained canned apples
    1 cup coarsely chopped walnuts

Cream butter and sugar until light. Add eggs, one at a time, beating well after each addition. Sift flour, baking powder, spices, and salt, and add to egg mixture. Stir in oats and apples and beat well. Fold in nuts. Drop by teaspoon onto greased cookie sheets. Bake in preheated moderate oven (350°F.) for about 15 minutes. Makes about 42.

UPSIDE-DOWN APPLE PIE

    ½ cup walnut halves
    ¼ cup butter or margarine, melted
    ⅓ cup firmly packed light brown sugar
      Pastry for 2-crust 9-inch pie, unbaked

½ cup granulated sugar
2½ cups (one 1-pound, 4-ounce can) apple slices, drained
2 tablespoons all-purpose flour
½ teaspoon ground cinnamon
¼ teaspoon salt
⅛ teaspoon ground nutmeg

Arrange nuts, flat sides up, in butter in deep 9-inch pie pan. Pat brown sugar over nuts and cover with circle of pastry rolled ⅛ inch thick; trim edges. Mix remaining ingredients and spoon into pastry. Cover with top crust, seal edges, and cut a few slashes in top crust. Bake in preheated moderate oven (375°F.) for about 40 minutes. Cool for 5 minutes; turn out on plate. Serve warm, plain or with whipped cream or ice cream. Makes 6 to 8 servings.

DRIED APPLES

SCHNITZ UND GNEPP
(Apples and Dumplings)

2 cups dried sweet apples
2 cups smoked ham, cubed
2 tablespoons brown sugar
2 cups sifted all-purpose flour
3 teaspoons baking powder
½ teaspoon salt
1 egg, beaten
2 tablespoons melted butter
½ cup milk (approximately)

Cover dried apples with water and soak overnight. Place apples and water in large saucepan. Add ham and cook slowly until apples are tender, adding additional water to keep level of liquid. Add brown sugar. Stir until dissolved. Sift flour with baking powder and salt. Beat egg with butter and milk. Add all at once to dry ingredients. Beat well. Add additional milk to make a moderately stiff batter. Drop batter from wet spoon into boiling ham and apples. Cover saucepan and simmer, without lifting lid, for 20 minutes. Makes 6 to 8 servings.

APPLE-NUT BARS

1 cup sifted all-purpose flour
¼ teaspoon baking powder
½ teaspoon salt
¼ cup butter or margarine, melted
1 cup granulated sugar
2 eggs, well beaten
1 cup chopped nuts
⅓ cup raisins
⅔ cup finely cut dried apples
Confectioners' sugar

Sift dry ingredients into bowl. Add remaining ingredients except confectioners' sugar. Mix well and pour into buttered pan (13 x 9 x 2 inches). Bake in preheated moderate oven (350°F.) for about 25 minutes. While still warm, cut into 27 bars, 3 by 1½ inches. Roll in confectioners' sugar.

DRIED-APPLE PIE

2 cups dried tart apple slices
2½ cups water
¾ cup sugar
½ teaspoon ground cinnamon
Pastry for 2-crust 9-inch pie, unbaked

Soak apples overnight in water. Cook slowly, covered, in same water until apples are soft, about 30 minutes. Force through coarse sieve or food mill. Add sugar and cinnamon and turn into pastry-lined 9-inch pie pan. Cover with top crust. Cut slits in top. Bake in preheated hot oven (425°F.) for 10 minutes. Reduce heat to moderate (350°F.) and bake for about 30 minutes longer. Makes 6 to 8 servings.

APPLE JUICE

CIDER SAUCE FOR MEATS

To 1 cup dark brown sugar add 1 cup liquid. Use any meat liquid, ham or steak drippings, with bouillon cube and water to make desired amount. Boil mixture to reduce to about half the volume. Reduce 1 cup cider to ⅓ cup. Add to first mixture with dash of cayenne, 1 teaspoon grated onion, and ¼ cup parboiled raisins, if desired. Heat and serve with baked ham or other smoked meat. Makes about 1 cup.

CIDER GELATIN SALAD

1 envelope unflavored gelatin
¼ cup sugar
Dash of salt
1¾ cups cider
2 tablespoons fresh lemon juice
1½ cups diced unpeeled red apples
½ cup diced celery
Salad greens
Mayonnaise
Chopped nuts

In saucepan mix gelatin, sugar, and salt. Add ½ cup cider. Let stand for 5 minutes. Heat, stirring, until gelatin is dissolved. Remove from heat and add remaining cider and lemon juice. Chill until thickened to consistency of unbeaten egg white. Fold in apple and celery and pour into 6 lightly oiled individual molds or a 1-quart mold. Chill until firm. Unmold on greens, top with mayonnaise, and sprinkle with chopped nuts. Makes 6 servings.

APPLE-HERB JELLY

Select dry or liquid pectin, using manufacturer's directions as a guide. Measure amount of apple juice required to make apple jelly. Bring to boil and pour over dried uncrumbled herbs such as leaf marjoram, leaf sage, or basil; use 2 teaspoons herb for each cup juice. Add dash of salt and let stand for 10 minutes. Strain through fine sieve or cloth bag. Complete jelly-making, adding sugar as called for in pectin recipe. Pour into hot sterilized jelly glasses and seal at once with paraffin.

APPLE-CRANBERRY FIZZ

Chill 2 cups apple juice and 1 cup cranberry-juice cocktail. When ready to serve, add 1 cup carbonated water. Pour into glasses and garnish each with a slice of lime or lemon. Makes 4 cups.

Above: Apricot Soufflé
Apricot Strudel
Apricots with Curried
Pork Chops

At right: Apricot Cream-Cheese Tarts
Apricot Refrigerator Cake

Apricots

Golden member of
the peach family, a delight
to the eye or the appetite—
in salads, desserts, main dishes.

APRICOT (*Prunus armeniaca*)—Oval-stoned fruit of a golden-yellow color which grows on a small tree belonging to the peach family. The apricot tree reaches a height of twenty to thirty feet and has ravishing pink flowers that come out before the leaves. Apricots hate frost and most varieties will grow only in warm temperate zones.

The tree is native to Asia, where it still grows wild. The Chinese cultivated apricots 2,000 years ago. From Asia, the tree came west to India, Persia, Armenia, and Egypt. It is said that Alexander the Great brought it from Persia to Greece, and from there it reached Italy. Apricots are grown extensively in the Middle East, in all of the Mediterranean countries from Turkey to Spain, in France, and to some extent, in espaliered form, in England. The first apricots in our country were probably those the Spanish missionaries brought to California in the 1770's. There it is still very much at home, both in private gardens and commercial orchards. Most commercial apricot shipments, fresh, canned, or dry, come from the Pacific Coast.

Apricots have been and are a staple food in many countries. The people of Hunza, a remote little kingdom in the high Himalayas, have attracted scientific attention because of their longevity and superb health; their chief food is apricots. In Persia, another country where apricots are widely eaten, poets have sung of the fruit and called it "the seed of the sun." The Chinese considered the apricot tree endowed with prophetic powers. Lao Tse, the famous Chinese philosopher, was born under one, and attributed his gifts to it. Confucius worked out his philosophy under an apricot tree. Syrians, Lebanese, Turks, Greeks, Romans, and Spaniards all doted and still dote on apricots, fresh, dried, raw, cooked, or made into ices. Few fruits are more delectable or more beautiful.

FRESH APRICOTS

Availability—June through August. The crop comes from California, Washington, and Utah.

Purchasing Guide—Well-matured fruit, which has true apricot flavor, is plump,

fairly firm, and a uniform golden to yellow-orange in color. Because apricots are highly perishable and not a great many are grown, they are sometimes difficult to find in the market. Apricots are graded by the U.S. Department of Agriculture in the same grades and count as listed under Fresh Apples.

☐ 1 pound = 8 to 12 apricots

Storage—Place ripe fruit in refrigerator in a covered container or perforated plastic bag. Green apricots should be allowed to ripen at room temperature, then stored in the refrigerator.

☐ Refrigerator shelf: 3 to 5 days
☐ Refrigerator frozen-food compartment, prepared for freezing: 2 months
☐ Freezer, prepared for freezing: 1 year

Nutritive Food Values—Excellent source of vitamin A, high in natural sugars.

☐ 3 medium = 54 calories

Basic Preparation—Wash, then strip off skin with a paring knife. If fruit is not ripe, it may be dipped into boiling water for 30 seconds, then into cold water, before peeling. Add a little lime or lemon juice to accent the flavor.

☐ **To Freeze**—Cut ripe washed apricots into halves, peeled or unpeeled, remove pits, and pack in heavy syrup (5½ cups sugar to 5 cups water). To avoid discoloration of fruit, add ½ teaspoon ascorbic acid to every 5½ cups sugar, or use a citric-acid compound available in food store dietetic departments, in amounts recommended on package. Fill container ⅓ with syrup; add fruit to within 1 inch of the top. Fill with syrup. Top with crumpled wax paper to keep fruit submerged. Cover with lid.

Also can be frozen after steaming pitted halves for 4 minutes. Crush fruit and pack with sugar, allowing ½ cup sugar to 1 quart fruit. Ascorbic acid or citric-acid compound is not needed in this method of packing for freezing.

CANNED APRICOTS

Availability—Peeled or unpeeled; packed in water, juice, or syrup; whole (pitted and unpitted), halves, or slices.

Apricots are also sold as strained and chopped infant food, in dietary packs, as preserves, and as juice, commonly called "nectar."

Storage—Store cans at room temperature. Rotate use of cans.

☐ Kitchen shelf, unopened: 2½ years
☐ Refrigerator shelf, opened and covered: 2 to 4 days

Caloric Value

☐ 4 medium halves with 2 tablespoons syrup = 97 calories

DRIED APRICOTS

Dried fruits have a large percentage of the moisture removed. They are treated with sulfur dioxide to retain their color.

Availability—Sold in bulk, in moisture-proof packages or plastic bags. Also sold in dried-fruit mixtures. They are sold only in halves.

Purchasing Guide

☐ 1 pound dried = 5 cups, cooked

Storage—Keep packages tightly sealed to keep fruit moist. Can be stored in carton, unopened, at room temperature for 2 to 5 months.

Nutritive Food Values

Dried apricots are a concentrated source of natural sugars which do not cause tooth decay.

☐ 4 large halves = 52 calories

Basic Preparation—Wash and cover apricots with water. Bring to a boil. Lower temperature, cover, and simmer for 15 to 20 minutes, or until tender, adding more water to keep up the level of the liquid. Sweeten to taste.

FRESH APRICOTS

APRICOT-CHEESE SALAD

1 pound creamed cottage cheese
2 teaspoons grated orange rind
2 tablespoons chopped maraschino cherries
Salad greens
6 fresh apricots, halved and pitted
Whole maraschino cherries
Mint sprigs (optional)

Blend cheese, orange rind, and chopped cherries. Arrange salad greens on 4 salad plates and put 3 apricot halves in center of each. Put cheese mixture around fruit and garnish with whole cherries and mint sprigs. Makes 4 servings.

FRESH APRICOT RIPPLE ICE CREAM

1½ cups puréed or mashed fresh apricots
1 tablespoon fresh lemon juice
¾ cup sugar
1 quart vanilla ice cream
½ cup heavy cream
¼ teaspoon almond extract

Mix apricot pulp with lemon juice and sugar. Chill for 30 minutes. Soften ice cream slightly. Whip cream and add flavoring. Mix apricot pulp, ice cream, and cream quickly, but not thoroughly. Freeze until firm. Serve with additional puréed fresh apricots. Makes 6 to 8 servings.

APRICOT CREAM-CHEESE TARTS

8 fresh apricots
Four 2½-inch tart shells, baked
½ cup sugar
¼ cup water
1 package (8 ounces) cream cheese
¼ cup milk
Mint sprigs

Wash and peel apricots; cut into halves and remove pits. Slice 8 halves and put in bottom of baked tart shells. Boil sugar and water until syrup forms a very soft ball in cold water (232°F. on a candy thermometer). Pour about half over sliced apricots. Mix cheese with milk until creamy. Put remaining apricot halves together with some of cream-cheese mixture. Put remaining cream cheese over sliced apricots. Top each tart with a filled apricot and cover with remaining syrup. Garnish with mint. Makes 4 servings.

APRICOT CRUMB PIE

    2 tablespoons quick-cooking tapioca
    ¾ cup granulated sugar
    ⅛ teaspoon salt
    2 pounds fresh apricots, halved and pitted
      Juice of ½ lemon
      Pastry for 1-crust 9-inch pie, unbaked
    ⅓ cup firmly packed light brown sugar
    ¼ cup all-purpose flour
    ½ teaspoon ground cinnamon
    3 tablespoons butter or margarine

Mix tapioca, granulated sugar, and salt. Combine with apricots and lemon juice. Pack into 9-inch pie pan lined with pastry. Mix brown sugar, flour, and cinnamon; cut in butter to form crumbs. Sprinkle over apricots. Bake in preheated hot oven (425°F.) for 15 minutes; reduce heat to moderate (375°F.) and bake for 30 to 35 minutes longer, or until apricots are tender. Makes 6 to 8 servings.

STEWED APRICOTS

Peel 12 large ripe fresh apricots. Cut into halves and discard pits, or leave whole. Bring to boil ¾ cup sugar, 1 cup water, and 4 whole cloves or a piece of cinnamon stick. Simmer for 5 minutes. Add apricots, cover, and simmer for 10 minutes, or until just tender. Chill. Replace ¼ cup of cooking water with ¼ cup white wine, if desired. Makes 4 to 6 servings.

CANNED APRICOTS

APRICOT AND BANANA CUP

Drain 1¼ cups (one 1-pound can) whole peeled apricots, reserving syrup. Mix syrup with the juice of ½ lemon or lime. Peel 2 bananas, score with fork, and slice into syrup. Add apricots, cover, and chill. Serve in sherbet glasses with mint sprig garnish. Or top with small scoop of lemon ice. Makes 4 to 6 servings.

APRICOTS WITH CURRIED PORK CHOPS

    8 small center-cut rib pork chops
    1 yellow onion, minced
    ¼ cup butter or margarine
    ¼ cup all-purpose flour
    1 teaspoon salt
    1 teaspoon (or more) curry powder
    ¼ teaspoon pepper
    2 cups milk
    ½ pound fresh mushrooms, sliced
    8 drained canned apricot halves

Brown chops quickly on both sides in skillet and put in casserole. Sauté onion in butter for 5 minutes. Blend in flour and seasonings. Gradually stir in milk and cook, stirring constantly, until thickened. Add mushrooms. Pour over chops. Cover and bake in preheated moderate oven (350°F.) for 1 hour, or until chops are tender. Top with apricot halves. Serve with rice and chutney. Makes 4 servings.

BROILED APRICOTS

Put drained canned apricot halves on

Apricot Cream-Cheese Tarts

Apricot Upside-Down Cake

Apricot Crumb Pie

Apricot Crescents

Apricot Delight

broiler rack. Brush with melted butter or margarine and sprinkle with lemon juice, sugar, and a little ground cinnamon, cloves, or nutmeg, if desired. Broil for about 8 minutes, 5 to 6 inches away from heat. Serve very hot with a mixed grill of lamb chops, kidneys, and sausages. Prepare 3 halves for each serving.

STUFFED APRICOT SALAD

1½ cups (one 1-pound can) apricot halves
1 package (3 ounces) cream cheese
2 tablespoons milk
Dash of salt
¼ cup chopped dates
Salad greens
Maraschino cherries (optional)
French dressing

Drain apricots and reserve syrup for other uses. Beat cheese, milk, and salt until light and fluffy. Stir in dates and stuff apricot halves with mixture. Put on salad greens and garnish each serving with a cherry. Serve with French dressing. Makes 4 servings.

APRICOT DELIGHT

2½ dozen almond macaroons
1½ boxes (11 ounces each) or 4 cups dried apricots
Water
2 envelopes unflavored gelatin
1½ cups unsalted butter
3 cups confectioners' sugar
6 eggs, separated
Rind and juice of 1 lemon
⅛ teaspoon salt
½ cup granulated sugar
1½ cups heavy cream, whipped
1⅔ cups (one 1-pound, 1-ounce can) unpeeled apricot halves, well drained
Chopped pistachio nuts

Break macaroons into small pieces and press enough on the bottom of a deep 9-inch springform or loose-bottomed pan to form a crust. Macaroons should be sticky. Cook apricots in 3 cups water until fruit is tender and water absorbed. Force through sieve or ricer, or whirl in blender. Cool. Sprinkle gelatin into ½ cup cold water. Let stand for 5 minutes to soften. Stir over hot water or very low heat until dissolved. Stir into apricots. Cream butter, add confectioners' sugar, and beat until blended. Beat in egg yolks, one at a time. Then beat in apricot mixture, lemon rind, and juice. Beat egg whites and salt until foamy. Add granulated sugar, 1 tablespoon at a time. Beat after each addition until stiff but not dry. Fold into apricot mixture. Pour about ¼ of mixture into pan. Add a layer of macaroon crumbs and continue alternating ingredients until all are used, ending with crumbs. Chill overnight. Remove sides of pan, leaving cake on pan base if preferred, and put cake on serving plate. Garnish with whipped cream, apricot halves, and chopped nuts. Makes 12 servings.

APRICOT SOUFFLÉ

12 to 20 apricot halves (one 1-pound can)
3 tablespoons butter
3 tablespoons all-purpose flour
Granulated sugar
1 tablespoon fresh lemon juice
Dash of salt
4 eggs, separated
Confectioners' sugar

Drain apricots, reserving syrup. Strain apricots through sieve and add syrup to make 1¼ cups. Melt butter and blend in flour. Add apricot pulp and cook until thickened. Remove from heat. Stir in 2 tablespoons granulated sugar, lemon juice, and salt. Beat egg yolks and add to mixture. Beat egg whites until stiff and fold into batter. Butter a 1½-quart soufflé dish and sprinkle with granulated sugar. Pour in mixture. Bake in preheated moderate oven (375°F.) for 25 minutes. Sprinkle with confectioners' sugar and serve with cream, if desired. Makes 4 servings.

APRICOT UPSIDE-DOWN CAKE

¾ cup butter or margarine
½ cup firmly packed brown sugar
½ teaspoon ground cinnamon
1½ cups drained canned apricot halves
½ cup granulated sugar
1 egg
1½ cups sifted all-purpose flour
2 teaspoons baking powder
½ teaspoon salt
½ cup milk

Melt ¼ cup butter in square pan (9x9x2 inches). Sprinkle with brown sugar and cinnamon. Arrange apricot halves, rounded side down, in pan. Cream ½ cup butter with granulated sugar until light. Beat in egg. Sift dry ingredients and add alternately with milk, beating until smooth. Spread on apricots. Bake in preheated moderate oven (375°F.) for about 30 minutes. Let stand for 10 minutes; turn out on serving plate and serve with whipped cream, if desired. Makes 6 large or 9 small servings.

Note: Halved, pitted, cooked prunes can be alternated with the apricots, for color contrast.

THE SIMPLEST APRICOT DESSERT

Served drained canned apricots with plenty of whipped cream that has been sweetened to taste and flavored with vanilla. Delicious.

APRICOTS WITH KIRSCH

Just before serving, put chilled canned apricot halves together with small scoops of vanilla ice cream. Place in individual serving dishes. Sprinkle lightly with kirsch (a colorless spirit distilled from cherries in Switzerland, Alsace, and Germany), or with red currant jelly that has been melted with a little hot water and then chilled.

DRIED APRICOTS

APRICOT CREAM

1 pound dried apricots
2½ cups water
⅛ teaspoon salt
½ cup sugar
1 tablespoon fresh lemon juice
1½ cups heavy cream

Cook apricots in water and salt for 15 to 20 minutes, or until tender. Stir in sugar and lemon juice. Press through sieve or whirl in a blender. Cool purée. Beat cream until stiff and fold into apricot purée. Chill. Makes 6 servings.

APRICOT-PRUNE PIE

2½ cups mixed cooked dried apricots and pitted prunes
Pastry for 2-crust 9-inch pie, unbaked
1 tablespoon cornstarch
½ cup sugar
⅛ teaspoon salt
¼ teaspoon each of ground cinnamon and nutmeg
½ cup cooking liquid from fruit
Juice of 1 lemon
1 tablespoon butter

Put fruit into 9-inch pie pan lined with pastry. Mix cornstarch, sugar, salt, and spices. Gradually stir in liquid. Cook, stirring constantly, until slightly thickened. Stir in lemon juice and butter; pour over fruit. Cover with remaining pastry. Moisten edges of pastry with water and press together with tines of fork. Trim edges and cut slits in top to allow steam to escape. Bake in preheated hot oven (425°F.) for about 30 minutes. Serve either warm or cold. Makes 6 to 8 servings.

APRICOT RICE PUDDING

½ cup raw rice (white or brown, not processed)
½ cup sugar
½ teaspoon salt
½ teaspoon ground nutmeg
2 quarts milk
¾ cup well-drained soaked dried apricots

Mix rice, sugar, salt, and nutmeg in shallow 2½-quart baking dish. Add 1 quart milk. Then, to prevent spilling, add second quart of milk after placing dish in oven. Bake in preheated slow oven (325°F.) for 2½ hours, stirring twice during first hour. Stir the brown crust into pudding several times during remainder of baking. Cut apricots into strips. Add 30 minutes before pudding is done. Then allow crust to form again. Serve with cream, if desired. Makes 6 to 8 servings.

FROZEN APRICOT MOUSSE

1 cup cooked dried apricots, sweetened to taste
2 eggs
⅓ cup sugar
½ teaspoon vanilla extract
⅛ teaspoon salt
1 cup heavy cream, stiffly whipped

Press apricots through a sieve or whirl in a blender. Beat eggs until fluffy. Gradually beat in sugar. Combine apricots with egg mixture, vanilla, and salt. Fold in whipped cream. Turn into refrigerator tray and place in freezing compartment. Set control at coldest setting and freeze until firm. Makes about 1½ pints.

APRICOT STRUDEL

12 ounces dried apricots
Boiling water
1 small orange, ground, including peel
1 small lemon, ground, including peel

Sugar (about 1⅔ cups)
1 cup chopped nuts
1½ teaspoons ground cinnamon
1 cup golden raisins
1 cup fine plain-cake crumbs
1 cup flaked coconut
   Melted butter or margarine
   Strudel Dough (see Apple Strudel, page 101)

Cover apricots with boiling water and soak for several hours or overnight. Drain. Chop apricots fine and add half of orange and lemon and ¾ cup sugar. Mix well. In another bowl, mix remaining orange and lemon, nuts, ¾ cup sugar, ½ teaspoon cinnamon, raisins, crumbs, coconut, and 1 tablespoon butter. Roll Strudel Dough as directed in recipe. Spread with nut mixture. Spoon a little butter evenly over top. Spread with apricot mixture and roll up. Slice into 1-inch pieces, but do not cut completely through. Sprinkle with a mixture of 2 tablespoons sugar and remaining cinnamon. Bake in preheated hot oven (400°F.) for about 1 hour. Remove from pan and complete slicing while still warm.

APRICOT-PINEAPPLE JAM

1 box (11 ounces) dried apricots
4 cups water
3½ cups (one 1-pound, 14-ounce can) pineapple chunks
6 cups sugar

In large saucepan mix all ingredients except sugar. Let stand for 1 hour. Then cook slowly until apricots are tender. Add sugar and cook slowly, stirring frequently, until thick and clear (220°F. on a candy-jelly thermometer). Pour at once into hot sterilized glasses and seal with paraffin. Cover with lids. Makes about 6 six-ounce glasses.

APRICOT REFRIGERATOR CAKE

1 pound dried apricots
2½ cups water
1 cup butter
2 cups sifted confectioners' sugar
4 eggs, separated
   Grated rind and juice of 1 lemon
⅓ cup granulated sugar
3 dozen ladyfingers, split
¾ cup heavy cream, whipped
   Canned apricot halves
   Fresh mint sprigs

Stew apricots in water until tender and liquid is absorbed. Put through ricer or sieve (there should be about 2⅓ cups thick pulp), and cool. Cream butter. Add confectioners' sugar and beat until light. Add egg yolks, one at a time, and beat well. Beat in apricot pulp, lemon rind, and juice. Beat egg whites until stiff, gradually add granulated sugar, beating until sugar is dissolved. Fold into apricot mixture. Line deep springform pan (9 inches) with split ladyfingers. Put in alternate layers of ⅓ of mixture and ⅓ of ladyfingers. Chill overnight, or a day or two. Remove sides of pan. Garnish with whipped cream and apricot halves. Decorate with mint sprigs. Makes 10 to 12 servings.

APRICOT PRESERVES

APRICOT GLAZE

This simple glaze is much used in French home- and professional cooking to give brilliance and glitter to any fruit tart, since the taste of apricot blends very well with that of other fruits. It can be used as a simple icing for cakes, cookies, and pies, or used inside a pastry shell to moistureproof it before the filling goes in.

Simply boil apricot preserves to between 225°F. and 228°F. Stir frequently. The preserve thus boiled will stiffen slightly as it cools and will not be sticky. Use a pastry brush in applying it.

Red currant jelly may be treated and used in the same way.

APRICOT CRESCENTS

½ cup soft butter or margarine
2 packages (3 ounces each) cream cheese, softened
¾ cup sifted all-purpose flour
⅛ teaspoon salt
1 tablespoon cold water
   Apricot preserves
   Minced nuts
   Confectioners' sugar

Cut butter and cheese into flour and salt. Add water and mix lightly with fork until blended. Chill until firm. Cut into 24 pieces. Keep dough chilled before rolling. Roll each piece very thin on floured board, to form 2½- to 3-inch squares. Spread each with apricot preserves and sprinkle with nuts. Roll up from one corner and bend ends in slightly to form crescents. Put folded side down on ungreased cookie sheets and bake in preheated very hot oven (450°F.) for about 10 minutes. Sift confectioners' sugar over cooled crescents. Makes 24.

APRICOT SAUCE

1½ cups apricot jam
½ cup water
1 tablespoon sugar
1 teaspoon fresh lemon juice or 2 tablespoons brandy

Combine apricot jam, water, and sugar in a small heavy saucepan. Bring to a boil. Simmer for 5 minutes, stirring constantly. Remove from heat and stir in lemon juice. Serve hot or cold. Excellent for ice cream, puddings, and cake. Makes about 2 cups.

APRICOT NECTAR

JELLIED APRICOT DESSERT

Use 1 can (12 ounces) apricot nectar. Sprinkle 1 envelope unflavored gelatin into ½ cup apricot nectar. Let stand for 5 minutes. Heat over hot water or over low heat, stirring until gelatin is dissolved. Add remaining nectar and juice of 1 orange and 1 lemon. Pour into 8-inch square pan and chill until firm. Cut into cubes, pile in dessert dishes, and serve with sweetened whipped cream or soft custard sauce. Makes 4 servings.

ARAB INFLUENCE ON FOOD—We

owe much of our knowledge of such everyday foods as sugar, fruits, and spices to the Arab world. The Arabs, traders since antiquity, introduced many new foods to the West. Especially welcome was their trading with spices, since spices, which were costly and very desirable, played a most important role in making palatable the monotonous and often improperly preserved foods of the past.

Many Arab plants, crops, and foods were introduced to the West during the 11th, 12th, and 13th centuries, the time of the Crusades. The Crusaders, for instance, brought back sesame, rice, millet, melons, apricots, shallots, and scallions and, most important, sugar, which until then was almost completely unknown, all the sweetening having been done with honey and fruits. The very word "sugar" comes from the Arabic.

AROMA—The word means a distinctive, agreeable fragrance which is more penetrating and persuasive than a smell, and has none of the negative meaning sometimes associated with the words smell and odor. Though one speaks of the aroma of a cigar, the word is usually applied to foods. Thus we say the aroma of coffee, of spices, of herbs, of meat cooking, of fruits, etc.

The aroma of foods greatly affects our enjoyment of them since the connection between the senses of taste and smell is an extremely close one. Instinctively, one thinks that if the aroma of a food is pleasant, the taste will be too. This is true in most cases (think of the aroma of a dish of strawberries), but it can be otherwise. Test this by biting into a clove.

There is also a close connection between aroma and memory. Few things are as evocative as the aroma of a certain food or drink; it may recall experiences long forgotten.

ARRACK—This name is given to two different strong liquors. One is a liquor distilled from rice. It originated in the former Dutch East Indies (now Indonesia) where it was known as Batavia arrack. It is used mostly as a flavoring in confectionery, desserts, and punches.

Arrack is also the name of a liquor with a pronounced anise flavor which is distilled from local grains or grapes in the Middle East, Turkey, and Greece. It is known as *arrack* in Lebanon, *raki* in Turkey, and *ouzo* in Greece. Though a clear spirit in itself, it turns milky and opalescent when mixed with water. It is said that you have to be born to *arrack*; *raki*, or *ouzo*, but those who are, love it.

ARROWROOT—The starch obtained from the tubers of several kinds of tropical plants. The roots are peeled, washed, and pulped to produce a white fluid. This is made into a powder which is then milled into the form we know.

Arrowroot is an excellent thickening agent and can be used in lieu of flour or cornstarch. It is neutral in flavor and produces soups, sauces, pie fillings, and puddings that are clear and sparkling, with none of the heaviness of other starches. Arrowroot is easily digested and therefore suitable for invalid cookery.

Arrowroot is not much known in modern American home-cooking, although our grandmothers used it to make their famous delicate blancmange and other puddings. It is now mainly used commercially as a thickening agent for various desserts. Arrowroot is very popular in Great Britain, and was a great standby of Victorian cooking, with its puddings and jellied sweet dishes of all kinds, all of which arrowroot makes to perfection. Victorian cook books are full of arrowroot recipes to suit the delicate tastes and constitutions of the ladies of the time.

Arrowroot is usually found on the spice shelves of grocery stores.

To Cook with Arrowroot—The delicate texture of arrowroot allows it to cook at a lower temperature and for a shorter time than other starches. It is thus ideally suited for sauces and custards containing eggs, which must not boil or are heat sensitive.

As a thickening agent substitute 1½ teaspoons arrowroot for 1 tablespoon flour.

ARROWROOT BLANCMANGE

⅓ cup arrowroot
1 cup cold milk
2 cups milk, scalded
⅓ cup sugar
1 teaspoon vanilla extract
Dash of salt

Mix arrowroot with milk. Gradually stir arrowroot mixture into scalded milk and cook over low heat, stirring constantly, until thickened. Add sugar, vanilla, and salt. Pour into 1-quart bowl and chill. Serve with stewed fruit or jam. Makes 4 to 5 servings.

ARTICHOKE—Globe or common artichokes are the leafy buds from a plant resembling the thistle. They have been widely cultivated as food in Europe for hundreds of years and cooked in a great many delicious ways. We know that they grew in the vicinity of Naples in the 15th century, and their popularity spread to other parts of Europe. In the 18th century French settlers brought them to Louisiana (they are sometimes called "French" artichokes). The Spanish brought artichokes to California, and they were also grown in Florida. Today they are cultivated in the United States where the climate is cool, foggy, and free of frost, mainly in the mid-coastal regions of California. Globe artichokes are not to be confused with Jerusalem artichokes, a completely different vegetable. Artichokes, like other vegetables, may be eaten in many ways. One way is to eat them with the fingers: pull off the leaves one at a time and dip them into a sauce which may be hot melted butter and lemon juice, hollandaise or mayonnaise, sour cream, or a French dressing. Eventually a core of thin, light-colored leaves is reached; this covers the choke and the heart. Eat the tender part of these leaves by drawing between teeth. Discard the remainder of the leaf. The fuzzy choke is scraped off with a knife or fork and discarded. The heart, also called "bottom," is eaten with a fork.

Availability—Fresh artichokes are available the year round; the main season is September to May, with the peak of production arriving toward spring.

Artichoke hearts or bottoms are available canned and ready for eating. Artichoke hearts are also available frozen and require a minimum of cooking.

Purchasing Guide—Look for uniformly solid heads with compact leaves. Loose, spreading, and discolored leaves indicate overmaturity or poor quality. Size has little to do with quality or flavor. Choose small, medium, or large, according to your preference or the way they are to be served. The small size is usually selected for pickling or baking with meat,

the medium or large for salads, and the large for the hearts.

Storage—Use fresh artichokes as soon as possible. Hold in a covered container in the refrigerator. Keep cool and moist.

☐ Fresh, refrigerator shelf: 4 days
☐ Fresh, refrigerator frozen-food compartment, prepared for freezing: 1 month
☐ Fresh, freezer, prepared for freezing: 1 year
☐ Canned, kitchen shelf: 1 year
☐ Canned, refrigerator shelf, opened and covered: 4 to 5 days

Nutritive Food Values—Artichokes contain small amounts of vitamins and minerals.

☐ Fresh, 1 cooked = 50 to 60 calories, depending on size
☐ About ½ cup, canned or frozen = about 40 calories; caloric values vary greatly.

Basic Preparation—**Important**—It must be remembered that artichokes discolor rapidly once they are cut. To prevent this, before starting to prepare the artichokes, have ready a bowl of water acidulated with vinegar or lemon juice, about 3 tablespoons to 1 quart water. Drop artichokes into this water as soon as they are prepared and keep them in the water until cooking time. This will keep them light.

☐ **To Cook, Whole**—Wash, drain, and cut off artichoke stem to a 1- or ½-inch stub. Pull off and discard any coarse or misshapen leaves. With kitchen scissors, trim off the thorny tip of each leaf; then cook immediately. Cook in boiling salted water uncovered until tender, about 15 to 40 minutes, depending on size and variety. If you are preparing several artichokes, keep them in acidulated water as described above.

☐ **To Cook, Hearts**—Slice off stem. Tear off tough outer leaves. Discard. Trim base piece smoothly with a sharp knife. Place artichoke on its side and cut off the pointed tips of the remaining leaves. Scoop out choke with a small spoon. Artichoke heart may be left whole or cut into halves or quarters. Drop into acidulated water. Drain. Cook in boiling salted water uncovered until tender, about 10 to 15 minutes, depending on size.

☐ **To Cook, Sliced**—Trim as above. Slice off all leaves, leaving ½ inch of the white leaf on base of artichoke. Dechoke as above. Slice firm base into ¼-inch slices and drop slices into acidulated water. The size of the artichoke slices will depend on the size of the original artichoke. Cook as above.

☐ **To Freeze**—Prepare as for cooking whole. Scald whole artichokes in boiling solution of 3 tablespoons lemon juice and 3 quarts water for 8 to 10 minutes after water has started to boil. Artichoke hearts, slices, or bottoms should be

ARTICHOKES

1 *Artichoke Omelet*
2 *Artichoke and Shrimp Salad*
3 *Artichoke Hearts au Gratin*
4 *Artichoke Halves*

1

2

3

4

scalded for 2 to 3 minutes. Cool for 15 minutes under cold or ice water. Drain and package.

FRESH ARTICHOKES

ARTICHOKE HALVES

Prepare artichokes as for eating whole. Stand upright in deep saucepan. Sprinkle with salt and put 2 teaspoons vegetable oil on each. Pour in about 1 inch of boiling water and add 1 or 2 minced garlic cloves and 1 sliced onion. Cover and simmer for about 45 minutes, or until the bases are very tender. Add more water if necessary. Lift out the artichokes with 2 spoons or tongs. Drain upside down and chill. Before serving, split lengthwise and remove and discard chokes. Arrange artichoke halves around the edge of a shallow serving dish or large round platter. Serve with French dressing, or oil and lemon juice, or with a thinned well-seasoned mayonnaise. Garnish with greens, parsley sprigs, and wedges of tomato, if desired.

TWO SIMPLE WAYS TO COOK ARTICHOKES

■ Cut trimmed artichokes into thin slices. Sauté in a little hot butter or olive oil until tender. Shake pan to prevent sticking. Season with salt and pepper, and serve with a squeeze of lemon.

■ Cut trimmed artichokes into thin slices. Dip into seasoned flour and fry in hot olive or salad oil. Drain on paper towel. Serve very hot.

ARTICHOKES WITH ROMAN PORK CHOPS

    2 large or 4 medium artichokes,
        trimmed and sliced
    3 tablespoons olive oil
    6 pork chops, trimmed of excess fat
        Salt and pepper
    1 garlic clove, minced
    ½ teaspoon rosemary, basil, or sage
    2½ cups (one 1-pound, 4½-ounce can)
        Italian-style stewed tomatoes

Keep sliced artichokes in acidulated water until ready to use (see Basic Preparation). Heat olive oil in deep skillet or shallow casserole. Fry pork chops until browned on all sides. Pour off excess fat from skillet. Arrange artichoke slices around meat. Add seasonings and herbs; cover with tomatoes. Simmer, covered, for 1 hour, or until meat and artichokes are tender. If sauce is too thin, simmer, uncovered, until sufficiently reduced. Makes 4 to 6 servings.

ARTICHOKE HALVES, GREEK STYLE

    6 large artichokes
    4 cups water
    3 lemons
    1 tablespoon all-purpose flour
    1 cup chopped onion
    1 cup olive oil
        Salt and pepper

Cut stems off artichokes. Remove bottom leaves and with scissors trim off brown thorny tips of all remaining leaves. Cut off tops and halve each artichoke.

Soak in the water and juice of 2 of the lemons. Meanwhile, sprinkle flour over onion and sauté in olive oil until lightly browned. Arrange artichoke halves, cut side up, in roasting pan or large skillet. Add salt and pepper and juice of remaining lemon to onion and oil, and pour over artichokes. Add small amount of water, about ½ cup. Cover and simmer over low heat until artichokes are tender. Serve warm or cold. Makes 6 servings.

CANNED OR FROZEN ARTICHOKES

ARTICHOKE AND SHRIMP SALAD

On individual plates arrange beds of finely shredded lettuce. Heap whole shrimp on lettuce and sprinkle with ¼ cup finely diced celery. Add mayonnaise to moisten if desired. Season with a few drops of fresh lemon juice and salt and pepper to taste.) Press hard-cooked egg yolk through a sieve, sprinkle on shrimp. Surround with artichoke hearts. Garnish with pimiento. Chill. Two medium artichoke hearts make 1 serving for luncheon main dish.

ARTICHOKE OMELET

    2 tablespoons butter
    3 cooked artichoke hearts, diced
        Equal amount of diced cooked
        mushrooms
    2 tablespoons tomato sauce
        Salt and pepper
        Dash of cayenne
    ½ garlic clove
    8 eggs
    1 small can flat anchovy fillets

In 1 tablespoon butter lightly sauté artichokes and mushrooms. Add tomato sauce and seasonings, mix well and set aside in warm place. Rub a bowl with garlic. Break eggs into bowl and beat with a fork. Cook omelet as usual in remaining 1 tablespoon butter. When omelet is cooked, top with artichoke mixture and fold over. Garnish with anchovies and serve at once. Makes 4 servings.

ARTICHOKE HEARTS AU GRATIN

    2 packages (9 ounces each) frozen
        artichoke hearts
    ¼ cup butter or margarine
    ¾ teaspoon salt
        Dash of pepper
    1 teaspoon onion salt
    ¼ teaspoon dry mustard
    ⅓ cup all-purpose flour
    1½ cups milk
    1 egg, slightly beaten
    ½ cup grated Swiss cheese
    1 tablespoon fine dry bread crumbs
        Paprika

Cook artichokes as directed on package. Drain; reserve ½ cup liquid. Melt butter in saucepan. Stir in seasonings and flour. Gradually stir in artichoke liquid and milk. Cook over low heat, stirring constantly, until thickened. Remove from heat. Stir hot sauce gradually into egg and half of cheese. Blend well. Put arti-

chokes in a layer in shallow baking dish. Cover with sauce. Sprinkle with remaining cheese, the crumbs, and paprika. Bake in preheated very hot oven (450° F.) for about 15 minutes. Makes 6 servings.

ARTICHOKE HEARTS PIQUANT

    2 carrots, sliced
    ½ cup water
    2 tablespoons salad oil
        Juice of 1 lemon
    1 small bay leaf
    1 teaspoon salt
        Dash of garlic salt
    1 package (9 ounces) frozen artichoke
        hearts

Put all ingredients except artichokes in a saucepan. Bring to a boil and boil for about 5 minutes. Add artichokes and cook until tender, 5 to 10 minutes. Drain and serve. Makes 4 servings.

ARTICHOKE HEARTS SALAD

    1 package (9 ounces) frozen artichoke
        hearts
    1 medium head lettuce, shredded
    1 cup small raw cauliflowerets
    1 large tomato, diced
    1 tablespoon chopped chives
    2 large ripe olives, sliced
    2 large stuffed olives, sliced
    2 tablespoons chopped dill pickle
        French dressing

Cook artichokes as directed on package. Chill. Lightly toss vegetables, olives, and pickle with dressing to moisten. Serve at once. Makes 6 servings.

ASPARAGUS—This vegetable, the fifth most popular in the United States, is a member of the lily-of-the-valley family. The name comes from a Greek word meaning "stalk" or "shoot." It is thought to be native to the eastern Mediterranean lands and Asia Minor, where it still grows wild. It spread to Europe; as early as 200 B.C. the Romans wrote down directions for growing and drying the vegetable. Later, the English developed a fondness for eating it raw. Undoubtedly some of our earliest settlers brought roots with them from Europe. We know that Thomas Jefferson grew asparagus in the greenhouses of his beautiful Monticello.

As pioneers traveled west, they took it with them, developing colloquial names for it. One was "sparrow grass," and even today, asparagus is known as "grass" in the vegetable trade. Yet asparagus, with its crisp stalks and tightly closed, tender tips, maintains a special place among vegetables, almost a symbol of pleasant eating. Not all of it is green. In some areas blanched, or white asparagus, somewhat milder in flavor, is available.

In Europe, asparagus is grown in a number of different varieties and ways. It is considered the most luxurious of vegetables, fit for a king. Great chefs have created some of their finest and most complicated dishes with asparagus; in aspics, for example, for which there are special molds tailored to the shape of the vegetable.

Especially prized is the variety of asparagus that yields very thick, white, fleshy stalks that are incredibly tender. These asparagus are grown in little individual mounds, and cut when only the green tip shows so that the stalks are still white. They are available at specialty markets or imported from Europe, canned in glass jars or metal cans.

Among the virtues of asparagus is that it not only tastes excellent with any kind of food, but it is equally good hot, lukewarm, or cold. Perhaps the most popular way of serving asparagus is boiled and hot, with either hot butter or hollandaise sauce, or cold, with a vinaigrette sauce, which is a simple French dressing.

Availability—The main market season for fresh asparagus may start as early as February with the southwestern (California) crop. The season continues until late June, when the northeastern (New Jersey) crop appears.

Canned and frozen asparagus is available in tips, spears, and cuts (pieces). Some white asparagus is canned.

Purchasing Guide—Tender asparagus has brittle, easily punctured, straight green stalks, and tips that are well formed and tightly closed. Spreading tips mean overmaturity, and very thin, wilted, or crooked stalks may be tough or stringy. Asparagus is sold mainly by weight, although it is often tied in bunches. Bunches are frequently standardized to weigh 2½ pounds.
☐ 1 pound = 16 to 20 stalks

Storage—Keep stalks in the refrigerator in a covered container or plastic bag until ready to use. If stalks seem a little limp, cut a thin slice from ends and stand in cold water for a short time before storing. Do not wash before storing. Cook as soon as possible.
☐ Fresh, refrigerator shelf or vegetable compartment: 4 days
☐ Fresh, refrigerator frozen-food com-

partment, prepared for freezing: 1 month
☐ Fresh, freezer, prepared for freezing: 1 year
☐ Canned, kitchen shelf, unopened: 1 to 2 months
☐ Canned, refrigerator shelf, opened and covered: 4 days

Nutritive Food Values—A good source of vitamin A, fair for vitamins B and C and iron.
☐ 3½ ounces, raw = 26 calories
☐ 3½ ounces, cooked, canned, or frozen = 21 calories

Basic Preparation—When ready to cook, wash in cold running water and lift from water to eliminate any sand or grit. Do not soak. Break or cut off the stalks as far down as they will snap easily. Usually the white portion is tough. Shear off heavy scales with a vegetable parer or sharp knife. Rinse stalks again, hold tips up. If you wish lots of stalk, strip the peeling from the ends with a vegetable parer. Stalks may be left whole, cut into 1½-inch pieces, or sliced diagonally. Tips may be used separately. Asparagus tastes best when cooked until almost tender. (A fork will pierce the tough ends easily.) It may be cooked by steam-boiling or boiling.

☐ **To Steam-boil**—Divide stalks into serving-size bunches; tie each loosely with a string; or tie in 1 bunch, if amount is not large. Stand each bunch upright in a deep pan, such as the bottom of a double boiler. Add enough boiling water to cover bottom of stalks about 1 inch. Salt or not, as desired. Cover with inverted top part of double boiler. Cook for about 15 minutes. (The tougher ends of stalks cook in water, the tender tips in steam.) Special pans and tongs to be used in cooking asparagus are available. Remove from pan by using tongs. Drain, arrange on serving plate, and season.

☐ **To Boil**—Arrange prepared stalks in a skillet or wide-bottomed pan; pour in about ½ inch of boiling water. Sprinkle with salt if you wish. Cover pan. Bring quickly to boil, then lower heat to medium or low. Cook for 10 to 12 minutes, or until stalks are almost tender. Lift from pan with tongs or 2 forks. Drain and serve at once with melted butter.

When asparagus is prepared in pieces, prepare as above, omitting tips. Cook, covered, for 2 minutes. Add tips and cook, covered, for an additional 6 to 8 minutes.

☐ **To Pan-cook Slices**—For a tender crisp vegetable in the Chinese manner, slice asparagus stalks slantwise about ¼ inch thick; leave tips whole. Melt enough butter to cover bottom of a skillet. Heat until butter is hot and bubbly but not brown. Add slices; sprinkle with salt (and pepper if desired). Cover pan; bring to steam, then lower heat and cook until

barely tender, 3 to 5 minutes. Serve.
☐ **To Freeze**—Use young crisp stalks with compact tips. Clean and scale and remove woody portion of the stalk. Wash in cold water. Scald whole stalks for 3 to 4 minutes in boiling water, using 1 gallon of water to each pint of asparagus. Scald cut asparagus for 2 to 3 minutes. Drain and chill quickly in cold running water or ice water. Drain, place in freezer container, allowing ½-inch headspace, and freeze.

FRESH ASPARAGUS

CHEESE-BROILED ASPARAGUS
Put cooked asparagus spears in shallow baking dish or pie pan. Sprinkle generously with grated Romano cheese. Put under broiler until heated.

ASPARAGI ALL' UOVO
1 bunch asparagus (2½ pounds)
6 tablespoons olive oil
Salt and pepper
⅓ cup grated Parmesan cheese
1 garlic clove
8 eggs
Paprika

Cook asparagus in boiling salted water until tender; drain well. Put whole asparagus spears in shallow baking pan. Pour 3 tablespoons oil over asparagus and sprinkle with salt, pepper, and cheese. Halve garlic and cook slowly in remaining 3 tablespoons oil for about 5 minutes; do not brown. Remove garlic. Put asparagus under broiler and brown lightly under medium heat. While asparagus is browning, drop eggs into oil; cover and cook slowly for 3 minutes. Serve 2 eggs on each portion of asparagus. Sprinkle with paprika. Makes 4 servings.

ASPARAGUS HAM ROLLS
16 asparagus stalks, cooked
4 thin slices of boiled ham
½ cup grated sharp Cheddar cheese
1 cup medium white sauce (2 tablespoons butter, 2 tablespoons flour, 1 cup milk, salt and pepper)
Toast points

Put 4 asparagus stalks on each ham slice; roll up. Fasten with toothpick. Broil for 5 minutes on each side. Add cheese to heated sauce. Stir until cheese is melted; pour over ham rolls. Broil to golden brown. Garnish with toast. Makes 4 servings.

ASPARAGUS AND MUSHROOMS IN CREAM
1 pound fresh asparagus
3 tablespoons salad oil
¼ cup water
1 small onion, minced
½ cup (one 4-ounce can) sliced mushrooms, drained
½ teaspoon salt
⅛ teaspoon pepper
¼ cup cream

Wash asparagus and slice diagonally into 1½-inch pieces. Put oil and water in large skillet and bring to boil. Add asparagus, onion, mushrooms, salt, and

Asparagi All'Uovo

Asparagus Soufflé

Sesame Asparagus Salad

Asparagus Ham Rolls

pepper. Cook, covered, for 8 to 10 minutes, shaking skillet occasionally. Add cream. Reheat slightly, but do not boil. Makes 4 servings.

SCALLOPED ASPARAGUS

1 bunch asparagus (2½ pounds)
6 tablespoons butter or margarine
¾ cup soft bread crumbs
¼ cup all-purpose flour
½ teaspoon salt
½ teaspoon paprika
½ teaspoon Worcestershire
⅛ teaspoon pepper
2 cups milk
½ cup grated Cheddar cheese
¼ cup sliced stuffed olives

Wash asparagus and cut into 2-inch pieces. Cook in boiling salted water until barely tender. Drain and put in shallow baking dish. Melt butter in top part of double boiler. Mix 2 tablespoons melted butter with crumbs. Blend flour and seasonings into remaining butter. Gradu-

ally stir in milk and cook over boiling water until thickened, stirring constantly. Add cheese and olives and stir until cheese is melted. Pour over asparagus. Top with crumbs. Bake in preheated moderate oven (375°F.) for about 15 minutes. Makes 4 servings.

ASPARAGUS SAUCE 1: HOLLANDAISE

½ cup butter, softened
¼ cup hot water
¼ teaspoon salt
⅛ teaspoon pepper
4 egg yolks, slightly beaten
2 tablespoons fresh lemon juice

Combine butter, hot water, salt, and pepper in top part of double boiler. Blend small amount of butter mixture, about 2 teaspoons, into beaten egg yolks. Gradually beat in remaining butter. Place over hot, not boiling, water. Beat with rotary beater or wire whip until thick and smooth. Blend in lemon juice. If sauce

curdles, add 1 teaspoon hot water and blend well. Makes about 1 cup.

ASPARAGUS SAUCE 2: QUICK BLENDER HOLLANDAISE

2 egg yolks
1 tablespoon fresh lemon juice
¼ teaspoon salt
⅛ teaspoon pepper
½ cup butter

Combine egg yolks, lemon juice, salt, and pepper in blender. Whirl slightly. Heat butter until bubbly. Do not brown. While eggs are whirling, drizzle butter slowly into blender. Whirl *only* until thick; this takes much less time than you may think. Makes about ¾ cup.

ASPARAGUS SAUCE 3: POLONAISE

¼ cup butter
½ cup fresh bread crumbs
1 hard-cooked egg, finely chopped
1 tablespoon chopped parsley

Heat butter. Brown bread crumbs in it. Add hard-cooked egg and heat through. Sprinkle with parsley. Spoon over hot cooked drained asparagus. Makes about ¾ cup.

ASPARAGUS SAUCE 4: SALSA VERDE

3 tablespoons cider vinegar
½ cup olive oil
¾ teaspoon prepared mustard
3 tablespoons mixed finely chopped parsley, raw spinach, and watercress
1 medium onion, minced

Combine all ingredients and blend thoroughly. Makes about ¾ cup sauce.
Note: This Italian sauce is also good for other vegetables served cold, for seafood and salads.

CANNED AND FROZEN ASPARAGUS

ASPARAGUS SOUFFLÉ

3 tablespoons butter or margarine
3 tablespoons flour
¾ teaspoon salt
⅛ teaspoon pepper
1 cup milk
6 eggs, separated
1 cup (1-inch pieces) canned asparagus, drained
1 tablespoon instant minced onion
1 chopped pimiento

Melt butter and blend in flour, salt, and pepper. Gradually stir in milk and cook, stirring constantly, until thickened. Cool. Beat egg whites until stiff. Then beat yolks until thick and lemon-colored. Stir first mixture gradually into yolks. Fold in whites and asparagus, onion, and pimiento. Pour into 2-quart casserole and set in pan of hot water. Bake in preheated moderate oven (350°F.) for 45 minutes, or until tip of knife inserted in center comes out clean. Serve at once. Makes 6 servings.

ASPARAGUS WITH HERB BUTTER

Cook 1 package (10 ounces) frozen asparagus spears until tender. Cream ¼ cup soft butter, dash each of cayenne and paprika, and a pinch each of rosemary and thyme. Blend in juice of ½ lemon. Serve on drained hot asparagus. Makes 2 or 3 servings.

SESAME ASPARAGUS SALAD

1 package (10 ounces) frozen cut asparagus
1 head romaine, broken in pieces
2 pimientos, diced
1 green onion, chopped
¼ cup toasted sesame seed
¼ teaspoon cracked pepper
¼ teaspoon herb seasoning
2 tablespoons each of lemon juice and salad oil
Salt to taste

Cook, drain, and chill asparagus. Add to next 3 ingredients. Mix sesame seed, pepper, herb seasoning, lemon juice, and oil. Add to first mixture; toss. Add salt. Makes 4 to 6 servings.

ASPIC—A clear, savory, nonsweet jelly used to decorate or to mold entrées, salads, and canapés of meat, fish, poultry, eggs, and the like. The origin of the word is French, meaning "lavender" as well as aspic, the food, and it may well be that the original aspic was a lavender-flavored jelly. In French culinary use, aspic refers not to the jelly, but to the whole decorated dish. The jelly itself is called "gelée."

How to Cook Superbly: Aspics

By Helen Evans Brown

A crystal-clear, shimmering aspic is a beautiful and impressive sight and one that any reasonably careful cook can make as perfectly as a trained chef. Aspics have three uses: the first, and best known, is for making molds in which various meats, poultry, seafoods, or vegetables are encased; a second use is for glazing and decorating previously cooked and chilled foods; the third use is for garnishing, the jelly being either chopped or cut into shapes for decorative purposes. In each case the aspic must be crystal clear, but this is easily accomplished as you'll learn below. Although a quick aspic can be made from canned bouillon, many dedicated cooks will prefer to make it from scratch. You'll have to start the day before you need it, but it's worth the trouble, truly. However, I'll give you the quick recipe, too.

☐ **Equipment**—Most kitchens have everything needed for a perfect aspic: a large pot (one with a capacity of 10 quarts), a large strainer or colander, a piece of closely woven cloth (sheeting, a dish towel, or a napkin, somewhat larger than the colander). A long-handled wire whip and a set of tiny cutters (usually called truffle cutters) are optional.

☐ **Ingredients**—For 2 quarts of regular aspic:

2 pounds beef shank (meat and bones)
2 pounds veal knuckle (meat and bones)
1 small stewing hen (or ½ a large hen, or 3 pounds chicken backs and necks)
1 calf's foot or 6 chicken feet (optional)
1 gallon cold water
1 peeled split onion
4 whole cloves
1 tablespoon salt
1 large carrot, sliced
2 large celery stalks, sliced
4 branches parsley
1 bay leaf
¼ teaspoon black peppercorns, crushed
1 cup port or Madeira or sherry (optional)
1 tablespoon minced parsley
½ teaspoon each of tarragon and basil
3 egg whites

Here's how—

1. Have meat and chicken chopped into pieces. (If you are able to find a calf's foot, have it skinned and split. Chicken feet should be scalded with boiling water and scraped. The calf's foot or chicken feet are used for their strong gelatin content; plain gelatin may be used instead, see step 6.)

2. Put meats all together in the 10-quart pot and add the water, onion, cloves, and salt. Bring slowly to a boil, skimming off the grayish scum as it forms on top.

3. When boiling, add the carrot, celery, parsley, bay leaf, and peppercorns. Turn heat down until the stock is simmering slowly, cover and cook for 5 or 6 hours, or until meat has fallen from bones and liquid has reduced one half.

4. Strain stock, discard the vegetables, seasonings, and tasteless meat and bones.

5. Cool the strained stock. Put into the refrigerator overnight.

6. Next day, remove the cake of fat that has formed on top of the jellied stock. If you have used the calf's foot or chicken feet, you should have a stiff enough jelly for any purpose (as stiff as a commercial gelatin dessert). Otherwise you'll have to add plain gelatin. If the jelly is fairly stiff, 1 envelope gelatin softened in ¼ cup cold water should do. Heat the stock and add the softened gelatin, stirring until dissolved. Pour a little in a cup and put in the refrigerator. If it doesn't set stiffly enough, add more gelatin, but you'll soon be able to judge how much. Sometimes the aspic is too stiff, in which case add boiling water, starting with a cupful and testing as above.

7. The next step is to flavor and clear the aspic. Melt the jellied stock. If you are using wine, simmer the wine until it has almost evaporated and add to the stock, along with the parsley, tarragon, and basil.

8. Beat the egg whites slightly, pour into the melted stock and bring the mixture to a boil, stirring constantly, preferably with a wire whip or slotted spoon.

The beauty and flavor of vegetables are captured in shimmering aspic to be served as an appetizer or in a sparkling salad.

When the mixture comes to a boil, it should separate in spots so that you can see the clear liquid.

9. Turn off heat and let settle for a few minutes, then skim the top.

10. Wring the cloth out in cold water and line the colander with it, then strain the stock through it. Don't let the cloth slip, because even a few drops of the unstrained liquid will cloud your masterpiece.

11. Taste and add salt if it's needed.

CHICKEN ASPIC

Make this the same way as the regular aspic, but use 2 small stewing hens or 6 pounds chicken backs and necks, and omit the beef and veal. If possible, include 6 scaled and scraped chicken feet, otherwise use gelatin if needed. The wine may be omitted or 3 tablespoons of Cognac can be substituted for it.

FISH ASPIC

Make this like the regular aspic, but use 6 pounds fish bones and scraps instead of the meats. Add ½ lemon to the cooking water. If you wish, use 1 cup white wine instead of the wines suggested above, or omit wine and use 3 tablespoons Cognac. Gelatin will probably have to be added.

QUICK ASPIC

Soften 1 envelope plain gelatin in ¼ cup cold water. Heat the contents of 2 cans (10 ounces each) beef bouillon or consommé and add the gelatin, 2 tablespoons port, sherry, or Madeira (optional) and the slightly beaten white of 1 egg. Proceed as for regular aspic.

☐ **To Decorate and Fill Aspic Molds—**

1. Pimientos, hard-cooked-egg whites, green peppers, black truffles or ripe olives, carrots, or any colorful food can be used for decoration. Slice them as thin as possible, then cut into fancy shapes with truffle cutters; or into squares, diamonds, or julienne pieces with a sharp knife. Thinly sliced stuffed olives or hard-cooked eggs, chives, or leaves of fresh tarragon can also be used.

2. Measure mold you are using and have corresponding amount of aspic, or less if large pieces of meats or other foods are to be jellied.

3. Cool melted aspic until it has the consistency of raw egg white by putting the bowl of aspic in a pan of ice and stirring with a metal spoon until the aspic reaches the proper consistency.

4. Have decorations ready and mold well chilled. If you want decorations on the sides as well as the bottom of the mold, have ready a pan larger than the mold, filled with cracked ice. Pour a small amount of the aspic in the ice-cold mold and tip and turn the mold so that the aspic glazes the entire inside. Put at once in the pan of ice. (If you wish to decorate only the bottom of the

Aspic can also be used as a glaze or, cut into decorative shapes, as a garnish.

tween head and tail, pieces of salmon steak, trimmed poached eggs, eggs *mollet* (cooked 5 minutes, then cooled and shelled immediately), decorative canapés, or even a whole salmon or chicken. Arrange food on a cake rack placed over a cookie sheet. Chill thoroughly. Have aspic at the raw-egg-white consistency as above. Spoon aspic over the food, using the side of a large metal spoon. (The excess will drop onto the pan and can be used again.) Chill, decorate as for molds, chill again, then add one more layer of aspic. When set, arrange on a cold platter and garnish with greens or with cut or chopped aspic.

☐ **To Garnish with Aspic**—Pour ½ inch of aspic into a baking pan (an 8- x 8-inch glass one is good) and allow to set. Using small cookie cutters, cut into shapes and use as a garnish, or turn out on a board covered with wax paper and chop the aspic into glittering pieces, then pile around the food on the platter. If you have chopped more than you need, slide aspic from paper into pan, melt and reset.

☐ **Jellied Soups**—If you want a particularly delicious jellied meat, fish, or chicken consommé, make any of the aspics as above, but add enough boiling water so that the aspic sets into a quivering jelly, one not quite as stiff as the usual canned jellied soups. Garnish with a slice of lemon, or with minced chives, or sour cream and red caviar, or with chopped fresh herbs.

EGGS IN ASPIC À LA FRANÇAISE
1 envelope unflavored gelatin
2 cups well-seasoned chicken bouillon
1 teaspoon instant minced onion
½ teaspoon monosodium glutamate
4 hard-cooked eggs, halved lengthwise
2 pimientos, cut into strips
Chopped parsley and chives
Salad greens
Mayonnaise

Soften gelatin in ½ cup of the bouillon for 5 minutes. Dissolve gelatin while stirring over hot water or low heat. Add to remaining bouillon with onion and monosodium glutamate. Pour half into an oiled pan (10 x 6 x 2 inches). Chill until firm. Chill remaining half until thickened to the consistency of unbeaten egg whites. Arrange eggs, cut side down, on firm mixture. Make a cross of pimiento on each. Sprinkle with herbs. Spoon remaining thickened mixture over eggs. Chill until firm. Cut into squares and serve on greens on individual plates with mayonnaise. Makes 4 servings.

JELLIED TONGUE RING
1 envelope unflavored gelatin
¼ cup cold tongue stock
1 beef bouillon cube
1½ cups hot tongue stock
¼ cup cider vinegar
1 tablespoon sugar
½ teaspoon Worcestershire
¼ cup chopped sweet pickle

mold, as in a loaf pan, pour a thin layer in the mold, then refrigerate until set.) If you want a thicker coating of aspic, repeat this process.

5. Dip decorations in the syrupy aspic and arrange in the desired design on the sides and bottom of the mold. They will stick in place if the mold is cold enough. Return to ice to set, then add another layer of aspic by again pouring in a small amount and turning until the decorations are covered. Again return to ice.

6. When set, add your chicken, fish, tongue, shellfish or vegetables, either sliced or cut into pieces, and fill to the top of the mold with the remaining aspic. Put in the refrigerator until completely set before unmolding.

☐ **To Unmold Aspic**—Loosen the aspic by pressing gently all around the edge of the mold or by running a small pointed knife around the inside. Dip the mold into warm water, making sure that none spills over the edge. Do this quickly;

it should not stand in the water. Put a plate over the top of the mold and reverse the mold quickly. Hold both plate and mold with both hands, on the table, and slide and shake mold back and forth a couple of times. Lift mold off carefully. (If aspic doesn't unmold, repeat process.)

☐ **To Serve Aspics in the Mold**—This is an easier version of aspic, since food is served from the dish or dishes in which it is molded. It's often used for eggs in aspic, for instance. Arrange the cold food in an attractive serving dish or, in the case of eggs *mollet,* in individual oval-shaped dishes. Cover the food with aspic and allow to set, then decorate as above. When decorations have set, pour another thin film of aspic over them and allow to set before serving in the dish.

☐ **To Glaze Food with Aspic**—The food to be glazed with aspic should be cooked and very cold. Favorite foods for coating are breast of chicken, neatly trimmed, whole trout with the skin removed be-

**Tomato Aspic
with Vegetables**

Tomato Aspic

¼ cup chopped green pepper
½ cup chopped celery
2 hard-cooked eggs, sliced
1¼ cups cold diced tongue

Sprinkle gelatin over cold stock. Let stand for 5 minutes. Dissolve bouillon cube in hot tongue stock. Add gelatin and stir until dissolved. Add vinegar, sugar, and Worcestershire. Chill until jelled to the consistency of unbeaten egg whites. Fold in remaining ingredients. Pour into a lightly oiled 5-cup mold. Chill until firm. Unmold on salad greens. If desired, serve with dairy sour cream or mayonnaise, seasoned with prepared mustard. Makes 4 servings.

Note: Make this the day before you plan to serve it.

TOMATO ASPIC
3½ cups tomato juice
1 celery stalk, cut up
1 onion, chopped
½ lemon, cut
1 teaspoon ground basil
1 teaspoon sugar
1 teaspoon salt
Dash of cayenne
2 envelopes unflavored gelatin
¼ cup cider vinegar

Combine tomato juice with vegetables and seasonings. Cover and simmer over low heat for 20 minutes. Strain. Add gelatin softened in vinegar and stir until dissolved. Pour into mold and refrigerate until firm. If vegetables, fish, or meat are to be added, chill until aspic is of the consistency of unbeaten egg white; fold in vegetables, fish, or meat and pour into a lightly oiled mold. Chill until firm. Makes 4 to 6 servings.

VEGETABLES IN ASPIC

Cook and cool 1 package (10 ounces) frozen mixed vegetables. Soften 1 envelope unflavored gelatin in ¼ cup chicken bouillon for 5 minutes. Stir over low heat until gelatin is dissolved. Stir into 1½ cups cold chicken bouillon; add 2 tablespoons chopped chives or green onion with tops, juice of 1 lemon, and salt and pepper to taste. Chill until thickened to the consistency of unbeaten egg white. Fold in mixed vegetables. Chill until firm in shallow dish; cut into squares and serve on greens with curry mayonnaise. Makes 6 servings.

ATTELET—This French word is derived from the Latin *hasta,* meaning "rod." An *attelet* is a kitchen accessory in the shape of a long pin or a little skewer, with a top in the shape of an ornament that might be an eagle, a flower, a harp, a design of scrolls, or arabesques, etc. *Attelets* are used only for decorat-

ing hot or cold dishes in the elaborate grand manner which is becoming rarer and rarer. To do so, bits of food such as truffles, shrimps, cocks' combs, or olives are threaded on the *attelets,* and sometimes separated by paper ruffles for greater effect. The *attelets* are then stuck into other foods or around them, giving the effect of a crown.

AU (plural, aux)—A French word which means in culinary usage "with," and is used in naming dishes. It is usually followed by an ingredient of the dish, as in *au gratin,* with cheese; *au lait,* with milk; *aux marrons,* with chestnuts; roast beef *au jus,* with natural gravy.

AU GRATIN—A cooking process done in a hot oven or under the broiler which produces dishes with a crisp, golden-brown crust. This is achieved by sprinkling the food with fresh or toasted bread crumbs, or with grated cheese, especially Parmesan, sprinkled with melted butter. But *au gratin* also applies to dishes that will crust of their own accord.

Foods to be finished *au gratin* may be raw or cooked, and they may or may not be blended with a sauce. The most frequently used sauce in foods served *au gratin* is white sauce.

To make a dish *au gratin* is to add taste, texture, and eye appeal, since the bubbly golden surface looks tempting. It is also an excellent way of utilizing leftovers of meat, fish, vegetables, cereals, and other foods, either singly or in combinations.

To gratin a dish, sprinkle top of food with 1 to 2 cups plain or buttered coarse bread crumbs, or with ¼ to ¾ cup grated cheese, depending on quantity of food to be gratined. Drizzle with a little melted butter. Brown under a preheated broiler, or bake uncovered in a preheated moderate oven (375°F.) until food is heated through and golden brown on top. If necessary to prevent overcooking, raise oven temperature to hot (400° to 425°F.) for 3 to 6 minutes, or until slightly browned.

FISH FILLETS AU GRATIN
1 pound fish fillets
⅔ cup canned condensed soup such as celery, mushroom, or asparagus
2 tablespoons milk
1 cup coarse bread crumbs or ¼ cup grated cheese
2 tablespoons melted butter

Arrange fish fillets in buttered baking dish. Combine soup and milk and heat.

Pour over fish. Sprinkle with bread crumbs. Drizzle with melted butter. Bake, uncovered, in moderate oven (375°F.) for 10 to 15 minutes, or until golden on top. Makes 2 to 3 servings.

AU JUS—A French term that describes meat served with its own natural juices, not with a gravy.

AU LAIT—A French term that describes a beverage, such as coffee, made or served with milk.

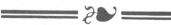

AU NATUREL—In culinary French, this term describes food prepared or cooked to resemble its natural state as much as possible, or in other words, food plainly done.

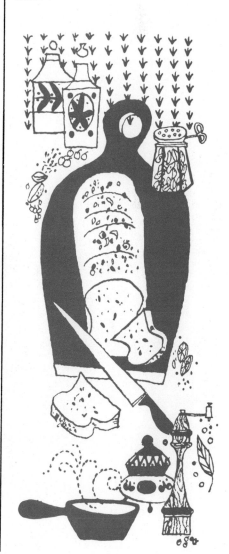

AUSTRIAN COOKERY

What makes Austrian food different from that of other Central European countries is its variety and liveliness. Austrian cooking has been influenced by the cooking of neighboring countries, some of which were once part of the Austrian Empire. They contributed dishes, seasonings, and ways of cooking to this charming country of luminous mountains, cool rivers and lakes, and picture-book towns.

From Hungary come the paprika dishes, and from Germany all kinds of dumplings. Italy sent pasta, tomato cookery, and the ubiquitous schnitzel, which started out as a Milanese veal cutlet. Serbia, Crotia, Bulgaria, and the rest of the Balkans contributed mutton, rice, vegetables, spices. To Poland, we trace an affection for sour cream, carp, and pike; to Czechoslovakia, fondness for goose, smoked pork, and noble yeast pastries. To the Turks, who besieged Vienna twice, goes the credit for Austria's heavenly coffee which is served in the country's innumerable coffeehouses in a dozen shades that range from black to white, each with its own name. Whatever the dish, in Austria's kitchens it became smoothed over, refined, expanded, richer, and generally improved to assume an expansive character of its own which is uniquely Austrian.

In Austria, women were rated on their ability to cook, and although no Austrian ever closed his eyes at the sight of a pretty face or a trim ankle, these were

not first considerations in the choice of a lifetime mate. Or, as the Austrian writer Adolf Glassbrenner has said: "Do not believe to be already in paradise when you see an apple tree."

From Austrian kitchens come the nourishing soups that are a cornerstone of all Austrian eating. The women were thrifty, making much of dumplings, pancakes, and cereal puddings, both savory and sweet. They were loving, cooking their pot roasts slowly, almost in their own juices to bring out every smidgen of the meat's flavor. They were canny, combining vegetables to make them more interesting, or putting them into soufflés. They were imaginative, devising dozens of ways to cook cabbage and potatoes.

When it came to desserts and cakes, Austrian women were temptresses out to capture kings. It would take a major poet to do justice to the infinite variety of Austrian *torten* rich with nuts, caramel, and chocolate, redolent with rum, and gussied up with billows of whipped cream reminiscent of the frills on imperial ball gowns. The most elaborate of these are served for dessert. And, if for nothing else, Austrian cooks must be praised for having introduced the use of a tart jam, such as red currant or apricot, as a filling for their cakes, to provide an unexpected and delicious flavor contrast.

The Austrians not only eat well, they also eat often. The day begins with coffee and milk and the rolls that we know and love as "Vienna rolls." To sustain life until lunch, which is really dinner and the main meal of the day, a *Gabelfrühstück*, fork breakfast, takes place in the middle of the morning in a restaurant or coffeehouse. *Kleinigkeiten*, that is, trifles, are served here—such as a small plate of goulash, or a sausage, or an egg dish, for, as the Austrians say, it is not healthy to come to the lunch table with an empty stomach.

The big meal is soup, meat, vegetables and potatoes, and dessert. Much entertaining is done at the midday main meal, which might then be increased to include a fish from the Danube or the much-prized venison of the Austrian Alps. Then comes the *Jause*, pronounced "yowzeh," a gossipy interlude in the late afternoon, over coffee and two or three

devastatingly tempting cakes, with whipped cream on the side. Supper is light, and it might be a soup, an omelet, or dumplings sweet or savory, with a salad or a compote. And if one feels weak during the day or night, there are sausage stands with very good sausages on crisp rolls and a dollop of spicy mustard!

So much excellent and rather rich food as well as the joyous Austrian wines have had the sunniest influence on the Austrian character. They infused it with a warmth, a charm, and a wit that found its expression in Johann Strauss' waltzes. Like these, it can be enjoyed in any country. Here, for your kitchen visit to Austria, a little culinary bouquet of the Austrian dishes Americans would enjoy most and a special collection of recipes for the country's beloved schnitzels.

GERSTENSUPPE (Barley Soup)

- 3 tablespoons butter or margarine
- ½ cup medium barley
- 1 celery stalk, minced
- 1 medium onion, minced
- 1 tablespoon flour
- 6 cups hot vegetable or chicken broth
  Salt and pepper
- ½ cup heavy cream

Heat butter in heavy saucepan. Sauté barley, celery, and onion in it. Sprinkle with flour. Gradually stir in hot broth. Season with salt and pepper. Simmer, covered, for about 1 hour, stirring occasionally, until barley is very tender. Remove from heat and add cream. Makes 4 to 6 servings.

Note: This soup can be prepared in advance without the addition of the cream. At serving time, heat and add cream.

KÜCHERLKRAUT (Beef and Sauerkraut)

- 4 to 5 pounds short ribs of beef, cut into cubes
- 2 pounds fresh sauerkraut
- 1½ teaspoons salt
- 4 large onions, sliced
- ½ cup lard or shortening
- ⅓ cup all-purpose flour

In a Dutch oven combine meat cubes, sauerkraut, salt, and 1 sliced onion. Mix well. Add enough hot water so that there will be about ¾ inch of water in pan. Cover and cook over low heat for 2 hours. When meat is almost done, melt lard in a saucepan and brown remaining sliced onions lightly. Add flour and brown well over low heat. Drain liquid from

meat. Gradually stir into flour mixture. Cook, stirring constantly, over low heat until thick and smooth. Add sauce to meat and sauerkraut. Blend well. Cook, covered, for 30 minutes longer, stirring occasoinally to prevent scorching. Serve with mashed potatoes or noodles. Makes 8 servings.

PICHELSTEINER FLEISCH (Pichelsteiner Casserole)

- 1 pound beef stew meat, cut into ¾-inch cubes
- 1 pound veal stew meat, cut into ¾-inch cubes
- 1 pound lean pork stew meat, cut into ¾-inch cubes
- 1 teaspoon salt
- 1 medium leek, white and green, cut into pieces
- 8 celery stalks, no leaves, cut into pieces
- 8 large raw potatoes, peeled and cubed
- 2 large onions, chopped
- 4 large carrots, diced
- 1 parsnip, diced
- 6 parsley sprigs, chopped
- ½ cup butter or margarine

Mix all meat cubes and sprinkle them with salt. Combine vegetables. In a casserole with tight-fitting lid, or a Dutch oven, spread a thin layer of vegetables, then a layer of meat. Dot each layer with butter. Continue in this way until all ingredients are used. Cover and bake for 1 hour in a preheated moderate oven (350°F.) for about 2 hours. Shake the pot often but do not remove the cover. Makes 8 servings.

PARMESANSCHLEGEL (Leg of Veal with Cheese)

- ½ pound sharp Cheddar or Parmesan cheese, in one piece
  One 4- to 5-pound boneless roast of veal
- 1 teaspoon salt
- ½ cup melted butter
- ¼ cup water or dry white wine

Cut cheese into strips 2 inches long and the thickness of a pencil. Punch holes in meat with a thick knitting needle or a knife. Push cheese into meat holes. Sprinkle meat with salt. Place roast on rack in roasting pan, and pour melted butter and water over it. Roast in preheated slow oven (325°F.) for about 2 hours, or until meat thermometer registers 155° to 160°F. Baste frequently with pan juices. If necessary, add a little more butter and water, about ¼ cup each.

Slice and serve hot with potatoes and a green vegetable, or cold with a tossed green or vegetable salad. Makes 6 servings.

Note: In Austria they use Parmesan, but a sharp Cheddar gives excellent results. The cheese will melt during the roasting.

KALBSGULASCH (Veal Goulash)

2 pounds boneless veal, cut into
   1½-inch squares
   Salt and pepper
¼ cup butter or margarine
2 medium onions, sliced
2 large tomatoes, peeled and quartered
1½ tablespoons all-purpose flour
⅔ cup dry white wine or beef bouillon
2 teaspoons caraway seeds
2 teaspoons paprika
   Juice of ½ lemon
¼ cup hot beef bouillon

Trim all fat and gristle from meat. Season with salt and pepper. Heat butter and brown meat in it, but only lightly. Add onions and tomatoes. Cook, uncovered, stirring constantly, until pan juices have cooked down. Sprinkle flour over meat and brown for 1 minute. Add wine, caraway seeds, paprika, lemon juice, and hot bouillon. Simmer, covered, for 45 minutes to 1 hour, or until meat is tender. Check at intervals; if too dry, add a little more hot bouillon. Serve with buttered rice or noodles. Makes 4 to 6 servings.

GERÖSTETE KALBSLEBER
(Calf's Liver, Sautéed)

½ cup lard or shortening
2 large onions, thinly sliced
2 pounds calf's liver, cut into small thin
   slices
¼ teaspoon crumbled marjoram
½ teaspoon pepper
   Salt

Heat the lard and sauté onions until they are light brown. Increase heat. Add liver, marjoram, and pepper. Sauté the liver for 3 to 4 minutes, stirring constantly. The liver is done when red juice has evaporated. Season with salt just before serving. If salt is added before cooking, liver will be tough. Serve on toast for lunch, or with a salad or plain risotto for supper. Makes 6 servings.

SCHINKENKRAUT (Ham and Sauerkraut)

2 cups cooked or canned sauerkraut
1 teaspoon caraway seeds
2 cups cooked smoked or fresh ham
2 cups thinly sliced cooked or raw potatoes
   Butter
   Salt and pepper

Place sauerkraut in baking dish. Sprinkle with caraway seeds. Add cubed ham. Top with potatoes. Dot with butter and sprinkle with salt and pepper. Bake, uncovered, in preheated hot oven (400°F.) until potatoes are tender and browned, 30 to 45 minutes if cooked ham and cooked potatoes are used, 1 hour if fresh ham and raw potatoes are used. Makes 4 to 6 servings.

SELCHFLEISCH (Smoked Butt)

Place a 2-pound smoked pork butt in enough water to cover. Simmer, covered, for 1¼ hours, or until tender. Slice and serve with puréed split peas and caraway-flavored sauerkraut.

SCHINKENFLECKERLN
(Noodles with Ham)

⅓ cup butter or margarine
1 medium onion, minced
3 cups cooked ham, cubed
4 cups (8 ounces) medium egg noodles,
   cooked
½ teaspoon salt
¼ teaspoon pepper
1 teaspoon caraway seeds

Heat butter or margarine in large skillet. Sauté onion in it until soft and golden. Add ham and cook over low heat for 10 minutes, stirring occasionally. Add noodles, salt, pepper, and caraway seeds and toss together. Cook for 5 minutes, or until thoroughly heated through, stirring frequently. Makes 4 servings.

Note: The Austrians use noodles in the shape of little squares for this dish. If you wish to be completely authentic, you can break your raw noodles into ¾-inch pieces, then cook them until tender.

BACKHENDL (Fried Chicken)

2 broiling chickens (2½ to 3 pounds each),
   quartered
   Seasoned all-purpose flour
2 eggs, beaten
2 tablespoons water
   Fine bread crumbs
   Fat or lard

Wash chickens and pat dry. Tuck wing tips back under second wing joint. With sharp knife cut leg tendon at the joint of drumstick and thigh. Dip pieces into seasoned flour, then into eggs beaten with water. Roll into fine bread crumbs. Fry in 3 inches of fat heated to 375°F. for 15 to 20 minutes. When chicken is browned on one side, turn and brown on the other side. Use tongs or a pancake turner to turn chicken, to keep from piercing skin. Place cooked chicken pieces on absorbent paper and put in very slow

oven (250°F.) to keep warm. Dip liver, gizzard, and heart into flour, egg mixture, and bread crumbs. Fry until brown. Serve with green salad, stewed fruit, or green peas. Makes 6 servings.

PAPRIKAHÜHNER (Paprika Chicken)

2 broiler-fryers (2½ to 3 pounds each),
   quartered
½ cup butter or margarine
1½ cups chopped onion
¼ cup all-purpose flour
2 teaspoons salt
1 cup chicken broth
1 to 2 teaspoons paprika
2 cups dairy sour cream

Wash chickens and pat dry. Heat butter in a large skillet and sauté onions until soft and light yellow. Lay chicken pieces over onions and sauté. Simmer, covered, over low heat for about 45 minutes. When chicken is tender, remove and keep warm. Stir flour and salt into onions. Gradually stir in chicken stock. Stir over low heat until thickened. Remove pan from heat and mix paprika into liquid. Amount depends on taste and color desired. Blend in sour cream. Add chicken to sauce. Spoon sauce over chicken. Reheat but do not boil. Serve with noodles or dumplings. Makes 6 servings.

HAUSENTE ALS WILDENTE
(Duck Cooked Like Wild Duck)

1 large duck
2 flat anchovy fillets, mashed
½ teaspoon crumbled dried thyme
¼ teaspoon pepper
12 juniper berries, crushed
   All-purpose flour
Marinade:
2 cups dry red wine
1 cup water
1 medium onion, sliced
2 parsley sprigs
2 celery stalks with leaves, chopped
1 large carrot, chopped

Clean duck and rub inside with anchovy, thyme, pepper, and juniper berries. Leave spices in cavity. Place duck in large bowl. Combine marinade ingredients. Bring to boil and pour over duck. Cover and refrigerate for 1 to 2 days, turning the duck 3 or 4 times. Place duck in covered roasting pan and add strained marinade. Bake, covered, in preheated slow oven (325° to 350°F.) for 2½ hours. Remove cover and cook for 30 minutes longer. Place bird on hot serving platter. Strain liquid, remove fat, and thicken with a little flour-and-water paste to make gravy. Serve with potato dumplings and black currant jelly. Makes 4 servings.

PARADEISKRAUT
(Cabbage with Tomatoes)

2 medium onions, sliced
2 tablespoons lard or shortening
1 tablespoon sugar
1 medium cabbage, shredded
   (1½ to 2 pounds)
1 teaspoon salt
½ teaspoon caraway seeds
1 to 2 tablespoons mild vinegar
½ cup water

3 large tomatoes, peeled and chopped
1 tablespoon all-purpose flour

In deep saucepan sauté onions in hot lard until soft and golden. Sprinkle with sugar. Add cabbage, salt, caraway seeds, vinegar, and water. Simmer, covered, over low heat for 30 minutes. Add tomatoes and simmer, covered, for 15 minutes more. Mix flour with 2 to 3 tablespoons of pan liquid to make a smooth paste. Stir into cabbage. Cook, uncovered, stirring constantly, until mixture thickens. Makes 4 to 6 servings.

GERÖSTETE MIT ROSMARIN
(Home-Fried Potatoes with Rosemary)

Add crushed dried rosemary to home-fried potatoes while they are cooking in the pan. Use about ½ teaspoon for each cup of potatoes, or more to taste.

KOPFSALAT MIT ERBSEN
(Romaine Lettuce with Peas)

1 large head Romaine lettuce,
  coarsely shredded
1 package frozen peas
¼ cup chopped parsley
2 teaspoons sugar
1 teaspoon salt
1 cup water
1 small onion, minced
2 tablespoons butter
2 tablespoons flour
  Salt and pepper

Combine lettuce, peas, parsley, sugar, salt, and water. Cook over low heat until peas are just tender. Drain; reserve vegetables and 1 cup of the liquid. Sauté onion in butter until soft. Sprinkle onion with flour. Stir in reserved vegetable liquid. Blend thoroughly to prevent flour from lumping. Add lettuce, peas, and parsley. Season to taste with salt and pepper. Simmer, covered, until thoroughly heated, 3 to 5 minutes. Makes 4 generous servings.

GURKENSALAT (Cucumber Salad)

3 medium cucumbers
1 large sweet onion
  Salt
  Ice water
¼ cup salad oil
¼ cup cider vinegar
1 cup dairy sour cream
  Pepper
  Chopped parsley and paprika

Peel cucumbers. Score with a fork. Thinly slice cucumbers and onion. Arrange alternate layers of cucumber and onion in a bowl, sprinkling each layer heavily with salt. Cover with ice water. Refrigerate for several hours. Drain and wash with running water. Drain well. Blend oil with vinegar. Pour mixture over cucumbers and onion and marinate for several hours. Drain. Stir in sour cream and pepper to taste. Top with chopped parsley and paprika. Prepare several hours ahead of serving. Makes 6 to 8 servings.

KAISERSCHMARRN
(The Emperor's Omelet)

4 eggs, separated
2 tablespoons sugar
1 cup sifted all-purpose flour
⅛ teaspoon salt
2 cups milk
2 tablespoons raisins
2 tablespoons butter

Beat egg yolks with sugar until light and pale. Combine flour and salt. Add to egg mixture alternately with milk, beating well after each addition. The batter should be smooth. Add raisins. Beat egg whites until stiff and gently fold into batter. Butter two 8-inch skillets with 1 tablespoon butter each. Heat. Pour half the mixture into one skillet. When one side is brown, turn pancake into second heated skillet. Repeat for second half of batter. Cook pancake until brown on both sides. Shred coarsely with 2 forks. Serve warm, with additional sugar and a sprinkling of cinnamon, or with a fruit compote. Makes 6 servings.

Note: A cross between a pancake and an omelet. Easy to make because it is shredded.

SALZBURGER NOCKERLN
(Dessert Puffs)

¼ cup butter or margarine
4 egg yolks
¼ cup all-purpose flour
⅛ teaspoon salt
4 egg whites
1 cup milk
1 teaspoon vanilla extract
1 teaspoon sugar
  Confectioners' sugar

Cream butter until fluffy. Gradually beat in egg yolks. Beat in flour and salt. Beat egg whites until stiff but not dry. Fold egg whites into mixture. In a 9-inch metal pie pan, heat milk, mixed with vanilla and sugar, to a boil. Stir egg mixture into milk. Bake in preheated moderate oven (350°F.) until golden

brown, about 15 to 20 minutes. Cut into wedges, lift out in pieces with a pancake turner or spatula. Sprinkle with confectioners' sugar. Serve at once. Makes 6 servings.

KANARI MILCH (Canary's Milk)

1 egg yolk
1 cup milk
¼ cup sugar
  One 1-inch piece vanilla bean or
  ½ teaspoon vanilla extract

Combine egg yolk, milk, sugar, and vanilla bean in top part of double boiler. Over hot, not boiling, water beat together until mixture rises slightly and is quite foamy. Remove vanilla bean before serving. Or, add vanilla extract. Serve hot or cold on strudels, apple desserts, pancakes, etc. Makes 3 to 4 servings.

WIENER EISKAFFEE
(Viennese Iced Coffee)

1 scoop rich vanilla ice cream, softened
1 cup cold strong black coffee
  Whipped cream
  Powdered sugar

Place ice cream in parfait glass. Pour coffee over it. Top with whipped cream and sprinkle with sugar. Stir as you drink. Makes 1 serving.

KUGELHUPF (Coffee Cake)

2 packages dry yeast or 2 cakes
  compressed yeast
½ cup water*
4 cups sifted all-purpose flour
1 cup butter or margarine
1 cup sugar
½ teaspoon salt
  Grated rind of 1 lemon
4 eggs
¼ cup blanched almonds
½ cup each of diced citron,
  white raisins, and currants

*Use very warm water (105°F. to 115°F.) for dry yeast; use lukewarm (80°F. to 90°F.) for compressed. Sprinkle dry yeast or crumble cake into water. Let stand for a few minutes; then stir until dissolved. Add 1½ cups of sifted flour; beat until smooth. Cover and let rise in warm place for 1 hour.

In an electric mixer, cream butter and beat in sugar; add salt and grated lemon rind. Add eggs, one at a time, beating well after each addition. Add yeast and remaining flour. Beat for 10 minutes. Butter a 9-inch Turk's-head pan (a fluted pan with tube), and decorate bottom and

sides with blanched almond halves. Pour in half the dough; sprinkle over the citron, raisins, and currants; cover with remaining dough; this should half fill the pan. Cover and let rise in warm place until dough just reaches top of pan. Cake will be coarse and dry if allowed to rise too long. Bake in preheated moderate oven (350°F.) for 45 to 55 minutes. Cool in pan for 5 minutes, then carefully remove to cake rack. Serve sprinkled with powdered sugar. Makes 6 to 8 servings.

DOBOSTORTE

(Hungarian Seven-Layer Cake)
    6 eggs, separated
    ¾ cup sugar
    1 cup sifted all-purpose flour

Beat egg yolks with electric beater until very thick. Gradually add sugar, beating well after each addition. Eggs should be beaten for about 8 to 10 minutes altogether. Sift flour over batter and fold in flour. Then fold in egg whites, beaten until stiff but not dry. Spread a few tablespoons in each of two or three 8-inch layer-cake pans, greased and lined on the bottom with wax paper. Batter should reach edge of pan evenly. Bake on lower rack of preheated moderate oven (350°F.) for 8 to 10 minutes, or until golden. Cool for about 3 minutes on rack. Remove while still warm and cool completely on rack. Peel off paper. Repeat baking process until 7 layers are made.

Chocolate Filling
    1½ cups semisweet chocolate pieces
    ⅓ cup coffee
    ⅓ cup sugar
    6 egg yolks
    ¾ cup butter, cut into small pieces

Melt chocolate pieces, coffee, and sugar together in top part of double boiler over hot water. Stir until completely smooth. Remove from heat. Beat in egg yolks, one at a time. Return to heat and cook until thickened. Cool to lukewarm. Beat butter into chocolate mixture until thoroughly blended and satiny. Cool or chill to spreading consistency.

Caramel Topping

Melt ¾ cup sugar in a skillet, stirring until caramel is smooth and brown. Put 1 layer of cake over inverted 8-inch layer-cake pan and pour boiling caramel syrup over it. Immediately, before caramel hardens, mark with long buttered knife into 12 wedges. Trim excess caramel from edges of cake.

■ **To assemble**—Spread layers (except caramel-topped layer) with chocolate filling and stack. Use about half of filling. Place caramel layer on top. Frost sides of cake with remaining filling. Sprinkle with one cup shredded filberts.

■ **To serve**—Place knife over previously marked lines and tap gently with another knife to crack caramel. Makes 12 servings.

ISCHLER TORTELETTEN

(Almond Butter Cookies)
    2 cups sifted all-purpose flour
    ½ teaspoon baking powder
    ¼ teaspoon salt
    1 cup sweet butter (must be butter;
        if salted butter is used, omit salt)
    1 cup ground blanched almonds
    ¾ cup sugar
    1 tablespoon fresh lemon juice
        Grated rind of 1 lemon
    ½ cup apricot jam
    4 ounces semisweet chocolate pieces
        Blanched almonds, halved

Sift flour with baking powder and salt. Cut 1 cup butter into small pieces. Add butter, ground almonds, sugar, lemon juice, and rind to flour. Knead with hands until dough is very smooth and firm. Chill for at least 2 hours. Roll small parts of dough between wax paper to ⅛- to ¼-inch thickness; keep remaining dough chilled until used. Cut into 1- or 2-inch rounds. Bake cookies on greased and floured cookie sheets in preheated moderate oven (350°F.) for 10 minutes, or until golden. Remove cookies carefully; very thin cookies are fragile. After cooling, put 2 cookies together with jam, sandwich fashion. Melt chocolate and 1 tablespoon butter over hot, not boiling, water. Beat until smooth. If necessary, add up to 1 tablespoon hot water to achieve spreading consistency. Frost cookies on top and sides. Place half an almond on center of each while frosting is still soft. Makes about 5 dozen 1-inch cookies, or about 2½ dozen 2-inch cookies.

NUSSKIPFERLN (Nut Crescents)
    1 cup finely ground walnuts or pecans
    1 cup butter (must be butter)
    ¾ cup sugar
    2½ cups sifted all-purpose flour
    1½ teaspoons vanilla extract
        Vanilla Sugar

Combine all ingredients, and with the fingers knead quickly to a smooth dough. Shape 1 teaspoon of dough at a time into small crescents, about 1½ inches long. Bake on ungreased cookie sheets in preheated moderate oven (350°F.) until slightly browned, about 15 to 17 minutes. Cool for 1 minute. While still warm, roll cookies in Vanilla Sugar. Cool completely and roll again in Vanilla Sugar. Makes about 70.

Vanilla Sugar

Break 2 to 3 vanilla beans into inch-long pieces. Place in a jar with 1 pound sifted confectioners' sugar. Let stand for 3 days. The longer the sugar stands, the more fragrant it becomes.

THE SAVORY SCHNITZELS OF AUSTRIA
By Marcia Colman Morton

Ask an Austrian what his country's proudest exports are, and he'll answer "The waltz, Freud, and schnitzel." But if it's an American he's talking to, chances are he'll only get two nods out of three: Yes, even our twisting teen-agers call for *The Blue Danube* at their proms, and every three-year-old knows he must relate to the group, but schnitzel? Let's see. Isn't that some kind of breaded meat?

This is not only slander, it's a self-deprivation. Not to know the rich range of schnitzelkind: the delectably creamed *Champignon Schnitzel,* the hot savor of a *Paprika Schnitzel!* Fortunately, my Austrian-born husband takes me back to his homeland now and then, and I've gathered a dozen recipes that prove schnitzel's abundant claim to waltz-and-Freud significance.

The very sound of the word, schnitzel, is chewy, mouth-watering. Literally it means "little cut" of meat, like the English cutlet. But in Austria if you want a slice of, say, pork, you must specify *Schweinsschnitzel.* Schnitzel, without a prefix, always means veal: veal chosen with care, pounded into tenderness, dipped into the just-right this, fried or sautéed with the just-right that, done to a golden brown. And not merely breaded! A schnitzel can be smothered in vegetables, melted through by cheese, simmered with curry. Each is a different dish, yet all have in common the gusto of Austrian cooking and the fine tooth-someness of veal.

Puszta Schnitzel

But first things first, and that means *Wiener Schnitzel,* which is breaded. This, the archetype schnitzel, the runaway national favorite, is named for Vienna (spelled *Wien* in German). But you can bet your *schillings* that wherever the Austrian flag flies, beneath it a *Wiener Schnitzel* is sending up redolent fumes. Rules amounting to a mystique surround the dish. It must be deep-fried, not in oil, not in lard, but in a mixture of the two for the perfect taste and texture. Ideally it's eaten in a portion large enough to overlap your plate, with a side dish of mealy boiled potatoes and a salad, for instance, peeled translucent-thin cucumber slices marinated in equal parts of water, vinegar, and olive oil with plenty of salt and pepper. For some reason the mystique forbids eating hot vegetables, except potatoes, with a *Wiener Schnitzel.* "We had an American family here last summer," one country innkeeper confided to me. "Imagine, they ate spinach with a *Wiener Schnitzel!*" As a matter of fact I imagined it very well. Spinach is an excellent accompaniment. But when I said so, he wrote me off as just another American.

His second horror tale got my complete sympathy, however. The young son of the Americans had used (could I believe it?) *ketchup!* "But it ruins the breading and this is why we like the *Wiener Schnitzel* so much!" mein host whispered, shocked still at the memory.

Because the breading is so important, a *Wiener Schnitzel* must be eaten immediately, out of the frying pan, onto your plate, no warming over, or the succulent coat of crumbs will be hard and tasteless. Even in the humblest Austrian restaurant the menu is divided into Freshly Made and Ready dishes, and the *Wiener Schnitzel* is always in the first list.

WIENER SCHNITZEL

To prepare the meat for this and every other schnitzel: Choose milk-fed veal, top quality, fine grained, and a soft bright pink in color. Use ¼-inch slices from the center of the rump, allowing approximately a 4-ounce slice per person. Trim all fat. Pound each slice as thin as possible (about ⅛ inch), or have the butcher do it for you. Make small vertical cuts all around the edges of the veal. Salt each veal slice. Dip first into a soup plate containing flour, and shake off excess; next into a soup plate of beaten egg (one egg will cover two 4-ounce slices, or you can stretch by beating egg with a little milk); finally into a soup plate containing fine, dry bread crumbs, pressing crumbs well in with the palm of your hand, then shaking off excess. Fry in deep fat, half olive oil, half melted lard, so hot that it smokes, for 2 to 3 minutes on each side, or until

heat is right when the breading ripples golden brown. You'll know your skillet as it fries; you'll know your schnitzel is done and tender when a fork goes right through the meat. Drain. Serve garnished with lemon wedges.

Austria is a nation of sports lovers who breathe happiest in the appetite-whetting mountain air that tingles through two-thirds of their country. Every Saturday, spring and fall, half the citizens get out their alpenstocks and knapsacks and head for the nearest hiking trail. At night they want to *eat!* Summer means Carinthia, the southern province barely discovered yet by Americans, whose two hundred mountain-ringed lakes are filled with sailing, swimming, water-skiing Austrians working up to a hearty lunch. In winter everyone heads for an Alpine ski town to swoop his days away and sit down to deservedly bountiful meals.

In a country where people get so hungry, eating is serious. Nobody blinks an eye at the hiker or skier who starts lunch with a brimming bowl of thick pea soup laced with frankfurter chunks; who goes on to a plump little trout; who has as a main dish a *Cordon Bleu;* and who finishes with a sigh and *Zwetsch-knödel,* the fist-sized potato-dough dumpling, stuffed with a whole plum, crusted with sugared buttered bread crumbs! To take only one course (and that's all you *can* take if you haven't just scaled a mountain peak), the *Cordon Bleu* is the only other breaded schnitzel. But breading is the least of it in this extravaganza.

CORDON BLEU

Salt each veal slice. Over veal, lay boiled-ham slice large enough to cover. Over ham, lay Swiss-cheese slice large enough to cover. Double the whole thing over, and fasten with wooden toothpicks. Dip in flour, beaten egg, bread crumbs, exactly as with *Wiener Schnitzel* (above).

Fry in smoking-hot deep fat, half olive oil, half melted lard, for 2 to 3 minutes on each side, or until golden brown. Drain, remove toothpicks. Serve with buttered peas or green beans.

Schnitzels can be light, too. In the city of Salzburg they often have to be. Every July and August, when the Salzburg Music Festival turns the lovely baroque town into a giant Mozartean music box, the calorie-counting international set crowds in for *Everyman* acted against the cathedral façade, and for chamber music played in old palaces. And Salzburg restaurants feature the *Pariser Schnitzel* (named for the French capital), lighter than the *Wiener* and easier on the waistline, but with all the family zest. To heighten the *Pariser Schnitzel's* diet-worthiness, you can go so far as to skip the everloving Austrian potatoes, and hold yourself to a salad of sliced tomatoes and chopped onions in the salted, peppered marinade of vinegar, oil, and water.

PARISER SCHNITZEL

Salt each veal slice. Dip only in flour, then in beaten egg. Deep-fry in smoking-hot half olive oil, half melted lard, for 2 to 3 minutes on each side, or until golden brown. Drain and serve.

If you want to make a real gesture of abstention, there's the still sparer *Natur* ("natural," in other words, untampered-with) *Schnitzel.* Since this leaves out the egg as well as the bread crumbs, the veal with its subtle texture and flavor has no batter to absorb the robust oil and lard. So a *Natur Schnitzel* is sautéed delicately in purest butter.

NATUR SCHNITZEL

Salt, and pepper just a little, each veal slice. Dip one side only into flour; shake off excess. Sauté in butter, floured side first, for 2 to 3 minutes on each side, or until golden brown. Serve floured side up (for its attractive color). Pour the butter gravy from skillet over schnitzel. Serve with shredded endive in oil-water-vinegar.

The *Natur Schnitzel* is so dainty a tidbit by Austrian standards that it's the standard dish for convalescents. Diners in the bloom of health add an anchovy here, a peach there, and feast on the sumptuous *Schnitzel à la Holstein,* named for a north German province, but undoubtedly invented there by an itinerant Austrian.

SCHNITZEL À LA HOLSTEIN

Prepare *Natur Schnitzel* as above. Garnish with an egg fried in butter. Crisscross egg with flat anchovies. Around egg, sprinkle capers and chopped onions. For still more elaborate effect, add caviar, sardines, strips of smoked salmon. Garnish with wedges of lemon and cucumber. Serve flanked by a bowl of tossed salad on one side, a bowl of stewed fruit (peaches, apricots, plums) on the other.

Lying between Germany and Italy, Austria (the Austrians like to say) is a happy blend of the two. Solid comfort they get from the North. The lilt in life wafts up from the South. In Tirol provinces, for example, the towns of Innsbruck and Lienz run day buses across the border to, respectively, Cortina and Venice. In their wake the buses leave such Latin touches as tapered-cut ski trousers, espresso coffee bars, and Neapolitan records for Tirolean jukeboxes. Lienz restaurants serve the homey lentil and bean soups of Austria, and the tangy Italian cheese soups as well, the *pavese* and the egg-flecked *stracciatella*. And the schnitzel you get is often Latinized into a *piccata*.

SCHNITZEL PICCATA

Salt each veal slice. Dip first into flour, shaking off excess; next into egg beaten with grated Parmesan cheese (1 egg to 1 teaspoon cheese). Deep-fry in smoking-hot half olive oil, half melted lard, for 2 to 3 minutes on each side, or until golden brown. Serve with rice and a salad of lettuce dressed in oil and vinegar.

But the most striking foreign accent in any Austrian province is the Balkan tint over the Burgenland on Hungary's border. Here the Alps are forgotten in vistas of steppelike plains; fir trees and the mountains' white water give way to rustling reeds around the huge, glassy Neusiedler Lake. Villages turn thatch roofed and gray steepled, with flocks of geese on flat, melancholy town commons. The men wear boots, breeches, and drooping mustaches. The women go babushkaed. You're this side of the Iron Curtain but just barely.

The Burgenland actually belonged to Hungary once and so, in a restaurant, as gypsy violinists in satin blouses bend over you with *czardas,* you eat (what else?) *Paprika Schnitzel.* The Austrian recipe retains all the old Magyar savor, but tames things a little by using sweet paprika. The cook with a Hungarian soul can try the sharp variety. But cautiously.

When Hungarians say "sharp," they mean it. And even sweet paprika grows fiercer if you cook it longer or use more of it.

PAPRIKA SCHNITZEL

Salt each veal slice. Dip one side only in flour, shaking off excess. Fry in deep, smoking-hot lard (the traditional Hungarian cooking fat) for 2 to 3 minutes on each side, floured side first, or until golden brown. Remove veal. In 2 tablespoons of same lard fry small onion, chopped, until soft. Replace veal; sprinkle with ½ teaspoon Hungarian sweet paprika (or more if desired) and 1 teaspoon flour. Keep turning veal, blending paprika and flour with lard and onions, for 3 minutes (longer for spicier schnitzel). Add to skillet ½ cup or more heavy sweet cream and about 1 tablespoon beef bouillon or soup stock (enough to give sauce the consistency you prefer). Keep mixing until sauce is hot and all ingredients are well blended. Serve schnitzel, smothered in sauce, with broad noodles.

For an even more Hungarian platter, garnish with strips of fiery red pepper and you have *Debrecziner Schnitzel,* named for a town in Hungary. Or, most Eastern of all, try the *Puszta Schnitzel* (*puszta* means "plains" in Magyar), which uses all the favorite Hungarian vegetables.

PUSZTA SCHNITZEL

Proceed as with a *Paprika Schnitzel.* After paprika, cream, and bouillon are well blended, add to skillet: chopped green pepper, sautéed sliced mushrooms, tomato cubes, diced boiled carrots, boiled peas; heat all in sauce. Serve with noodles and green salad.

By now it should be clear that to be Austrian is to eat schnitzel. Yet a few years ago, in the very capital of the nation, this was challenged.

To set the stage, you must know that in Vienna, if a Hapsburg prince once wined and dined his mistress in a certain restaurant, the place was crested with chic forevermore. The more famous the romance, the more brilliant the dining room that beheld it. Imagine, then, the hallowed elegance of the Kerzenstuberl. Its red-damask walls, silk-tapestry chairs, and crystal chandeliers have framed the midnight suppers of Crown

Prince Rudolph and Countess Marie Vetsera, the legendary lovers who killed themselves at Mayerling.

The restaurant determined to match its menu to its pedigree, to banish the homely, native schnitzel in favor of a purely international cuisine. The edict lasted one week. Outraged Viennese set up such a clamor that the exiles were back before you could say Kerzenstuberl.

That is, a compromise was effected. The menu still doesn't list schnitzels openly, but there's a discreet little note, "Our chefs are ready at any time to execute your culinary wishes," that most Austrians take to mean "your schnitzel wishes." In a bow to the gourmet atmosphere, however, they order such stylish variations as the *Champignon Schnitzel.*

CHAMPIGNON SCHNITZEL

Prepare *Natur Schnitzel* (see page 126). Remove veal. In skillet butter, sauté fresh mushrooms, finely sliced lengthwise. Add ¼ cup heavy sweet cream, blend well. Heat veal in sauce for 1 to 2 minutes. Serve, smothered in mushroom-cream sauce, with white rice and peas.

As I say, the menu doesn't list a single schnitzel. But there is something called *Piccata à la Kerzenstuberl* and what would *you* say it is?

PICCATA À LA KERZENSTUBERL

Prepare *Champignon Schnitzel.* But mushrooms are diced (instead of sliced) and sautéed with an equal amount of diced boiled ham. Serve, smothered in mushroom-ham-cream sauce, with Austrian *Risibisi*—boiled white rice mixed with boiled green peas.

Again not on the printed menu, but ready to fulfill the culinary wish of any Maharajah who wanders in, is the chef's supreme exotic triumph, the *Curry Schnitzel.*

CURRY SCHNITZEL

Prepare *Natur Schnitzel* (see page 126). Remove veal. In skillet butter, sauté ½ an onion, chopped, until soft. Replace veal; sprinkle with ¼ teaspoon curry powder (or more if desired) and 1 teaspoon flour. Keep turning veal, blending curry and flour with butter and onion for about 3 minutes. Add ½ cup or more

heavy sweet cream and about 1 table-spoon beef bouillon or soup stock (enough to give sauce consistency you prefer). Keep mixing until sauce is hot, well blended. Serve schnitzel, smothered in sauce, topped with sautéed chopped almonds, with side dishes of chutney and sautéed sliced bananas.

Clearly, the *Curry Schnitzel* is a pukka adaptation of the *Paprika Schnitzel*. But with it the Kerzenstuberl goes beyond even the international and attains the intercontinental. If they're still brooding, though, I have happy news for them. When I had dinner at the world-famous Madrid restaurant, Horchers, the menu was in English, and from it I ordered "Veal Escalope Florentine." Of course, this turned out to be the familiar Austrian Schnitzel Florentine, a super dish that reminds me of my anti-spinach inn-keeper.

SCHNITZEL FLORENTINE
Cover a mound of freshly boiled spinach with *Natur Schnitzel* (see page 126). Over schnitzel, pour hollandaise sauce into which grated Parmesan cheese has been blended. Oven-brown the whole thing.

So the schnitzel has a respected place on one of Europe's great menus. The Kerzenstuberl can stop worrying and Americans can start cooking.

AVOCADO (Alligator pear)—This fruit is native to Central or South America and references to it have been found

Chilled Avocado Soup

Avocado Lime Pie

Puerto Rican Avocado Shrimp Boats

Guacamole

in records kept by Spanish explorers as far back as 1519. The word is said to come from the Central American Indian word *ahuacatl,* which was modified by the Spanish explorers into *aguacate.* More and more North Americans have become enchanted by the delicately nutty flavor and buttery texture. Today avocado orchards flourish along our southern coast from California to Florida, especially in the Rio Grande Valley. The fruit may vary from the small round ball variety, shiny green, to the huge pear-shaped, slightly russet-coated fruit; the fruit may weigh from five to six ounces to two to three pounds. Avocados have a coarse shell-like skin or a smooth thin skin, depending on the variety. They are yellowish-green with a fairly firm flesh and a single large seed, round or conical. If you enjoy cultivating house plants, you'll use the seed to add to your indoor garden. Prop it on the rim of a glass of water with three toothpicks until roots form. Then plant it in soil, stand in a warm sunny spot, and water it frequently. The result: a beautiful, lush, leafy plant.

Availability—The peak period is from December to April, with smaller amounts available the remainder of the year. Florida and California produce most of the crop.

Purchasing Guide—Select fruit that is heavy and fairly firm or just beginning to soften. The skin should be uniform in color and without cracks, bruises, or punctures. When touched, the avocado skin should yield to light pressure. They are sold by the pound or by the unit.

Storage—If firm to hard, keep at room temperature for two to three days until soft to the touch. An hour or two before using, put in your refrigerator, but away from the cooling unit. Never put avocados in the refrigerator unless they are ripe.

☐ Room temperature: 1 to 2 days after they are ripe
☐ Refrigerator shelf, whole: 2 to 4 weeks
☐ Refrigerator shelf, cut and covered: 1 to 2 days
☐ Refrigerator frozen-food compartment, prepared for freezing: 2 months
☐ Freezer, prepared for freezing: 1 year

Nutritive Food Values—Avocados offer fair amounts of thiamine, riboflavin, and

Crabmeat Stuffed Avocados

vitamin C. Unlike most fruits, they have a high fat content which varies from less than 5 per cent to more than 20 per cent.

☐ 3½ ounces, raw = 167 calories

Basic Preparation—Cut in half lengthwise, using a stainless-steel knife. (Always use stainless-steel utensils when cutting or mashing avocados, to keep them from darkening.) Twist halves slightly to get them apart, and remove seed. If you are removing the skin, place the shell cut side down on a counter. Cut off the skin with a paring knife or pry it off, using a teaspoon with the back of the spoon under the skin. Avocados are usually used raw or baked. Halves can be sliced, diced, mashed, or sieved. Since avocados discolor quickly, sprinkle immediately with lemon juice, weak cider vinegar, or one of the commercial fruit-darkening preventatives.

☐ **To Freeze**—Use ripe avocados free of dark blemishes. Cut in half, peel and remove seed. Mash well and blend with ⅛ teaspoon ascorbic acid to 1 quart mashed avocado. Package with 1-inch headspace and freeze.

APPETIZERS

GUACAMOLE

1 large ripe avocado
2 teaspoons fresh lemon juice
1 teaspoon chili powder
1 garlic clove, crushed
2 tablespoons mayonnaise
  Salt

Peel avocado and remove seed. Mash pulp completely. Add lemon juice and mix well. Add chili powder, garlic, and mayonnaise. Season. Serve with king-size corn chips. Makes about 1½ cups.

AVOCADO DIP

1 large ripe avocado
¼ teaspoon onion juice
  Dash each of pepper, curry powder, and cayenne
1 tablespoon white-wine vinegar
¼ teaspoon salt

Peel avocado and remove seed. Mash to smooth pulp and mix with remaining ingredients. Use as dip for potato chips, cauliflowerets, diagonally cut carrot slices, or tiny cheese crackers. For variety, use horseradish or Worcestershire in place of curry powder. Makes 1 cup.

SOUP

CHILLED AVOCADO SOUP

1 large ripe avocado
2 cans clear consomme madrilene
1 cup dairy sour cream
  Salt, chili powder, and cayenne to taste
  Grated onion
  Minced fresh dill or crushed dillseed

Peel avocado and remove seed. Whirl until smooth in electric blender or force through sieve or food mill. Mix with consommé and sour cream. Season with salt, chili powder, cayenne, and onion. Chill until mixture jells. Serve in bouillon cups with a garnish of dill. Makes 4 servings.

SALADS

AVOCADO CRABMEAT SALAD À LA RITZ

½ cup diced cooked lobster
1 cup flaked cooked crabmeat
1 tablespoon chopped peeled fresh tomato
½ teaspoon chopped chives or green onion tops
¼ teaspoon crumbled dried tarragon
½ teaspoon salt
3 tablespoons mayonnaise
¼ teaspoon chili powder
1 large ripe avocado, halved and seeded
4 strips pimiento

Combine first 8 ingredients and toss gently to mix. Spoon mixture into avocado halves. Top each with 2 crossed strips of pimiento. Serve on lettuce leaves. Makes 2 servings.

PUERTO RICAN AVOCADO SHRIMP BOATS

2 large ripe avocados
  Lemon juice
2 medium tomatoes
1 teaspoon sugar
½ teaspoon salt
  Pepper
⅛ teaspoon ground tumeric
1 teaspoon chopped parsley
2 green onions, minced
  Sprig of fresh mint, chopped fine
½ tablespoon cider vinegar
½ tablespoon water
  Dash of cayenne
2 tablespoons French dressing
1 cup cooked shrimps
  Watercress

Halve avocados and remove seed. Scoop out pulp and dice. Rub shells with lemon juice and set aside. Peel and chop tomatoes. Mix all remaining ingredients except shrimps and watercress. Pour over tomatoes and avocado pieces. Mix carefully. Fold in shrimps. Pile mixture in avocado shells. Top with watercress sprigs. Chill. Makes 4 servings.

CHICKEN-AVOCADO SALAD

2 cups finely chopped cold cooked chicken
½ cup finely chopped celery
  Salt and pepper
1 tablespoon fresh lemon juice
  Dash of hot pepper sauce
½ cup mayonnaise
2 large ripe avocados
2 hard-cooked eggs, sliced

Combine all ingredients except avocados and eggs. Halve avocados and remove seeds. Scoop out pulp and reserve avocado shells. Dice pulp and add to chicken mixture. Fill shells with mixture. Top with egg slices. Makes 4 servings.

AVOCADO GELATIN SALAD

2 envelopes unflavored gelatin
¼ cup cold water
1 cup boiling water
  Juice of 1 lemon
  Dash of hot pepper sauce
1 teaspoon salt
⅛ teaspoon pepper
1 teaspoon onion juice
2½ cups mashed avocado pulp (2 or 3 avocados)
1 cup dairy sour cream
1 cup mayonnaise or salad dressing

Soften gelatin in cold water for 5 minutes. Dissolve gelatin in boiling water. Add lemon juice, hot pepper sauce, salt, pepper, and onion juice. Cool. Stir in mashed avocado, sour cream, and mayonnaise. Beat to blend. Pour into 1½-quart mold. Chill until firm. Unmold and serve on greens. Makes 8 servings.

CRABMEAT STUFFED AVOCADOS

Stuff avocado halves with canned or thawed frozen crabmeat. Squeeze a little fresh lime juice over top. Put a dollop of mayonnaise on top of each, and sprinkle with shredded hard-cooked egg yolk. Serve with cooked green beans marinated in a little French dressing. Garnish with ripe olives, and serve with additional French dressing, if desired. Makes 6 servings.

DESSERTS

AVOCADO-CITRUS DESSERT

Halve unpeeled avocados and remove seeds. Sprinkle avocados with lemon juice and fill cavity with grapefruit or orange segments. Add honey to taste and garnish with fresh mint. This can be served as a salad, too.

AVOCADO CREAM

2 ripe avocados
  Juice of 1 lemon
¼ cup sugar

Halve avocados and remove seeds. Peel avocados and slice into blender containing lemon juice. Add sugar. Whirl until smooth. Fill punch cups or dessert dishes. Chill thoroughly. Makes 4 servings.

AVOCADO LIME PIE

1 large ripe avocado
1 can (14 ounces) sweetened condensed milk
  Grated rind of 1 lime
½ cup fresh lime juice
2 egg yolks
  Dash of salt
1 baked 9-inch pie shell
  Avocado for garnish
  Chopped nuts

Mash avocado well (there should be about 1¼ cups). Combine sweetened condensed milk, lime rind, lime juice, well beaten egg yolks, and salt. Stir until mixture is thickened. Fold in avocado. Turn into baked pastry shell and chill for several hours. Garnish with avocado balls. (Cut avocado in half and scoop out balls with melon cutter. Cover with fresh lemon juice.) Sprinkle with chopped nuts. Makes 6 to 8 servings.

BABA—This French dessert cake is made with a yeast dough which contains raisins. The finished cakes are steeped in a rum and sugar syrup. Babas come large or small, and they are baked in tall, often fluted molds. Thanks to their lightness, they are one of the most popular dessert cakes on both sides of the Atlantic.

A Polish king is credited with the invention of babas, and it is said that he named it after his favorite hero in the *Thousand and One Nights* tales. More accurately, the king invented a new way of eating *Kugelhupf,* an old, well-established Central European cake, by pouring rum over it.

Sticklers for accuracy should note that savarins, though made with baba dough, are baked in ring molds and contain no raisins. They, too, are doused with a rum syrup.

Babas, as well as savarins, were especially popular during the 19th century, when they brought fame and money to several pastry cooks. They are well worth making and serving since they appeal to both men and women as desserts.

BABA AU RHUM

1 package active dry yeast or 1 cake compressed yeast
¼ cup warm milk*
  Sugar
2 cups sifted all-purpose flour
4 eggs, slightly beaten
½ teaspoon salt
⅔ cup soft butter or margarine
⅓ cup raisins
¼ cup currants
  Saffron
  Rum Syrup
  Whipped cream

*Use very warm milk (105°F. to 115°F.) for dry yeast; use lukewarm (80°F. to 90°F.) for compressed. Sprinkle dry yeast or crumble cake into milk and add a pinch of sugar. Let stand for a few minutes, then stir until dissolved. Put flour in large mixing bowl and make a well in the center. Add eggs, salt, 1 tablespoon sugar, and yeast mixture. Mix well and then knead in the bowl with hands. Cover and let rise in warm place until double in bulk, about 45 minutes. Stir down; add butter, raisins, currants, and a pinch of saffron. Beat or knead in bowl for about 4 minutes. Fill greased muffin or popover pans one third full. Let rise until batter doubles again. Bake in preheated hot oven (425°F.) for 10 minutes; reduce heat to moderate (350° F.) and bake until brown. Turn out on rack and cool to lukewarm. Drench with warm Rum Syrup. Serve warm, topped with whipped cream. Makes 8 servings.

If raisins and currants are omitted and dough is baked in a well-buttered angel-cake pan, it is called a savarin.

Rum Syrup

Simmer 1 cup sugar and 1½ cups water for 35 to 40 minutes. Stir in ½ cup light or dark rum.

QUICK BABA AU RHUM

2 eggs
½ cup sugar
1 cup sifted all-purpose flour
1 teaspoon baking powder
¼ teaspoon salt
1 teaspoon vanilla extract
⅓ cup melted butter
1 cup currants
    Rum Syrup (see above)

Preheat oven to moderate (375°F.). Grease a 1½-quart fluted tube pan. Beat 2 egg whites until fluffy, gradually adding ¼ cup of the sugar; then beat until stiff. In another bowl beat egg yolks with remaining sugar. Add all at once to the whites, stirring lightly but well. Sift flour, baking powder, and salt together; fold into egg mixture gently. Stir in melted butter and vanilla. Fold in currants. Pour into pan and bake in preheated moderate oven (375°F.) for 30 minutes, until top feels springy when touched and toothpick inserted in cake comes out clean. Let stand for 5 minutes, then turn out on serving plate. Prick with a fork and spoon Rum Syrup over Baba. Let stand until syrup is absorbed. Makes 6 servings.

BACCHUS The Roman god of wine, portrayed in Greek and Roman painting and sculpture, may be easily identified by his raised wine glass or basket of grapes. Called Dionysus by the Greeks, his worship was banned by the Roman Senate in 186 B.C.

BACON—The cured and smoked fat and lean meat from the side of the pig, after the spareribs have been removed. Canadian-style bacon, which resembles ham rather than ordinary streaky bacon, is the eye muscle that runs along the pig's back. The word bacon, originally French, meant pork and cured pork products. Even in England, as late as Shakespearean times, the word bacon was used for pork.

Bacon has played an extraordinarily important part in the nutrition of the Anglo-Saxon world. Pork is the only meat that is tastier cured than fresh, a most important fact during the many centuries when curing was the only way

of preserving meat—that is, until modern food refrigeration and preservation methods were invented. A bit of bacon, easily carried, went a long way in making bland food, such as beans, into a palatable and appetizing dish, adding much nutrition as well. The British Isles, Ireland, and all English-speaking lands lean heavily on bacon for breakfast and for other meals. However, because of different methods of meat-cutting in the various countries, many cuts of English "bacon" correspond to our salt pork, ham, picnic shoulders, butts, etc. They may also taste differently from their American cousins, because methods of feeding the pigs and curing the meat are not alike.

Bacon is usually ready-sliced, thick, regular, or thin, and packaged by the manufacturer. It is possible to buy unsliced slab bacon and have it sliced either by the butcher or at home.

Availability—Bacon is available in grocery stores throughout the country all year round.

Purchasing Guide

SLAB BACON—Side meat with the spareribs removed, squared up, cured, and smoked. May be derinded and sliced in the market, or sold by the piece. Cures and weight ranges vary. (The bacon square is a square-cut piece of jowl meat, cured and smoked like bacon.)

SLICED BACON—Derinded bacon that is machine-sliced to uniform thickness and packaged. Available in ½-pound and 1-pound packages. Pound contains an average of 16 to 20 slices. Also sold thick sliced, about 12 slices to a pound. Imported bacon is sold usually in cans.

SALT PORK—(Sides 16%, fat back 6%, jowl 3% dressed weight.) Known as white bacon in some sections. Dry-salt or brine-cured. Not smoked. Used as bacon, for seasoning vegetables, and to supply needed fat for larding for roasting lean meats, poultry, and fish.

CANADIAN-STYLE BACON—Boned pork loins with tenderloin removed. Very lean. Sugar-cured and smoked like ham. Sold in a casing in 2- to 4-pound pieces, or sliced in vacuum packs, or canned.

Storage—Should be used as quickly as possible to prevent fat from becoming rancid and to prevent molding.
☐ Refrigerator shelf, well wrapped in foil or original waxed wrapper: 6 to 7 days
☐ Refrigerator frozen-food compartment, tightly wrapped for freezing: 2 weeks
☐ Freezer, wrapped for freezing: 1 month

Caloric Values

☐ Bacon, 3½ ounces, raw = 665 calories
☐ Bacon, 3½ ounces, cooked, broiled, or fried, drained = 611 calories
☐ Salt pork, 3½ ounces, raw = 738 calories
☐ Canadian-style bacon, 3½ ounces, raw = 277 calories

Basic Preparation

☐ **To Use Uncooked**—Bacon or salt pork may be used raw for vegetables, beans, chowders, for larding, etc. Use slab bacon, sliced bacon, or salt pork (freshen salt pork in cold water and drain before using).

☐ **To Pan-broil**—Place bacon in cold skillet and cook over *low* heat. Separate slices as they begin to cook so that each piece is flat in the pan. Turn slices often. Never let the fat smoke or the bacon will have a burned flavor. When browned evenly, drain on absorbent paper. Drain fat several times during cooking to keep slices crisp.

☐ **To Bake**—Arrange bacon slices on rack in shallow pan. Bake in hot oven (400°F.) for 10 to 15 minutes. This is a good way to cook a quantity of bacon, for the bacon requires less watching and needs no turning at all.

☐ **To Broil**—Place bacon slices on rack 3 to 4 inches below heat source. Broil for 2 to 3 minutes to a side, turning once. Drain on absorbent paper.

☐ **To Save Drippings**—Use a large coffee can. When it is full, scoop the drippings into a large pan, add 1 cup water, and sprinkle 3 tablespoons flour on top. The flour settles any particles to the bottom. After the drippings have come to a boil, set them aside to cool, then strain into clean can or jar for storage in the refrigerator. Snowy white, the drippings are indistinguishable from lard. Use drippings for seasoning vegetables, in baking, and in many other dishes where lard is used.

☐ **To Roast Canadian-style Bacon**—Roast in moderate oven (350°F.) for about 25 minutes to the pound, or until meat thermometer registers 160°F.

☐ **To Pan-broil Canadian-style Bacon**—Lightly grease the skillet. Cook slices of Canadian bacon over low heat, turning frequently. Cook for 5 to 10 minutes depending on thickness of slices.

BACONY BEANS

1 pound dried marrow beans, washed and drained
6 cups water
1 onion, chopped
¼ cup dark molasses
1 tablespoon Worcestershire
1 tablespoon salt
1 teaspoon dry mustard
⅛ teaspoon pepper

1 pound bacon ends, cut up

Bring beans and water to boil in large saucepan. Boil for 2 minutes. Remove from heat and let stand for 1 hour. Continue cooking until tender, replacing water when necessary to keep up level of liquid. Liquid should nearly cover beans when done. Add remaining ingredients except bacon ends and put in a 2-quart baking dish. Pan-broil bacon ends for 5 minutes. Add bacon and ⅓ cup of the bacon fat. Mix well. Cover and bake in moderate oven (350°F.) for 1½ hours. Uncover and bake for 30 minutes longer. Makes 4 servings.

BACON AND EGG SKILLET

¼ pound sliced bacon
3 tablespoons all-purpose flour
½ teaspoon salt
½ teaspoon white pepper
1½ cups milk
6 hard-cooked eggs
½ cup crumbled crisp corn crackers
   Paprika

Panbroil bacon in skillet; drain on absorbent paper and crumble. Reserve bacon fat. Put 3 tablespoons fat in skillet. Add flour and seasonings and blend. Gradually stir in milk. Cook until thickened, stirring constantly. Slice eggs and arrange on mixture. Sprinkle with bacon; top with crumbled crackers and sprinkle with paprika. Cook, uncovered, without stirring, over moderate heat for 5 to 10 minutes, or until heated through. Makes 4 servings.

BACON-KRAUT-POTATO SKILLET

¾ pound sliced Canadian-style bacon
2 tablespoons fat
1 can (1 pound, 13 ounces) sauerkraut
1 tablespoon brown sugar
2 cups (one 1-pound can) potatoes,
   undrained

Brown Canadian bacon slices in hot fat in a skillet. Remove slices. Spoon sauerkraut into skillet. Top with Canadian bacon slices. Sprinkle with brown sugar. Place potatoes around outside edge of skillet. Pour can juices over all. Cover and simmer for 15 minutes. Makes 4 servings.

BACON AND BEEF SUCCOTASH

6 slices of bacon
¾ pound beef chuck, ground
1 onion, chopped
2 cups fresh or frozen shelled Lima beans
1 cup water
2 cups canned drained whole-kernel corn
   Salt and pepper

Pan-broil bacon until crisp. Remove bacon and reserve. Heat 2 tablespoons of bacon fat. Sauté beef and onion in fat, breaking up meat with a fork. Add Lima beans and water and simmer, covered, for about 15 minutes. Add corn and simmer for another 5 minutes. Season to taste. Serve in bowls with bacon crumbled on top. Makes 4 servings.

Sliced Bacon

BACON SAUCE WITH PEAS

4 slices of bacon, diced
1 small onion, minced
1 garlic clove, minced
Few parsley sprigs, minced
1 celery stalk, minced
2⅓ cups (one 1-pound, 3-ounce can) tomatoes
1 tablespoon tomato paste
½ cup water
1 cup frozen peas
Salt and pepper

Pan-broil bacon until almost crisp. Heat ¼ cup bacon fat. Add onion, garlic, parsley, and celery. Sauté for 5 minutes. Add tomatoes, tomato paste, and water. Simmer, uncovered, over very low heat, stirring frequently, for 30 minutes. Add peas and simmer for 10 minutes. Add salt and pepper to taste. Makes 2 cups sauce.

HOT POTATO SALAD WITH BACON

4 slices of bacon, quartered
1½ tablespoons all-purpose flour
1 tablespoon sugar
1 teaspoon salt
1 tablespoon prepared mustard
½ cup cider vinegar
½ cup water
4 cups sliced cooked peeled potato

Pan-broil bacon until crisp. Remove bacon and reserve. Heat 2 tablespoons bacon fat. Blend in flour, sugar, salt, and mustard. Add vinegar and water gradually, stirring until smooth. Cook over low heat, stirring, until thickened. Add potato and heat, mixing lightly. Sprinkle with reserved bacon. Makes 4 servings.

BACON, EGG, AND CORN CAKES

½ cup chopped bacon ends
1¼ cups yellow cornmeal
¼ cup all-purpose flour
½ teaspoon baking soda
1 hard-cooked egg, chopped
1 egg, beaten
1 cup buttermilk

Panbroil bacon until crisp; reserve fat. Mix dry ingredients; add crisp bacon and chopped egg. Mix bacon fat, raw egg, and buttermilk. Add to dry ingredients and mix well. Spoon onto hot greased skillet; shape into small cakes. Brown on both sides. Makes 4 servings.

BACON BISCUITS

2 cups sifted all-purpose flour
2 teaspoons baking powder
½ teaspoon salt
¼ cup bacon fat, chilled
⅔ cup milk (about)

Sift dry ingredients. Cut in bacon fat until mixture resembles cornmeal. Stir in milk to make a soft dough. Turn out on floured board and knead lightly a few times. Roll or pat to ¾-inch thickness. Cut biscuits and place on ungreased cookie sheet. Bake in preheated very hot oven (450°F.) for 10 to 12 minutes. Makes about 18 two-inch biscuits.

PEANUT BUTTER AND BACON SANDWICH

Season smooth or chunky peanut butter to taste with pickle relish, and moisten with mayonnaise. Spread on whole-wheat bread and sprinkle with crumbled crisp bacon. Serve sandwich open face or top with another slice of bread.

BAGEL—A bland doughnut-shaped pastry made of nonsweet raised dough that is first simmered in water, then baked. This process gives the bagel a hard glazed crust and a chewy white interior. It is also known as a water doughnut.

Bagels are a distinctive part of Jewish cuisine. In the United States, especially in New York, it has become traditional to serve bagels with cream cheese and lox, that is, smoked salmon.

Bagels are seldom made at home. However, it can be done by the determined, as shown in the following recipe.

BAGELS

3 cups sifted all-purpose flour (plus 3 tablespoons for kneading board)
1½ teaspoons salt
2 tablespoons sugar
1 package active dry yeast or 1 cake compressed yeast
⅔ cup water*
3 tablespoons salad oil or shortening
1 egg
4 quarts boiling water to which add
2 tablespoons sugar

Sift dry ingredients together into a deep mixing bowl. Dissolve yeast in one third of the water. *Use very warm water (105°F.) to 115°F.) for dry yeast; use lukewarm (80°F. to 90°F.) for compressed. Sprinkle dry yeast or crumble cake into water. Let stand for a few minutes; then stir until dissolved. Add oil or melted shortening to the remainder of warm water and stir into dissolved yeast. Make a well in the center of flour mixture and stir in the liquid, adding slightly beaten egg when half the liquid has been used. Stir briskly to form a ball of dough and knead on a lightly floured board for 2 minutes. Return dough to mixing bowl, smooth side up, and punch down 3 times. Cover and let rise at room temperature for 30 to 45 minutes, or until the dough has come to the top of the bowl. Knead again on board until smooth and elastic as for rolls. Divide dough into 12 equal portions. Form into lengths not more than ¾ inch thick, pinching ends together. Place on a floured cookie sheet and slip under broiler for 3 minutes. Drop each bagel into rapidly boiling water, in a deep kettle (only a few at a time so they will not touch each other), and cook over moderate heat for 15 to 20 minutes. Skim out and place on a cookie sheet. Bake at 375°F. (moderate) for 15 minutes, then increase heat to 400°F. (hot) for 10 minutes, or until bagels are browned and crust is golden brown and crisp. Makes 1 dozen.

BAIN-MARIE—The literal translation of this French culinary term is "Mary's bath." The term is used for the hot-water bath in which cooking vessels are placed to cook or to keep foods hot, as in a double boiler. However, the *bain-marie* is much larger than the bottom part of a double boiler and does not fit tightly around the saucepans placed in it, therefore the water does not steam or boil as it may do in a double boiler.

BAKE—This basic cooking process is carried out with dry heat, at any kind of temperature, and usually in a confined space, such as an oven. However, foods have been baked over open fires, by hot coals and on hot rocks, under hot ashes, and even by the heat of the sun.

Baking is an extremely ancient art, and bake ovens are almost as old as baking. Two thousand years ago, the Egyptians, always proficient bakers, used simple ovens without flues. In early Greece, baking was done in heated huge bowl-like clay ovens. Throughout Roman days, medieval times, and well into our own day, baking took place in a simple masonry chamber placed above a fire box.

In colonial America, baking was done in Dutch ovens, in front of the fireplace, or connected with it, or in alcoves with flues built into the backs of the wide masonry kitchen fireplaces. These ovens were heated by a hot wood fire built within them. When the bricks were thoroughly hot, the ashes were swept out into an ash pit below, or into the kitchen. The flue of the oven was then closed, and the food to be baked pushed in by a long-handled shovel. An experienced colonial housewife knew the exact spot in her oven in which its heat would give her the best roasts, breads, or pies.

Metal ovens and kitchen ranges appeared in England and the United States in the latter part of the 18th century, but they were at first dimly viewed by colonial housewives. A cook book of the times tells the unfortunate owner of such a newfangled contraption not to use it, but to send her bread to the baker instead.

Metal ovens and baking remained pretty much the same until well into the 20th century, when modern fuels, such as gas and electricity, and the resulting ability to control temperatures, made baking much more exact.

At all times, baking has been a highly skilled occupation, and bakers have always been key figures in a community. In dollar volume, baking is second only to the meat-packing industry. The importance governments have given to bakers and baking is shown by the constant rules and regulations of the trade from the days of the ancient Egyptians, to insure honest bread, and to prevent bread riots as well.

Until quite recently, there was a close connection between baking and cleanliness. Our female ancestors had definite days for doing their chores, and Saturday was reserved for baking and baths. In an age when hot water did not simply come out of a faucet, the kitchen range provided not only the heat for baking everything from meats to cookies, but also the hot water needed for cleaning up for Sunday's churchgoing. The baking began Saturday morning, the baths Saturday afternoon.

GUIDE TO UP-TO-DATE BAKING

The many foods requiring baking may be divided into two main groups. The first group, which includes cakes, pies, muffins, cookies, breads, cream puffs, and soufflés, requires pampering and its preparation is an exact science. There are chemical reactions involved that call for accuracy in measuring, mixing, and baking. The oven temperature recommended in the recipe, the type and size of pan,

and the baking time must be carefully observed. A reliable recipe is the starting point. Next comes accurate measurement of ingredients, and these should be the exact products called for in the recipe. Don't substitute unless you're certain you know how. Directions for mixing should also be followed to the letter. Your oven plays an important part; know how to use it properly.

The second group includes the less sensitive foods, such as baked stuffed peppers, potatoes, and other vegetables, baked apples, cobblers, meat and chicken pies, and casseroles of all kinds. While it is true that each of these has a recommended baking temperature, it is possible to use considerable leeway and still come up with good results. For instance, one usually bakes potatoes for about one hour at 400°F., but if you have a roast in the oven at 325°F., potatoes can bake along with it if more time is allowed. Or, most casserole dishes can be baked at a temperature 25° higher or lower than stated in the recipe, with proper adjustment of time. The exceptions would be those dishes which include heat-sensitive ingredients, such as cheese or eggs,

which might be toughened by a too-high temperature.

It Pays To Know Your Oven

If your range does not have automatic temperature regulators or thermostats, you need to use a portable oven thermometer to guide you. Place the thermometer toward the front and at one side of the rack on which the baking is done. Turn the heat on full and, after 10 to 15 minutes, look at the thermometer and adjust the heat according to the temperature you want.

Almost all ranges made today have automatic oven temperature controls which regulate the heat for you. These give a more constant temperature and consequently more dependable results. However, a thermostat may get out of kilter during shipment or from some unknown cause during use. If you're having trouble, here's how to check or adjust it. If the temperature is off only 15° to 25°, you can, for the time being, compensate by setting the oven control dial that much above or below the temperature you need, as the case may be. Keep in mind that an oven may be accurate at

one temperature, say 300°, but be off at the 400° setting. To test oven temperatures, check with your thermometer when the thermostat is set at a low, a moderate, and a high temperature. Be sure to leave the control set at each of the three temperatures for at least thirty minutes. Use a reliable thermometer.

If the situation appears to need further attention, you should call your electric or gas utility, and ask to have a home service representative or service man come to your home to adjust the controls.

You Don't Have To Bake in the Kitchen

New electric housewares let you bake wherever you choose. For instance, a small portable oven is large enough to bake pies, layer cakes, biscuits, or a casserole. It has controlled heat up to a temperature of 450°F. and can be plugged into any convenient outlet. Other portable ovens provide for rotisserie cooking, as well as baking.

Upside-down cakes, quick breads, and the like bake nicely in the electric frying pan. For some foods, you can use the electric Dutch oven or saucepan. These appliances have automatic temperature control and directions for baking are included in their instruction booklets.

Know Your Pans

Always use the correct size pan in proportion to the amount of food to be baked. Inside measurements of pans are the ones referred to in recipes. For pie pans, measure the size of the opening across the top of the pan. To measure cake pans, check the inside diameter of round pans and depth, width, and length of others.

The arrangement of pans in the oven can make a great difference in the evenness of baking. When baking one item, center it in your oven, top to bottom, front to back, and side to side.

When you use two or more pans in the oven, place them at least one inch from the sides and back of the oven and allow space between pans on the same rack. When two racks are used, place one rack just above the center set of guides and the other just below center. Never place one pan directly above the other on different racks. There must be room for the heat to circulate freely in order to give even baking.

Pans for Cakes—Use the size pan called for in the recipe. Cakes do not brown well on top if the pan is too large because the batter cannot rise to the top. Use shiny metal or glass pans. Dark pans absorb the heat and cakes may brown

excessively. When you bake in glass, use a temperature 25° lower than called for in the recipe. Glass absorbs and holds the heat, and the lower temperature compensates for this.

Warped pans may cause cakes to rise and bake unevenly.

If you don't find the shape pan you want, make your own from a double layer of heavy aluminum foil. Crease foil firmly at the corners so that the shape will hold during baking.

Pans for Pies—To get good browning of the crust, a pie pan should absorb and hold heat. Oven glassware answers these requirements.

Pie pans with high sides, both glass and metal, are especially good for fruit pies, because juices are less likely to boil over in the oven.

Pans for Cookies and Biscuits—Use a bright metal baking sheet or a pan with very low sides. High sides shield the food from the heat and prevent good browning.

The baking sheet should not touch sides or back of oven, as this interferes with circulation of heat in the oven.

If you do not have a baking sheet, you can bake cookies or biscuits on the bottom of an inverted cake or roasting pan.

To speed up cookie-making, place rolled or drop cookies on sheets of aluminum foil ready for baking. As a pan of cookies comes from the oven, slip the unbaked sheet onto the pan, then into the oven without delay. With heavy foil and care, you may place a sheet of foil with cookies directly on the oven rack without a pan underneath.

Tips for Picture-Perfect Pies and Cakes

For perfection, cakes and pies must come out of pans smoothly, with crusts evenly browned.

■ A square of aluminum foil in the center of a cake pan (it doesn't need to cover the bottom completely) will prevent a cake from sticking in the center. If you leave a tab of foil higher than the pan on one side, you can tug on this to loosen the cake.

■ When frosting a cake, place wide strips of wax paper on the plate under the cake before you frost it. Later, the paper strips with the frosting dribbles can be pulled out, leaving the rim of the plate clear.

■ For muffins, place a strip of foil in each pan with one end hanging out so you can pull it for quick release of the muffins.

■ Crimp a strip of aluminum foil about

1½ inches wide or use pie tape over the fluted edge of a two-crust pie before baking. Remove it about twenty minutes before pie is done. This will prevent excessive browning of the crust.

■ To keep juicy fruit pies from boiling over in the oven, use a bubbler in the center. You can make a simple one by rolling a double thickness of aluminum foil around a pencil. It should be about four to five inches high. Remove pencil and insert roll into the opening of the top crust so that juices will run up into it and back into the pie as it cools.

BAKED ALASKA—Cake, ice cream, and meringue are the ingredients of this spectacular dessert. The cake is topped with ice cream and covered on all sides with a meringue. Then the whole is browned quickly in a hot oven and served immediately.

Baked Alaska is a dessert that was created in New York's luxurious Delmonico restaurant, whose fame for gourmet food was unparalleled and completely justified. It was introduced to an adoring public in the 1870's in honor of the American purchase of the Territory of Alaska, now our forty-ninth state. Since then, it has occupied a post of honor among the more fanciful desserts of the American table, both in restaurants and in homes.

The interest of this dessert lies in the fact that you can bake ice cream without melting it, and in the flavor and texture contrast between the hot and cold ingredients of the dish. A Baked Alaska looks difficult to make, but it is not, if a few simple rules are followed. The ice cream, to prevent quick melting, must not contain water, but only milk or cream and it must be frozen very hard. Since the air in the meringue that tops the ice cream acts as an insulator to keep the heat of the oven away from the ice cream, it is extremely important that the ice cream is completely and thoroughly covered by the meringue. Otherwise the heat will penetrate and melt the ice cream.

BAKED ALASKA

Loaf cake or spongecake
⅛ teaspoon salt
3 egg whites
6 tablespoons sugar
2 bricks (1 pint each) ice cream,
    any flavor

Cut cake to make a layer 1 inch thick and ½ inch wider and longer than brick of ice cream. Put on a sheet of brown paper on cookie sheet. Add salt to egg whites and beat with rotary beater until foamy. Gradually beat in sugar, 1 tablespoon at a time; beat until stiff but not dry. Put very firm brick of ice cream on cake and spread top and sides of both with meringue, being careful to cover completely. Bake in preheated very hot oven (450°F.) for 5 minutes, or until delicately browned. Transfer from cookie sheet to cold serving plate. Cut into slices and serve at once. Makes 6 servings. If you wish to use a ready-to-use round spongecake layer instead of an oblong, soften the 2 bricks of ice cream and press them into an 8-inch layer-cake pan, 1½ inches deep, lined with wax paper or foil. Refreeze. Turn out on spongecake layer. Remove wax paper or foil. Proceed as above.

Caution: Always make certain the ice cream is very hard. If it is soft, put it on whatever base is to be used and slide it into the freezer until it is hard again. Then apply meringue.

■ **Variation I**—Use 2 bricks (1 pint each) of 3-flavored ice cream to prepare a 3-toned Neapolitan-type Baked Alaska.

Slivered almonds or shredded coconut may be sprinkled on meringue before baking.

■ **Variation II**—Cut oranges or grapefruit into halves. Carefully scoop out pulp and reserve for other uses. Chill shells. Fill with ice cream. Brown quickly in hot oven.

BAKING POWDER—This is a leavening agent used in batters and doughs to make them rise and become light and porous during baking. In mixtures it produces carbon dioxide, one of the three leavening gases (the other two are air and water vapor or steam). Once upon a time recipes for cakes and other baked goods called for cream of tartar and bicarbonate of soda (baking soda), which came in solid or lump form and had to be painstakingly crushed and measured and mixed before they could be used. Commercial baking powder was first made in the United States in 1855 in Boston, Massachusetts.

Today's cooks are fortunate; they can use commercial baking powders, which contain at least three ingredients:

Baking soda, also known as sodium bicarbonate or bicarbonate of soda and, in its less-refined form, saleratus.

An acid salt which produces carbon dioxide, the leavening agent, which may be a tartrate compound, a phosphate compound, or sulfate and phosphate combinations.

Starch, used as a stabilizer, to keep the powder from caking and reacting in the can.

There are three different kinds of baking powders, named according to the type of acid salt used in the baking powder. The common names sometimes found in recipes are:

Tartrate which contains cream of tartar and tartaric acid. This type releases most of its gas quickly in the batter or dough at room temperature. To allow for this, larger quantities of this type of powder are specified in recipes. The cake or cookies should be baked immediately to prevent loss of too much gas, which would produce a heavy product instead of a well-leavened product.

Phosphate which contains calcium acid phosphate, which may also be combined with sodium acid pyrophosphate. This type of powder releases two thirds of its gas at room temperature and the remainder when heat is applied. It is a little slower acting than the tartrate powder.

Double-acting or **SAS-phosphate** in which the acids are sodium aluminum sulfate (s.a.s.) and calcium acid phosphate. This type releases a small portion of gas when the ingredients are combined at room temperature, but the greater amount is released in the oven. Baking can be delayed a few minutes. The batter or dough can even be refrigerated for baking later in the day.

BAKING SODA (Bicarbonate of Soda)—The chemical formula of this product is $NaHCO_3$. Its home use lies mostly in baking, to leaven cakes containing acid ingredients such as buttermilk, vinegar, molasses, and fruit juices. It is also used along with cream of tartar or baking powder where the amount of acid in the ingredients being combined varies a great deal, as it does when such things as chocolate, brown sugar, honey, sour cream, apples, etc., are used together. The acid in the ingredients combines with the baking soda to produce a gas which leavens the dough. A dough containing baking soda should be baked without delay since most of the leavening gas is produced at room temperature and will escape.

Formerly known as saleratus, baking soda was used in baking and for cleaning butterchurns and other homely articles. It was made in this country as early as 1839 and made a formidable competition for soda imported from England. It is easy to see why: saleratus was packaged in a bright-red wrapper, each pound with its free recipe card for the ladies. This was a colorful era of salesmanship.

One can imagine the delight of the children and all onlookers as the soda salesman drove into town in a colorfully decorated wagon drawn by plumed horses. There was the jingle of bells and a trumpet blast. One of the most memorable, and surely one of the most successful, salesmen was Colonel Powell, a former Barnum giant, who stood nine feet tall with the aid of a very high hat and a pair of extremely thick-soled shoes.

Aside from baking, the virtues of $NaHCO_3$ are as many as they are varied. It will clean such diverse items as painted walls, plastic table mats, car windshields, crystal, costume jewelry, and even the family dog. Take baking soda on a fishing trip? Certainly! It will brighten up those dull or rusted lures and hooks, rid your hands of fishy odors, take the soreness out of an accidental sunburn, and soothe the itch or sting of bug bites.

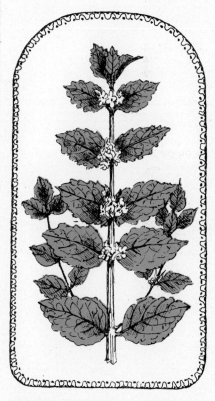

BALM (Lemon Balm) (Melissa officinalis)—A hardy perennial which reaches a height of from one and a half to two feet. It has broad, dark-green leaves, with a faint lemon flavor, and flowers growing in pale yellow clusters. Balm thrives in all temperate climates and may be used attractively as a garden border.

Balm is probably the most quoted of all herbs. Its name has become synonymous with a healing substance. Macbeth bewails the fact that he has killed sleep, that "Balm of hurt minds." One thinks immediately of Jeremiah's poignant cry, "Is there no balm in Gilead, is there no physician there" (Jeremiah 8:22), although, strictly speaking, the prophet's balm belongs to a small evergreen tree of the poplar family which yields a fragrant balsam.

There is little doubt that the lemon balm of today is the same herb ancient Greeks and Orientals crushed in their teas and in wine drinks. Arabs praised tea made from balm leaves because it made "the heart merry and joyful." Dioscorides, the early Greek physician and authority on medical plants, says balm leaves "being drunk with wine and also applied, are good for the scorpion-smitten and the dog-bitten. Being smeared on they will assuage the pains of gout." The ancients appreciated as well the bee-attracting quality of this fragrant herb. Virgil tells how beekeepers must quickly spread bruised balm and honeywort to lure bees back as they swarm from their hive. Balm is still kept on the Ionian Islands for the bees. Lemon balm is not to be confused, however, with bee balm (bergamot), an herb used by the American Indians.

The soothing powers of balm continued to sustain men of the Middle Ages. An old herbal claims: "The dried leaves laid on top of the head will draw out the congestion and leave one light-headed." Balm tea is still used in some European countries as a remedy for fainting and the fever of colds.

Leaves and tender sprigs lend a subtle, charming flavor to lemonade, teas, meats, sauces, stuffings, soups, and salads. Industrially, balm is used in making perfume and liqueurs, especially Benedictine and Chartreuse.

COMPOTE OF FRESH FRUITS WITH LEMON BALM

4 pears
8 plums or fresh prunes
2 peaches
½ cup water
Fresh lemon balm leaves
1¼ cups sugar

Select firm fruit. Peel, core, and quarter pears. Cut plums or prunes into 4 sections through to stone; leave pulp attached to stones. Peel peaches and cut into halves. Save stones. Put fruit and peach stones in heavy saucepan; add water, lemon balm leaves, and sugar. Cover and cook slowly over very low heat for 20 minutes, or until tender. Chill, and remove fruit stones before serving. Makes 4 to 6 servings.

BAMBOO SHOOT—The inner white part of the young shoot of the bamboo, a tropical plant, prepared by stripping off the tight, tough, overlapping outer sheaths of the plant. The shoots are then cut into strips and are ready for cooking.

Bamboo shoots are a basic ingredient in Chinese, Japanese, and other oriental cooking. There are different kinds, depending on the season (winter, early spring, and spring bamboo shoots; summer ones are bitter), and sizes, from one inch to eight inches in diameter. Not all bamboo plants produce edible shoots. It is essential that bamboo shoots be tender, which they are only when young, before they become grown-up bamboo. On the whole, they grow fast. A Chinese proverb says: "It is like spring bamboo shoots after rain."

In this country, we buy bamboo shoots in cans, peeled, chunked, boiled, and ready to use. They are imported from Taiwan and Japan, and come packed in either water or brine. Bamboo shoots are used mainly as fillers in Chinese cooking; their flavor is reminiscent of that of the artichoke. They can be deep-fried, pickled, or put into soups, stews, and other dishes much in the way mushrooms are used.

If a recipe calls for fewer bamboo shoots than are contained in a can, the remaining ones can be kept for a considerable amount of time by placing them in a clean glass jar, covering them with cold water, and sealing the jar with an airtight lid. The jar should be placed in the warmest part of the refrigerator, and the water changed at least every other day.

Caloric Value

☐ 3½ ounces = 27 calories

SAUTÉED BAMBOO SHOOTS

2 cups canned bamboo shoots, drained
1 chicken breast
3 tablespoons salad oil
1 tablespoon chopped onion
¼ cup chicken bouillon
1 tablespoon soy sauce, or more to taste

Cut bamboo shoots into slivers. Skin and bone chicken breast. Cut against the grain into thin slices. Heat salad oil in skillet. When very hot, cook onion in it for 1 minute. Add chicken and cook for 1 minute. Add bamboo shoots, bouillon, and soy sauce. Simmer, covered, for about 10 minutes, or until flavors have blended. Makes 2 to 3 servings.

BANANA—Bananas are seedless fruit grown on a plant that resembles the palm, each plant bearing a single bunch of fruit. To those who enjoy the smooth softness of ripe bananas, it may come as a surprise to learn that this plant is first cousin to the tough, fibrous Manila hemp plant. Bananas are harvested green, and their food value and flavor are the result of carefully controlled conditions and temperatures during ripening, when their starch is converted to sugar. The skin of the partly ripened fruit is usually yellow, but there are also red-skinned varieties. Originally the banana tree was native to tropical Asia, perhaps India, for ancient Greek and Arabian writers have called it "the remarkable Indian fruit tree." Judging from the quantity of fresh bananas sold in this country, they are the third most popular American fruit. It is clear that they have always been held in high esteem, for their botanical name (*Musa sapientum*) means fruit of the wise men. But man, wise or foolish, isn't the only creature to find them delectable. A tropical American oriole is so fond of the fruit that it is called the banana bird.

There are some thirty species of bananas, which look and taste quite differently from each other. There are red bananas, and greenish bananas, and bananas with a flavor reminiscent of apples and peaches, and some with a more delicate or a richer flavor. The *plantain* is the best known of these varieties, with a fruit that is larger, less sweet, and starchier than the usual banana. Some bananas are not suited for eating raw, but must be cooked, fried, boiled, or baked to become palatable. These are often used as a vegetable rather than as a dessert, and are found in stores in Puerto Rican neighborhoods.

Bananas are one of the diet mainstays in the West Indies, Central and tropical South America, the Pacific Islands, and throughout Central Africa. They sustain life better than other tropical starches, such as arrowroot or tapioca, and when only a small amount of growing space is available, bananas will support more people than wheat. Any house or hut in the banana-eating countries has its own little grove of trees nearby, where the fruit grows like weeds. Commercially, bananas are grown on enormous plantations.

The banana tree itself has enormously long pointed leaves which usually hang in shreds, giving the tree a disheveled appearance. This raggedness is one of nature's ways of guarding its own against damage from the elements, causing the leaves to shred rather than to break off under the pressure of tropical storms and torrential rains. If the leaves broke off, they could no longer fulfill their purpose of sheltering the growing fruit.

Availability—Available all year round with peak season in March, April, May, and June. Sources are Ecuador, Costa Rica, Panama, Honduras, Guatemala, and other Central and South American countries.

Purchasing Guide—Look for firm, unblemished, plump fruit, irrespective of size.

Sold now in small bunches, mainly by weight. It is better to buy them by the bunch than singly, for single bananas deteriorate more rapidly.

Fully ripe bananas have brown flecks on the yellow skin; plan to use these immediately. Choose yellow (partly ripe) fruit for cooking and for future use.

Bananas are sold packaged, dehydrated in powder or flakes.

Storage—For green or slightly green, room temperature is best.

Let ripen slowly and naturally to the point desired: slightly green for cooking, yellow skin with brown flecks when fully ripe and suitable for eating. Chill only before using.

☐ Room temperature, when green: 5 days
☐ Refrigerator frozen-food compartment, prepared for freezing: 1 week
☐ Freezer, prepared for freezing: 1 year

Nutritive Food Values—Bananas provide vitamin C with good quantities of vitamin A and some vitamins B_1 and G. They are low in protein and fat. When completely ripe, they are easily digested.

☐ 1 medium banana = 85 calories

Basic Preparation—Peel, then slice directly into food in which it is used (salad, fruit cup, gelatin, etc.).

To serve plain: peel, slice lengthwise or crosswise, sprinkle immediately with lemon, orange, pineapple, or other fruit juice, or with an ascorbic-acid mixture to prevent darkening. Chill in refrigerator for 2 to 3 hours before serving.

To decorate slices: remove peeling completely, brush with fruit juice, score lengthwise using tines of stainless-steel fork. Then slice as desired.

☐ **To Freeze**—Mash ripe bananas. Add lemon juice or ascorbic acid or a citric-acid preparation to prevent darkening. Citric acid preparation is sold in the dietetic department of grocery stores and is used in amounts specified on the package.

Defrost and use in cooking where mashed bananas are a recipe ingredient.

BANANA-SHRIMP CURRY

2 pounds raw shrimps
  Butter or margarine
1 onion, minced
6 tablespoons all-purpose flour
2½ teaspoons curry powder
1½ teaspoons sugar
¼ teaspoon ground ginger
2 cups milk
1 cup chicken bouillon
1 teaspoon fresh lemon juice
  Salt to taste
4 bananas
3 cups hot cooked rice

Cook, shell, and devein shrimps. In a saucepan melt ⅓ cup butter. Add onion and sauté for 2 to 3 minutes. Blend in flour, curry powder, sugar, and ginger. Gradually stir in liquids and cook over low heat, stirring, until thickened. Add lemon juice and salt to taste. Add shrimps and heat. Sauté bananas in butter until lightly browned. Put on rice in serving dish. Pour curry over top. Makes 4 to 6 servings.

BANANA FRITTERS

4 medium firm bananas
  Juice of ½ lemon
2 tablespoons confectioners' sugar
½ cup biscuit mix
1 tablespoon sugar
1 egg
¼ cup milk
  Fat for deep frying

Cut each banana into 3 chunks, and sprinkle with lemon juice and confectioners' sugar. Let stand for 20 minutes. Mix biscuit mix, sugar, egg, and milk. Dip banana chunks in the batter and fry in hot deep fat (375°F. on frying thermometer) in electric cooker-fryer or deep skillet until brown. Serve as dessert, with maple syrup, if desired. Makes 4 servings.

BANANA-NUT BREAD

½ cup cooking oil
1 cup sugar
2 eggs, beaten
3 ripe bananas, mashed
2 cups all-purpose flour
1 teaspoon baking soda
½ teaspoon baking powder
½ teaspoon salt
3 tablespoons milk
½ teaspoon vanilla extract
½ cup chopped nuts

Beat oil and sugar together. Add eggs and banana pulp and beat well. Add sifted dry ingredients, milk, and vanilla.

Mix well and stir in nuts. Pour into greased and floured loaf pan (9 x 5 x 3 inches). Bake in preheated moderate oven (350°F.) for about 1 hour. Cool well and store overnight before cutting. Makes 1 loaf. Good with cream cheese for tea sandwiches.

BANANA CREAM PIE

½ cup sugar
6 tablespoons all-purpose flour
¼ teaspoon salt
2½ cups milk
2 egg yolks or 1 whole egg
1 tablespoon butter
½ teaspoon lemon or vanilla extract
3 ripe bananas
1 baked 9-inch pie shell
½ cup shredded coconut
½ cup heavy cream, whipped

Mix sugar, flour, and salt in top part of double boiler. Gradually stir in milk and cook over boiling water until thickened, stirring constantly. Cover and cook for 10 minutes longer, stirring occasionally. Beat egg and add a small amount of milk mixture; return to double boiler and cook for 2 minutes over hot, not boiling, water, stirring constantly. Remove from heat and add butter and extract; cool. Slice 2 bananas into baked shell. Pour cooked mixture over bananas at once. Chill for at least 1 hour. Put coconut in shallow pan and toast by baking in moderate oven (350°F.) for 10 minutes, or until lightly browned, stirring occasionally; cool. Just before serving, spread pie with whipped cream. Peel remaining banana and score lengthwise with fork; slice thin and arrange around edge of pie; put toasted coconut in center. Makes 6 to 8 servings.

BAKED BANANAS IN FRESH ORANGE JUICE

Peel whole bananas and place in a baking dish. Pour 2 tablespoons fresh orange juice and 1 teaspoon fresh lemon juice over each banana. Bake in preheated hot oven (400°F.) for 10 to 15 minutes. Serve as a meat accompaniment.

BAKED BANANAS WITH HONEY

Peel bananas and cut into halves lengthwise. Arrange in a shallow baking dish. Sprinkle 1 tablespoon strained honey mixed with 1 teaspoon fresh lemon juice over each banana. Bake in preheated hot oven (400°F.) for 10 to 15 minutes. Serve as a meat accompaniment or for dessert.

BAKED BANANAS IN CURRANT JELLY

Peel bananas and cut into halves lengthwise. Arrange in a shallow baking dish. For each banana mix 1½ teaspoons currant jelly, ½ teaspoon butter or margarine, and 1 teaspoon hot water. Pour over each banana. Bake in preheated hot oven (400°F.) for 10 to 15 minutes. Serve as a meat accompaniment.

BANANA CREAM PIE

BANANAS • Straight from the tropics

Banana-Filled Orange Layer Cake

Banana and Cantaloupe Salad

BANANA FRITTERS

to your table, to eat out-of-hand or to cook. *Delicious eating!*

Banana Meringue Pudding

BANANA AND CANTALOUPE SALAD

1 medium cantaloupe, peeled and diced
2 large bananas, sliced
1 cup miniature marshmallows
½ cup pecans
½ cup mayonnaise
½ cup strawberry or peach ice cream
  Salad greens

Mix fruits, marshmallows, and nuts lightly. Blend mayonnaise and ice cream and stir lightly into first mixture. Serve on greens. Makes 6 servings.

BANANA MERINGUE PUDDING

1 cup sugar
⅓ cup cornstarch
¾ teaspoon salt
3 cups milk
3 eggs, separated
1½ teaspoons vanilla extract
24 small or 16 large vanilla wafers
3 large ripe bananas

In the top part of double boiler, mix ⅔ cup sugar, cornstarch, salt, and milk. Put over boiling water and cook, stirring, until thickened. Cover and cook for 10 minutes, stirring occasionally. Add small amount to egg yolks, stirring. Put back in double boiler and cook for 2 minutes, stirring. Cool and add vanilla. Arrange alternate layers of wafers, banana slices, and pudding in 1½-quart casserole, ending with pudding. Whip egg whites until foamy; add sugar gradually, continuing to whip until stiff. Pile lightly on pudding. Bake in preheated hot oven (400° F.) for 5 minutes. Makes 6 servings.

BANANA-FILLED ORANGE LAYER CAKE

¾ cup soft butter or margarine
1¼ cups sugar
8 egg yolks
  Grated rind of ½ orange
2¾ cups sifted cake flour
2¾ teaspoons baking powder
½ teaspoon salt
¾ cup milk
  *Fluffy White Frosting
5 ripe bananas

Cream butter well; add sugar gradually, beating until fluffy. Beat egg yolks until thick; add with rind to creamed mixture. Mix all sifted dry ingredients together and add alternately with milk, beating until smooth. Pour into 3 greased and floured 9-inch round layer-cake pans. Bake in pre-heated moderate oven (375° F.) for about 20 minutes. Cool for 5 minutes; turn out on racks. Spread part of frosting and some sliced bananas between layers. Use remaining frosting on top and sides. Decorate top with a circle of sliced bananas.

*Use recipe on page **46** for the frosting or use Fluffy White Frosting mix.

BANBURY TART—This comes from England. It is a small pie or turnover filled with currants and raisins. It is also called a Banbury Cake. As with so many traditional pastries, the shape may vary slightly; sometimes they are round, at other times oval, and again, they may be baked in a half-moon shape. The pastry used varies too; it may be flaky, short, or any of the varieties of pastry dough. Banbury tarts date back over 300 years; they brought fame and money to the small market town of Banbury in Oxfordshire. Many of us know Banbury from the Mother Goose rhyme that says: "Ride a cock-horse to Banbury Cross, To see a fair lady ride a white horse." Banbury tarts make pleasant eating with coffee or tea, or as a dessert.

BANBURY TARTS

Pastry (2 cups flour recipe), unbaked
Beaten egg

Cut rolled-out pastry into rounds 3 inches in diameter. Place about 2 teaspoons Filling in center of each round. Cover with another round, press edges together and crimp with fork. Brush over with beaten egg. Bake in preheated moderate oven (350°F.) for 15 to 20 minutes, or until golden brown.

Filling

½ cup raisins
½ cup currants
¼ cup chopped citron
¼ cup water
1 cup sugar
2 tablespoons all-purpose flour
  Grated rind and juice of 1 large lemon
½ cup chopped walnuts

Combine all ingredients except walnuts and cook over low heat until thick. Remove from heat, add walnuts, and cool before using. Enough for about 12 to 16 tarts.

BANNOCK—This substantial round Scottish oatmeal or barley cake was baked on a griddle and often served toasted with butter and jam as a breakfast and supper food. Bannocks are to the Scottish people what biscuits are to Americans from the southern United States. The word comes from the Gaelic and means "cake." Since bannocks have been basic fare in Scotland for centuries, there are many varieties and many customs connected with them. There was a sweet "cryin' bannock" served to the people in attendance when a child was born; a "teethin' bannock" of oatmeal and butter or cream, with a teething ring in it for children cutting their teeth. A salt bannock served in the Highlands on Halloween made those who ate it dream of the future, provided they neither spoke nor drank water after eating it. In America, pioneers of Scottish descent made their bannocks with cornmeal.

DROP BANNOCKS

2 cups milk
1 egg, beaten
2 cups old-fashioned rolled oats
¼ teaspoon baking soda
½ teaspoon salt

Heat milk to lukewarm. Add egg. Stir in rolled oats. Let stand for 30 minutes until oats soften and liquid is absorbed. Add baking soda and salt and mix. Drop by tablespoon onto a greased griddle. Cook until bubbles form on top, then turn. Makes about 24. Serve with butter and jam.

BANQUET—A banquet is a sumptuous, formal meal given for a large number of guests. The word comes from the French *banc* or bench, and may be interpreted to mean that people sat on benches while partaking of a common meal, rather than eating it haphazardly.

Eating together in a festive manner is a habit as old as civilization, but banquets became possible only with the invention of cooking vessels big enough to feed large gatherings of people at the same time, since it is the essence of a banquet that people eat together, not after one another. Book after book could be written about banquets in every part of the world, and through the ages, from the elaborate meals of antiquity to modern streamlined American banquets, and from the highly ornamented foods of the civilized countries to the simple feasts of primitive people.

The banquets of the ancient Assyrians, Egyptians, Greeks, Romans, and Persians were of a lavishness that defies belief, and they were rivaled by those of the Chinese. These banquets lasted for many days, and were held in premises hung with sumptuous tapestries of silk, silver, and gold. Guests dressed in special garments and rested on couches of silver and gold on floors of alabaster and marble. Precious wines were poured into golden vessels, and rare foods were served

on silver dishes by colorfully costumed slaves, while music and flowers filled the air with sweet sounds and scents.

The Bible speaks of banquets in the Books of Esther (5:4), Job (41:6), Solomon (2:4), Daniel (5:10), and Amos (6:7). The most famous Roman banquet was the Feast of Trimalchio, for which sculptors created special works of art, and which featured foods within foods, such as live thrushes sown into the belly of a boar and pastry eggs containing roast birds, as well as a hare with wings fastened to his back to resemble Pegasus, the winged horse which is the symbol of poetic inspiration, plus an articulated silver skeleton which inspired Trimalchio, th host, to utter an elegy on the shortness of life.

The courts of Europe in the 15th century featured dinners comprising four courses, each of which was composed of ten pairs of dishes. For regal feasts, the royal chefs slaved to make such creations as a ship of confectionery, with guns charged with actual powder, and a castle of pies, containing live frogs and birds. Spices were so necessary for preserving and flavoring that royal fortunes were spent on explorations to procure them, and thus the paths of empire were blazed. One of the adventurers, Columbus, in search primarily of black pepper, discovered America instead, as well as many previously unknown foods which delighted European palates.

As time went on, banquets became simpler though some of the great chefs of the 18th and 19th centuries, such as Carême, created edible sculptures that would stagger our modern eyes. An important historic dinner eaten by Czar Alexander II of Russia and William I, King of Prussia, in 1867 in Paris consisted of only sixteen dishes served in five courses, which was paltry indeed by past banquet standards. Today's banquets are at best a pallid echo; the custom of today is to serve a well-planned four- or five-course dinner.

We are indebted to banquets for the creation of table accessories and decorations of great artistry. These include the exquisite dinner services of Europe's great porcelain factories in Sèvres, Meissen, Copenhagen, and Capodistria, English Spode, the glassware of Baccarat, and the superlative silver of French and English silversmiths. Banquets were more than an orgy of food and drink; they were pacesetters for gracious living, and no small influence in the history of civilization.

BARBECUE

BARBECUE—This familiar word has several related meanings. It covers food cooked over an open fire, over coals, in a pit, or on a spit in front of a fire. The food can be a whole animal, large or small, such as an ox or a pig, a bird, or a fish. It can also be cuts of any of these. A barbecue is an outdoor party, where these foods are prepared for a large group of people. The word also includes any equipment, simple or elaborate, used for the purpose, and finally the sauces used for basting the foods that are being barbecued.

The word "barbecue" comes from the Spanish word *barbacoa,* meaning a frame made of sticks, on which meat was set for roasting. This frame was set over a deep pit which held the fire.

Meats should be marinated or brushed with a barbecue sauce before or during cooking to prevent drying.

Keep menu simple, making full use of the cooking surface of the grill. Use the heat remaining in the coals after main meal is cooked to toast marshmallows, grill banana chunks, pop popcorn, etc.

EQUIPMENT

■ A brazier with holes in the fire pan to allow air to circulate through coals, with racks that can be raised or lowered.

■ A battery- or electric-powered rotisserie.

■ Two-sided broilers, wire basket, or wire racks to use when broiling frankfurters or other small loose pieces, which allow for quick turning and removal from heat.

■ Barbecue tools with long handles.

■ Long insulated gloves, asbestos, if possible.

■ Foil to cover food or to make drip pans for rotisserie-roasted meats.

■ Sand or water to control fire if it flares when drippings hit it, or to put out fire.

HOW TO BUILD A FIRE

■ Start fire 45 minutes to 1 hour before actual cooking starts.

■ Use charcoal briquettes for an even intense fire.

■ To kindle, start with a few rolls of newspaper or kindling wood. Fan flames to keep fire burning. Burn coals until they are glowing and coated with white ashes. Do not cook over flames or food will burn.

BARBECUE MENUS AND RECIPES

BROILED WHOLE TENDERLOIN
Serve with:

BORDELAISE SAUCE
MUSHROOMS IN FOIL
POTATOES AU GRATIN
AVOCADO SALAD
COFFEE AND CHOCOLATES

A whole tenderloin is not as extravagant as it may seem. It has no waste; it may

There is nothing that helps a barbecued dish like a good barbecue sauce,

be served to suit each appetite.

Brush the tenderloin with melted butter or oil and broil over a medium-hot fire for 25 to 50 minutes, depending on how rare you want it. While it is cooking, wrap 6 two-inch pieces of marrow bone in foil and cook at the edge of the grill. Slip marrow from the bones, slice it, and add it to the sauce just before serving.

Bordelaise Sauce

2 tablespoons butter
2 tablespoons minced shallots or 1 tablespoon minced onion
¾ cup dry red wine
1½ cups canned beef gravy
2 tablespoons lemon juice

3 tablespoons minced parsley
Salt
Cayenne
¾ cup sliced mushrooms, sautéed in 1 tablespoon butter (optional)

Melt butter and sauté shallots or onions in it until soft and transparent. Add wine and simmer until reduced to half its volume. Stir in beef gravy, lemon juice, parsley, salt and cayenne to taste, and mushrooms. Heat through before serving. Makes about 2 cups sauce.

Mushrooms in Foil—Put enough mushrooms for each serving on a square of heavy foil. Add a pat of butter, salt, and pepper, with perhaps a whisper of tarragon. Fold in a packet, sealing the edges,

especially when the natural flavor of the food is enhanced by the choice of a zestful sauce.

and broil for about 10 minutes, turning at least once. Serve in the foil.

CHARCOAL-BROILED SALISBURY STEAK
Serve with:

ROAST CORN
TOASTED CHEESE BREAD
SWEET ONIONS WITH OREGANO
CHERRY TOMATOES
BROWNIES AND COFFEE

Not new, this, but not often served at home. Have 3 pounds of beef from the round, rump, or shoulder ground not too fine and combine it with 1 tablespoon salt, ½ teaspoon pepper, and 2 eggs. Form into a large patty, 1½ to 2 inches thick. Brush with soft butter or beef drippings and broil in a hinged broiler until done to your liking.

Roast Corn—Pull back husks and remove silk, then replace husks and tie with a strip of the outer husk. Soak in cold water for at least 30 minutes. Roast around the edge of the fire, turning a few times. The outer husks will burn off and also the "tie," so that a little of the corn will be exposed. A few browned spots are delicious.

Toasted Cheese Bread—Split a long loaf of French or Italian bread lengthwise and toast it over the coals on both cut and crust sides. Then spread with ½ cup but-ter mixed with 1 cup grated Cheddar cheese. Put near the fire so that the cheese will melt. If you want the topping beautifully bubbly brown, fill a fine-meshed hinged broiler, preferably the "basket" type, with hot coals and hold it over the top of the bread. This may also be used for browning other foods that can't be put face down to the coals. Cut bread into slices.

Sweet Onions with Oregano—Peel and thinly slice large sweet red onions. Sprinkle them with salt and a little ground oregano. Cover with a mixture of 1 part vinegar to 2 parts water. Chill for half a day before serving.

BROILED LOBSTER
Serve with:

FOIL-BAKED POTATOES
GREEN-BEAN AND DILL SALAD
ASSORTED CUPCAKES OR PETITS FOURS

Buy a live lobster for this, if possible. Split; remove the intestinal vein and stomach. Brush the meat well with softened butter and cook for a minute or two, flesh side down; then turn and cook, shell side down, for about 15 minutes, basting the top generously with butter. The lobster will be done when the meat is opaque. Do not overcook. Cooked lobsters should be broiled only until hot and browned.

The <u>salad</u> is made with chilled cooked green beans, sprinkled with dill, then covered with French dressing.

CHARCOAL-BROILED CHICKEN
Serve with:

BROILED PINEAPPLE
TOASTED CORN BREAD
LIMA-BEAN SALAD
CRACKERS AND CHEESE

Next to steak, broiled chicken is probably the country's favorite barbecue dish. Allow half a broiler for each serving and cook over a medium fire, skin side down, until browned, then turn and cook other side. Baste with a mixture of ½ cup melted butter or margarine, ½ cup cooking oil, ½ cup white wine, and 1 tablespoon dried tarragon. A chicken will take from 25 to 60 minutes, depending on its size.

<u>Broiled Pineapple</u>—Brush slices of canned or fresh fruit with butter or oil. Cook in a hinged broiler until brown on both sides.

<u>Split the corn bread</u>—before toasting it over the coals.

<u>Lima-Bean Salad</u>—Combine 3 cups cooked baby Lima beans, 1 cup diced celery, ¼ cup each of minced parsley and chives, and 2 teaspoons minced dill. Dress with ½ cup each of mayonnaise and sour cream, 1 tablespoon lemon juice, and salt and pepper to taste. Serves 6 to 8.

SHISH KEBAB
Serve with:

PILAF
GREEN SALAD
ASSORTED CHEESES
RED WINE

Here's an old favorite that has dozens of variations. Basically, it's chunks of meat, marinated and strung on *skewers, alternating with various vegetables. Use lamb, mutton, beef, or even veal, and cut it into 1½-inch cubes. For vegetables have any or all of the following: quartered tomatoes or whole small ones, slices of onion or whole parboiled small ones, cubes of eggplant or zucchini, pieces of green pepper, and sometimes pieces of bacon. Bay leaves are often threaded

next to the meat, too. A good marinade for the meat (used for at least a day before stringing meat on the skewers) is made with 1 cup red wine, 3 tablespoons red-wine vinegar, ½ cup olive oil, 1 garlic clove, crushed, 1 large onion, sliced, and the herb or spice of your choice—bay leaf, oregano, marjoram, thyme, cumin-seed, perhaps. A simpler marinade, and a good one, is 1 part lemon juice to 3 parts olive oil. When stringing the meat and vegetables on the skewers, push them close together if you want the meat rare and juicy; leave a space between if you want it crisp and well done. It will take from 10 to 30 minutes, depending on your taste.

<u>Pilaf</u>—Cook 1 cup uncooked rice and ¼ cup minced onion in ¼ cup butter until golden. Add 2 cups chicken bouillon, cover, and cook until rice is tender. Add 2 tablespoons butter and a little ground oregano.

*SUGGESTIONS FOR SKEWERED DISHES
■ Cubes of cooked pork alternating with cubes of cooked sweet potato and pineapple.
■ Cubes of liver wrapped in bacon and alternating with parboiled baby onions and canned or parboiled new potatoes.
■ Whole peeled jumbo shrimps, with green-pepper squares and pineapple chunks.
■ Cubes of fish with onion, tomato, green pepper, and bacon. These are called "fish kebabs."
■ Oysters wrapped in bacon, with mushroom caps.
■ Scallops wrapped in bacon, with mushroom caps.
■ Cubes of raw turkey breast, with bacon and pitted ripe olives.

ROAST LOIN OF PORK
Serve with:

FOIL-BAKED APPLES
FOIL-ROASTED YAMS
ROAST CORN, COLESLAW
BLUEBERRY CUPCAKES

Rub the outside of a whole or half pork loin with salt, pepper, and ground oregano. Insert spit parallel to the backbone. Roast over a slow fire until the thermometer reaches 170°F. to 175°F., which is well done, as pork should be, but juicy. A loin any length will take from 2 to 2¾ hours to cook.

<u>Foil-Baked Apples</u>—Core apples, one to a serving, and fill the centers with a mixture of sugar and butter mixed, if you like, with a little cinnamon or nutmeg. Wrap in foil and cook on the outside of the fire for 30 minutes or longer. They may be tested by forking through the foil.

BROILED BONED LEG OF LAMB
For those who don't have a spit, this is a marvelous way to cook a whole leg of lamb

Have your butcher bone and split a leg of lamb. Open the leg out flat, rub it with a cut garlic clove, and brush with a little oil. Broil it, preferably in a hinged grill, exactly as you would a steak. This will take from 45 minutes to 1¼ hours, depending on just how well done you like it.

FISH IN FOIL
Use skinned pike steaks or fillets. For small pan fish, it is best to use them whole, dressed but with the skin left on. Place each serving of fish on a square of heavy-duty aluminum foil. Sprinkle with salt and a little crumbled dried thyme; add a slice of lemon, a slice of onion, and a piece of bay leaf. Wrap securely and cook *directly on the coals,* turning once, for about 8 minutes, or until the fish is white and flaky.

BARBECUE SAUCES

TEXAS HOT SAUCE
In a saucepan mix 2 cups ketchup, ⅔ cup Worcestershire, ½ cup cider vinegar, 1 teaspoon salt, 2 garlic cloves, minced, dash of cayenne, and 2 tablespoons cooking oil. Bring to boil and simmer for 20 minutes. Makes about 3½ cups.

ORANGE BARBECUE SAUCE
1 can (6 ounces) frozen orange juice
   concentrate
¾ cup water
⅓ cup firmly packed brown sugar
½ cup wine vinegar
¼ cup honey
1 teaspoon prepared mustard
1 teaspoon soy sauce
½ teaspoon salt
½ teaspoon seasoned pepper

Thaw orange juice. Add remaining ingredients and stir until mixed. Makes 2¼ cups. Good on pork, lamb, chicken, turkey, rabbit, duck, ham, bologna roll, frankfurters, carrots, onions, corn, peaches, and pears.

SAVORY LEMON BARBECUE SAUCE
1 cup butter or margarine, melted
⅓ cup fresh lemon juice
½ teaspoon onion salt
2 teaspoons Worcestershire
½ teaspoon monosodium glutamate
   Chopped parsley

Combine all ingredients, except parsley. Just before serving, sprinkle with parsley. Makes 1⅓ cups. Good on fish, seafood, chicken, veal, green beans, and carrots.

GREEK BARBECUE SAUCE
1 pint wine vinegar
¼ cup olive oil
1½ teaspoons onion salt
1 teaspoon oregano
½ teaspoon each of seasoned salt
   and pepper

Combine all ingredients and let stand several hours or overnight to blend flavors. Makes 2 cups. Good on lamb, chicken, rabbit, onions, potatoes, peppers, and green beans. If you wish, marinate meat in sauce 4 to 5 hours before cooking.

APRICOT BARBECUE SAUCE

¼ cup cooking oil
¼ cup vinegar
½ cup apricot nectar
½ cup ketchup
2 tablespoons brown sugar
2 tablespoons grated onion
½ teaspoon Worcestershire
1 teaspoon salt
½ teaspoon oregano
    Dash of hot pepper sauce

Combine all ingredients and bring to boil. Makes 1¾ cups. Good on beef, pork, lamb, veal, turkey, chicken, liver, kidneys, bologna roll, frankfurters, meat loaf, hash, carrots, corn, potatoes, peppers, Limas and green beans, peaches, and pears.

BARD—An important food preparation process by which a piece of meat, poultry, game, or fish is wrapped with thin slices of bacon, salt or fresh pork. The food is then cooked and the barding fat removed before serving, with the exception of the barding on roast game birds.

The purpose of barding a food is to protect it from too rapid cooking and to lubricate meats that are too lean to be tender, such as filet mignon, breast of chicken, game birds, and venison.

BAR-LE-DUC—A town in the French province of Lorraine, famous for its delicious red-currant preserve, which is called Bar-le-Duc. The preserve is most painstakingly seeded and each berry is pierced to retain its original shape during cooking.

In France, Bar-le-Duc is eaten for dessert and served with cream cheese and crisp bread or crackers.

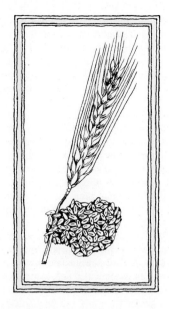

BARLEY—This hardy cereal grass is related to wheat, which it resembles. It comes in a number of varieties and seldom grows higher than three feet.

Barley grows in a larger range of climates than other cereals. It has a short growing season, and therefore can be grown at high altitudes and up to the shores of the Arctic seas. It is an important crop in temperate and even subtropical climates.

Barley is one of the oldest of food plants. The Lake Dwellers of Switzerland, about 3,000 years ago, knew at least three kinds. The Bible mentions barley as one of the foods that was destroyed by the plagues of Egypt (Exodus 9:31). The ancient Greeks and Romans used barley, and it was extensively grown later in England. In America, barley was sown on Martha's Vineyard very early in the 17th century.

Barley is high in nutritive values. Until the 16th century, it was the main source of bread, though its deficiency in gluten makes it poor bread flour. In prosperous countries it was supplanted by wheat which is more palatable and better suited for baking since bread made from wheat flour is much lighter than barley bread. However, barley has an excellent, nutty flavor and is extremely satisfying as a filler or as a side dish with meats, instead of potatoes. People have grown strong on it: Scandinavians, Scots, and Turks, for example.

Barley is an essential ingredient in the brewing of beer and in the distillation of Scotch whisky.

Barley water, a drink that is both refreshing and mild, was once a standard beverage in English households, especially in Victorian times.

Availability—In food stores.

Purchasing Guide—Sold in 1-pound packages with bran removed and polished as pearl barley in fine, medium, and coarse

sizes. Scotch barley is husked grain roughly ground. It is not readily available but can be found in health-food and specialty stores.

Barley is also available as a baby cereal.

Storage

☐ Kitchen shelf, in a cool, dry spot: indefinitely

☐ Refrigerator shelf, cooked, covered: 2 to 4 days

Nutritive Food Values—High in carbohydrates with moderate amounts of protein, calcium, and phosphorus, and small amounts of B vitamins.

☐ Pearl barley, 3½ ounces, raw = 349 calories

☐ Scotch barley, 3½ ounces, raw = 113 calories

Basic Preparations—Cook pearl barley in water to cover from 1 to 1½ hours, or until tender. Old-fashioned Scotch barley must be soaked for 12 hours before cooking.

SCOTCH BROTH

3 pounds lamb or mutton, any cut, cubed
    Water
1 teaspoon salt
½ cup pearl barley
2 carrots, diced
2 turnips, diced
3 onions
½ cup chopped parsley

Place lamb or mutton in deep kettle and cover with water. Add salt. Bring to a boil and reduce heat to very low. Skim off scum whenever necessary. Simmer, covered, for 1 hour. Add barley and vegetables except parsley. Continue simmering, covered, for another 1½ to 2 hours. Skim fat from soup. Before serving, stir in parsley. Makes 6 servings.

BARLEY CASSEROLE

6 tablespoons butter or margarine
1 cup pearl barley
1 large onion, minced
¾ to 1 cup sliced raw mushrooms
    or drained canned mushrooms
3 cups consommé or chicken bouillon,
    boiling
    Salt and pepper

Heat 2 tablespoons butter and sauté barley in it. Transfer barley to heavy casserole. Heat 2 more tablespoons butter and sauté onion in it. Add to barley. Sauté mushrooms in remaining butter and add to other ingredients. Stir in hot consommé and salt and pepper to taste. Cook, covered, over lowest possible heat until barley is tender and has absorbed the consommé. Depending on the kind of barley used, this will take from 25 to 45 minutes. Stir occasionally. Makes about 6 servings.

BARLEY WATER

¼ cup pearl barley
1 quart water
    Rind and juice of 2 lemons
    Sugar to taste

Combine barley, water, and lemon rind in a saucepan. Bring to a boil. Lower heat and simmer, covered, over lowest possible heat for 2 hours. Strain; add lemon juice and sugar to taste. Chill before serving. Makes 1 quart.

BASIL (Ocimum basilicum)—There are five or six varieties of basil, which belongs to the mint family, all differing in height, color, and taste. Each variety of this annual is very hardy and will grow in most climates. The exact species determines leaf color, ranging from light to dark green to purple. White flowers are common to all, appearing at the tops of the branches. The basil most often used in this country is of the two tall varieties of sweet basil (Ocimum basilicum). Reaching a height of one to two feet, its branches will spread out almost as far. Dwarf basil (Ocimum minimum) grows from six inches to one foot tall, in either the green-leaf or the purple-leaf variety. These will form small bushes, making excellent garden borders. The French use them frequently in formal gardens. All basil varieties have a unique fragrance and taste that add zest and flavor in cooking.

The word basil comes from the Greek *basilikon* meaning "royal" or "king." Whether its purple color, used in classical times by royalty, or its use in some royal preparation or medicine, inspired such an elevated name is unknown. Basil is native to the Middle East and the Mediterranean and in India is called *tulasî*. The Hindus regard it as a sacred herb, cultivating it near temple and home as a protection against the misfortunes of life and as a guide to heaven in death. Basil offered protection against the dread malaria, as well as the assurance of fertility to those desiring children. Beads were made of the root to adorn the neck and

arms and a rosary was made from the seeds. A leaf of basil was placed on the breast of the pious Hindu in death. Good fortune comes to those who build their houses where *tulasî* grows well, but only evil to those who inadvertently uproot the holy herb.

Basil was *rayhan* to the Persians and could be found in cemeteries. Egyptians also regarded this herb as having a funereal symbolism. For the ancient Greeks, basil appeared as a symbol of hatred, but present-day Greeks have a different opinion, for one sees this fragrant herb happily growing in blue pots on window sills, all over their country.

We must thank the Italians for finding a happy use for this herb: with a sprig of basil tucked behind her ear or in her dress, the peasant girl sets out to win her sweetheart. Basil is called *amorino* in Turkey. In Rumania the enchanted herb, when given to a youth by a girl, makes him forever hers. This symbol of love takes on curative properties in Africa, where it is said that if one eats basil after a scorpion bite one feels no pain.

Sweet basil is a delicious culinary seasoning. It is useful in almost any dish that can be herbed and is especially pleasing in seafoods, salads, potatoes, vegetable soup, and dishes that contain tomatoes. Basil may be used fresh or dried. It makes a delightful, easily potted plant, especially the purple variety.

PESTO GENOVESE
    4 to 6 garlic cloves, chopped
    16 large fresh basil leaves
    2 parsley sprigs
    6 tablespoons Parmesan cheese
    ¼ cup chopped pine nuts or walnuts
    ½ teaspoon salt
    ½ cup olive oil (do not substitute)

In mortar and pestle or in electric blender, crush or blend all ingredients except the oil to a smooth paste. Slowly blend in oil and stir until smooth. Serve with hot pasta; toss pasta with 1 to 2 tablespoons butter with *pesto* to taste. Leftovers may be placed in a small jar, covered with olive oil, and refrigerated. Makes about ¾ to 1 cup sauce.

BASS—The name covers more than a dozen spiny-rayed North American food and game fish that belong to at least half a dozen different fish families.

Some bass are freshwater fish; others, saltwater fish. They are well distributed throughout the rivers and lakes of the country and in the surrounding oceans, and all are the sportsman's joy. Most bass give gourmets great pleasure, since the flesh is delicately flavored, tender and juicy.

The most common freshwater varieties include: white or silver bass and yellow bass. White or silver bass are found in the upper Mississippi River system, the Great Lakes, and in the east central longitudes of the United States. This species seldom exceeds three pounds, and is caught by angling in lakes and rivers. Yellow Bass is to be found in the eastern part of the United States. In size, it is similar to the white bass, and it also bears some resemblance to the striped bass, with its black, longitudinal lines. Five members of the sunfish family are also called bass. They are the large- and small-mouthed black bass, the spotted bass, the rock bass, and the calico bass.

The best-known saltwater basses are: common sea bass, an abundant fish caught in the Atlantic, which ranges from one to four pounds in size, and striped bass, originally native to the Atlantic, which is now also found in the Pacific. It runs up to some twenty pounds in weight.

Storage
☐ Refrigerator shelf, raw: 24 hours
☐ Refrigerator shelf, cooked and covered: 1 to 2 days
☐ Refrigerator frozen-food compartment, prepared for freezing: 1 month
☐ Freezer, prepared for freezing: 6 months

Nutritive Food Values—It is a good source of protein and phosphorus.
☐ 3½ ounces, raw = 104 calories

Basic Preparation—All bass may be broiled, sautéed, fried, or stuffed and baked. It is served with any of the fish sauces such as browned butter or hollandaise.
☐ **To Freeze**—Scale and clean fish. Remove head and fins. Wrap tightly in freezer paper, seal, tape and date.

STUFFED BAKED BASS
    1 striped bass (about 3 pounds)
    3 eggs
    1 tablespoon water
    1 tablespoon each of finely chopped
       parsley and chives
       Salt and pepper
       Chopped shallots, scallions, or onions
    1 cup dry white wine
    ½ cup light cream
    2 egg yolks
       Lemon slices

Clean and split fish. Make an omelet with eggs, water, finely chopped herbs, and salt and pepper. Stuff fish with the omelet and sew it up with thread or skewer. Coarsely chop enough shallots to make a bed for the fish in a flat oval or round greased baking dish. Sprinkle fish with salt and pepper. Place fish on vegetables. Add white wine. Bake in preheated hot oven (400°F.) for about 30 minutes, or until fish is cooked through. (Fish should never be overcooked.) Baste fish frequently during the baking process. Carefully pour off pan juices and strain into a saucepan. Reduce to half the amount. Beat together cream and egg yolks. Stir pan juices into egg mixture. Return to saucepan. Cook over low heat, stirring constantly, until slightly thickened. Pour sauce around fish in baking dish. Decorate with fresh lemon slices. Makes 4 servings.

POACHED WHOLE BASS

- 1 quart water
- ⅓ cup cider vinegar
   or 1 cup white wine
- 1 carrot
- 1 onion, stuck with 2 cloves
- 1 parsley sprig
- 1 celery stalk
- 1 tablespoon salt
- 2 lemon slices
- 1 whole striped bass (3 to 4 pounds)

Place all ingredients except fish in a large flat pan; bring to boil and cook for 10 minutes. Wrap fish in cheesecloth, lower into liquid, and simmer, covered, for 16 to 20 minutes. Serve hot with hollandaise sauce. Makes 4 servings.

BASTE—To brush or pour liquid over meat or other food while it is cooking. The purpose is to enhance the flavor, to prevent the drying of the surface, and to give it a nice finish. The most frequently used liquids: pan drippings, fruit juice, melted fat, or a sauce.

BATTER—A mixture of flour, liquid, and other ingredients, to cook as is (as in pancakes or cakes), or to be used as an outer coating for foods that are to be fried. The consistency of the batter depends on its purpose. Batters containing beer are excellent for frying, since they are lighter, thanks to the fermentation of

the beer. All alcohol vanishes during the cooking.

When coating foods with batter, it is essential that the foods be absolutely dry, or the batter won't adhere, and will come off in the frying. You should also remember not to overbeat batters since this makes them tough. It is preferable to let a batter rest before using it, if at all possible.

FRENCH BEER BATTER

- 1⅓ cups sifted all-purpose flour
- 1 teaspoon salt
- 1 tablespoon melted butter
- 2 eggs, separated
- ¾ cup stale beer

Combine flour, salt, melted butter, egg yolks, and stale beer. Beat only until smooth. Cover and let stand in cool place from 1 to 12 hours. Just before using, beat egg whites until stiff and fold gently into batter.

Stuffed Baked Bass

BATTERIE DE CUISINE

BATTERIE DE CUISINE—The literal translation of this French expression is "kitchen battery." What it denotes, however, is the standard equipment of a French kitchen, that is, all the pots and pans and odds and ends one needs for cooking.

A French *batterie de cuisine* has many copper utensils, since the French like to cook in copper because it keeps a slow, even heat. Standard items include *sauteuses,* or deep skillets, *cocottes,* or oval or round casseroles with tight-fitting lids, deep round kettles for boiling, fish cookers, rectangular *braisières* for pot roasting, oval baking dishes for gratins, as well as sieves, whisks, molds, a mortar and pestle, a coffee grinder, a salad basket, forks, spoons, good kitchen knives, and all the other things that are also found in American kitchens, all lovingly tended.

BAVARIAN CREAM

BAVARIAN CREAM—A dessert made from an egg custard stiffened with gelatin and enriched with whipped cream. It is then molded and chilled, and served with or without a sauce. No one is certain of the origin of the name.

Bavarians are among the most popular desserts since they are delicious to taste and spectacular to look at, especially when done in a fancy mold. They lend themselves to a great variety of flavors and are not difficult to make. Bavarians were great favorites in the middle and latter part of the 19th century, which was the golden age of fancy puddings, with a special predilection for delicately quivering ones, such as Bavarians.

To be unmolded successfully, a Bavarian must have been chilled for a minimum of four hours, and preferably ten to twelve, covered, so that it won't absorb foreign flavors. Have ready a chilled plate large enough to take the Bavarian and a garnish. Moisten the plate slightly since this prevents the pudding from sticking and makes it easier to center. Run a thin knife under the Bavarian at several points on the rim of the mold to release the vacuum. Reverse the mold on the plate. If the Bavarian does not come loose, wring out a kitchen towel in warm water and place on mold for a few seconds. If the Bavarian still won't slide out, shake the mold very gently against the serving dish. Some cooks advocate placing the mold in warm water for a few seconds, but this is not advisable since the water is usually too hot, causing the first layer of pudding to melt and run.

LEMON BAVARIAN
Grated rind of 2 lemons
¾ cup boiling water
1 envelope unflavored gelatin
½ cup sugar
Dash of salt
3 egg yolks
½ cup fresh lemon juice
2 tablespoons fresh orange juice
1 cup heavy cream, whipped
½ cup sifted confectioners' sugar

Steep rind in boiling water. Combine gelatin with sugar and salt in saucepan. Beat egg yolks until thick; add rind and fruit juices. Blend egg mixture into gelatin and cook over low heat, stirring constantly, until gelatin is dissolved. Remove from heat and chill until mixture mounds slightly when dropped from spoon. Fold in cream whipped with confectioners' sugar. Pour into 1½-quart mold. Chill for at least four hours, or until firm. Unmold and garnish with whipped cream, strawberries, or chopped candied ginger. Makes 6 servings.

BAY LEAF OR LAUREL LEAF (Laurus nobilis)

BAY LEAF OR LAUREL LEAF (Laurus nobilis)—The true bay or laurel comes from the evergreen sweet bay or laurel shrub or small tree, native to the Near East and the Mediterranean. It is also grown in the southern United States. The California laurel is much larger and its leaves are used less as a flavoring than for their volatile oil.

In Greece, the laurel tree, which grows there to heights of over fifty feet, has been admired ever since antiquity, occupying a semimystical position in Greek life and mythology. A laurel leaf was placed on the brow of the winner of the Olympic games, giving origin to the expression, "winning one's laurels." Zeus, chief of the gods, was also crowned with laurel, and so were the gods, the emperors, and the heroes of ancient Rome. Laurel crowns were placed on the poet's brow, and the word baccalaureate (from which bachelor is derived) means "laurel berry." Apollo's temple stood in a laurel grove, and the Delphic oracle, sitting in her inner sanctum, munched a few leaves before she began prophesying. The nymph Daphne, pursued by Apollo, was saved by being changed into a laurel tree, a legend which has produced some of the finest Greek sculpture of the nymph, half maiden, half laurel tree.

Bay leaves are chiefly used dried and one leaf, crushed, can give a wonderful flavor to a simple dish of potatoes, onions, and other vegetables and can add distinction to tomato-flavored dishes. French cooking can't be imagined without a trace of *laurier,* which is also one of the chief ingredients of the *bouquet garni,* a combination of herbs used for flavoring almost any French dish. And bay leaves are almost as popular in all Mediterranean cooking.

HOW TO USE BAY LEAVES
■ Add 1 to 2 leaves to chowders and soups.
■ Add crushed bay leaf to kabobs.
■ Use 1 to 3 bay leaves in marinades.
■ Add bay leaves to all venison and game dishes.
■ Add 1 or more bay leaves to stews, pot roasts, chicken casseroles, and to the water in which corned beef, ham or tongue is cooked.
■ Add ½ crushed bay leaf to dishes with shrimps, lobster, scallops, and other fish and seafood, whether hot or in a salad.
■ Add a bay leaf to the water in which fresh or frozen vegetables are cooked.
■ Add 1 or more bay leaves to all dishes containing tomato.

BEACH PLUM

BEACH PLUM—The full botanical name of this member of the prune tree family is *Prunus maritima*. Beach plums grow wild. Though the fruit is highly prized for jams and jellies, the plums are seldom cultivated. They are native to the Atlantic seacoast from Canada to Virginia. They grow in low bushes chiefly in sandy soil. The charming flowers are white. The fruit is small and dark purple-blue when ripe, with a thick tough skin and bullet-hard small seed. The flavor is a combination of grape, plum, and cherry, on the bitter and sour side. They are hardly worth eating raw, but are wonderful when cooked.

The Indians knew and used beach plums. One of their legends says that the Great Spirit created the beach plum especially for man since the birds ate all the other fruits of the season. In fact, birds seem to shun the bushes thickly hung with ripe fruit.

Gathering beach plums on a clear, sunny, wind-swept, late summer day, when the beaches of the Atlantic are empty and no noise is heard save that of the seabird's crying and the beating of the surf, is one of the most delightful occupations, second only to eating the resulting beach plum jam or jelly.

BEACH PLUM JAM
Stem and wash beach plums. Remove seeds by inserting the rounded end of a big hairpin into the stem end and hooking out the pit. Or else, the pits can be removed by cutting the plums into halves with a small paring knife and by prying the pit out of the flesh with the knife. The hairpin process is easier, faster, and less messy.

Cover and cook as for jelly until soft. Measure pulp and add ½ to ¾ cup sugar for 1 cup pulp, depending on taste. Boil gently until thick, stirring carefully to prevent burning. Pour while hot into hot sterilized jars and seal.

The gourmet's delight
and the budget's best friend as
a main dish, casserole, soup, salad.
Every country in the world
has a favorite bean dish!

BEAN—Beans are the seed or seeds of many plants, both trailing vines and erect bushes, which are easily cultivated. They belong to the group of foods called legumes, which also include peas, lentils, and peanuts. Next to cereals, it is the legume family which contributes most substantially toward feeding the people of the world. Thanks to their high protein content, beans are an absolute necessity in countries where little meat is eaten.

Broad beans were one of the oldest cultivated plants. They have been found in Bronze Age deposits in Europe (around 3000 B.C.) and we know that they were grown by the ancient Egyptians, Greeks, and Romans. Beans played a prominent part in their rituals, as offerings of food for the dead and to the powers of the afterworld. In China, as far back as the 1st century A.D., records show that many a merchant made a fortune on bean relishes.

The common field, garden, or kidney beans are native to the New World. Domesticated possibly by the Incas of Peru, they were used extensively by the Indians of both South and North America. The Indians appreciated the fact that beans could be cultivated in poorer soil than corn, that they could be dried for easy storage, and that they contained a high-energy content most important in the cold winter. When the meat supply dwindled, beans became an excellent source of protein. Knowledge of bean cultivation, learned from the Indians, was greatly appreciated by the early settlers. Folklore seems to follow the bean wherever it goes. The Seneca Indians believed beans to be a special gift of the Creator to man. One of the major ceremonies of the Hopis is the Bean Festival. Beans were grown as a farm crop for the first time in 1836 in the eastern part of New York State. As a farm industry it was given great impetus when the government started to buy beans for the army during the Civil War. Today the young pods (green or snap beans), the unripe seeds (shell beans), and the dried ripe seeds are all used for human consumption, while the whole plant is used for forage.

The garbanzo bean, or chick-pea, is a native of southern Europe, brought to this country by Spaniards. Lima beans came north to us from Peru and Brazil. The soybean is a most important legume in the Far East. It is the richest natural vegetable food known.

For centuries beans have been the principal ingredient in rib-sticking, delicious French cassoulets, Italian bean soups, Greek bean stews, Spanish rice and bean combinations, to name but a few of the many basic bean dishes. On this continent, where beans were already being grown before the first settlers arrived, they have wandered across the country with the settlers, and have long been featured in many well-known regional dishes: succotash, Boston Baked Beans, Southern Black Bean Soup, Western Chili, and Mexican Refried Beans.

Last but not least comes the magical bean. Folktales are full of magic beans; beans that spanked wrongdoers, beans that laughed until their sides split, and children love all the tales ever told about the magical beans.

FRESH SNAP BEANS, GREEN OR WAX

Availability—All year round, sold in bulk, peak crop from May to October. Major sources are Florida, South Carolina, Louisiana, Georgia, and California.

Purchasing Guide—Look for straight pods that are crisp enough to snap easily, free from scars and rust, as well as smooth and well filled but with immature seeds. Usually sold by the pound.

☐ 1 pound, cooked = 3 cups

Green beans are also sold dried but are available only in limited quantities. They are a Pennsylvania Dutch specialty.

Storage—Place in the refrigerator in a bag or moistureproof covered container. Plan to use as soon as possible. Beans may seem indestructible, but in time they will toughen and lose some of their fresh flavor and color.

☐ Refrigerator shelf, raw: 3 to 5 days
☐ Refrigerator shelf, cooked and covered: 1 to 4 days
☐ Refrigerator frozen-food compartment, prepared for freezing: 1 month
☐ Freezer, prepared for freezing: 10 months

Nutritive Food Values—When cooked for a short time in a small amount of water, they are a fair source of vitamins A and C.

☐ Green beans, 3½ ounces, raw = 32 calories
☐ Green beans, 3½ ounces, boiled and drained = 25 calories
☐ Wax beans, 3½ ounces, raw = 27 calories
☐ Wax beans, 3½ ounces, boiled and drained = 22 calories

Basic Preparation—Wash well in cold water; sort according to size if necessary. Remove stems and tops with paring knife and:
1. Leave whole.
2. Snap or cut straight across into 1-inch pieces.
3. Cut on the diagonal into thin shreds.
4. French cut: slice one or more times lengthwise with a sharp knife, or put through a bean slicer.

☐ **To Cook**—Have about 1 inch of water boiling in a saucepan. Add beans and, if you wish, ½ teaspoon salt per pound. Bring to rapid boil and cook for 2 to 3 minutes. Cover pan and lower heat to point where it will just continue to boil.

Whole, cook for 20 to 30 minutes; pieces, for 15 to 30 minutes; shreds or French cut, for 10 to 20 minutes. Cook the shortest time possible to "just tender" for the best-flavored beans. Drain, season, add butter, and serve.

☐ **To Freeze**—Wash and trim beans. Leave young beans whole, or cut into 1-inch pieces, or French. Scald in boiling water for 3½ minutes. Cool quickly in ice water. Drain; pack with ½-inch headspace in freezer containers.

FRESH LIMA BEANS

Availability—Baby Limas or Fordhook Limas are available all year round with peak crop from June to September. Sources are New Jersey, New York, Virginia, Ohio, California.

Purchasing Guide—Choose clean, well-filled, fresh, dark-green pods. Usually shipped unshelled. Some markets shell and sell by weight as a service feature.

☐ 2 pounds in pods = about 2½ cups shelled

Storage—Shell when ready to cook. Store in refrigerator, unshelled, in moistureproof container.

☐ Refrigerator shelf in pod, raw: 3 to 5 days
Refrigerator shelf, cooked and covered: 1 to 4 days
☐ Refrigerator frozen-food compartment, prepared for freezing: 1 month
☐ Freezer, prepared for freezing: 10 months

Nutritive Food Values—Higher in protein than most vegetables, fair amounts of vitamins A and C.

☐ 3½ ounces, raw = 123 calories

Basic Preparation—Cut thin strip from inner edge of pods with scissors or snap pods open with fingers. Remove beans.

Cook in small amount of boiling salted water for 20 to 25 minutes, or until tender. Drain. Add seasonings, butter, and serve.

FRESH FAVA OR FABA BEANS

They resemble the Lima but are rounder and have a somewhat larger and thicker pod. They are also known as the English broad bean. They are the world's third most important bean; Europe's most important bean. In general, the buying, preparing, and cooking instructions for Lima beans will apply to the fava. They require a slightly longer cooking period. Choose pods filled with smaller beans, as large bulging pods indicate overmaturity. Fava beans have a slightly bitter taste and are best cooked with bacon.

DRIED BEANS

The oldest type of beans and still a staple today, whether low-cost meals or high-flavor dishes are the criterion. Many dried beans are ground into flour and used as protein supplement for allergy diets. In

the Far East particularly, these bean flours are often a diet mainstay.

Dried Bean Varieties:

1. **Black or turtle beans,** of which there are many varieties, are smaller than red kidney beans, oval in shape. The off-black skin hides a whitish inside. They are extensively used in soup, especially in the South, where they are grown. South Americans use them in many other bean dishes.

2. **Blackeye and yelloweye beans** are called "peas" in the South. They are oval with either a black or a yellow spot. Blackeye "peas" are favored for Hopping John, a Southern specialty.

3. **Chick-peas** are also known as Spanish beans, garbanzo beans, or *ceci* peas. They have an irregular shape, firm texture, and a nutlike flavor. Good in Spanish Stew and Italian Minestrone. Especially popular on the West Coast.

4. **Cranberry beans,** called "shellouts" in Ohio and Indiana, are similar to the pinto except that markings are pink instead of brown. A popular dish in New England using them is Cranberry-Bean Succotash.

5. **Lima beans** are flat, kidney-shaped beans, grown extensively in California. There are both large and small varieties. In the South large Limas mottled with purple are called "calico" or "speckled butter beans."

6. **Pinto and pink beans,** although related and interchangeable in recipes, do not look alike. The pintos are pale pink, speckled with brown. The pinks are smoother and more brownish red than the name implies, and are sometimes called "red Mexican" or "red miners." Both varieties turn red-brown during cooking.

7. **Red beans,** known as Mexican "chili beans," are a favorite in making chili con carne and various Spanish dishes. They are darker red than pink beans.

8. **Red kidney beans,** the world's second most important bean, with a bright red-purple color and distinctive flavor, are popular in the United States for use in chili con carne, soups, and salads. They are also a favorite in Scandinavian countries, France, and England. Grown in this country in Michigan, New York, and California.

9. **Soybeans,** the world's most important bean, are the size of a pea. In the most highly populated areas of the world they are extensively used as a source of food and oil. Their skin can be yellow, green, brown, black, or bicolored. They are very high in nutritive value but have a distinctive flavor some people do not care for.

10. **White beans** are four in number:
    a. *Marrow beans,* the largest and

roundest of the white beans, are grown chiefly in the East but are popular throughout the United States in many types of bean dishes.

b. *Great Northern beans* are very large and have a distinctive, delicate flavor. They are grown in the Midwest and are a favorite for baked bean dishes.

c. *Navy beans,* grown mainly in Michigan, are somewhat smaller than the Great Northerns. They are used extensively by canners of pork and beans. Some producers do not differentiate between navy and pea beans.

d. *Pea beans* are the smallest of the white beans. They are in great demand in New England and along the Atlantic Coast for Boston Baked Beans.

Purchasing Guide—Dried beans should be clean, uniform in size and quality. Since today they are usually packaged, a reliable brand will guarantee clean, uniformly sized beans.

☐ 1 pound, raw = approximately 2 cups

☐ 1 pound, cooked = approximately 6 cups

Storage—After opening the package, place unused beans in a clean, covered container on the pantry shelf.

☐ Kitchen shelf: 1 year

☐ Refrigerator shelf, cooked and covered: 1 to 4 days

☐ Refrigerator frozen-food compartment, cooked beans and bean dishes, prepared for freezing: 1 month

☐ Freezer, cooked beans and bean dishes, prepared for freezing: 4 to 6 months

Nutritive Food Values—The protein content in dried beans is very good, although the protein quality is inferior to that of meat, eggs, milk, or cheese. These bean-family foods are more valuable if supplemented or combined with some of the high quality protein foods. They contain a fair amount of thiamine and are a very good source of iron. A cupful of cooked beans furnishes almost half the daily requirement of iron.

☐ 3½ ounces, dried Lima beans, cooked = 138 calories

☐ 3½ ounces other dried beans, cooked = approximately 118 calories

Basic Preparation—Packaged beans are usually sorted and washed before packaging, so need only be rinsed. Beans bought in bulk should be sorted carefully, discarding broken or defective ones, and washed until water is clear. It is necessary to soak beans to replace the water that was lost in drying. In general, if directions are not given on the package, use the amount of water called for in the recipe; *save the nutritious soaking water* to use in cooking the beans. There

are two ways of soaking:

1. Quick method: Measure the soaking water into a large, heavy pot. Add washed beans and bring to a boil. Cover pot and cook for 2 minutes; remove from heat. Let stand for 1 hour, then cook according to recipe directions.

2. Overnight method: Measure soaking water into a large pot; add washed beans, cover pot, and let stand for 6 to 8 hours. To prevent souring and hard skins, the 2-minute boil is also recommended, even when beans are soaked overnight.

Add salt to the pot of soaked beans (1 teaspoon salt for 1 cup dried beans). If ham, bacon, or salt pork is to be added to the beans, use less salt. Always cook in the soaking water. Cover pot, bring to a boil, reduce heat, and simmer for the time stated in the recipe. Stir carefully but not too often; overstirring can break the beans. When done, they should hold their shape as well as be tender. (Exception: Beans for baked dishes or soups should be cooked only until they are barely tender.) Cooking time required is usually about 1½ to 2 hours. The remaining liquid should be of the consistency of a medium-thick gravy.

Cooking Hints

■ Fast cooking causes beans to break. Simmering keeps them whole and prevents sticking to the bottom of the pot.

■ A tablespoon of butter, salad oil, or drippings, added to beans during cooking, keeps down foam.

■ In hard-water areas and in high altitudes, increase the cooking time.

■ Chopped onion, green pepper, pimiento, celery, herbs, or meat, added during the cooking period, will give special flavor to bean dishes.

■ Be sure to wait until close to the end of cooking time to add tomatoes, lemon juice, vinegar, or wine to beans. The reason: Acid slows down the softening process.

■ Stick a sample bean or two with the point of a sharp knife or a fork to see if they are tender.

■ In a pressure cooker, beans will not foam or clog the pressure vent if the cooker is no more than ⅓ full and if 1 tablespoon butter or drippings is added. Also, during cooking, the pressure should not fluctuate; when done, remove cooker from the heat so that pressure will drop gradually.

■ Cooked beans and bean dishes freeze well.

CANNED BEANS

A great variety of fresh and dried beans are canned. Canned beans are precooked. They may be used as they come from the can in soups, stews, etc., or rinsed quickly under cold water, then drained

well, for salads. They have the same caloric value as home-cooked beans.

Storage

☐ Fresh, kitchen shelf: 36 months

☐ Fresh, refrigerator shelf, opened but covered: 1 to 4 days

☐ Dried, kitchen shelf: 1 year

☐ Dried, refrigerator shelf, cooked but covered: 3 to 4 days

INSTANT BEAN POWDERS

These have recently appeared in grocery stores. They can be used for soups, purées (use as a substitute for mashed potatoes), fried and refried dishes, dips, breads, casseroles, and soufflés. Also use them as a substitute for bread crumbs or oatmeal in bread and meat loaf, or add to bread crumbs for coating foods. Gravies and sauces may also be thickened with the powder. Since bean powder is a protein extender, its addition naturally increases the nutritive value of a food.

FRESH BEANS

Note: Fresh, canned, or frozen green or snap beans, Italian green beans, and wax beans can be used interchangeably in the following recipes.

Fresh, canned, or frozen Lima beans, baby or Fordhook, and fava or broad beans, can be used interchangeably in the following recipes.

GREEN BEANS AND MUSHROOMS

¼ pound fresh mushrooms, sliced
½ small onion, minced
2 tablespoons butter
1 package (9 ounces) frozen cut green or ¾ pound fresh green beans
½ cup water
Salt and pepper
¼ cup heavy cream

Sauté mushrooms and onions in hot butter. Add frozen or fresh beans, water, and salt and pepper to taste. Bring to a boil, lower heat, cover, and simmer until tender. Add cream and reheat. Do not boil. Makes 4 servings.

STEWED GREEN BEANS WITH TOMATOES

1 garlic clove, minced
1 cup thinly sliced onion
⅔ cup chopped green pepper
⅔ cup diced celery
2 tablespoons butter
2 cups chopped fresh tomatoes
2 cups cut fresh or canned green beans
½ cup chopped parsley
Salt and pepper

Sauté garlic, onion, green pepper, and celery in butter in heavy skillet for about 3 minutes. Add tomatoes, beans, and parsley. Cover and cook for 15 minutes, or until beans are tender or until canned beans are heated through. Season to taste. Makes 4 servings.

THREE-BEAN SUCCOTASH

1 onion, chopped

White and
Red Bean Salad

Hoppin John

New England Baked Beans

Beans, Creole Style

Baked Beans Southern Style

Black Beans and Rice

New England Bean Dinner— hearty eating for every member of the family.

2 tablespoons butter
1 cup water
1 cup Lima beans
1 cup cut green beans
1 cup cut wax beans
  Salt and pepper
1½ cups fresh corn kernels
½ cup heavy cream

Sauté onion in butter in large skillet for about 3 minutes. Add water, beans, salt, and pepper. Cook for 15 minutes, or until vegetables are almost tender. Add corn and cook, uncovered, for 3 minutes, or until water is almost evaporated. Add cream and more salt and pepper, if desired. Heat and serve. Makes 4 to 6 servings.

BEANS AU GRATIN

One 9-ounce package frozen cut green
  beans or Italian green beans
One 9-ounce package each of wax beans
  and Lima beans
¼ cup butter or margarine
2 tablespoons all-purpose flour
1 teaspoon salt
  Dash of pepper
  Dash of Worcestershire
1 cup medium cream
½ cup grated Parmesan cheese

Cook beans separately according to package directions; drain. Mix lightly and put in shallow baking dish. Melt 2 tablespoons butter; stir in flour, salt, pepper, and Worcestershire. Gradually stir in cream and cook over low heat, stirring constantly, until thickened. Pour over beans. Dot with remaining butter and sprinkle with cheese. Bake in preheated moderate oven (375°F.) until hot and browned. Makes 6 servings.

WAX BEAN AND ONION SALAD

1 pound wax beans or one 1-pound can
  wax beans
1 medium onion, sliced thin
2 tablespoons highly seasoned French
  dressing

Wash beans and remove stem ends. Cut beans into halves or thirds. Simmer, covered, in 1 inch of boiling water for 15 minutes, or until just tender. Drain and cool, or drain canned beans. Put in bowl; add onion, drizzle with French dressing, and toss lightly. Cover and refrigerate for several hours. Add more salt and pepper, if necessary. Makes 4 servings.

DRIED BEANS

Note: Generally speaking, dried beans are interchangeable in the recipes that follow, but the appearance and flavor of the dish will vary depending on the beans used.

SENATE BEAN SOUP

1 pound dried white beans, washed and
  drained
1 large smoked ham hock
3 potatoes, cooked and mashed
2 onions, chopped
1 cup diced celery
2 garlic cloves, minced
  Salt and pepper

Cover beans with water, bring to boil, and boil for 2 minutes. Remove from heat. Cover pan and let stand for 1 hour. Drain beans and measure liquid; add enough water to make 5 quarts. Bring again to boil and simmer, covered, for 2 hours, or until beans begin to mush. Add remaining ingredients except salt and pepper and simmer, covered, for 1 hour longer. Remove bone, cut up meat, and return meat to soup. Season to taste. Makes about 4 quarts.

PORTUGUESE BEAN SOUP

1 cup dried red beans
2 quarts water
3 onions, sliced
2 garlic cloves, minced
¼ cup bacon fat
6 potatoes, diced
2 bay leaves
1 teaspoon ground allspice
1 can (8 ounces) tomato paste
Salt and pepper

Put beans and water in kettle and bring to boil. Boil for 2 minutes. Remove from heat, and let stand for 1 hour. Then bring again to boil, and simmer, covered, for 1½ hours or until beans are tender. Cook onions and garlic in bacon fat until lightly browned. Add with remaining ingredients, except salt and pepper, to beans. Simmer, covered, for 1½ hours. Season to taste. Makes 3 quarts.

WESTERN BEAN STEW

2 cups (1 pound) dried pinto beans
Ham bone
1 teaspoon salt
⅛ teaspoon hot pepper sauce
¼ cup bacon fat or lard
1 large onion, chopped
1 chopped garlic clove
4 medium tomatoes, chopped or 1¼ cups canned whole tomatoes
¼ cup minced parsley
½ teaspoon ground marjoram
1 tablespoon chili powder or more to taste

In deep kettle, soak beans overnight in cold water to cover. The next day, add ham bone, salt, and hot pepper sauce. Bring to a boil. Reduce heat. Simmer, covered, for about 1 hour or until beans are tender. Drain beans and reserve liquid. When beans are almost tender, heat bacon fat in large skillet. Add onion and garlic and cook until golden. Add tomatoes, parsley, 1 cup of the reserved bean liquid, marjoram, and chili powder. Taste for seasoning; if necessary, add a little more salt. Cook, covered, over low heat, stirring frequently, for about 45 minutes. Combine skillet contents with beans. Simmer, covered, over low heat for 15 more minutes. Remove ham bone before serving. Makes 6 to 8 servings.

BAKED BEANS WITH HAM

1 pound dried white beans, washed and drained
6 cups water

1 onion, sliced
2 teaspoons salt
¼ cup ketchup
¼ cup light molasses
1 tablespoon cider vinegar
¼ teaspoon hot pepper sauce
1 teaspoon dry mustard
Smoked ham shank (3 pounds)

Cover beans with water, bring to boil, and boil for 2 minutes. Cover pan and let stand for 1 hour. Add onion and salt; cook until tender, adding more liquid if necessary. Drain, reserving 1½ cups liquid. Mix liquid with ketchup and next 4 ingredients. Put ham in 3-quart casserole. Put beans around ham and pour liquid over top. Cover and bake in preheated slow oven (325°F.) for 1½ hours. Remove ham and put beans back in oven. Bake, uncovered, for 1 hour more. Remove rind from ham and cut meat into bite-size pieces. Add to beans and bake for 30 minutes longer. Makes 6 servings.

BEANS WITH BREAST OF LAMB

1½ cups dried Lima beans, washed and drained
Water
3 pounds breast of lamb, cut into pieces
¼ cup cooking oil
1 onion, sliced
Seasoned salt
Garlic salt
Pepper

Cover beans with 4 cups water, bring to boil, and boil for 2 minutes. Cover pan and let stand for 1 hour. Brown lamb in oil and put in 3-quart casserole. Add onion and 1 cup hot water. Cover and bake in preheated moderate oven (350°F.) for 1 hour. Pour off fat and liquid. Add beans with bean liquid. Season meat and beans. Cover and bake for about 1½ hours longer, adding more water if necessary. Makes 4 servings.

BLACK BEANS AND RICE

1 pound dried black beans, washed and drained
6 cups water
1 cup chopped onion
1 green pepper, chopped
1 garlic clove, minced
½ cup olive oil
2 bay leaves
2 teaspoons salt
¼ teaspoon pepper
1 smoked ham bone (optional)
1 slice of bacon, minced
¼ cup wine vinegar
Cooked rice
Hard-cooked egg
Onion rings

Cover beans with water, bring to boil, and boil for 2 minutes. Cover pan and let stand for 1 hour. Sauté chopped onion, green pepper, and garlic in olive oil for 5 minutes. Add to beans with bay leaves, salt, pepper, ham bone, and bacon. Bring to boil and simmer, covered, for 2 hours, adding more water if necessary. Add wine vinegar. Serve with

rice. Garnish with hard-cooked egg and onion rings. Makes 6 to 8 servings.

TOMATO-CHEESE SOYBEANS

1 cup dried soybeans, washed and drained
4 cups water
2 cups cooked kernel corn
2⅓ cups (one 1-pound, 3-ounce can) tomatoes
1 teaspoon sugar
1 teaspoon seasoned salt
½ teaspoon monosodium glutamate
⅛ teaspoon pepper
1 cup buttered soft bread crumbs
½ cup grated Cheddar cheese
Paprika

Cover beans with water, bring to boil, and boil for 2 minutes. Cover and let stand for 1 hour; then cook until tender. Drain and arrange beans in alternate layers with corn in a shallow baking dish. Mix tomatoes, sugar, and seasonings; pour over bean mixture. Top with crumbs and sprinkle with cheese and paprika. Bake, uncovered, in preheated moderate oven (375°F.) for about 30 minutes. Makes 6 servings.

BAKED BEANS, SOUTHERN STYLE

1 pound dried marrow beans
6 cups water
2 garlic cloves, minced
1 onion, sliced
1 small dried hot red pepper
1 bay leaf
¾ pound salt pork, sliced
3 tablespoons molasses
¼ cup ketchup
1 teaspoon powdered mustard
½ teaspoon ground ginger
1½ teaspoons Worcestershire
½ teaspoon salt
¼ cup firmly packed brown sugar

Cover beans with water, bring to boil, and boil for 2 minutes. Cover and let stand for 1 hour. Add next 5 ingredients and cook until beans are tender. Drain, reserving liquid. To 2 cups liquid (or water) add remaining ingredients, except sugar. Put beans in shallow 2-quart baking dish. Arrange pork slices on top. Add liquid. Sprinkle with sugar. Bake, uncovered, in preheated hot oven (400°F.) for about 1 hour. Makes 6 servings.

BEANS, CREOLE STYLE

1 pound dried large Lima beans
6 cups water
½ pound bacon, diced
1 onion, chopped
1 green pepper, diced
1 tablespoon all-purpose flour
2 teaspoons seasoned salt
½ teaspoon salt
¼ teaspoon pepper
2 teaspoons prepared mustard
1 teaspoon Worcestershire
2 tablespoons brown sugar
2⅓ cups (one 1-pound, 3-ounce can) tomatoes

Cover washed beans with water, bring to boil, and boil for 2 minutes. Cover and let stand for 1 hour; then cook until tender. Drain. Cook bacon in large skillet until crisp. Remove bacon and drain. Add onion and green pepper to fat in skillet and cook for 5 minutes. Blend in flour, seasonings, and sugar. Add tomatoes and simmer, uncovered, for 10 minutes. Add beans and heat. Sprinkle with bacon. Makes 6 to 8 servings.

NEW ENGLAND BAKED BEANS

2 cups dried yellow-eye or pea beans
¼ pound lean salt pork
1 teaspoon salt
½ cup light molasses
½ teaspoon powdered mustard
1 tablespoon brown sugar

Cover washed beans with 6 cups water, bring to boil, and boil for 2 minutes. Cover and let stand for 1 hour; then cook until tender. Drain, reserving liquid. Put beans in pot. Cut through pork rind every ½ inch, making cuts 1 inch deep. Bury the salt pork in the beans, leaving rind exposed. Mix 1 cup liquid and remaining ingredients; pour over beans. Add enough liquid to cover beans. Cover; bake in preheated slow oven (300°F.) for 6 to 8 hours. Uncover pot last hour. Makes 6 servings.

KIDNEY-BEAN SALAD

Cover 1½ cups washed, dried red kidney beans with 6 cups water, bring to boil and boil 2 minutes. Cover and let stand for 1 hour; then cook until tender. Drain and cool. Add 3 diced hard-cooked eggs, 1 minced small onion, ½ cup diced celery, ½ cup mayonnaise, 2 tablespoons vinegar, ¼ pound slivered hard salami; season to taste. Mix well; chill. Makes six servings.

CHUTNEY BAKED BEANS

1 pound dried white beans, washed and drained
6 cups water
1 garlic clove, minced
1 onion, chopped
⅓ cup butter or margarine, melted
1 teaspoon salt
3 tablespoons dark corn syrup
¼ teaspoon dry mustard
¼ teaspoon ground ginger
⅔ cup (9-ounce jar) chutney, chopped

Cover beans with water, bring to boil, and boil for 2 minutes. Cover pan and let stand for 1 hour. Add garlic and onion; simmer until tender, adding more liquid if necessary. Drain; reserve liquid. To 1 cup bean liquid add remaining ingredients. Add to beans; put in 2-quart baking dish. Add enough bean liquid to cover beans. Bake in preheated moderate oven (375°F.) for 1 hour. Makes 6 to 8 servings.

CRANBERRY-BEAN SUCCOTASH

Shell and wash enough ripe but not dry cranberry beans (shell beans) to make 2 cups. Cover with boiling water. Bring to a boil. Simmer, covered, 1½ hours, or until beans are tender. Add 2 cups fresh corn cut from the cob. Simmer 10 minutes longer. Add salt and pepper and butter to taste. Makes 4 to 6 servings.
Note: One can (19 ounces) shell beans can be substituted for the cranberry beans. Bring to boil, add corn, and proceed as directed.

BRETON BEANS

1½ cups dried pea beans, washed and drained
6 cups water
1 cup chicken bouillon
1 cup strained canned tomatoes
1 onion, minced
1 garlic clove, minced
¼ cup melted butter or margarine
Salt and pepper to taste
4 pimientos, mashed

Cover beans with water, bring to boil and boil for 2 minutes. Cover pan and let stand for 1 hour. Cook beans until tender, adding more liquid if necessary. Drain beans and place in a 2-quart casserole. Mix remaining ingredients and add to beans. Cover and bake in preheated moderate oven (350°F.) for 1 hour. Uncover and bake for 30 minutes longer. Makes 4 to 6 servings.

BLACKEYE BEANS, SOUTHERN STYLE

2 cups dried blackeye beans, washed and drained
3 cups water
2 tablespoons bacon fat
1 tablespoon all-purpose flour
1 teaspoon salt
¼ teaspoon pepper
⅛ teaspoon ground red pepper or cayenne
2 onions, minced

Cover beans with water, bring to boil, and boil for 2 minutes. Cover pan and let stand for 1 hour. Melt bacon fat in deep skillet; stir in flour, seasonings, and onions. Cook until onions are lightly browned. Pour bacon mixture into beans. Cover and cook over medium heat until beans are tender, about 1 hour. If necessary, add more water to keep beans from sticking. Makes 4 servings.

WHITE AND RED BEAN SALAD

1 cup each of dried white and red kidney beans, washed and drained
6 cups water
2 tablespoons olive oil
½ teaspoon ground sage
2 garlic cloves
2 teaspoons salt
Dash of cayenne
½ teaspoon paprika
¼ cup cider vinegar
1 tablespoon tarragon vinegar
¼ cup minced green pepper
2 tablespoons chopped cucumber pickle
Few parsley sprigs, chopped
2 tablespoons dried chives
or 1 tablespoon instant minced onion
Romaine or other salad greens
2 pimientos, cut into strips

Cover beans with water, bring to a boil, and boil for 2 minutes. Cover pan and let stand for 1 hour. Add oil, sage, and garlic; then cook until tender, adding more water if necessary. Drain and cool; remove garlic. Add remaining ingredients, except last 2; mix well and chill. Put in bowl lined with romaine. Garnish with pimiento. Makes 6 to 8 servings.

SPAGHETTI WITH GARBANZO SAUCE

1 onion, chopped
1 garlic clove, minced
½ cup celery and tops, chopped
3 tablespoons olive oil
2 cups (one 1-pound, 3-ounce can) undrained garbanzo beans
2⅓ cups (one 1-pound, 3-ounce can) tomatoes
1 can (6 ounces) tomato paste
1 bay leaf
1 teaspoon salt
Dash of cayenne
½ teaspoon ground oregano
1 pound spaghetti, cooked
Grated Parmesan cheese

Sauté onion, garlic, and celery in olive oil until golden. Drain garbanzos, reserving liquid. Measure liquid; add water to make 2½ cups. Add with garbanzos, tomatoes, tomato paste, bay leaf, salt, cayenne, and oregano to onion mixture. Simmer, uncovered, for 2 hours, stirring occasionally. Serve on spaghetti; sprinkle with cheese. Makes 8 servings.

BEAN SPROUTS—This popular oriental vegetable, the pale, tender shoots of the soya, mung, or curd bean, is an important, if not essential, ingredient in chop suey, chow mein, and other Chinese and oriental dishes. Westerners also enjoy their bland flavor in salads, stews, and soups. They are available canned and may be found fresh in areas with a large Chinese population such as New York City and San Francisco.

Caloric Value

☐ 3½ ounces, cooked, drained = 28 calories

SAUTÉED BEAN SPROUTS

2 cups (one 1-pound can) bean sprouts, drained
1 tablespoon salad oil
1 small onion, sliced
½ teaspoon salt

Rinse and drain bean sprouts. Heat oil in skillet and fry onion in it for 2 minutes. Add salt and bean sprouts. Cook over medium heat for 3 minutes, stirring constantly. Serve immediately. Makes 4 servings.

100 Menus
to help you plan
more varied meals
for your family with
the recipes in this volume

*Recipes for all starred dishes found in this volume.

BREAKFAST or BRUNCH

Sliced Peaches and Oranges
with Honey
Fried Chicken with Puffs
and Gravy*
Sliced Tomatoes

Grapefruit-Cantaloupe Cup
Fried Catfish Home Style*
Bacon Biscuits*
Butter

Gingered Melon*
Smothered Steak*
Hominy Grits
Pike's Peak Raised
Potato Biscuits*
Butter
Wild-Plum Jelly*

Stewed Prunes
Crisp Bacon or Sausage
Hoosier Fried Tomatoes,
Creamy Gravy*
Grilled Corn Mush*

Baked Bananas in Fresh
Orange Juice*
Canadian-Style Bacon
Liberal Pancakes*
and Melted Butter
Sorghum or Cane Syrup

Cranberry Juice
Fried Tripe*
Two-Bean Succotash
with Pork Cubes*
Blueberry Coffeecake

Thompson Seedless Grapes
in Sour Cream*
Baked Smithfield Ham*
Cheese Blintzes
Prune Butter

Fruit Juice
Prune Kolache*
Toasted Raisin Muffins
Butter
Coffee

LUNCH or SUPPER

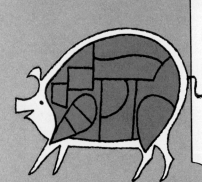

Applesauce
Green-Corn Cakes*
Maple Syrup
Sausages
Coffee

Mandarin Orange Sections
Smoked Pork Chops
Scrambled Eggs
Fruit Ketchup*
Johnnycake*
Whipped Butter

Baked Apples with Cream
South Carolina Scrapple*
Hot Spiced Whole Tomatoes*
Toasted Cracked-Wheat Bread

Cereal with Sliced Bananas
Pan-Fried Smelts*
Corn Dodgers*
Blueberry Muffins

Shrimp à la King
Tomato Aspic*
Blueberry Betty*

Turkey and Beef
Tenderloin*
Tossed Salad
Hot Muffins
Arizona Pecan
and Date Pie*

Squaw Corn*
Sourdough Biscuits
Apple Brown Betty*

Pepper Pot Soup*
Crisp Relishes
Cornmeal Griddle Cakes
Apricot Refrigerator
Cake*

Barbecued Beef Patties
Warm Buns
Relish Ketchup
Hot Bean Pot*
Lemon Tarts

Kentucky Burgoo*
Assorted Warm Biscuits
Raw Vegetable Relishes
Assorted Pickles
Strawberry Chess Tarts*

Apple and Cranberry Juice
Veal Stew with Almonds
in Sour Cream*
Hot Rice
Assorted Cookies
Saltwater Taffy*

Autumn Apple Bread*
Sandwiches Filled
with Cream Cheese
Deviled Ham and Relish
Sandwiches
Coffee Ice Cream
Frosted Brownies

Watermelon Cocktail*
Cold Roast Turkey
Stuffed Apricot Salad*
Warm Onion Rye Bread
Chocolate Soufflé

Liederkranz Appetizer
Cheese Balls*
Koenigsburger Klops*
Coleslaw
Rolls
Raspberry Sherbet

Wiscasset Lobster Stew*
Crisp Relishes
Hot French Bread
Maple Sugar on Snow*
Baked Indian Pudding*

Fruit Punch
Cakes
Crisp Crackers
Potato Chips
Cream-Cheese and Clam Dip*
Assorted Cold Cuts
Assorted Breads, Relishes

Oyster Fricassee*
Broiled Tomato
Spinach Salad
Crisp Rye Crackers
Ambrosia de Luxe*
Cookies

Hog and Hominy*
Turnip Greens with
Raw Vegetable Relish*
Hush Puppies
Party Pudding*

Tomato Caviar*
Game Mulligan*
Tossed Green Salad
Individual Loaves of Bread
Snickerdoodles*

Chutney Baked Beans*
Apple Sandwiches*
Figs Stuffed with Almonds*
Milk

Apple Snacks*
Baked Beans with Ham*
Coleslaw
Peach Leather*

Senate Bean Soup*
Banana-Nut Bread*, Buttered
Crisp Relishes
Cheesecake

Campfire Trout*
Cucumber Salad
Virginia Batter Bread*
Spiced Blueberries*

Meatball Soup*
Grilled Cheese and
Ham Sandwich
Shoofly Pie*

Fried Freshwater Fish*
Kidney-Bean Salad
Sourdough Pancakes*

Nebraska Corn Fritters*
Sliced Ham
Mustard Relish
Sweet-Potato Pudding*

Nutmeg State Crab Soup*
Baked Hominy Grits
with Cheese*
Tossed Green Salad
Sourdough Doughnuts*

Hamburgers
with Apple Rings*
Toasted Buns
Crisp Relishes
Ice Cream Sundae

Poached Eggs à la Romana*
Watercress Salad
Italian Bread
Wild Huckleberry Pie*

Almond-Chicken Salad*
Assorted Crisp Crackers
Stewed Apricots*
Cookies

Sliced Cold Ham
Hopping John*
Whole-Wheat Bread
Baked Apple Tapioca*

Maine Seafood Chowder*
Tossed Salad with
Herb Croutons
Soda Crackers
Buckeye Maple Syrup Cake*

Charleston She-Crab Soup*
Artichoke Halves,
Greek Style*
Assorted Warm Biscuits
Apple Strudel*

Sheepherder's Stew*
Bibb Lettuce Salad
Fresh Fruit Dessert
Cookies

Apple Pancake*
Maple Syrup
Celery and Cucumber Sticks
Ice Cream

South Carolina Scrapple*
Chuck Wagon Boiled Beans*
Hard Tack
Dried Fruit

DINNER

Cold Chicken or Turkey
Bean Salad*
Autumn Apple Bread*
Candy Bars

Fruit Salad with
Honey Cream Salad Dressing*
Cheese Soufflé
Polynees*

Green Corn Soup
Cold Baked Ham
Potato Salad
Assorted Warm
Sliced Breads
Ozark Pudding*

Scalloped Scallops*
Broccoli with Lemon Butter
Hot Bread Sticks
Apricots with Kirsch*

Lamb on Skewers*
Baked Potatoes
Tossed Salad
Sesame-Seed Crackers
Bluegrass Sorghum Cake*

Roast Turkey with
Giblet-Butternut Stuffing*
Rutabaga Ring*
Mashed Potatoes
Creamed Peas and Onions
Cranberry Sauce
Homemade Biscuits
Avocado Lime Pie*

Menus

Cranberry-Glazed Ham*
Parsnip Fritters*
Buttered Broccoli
Beet and Cucumber Relish*
Pumpkin Pie

———◆———

Barbecued Pork Ribs*
Toasted Buns
Tomato and Lettuce Salad
Roasted Corn on Cob
Fresh Fruit Bowl
Peanut Brittle*

Guacamole* with
Corn Chips
Braised Pork Chops
Scalloped Potatoes
Raw Vegetables
Cheese Board*
Fresh Fruit

———◆———

Broiled Chicken, Brown Rice
Turnip Greens
Crisp Raw Relishes
Corn Bread
Oregon Filbert Squares*

Baked Red Snapper
Buttered Noodles
Fruit Salad Bowl*
Pecan Pie

———◆———

Roast Crown of Pork,
Florida Style*
Boiled Potatoes
Sauerkraut
Warm Biscuits
Wilted Cucumbers with
Watercress
Fried Squaw Bread*

Broiled Pompano*
Stewed Tomatoes
Buttered Green Beans
Corn Muffins
Apricot Cream-Cheese
Tarts*

———◆———

Nutmeg State Crab Soup*
Corn Oysters*
Mixed Green Salad
Election Cake*

Wiener Schnitzel*
Geröstete mit Rosmarin
(Home-Fried Potatoes
with Rosemary)*
Green Beans with Dillweed
Kugelhupf*

———◆———

Old-Time Salt-Pork Soup*
with Dumplings
Green Cabbage Slaw
with Cheese Cubes
New Hampshire Turnover
Apple Pie*

Hot Pickled Beef*
Boiled Potatoes
Mixed Green Salad
Baked Doughnuts*

———◆———

Roast Long Island
Duckling*
Baked Acorn Squash
Supreme*
Waldorf Salad*
Seeded French Bread
Sherry Jelly*

Grandmother's Steak*
Celery Fritters*
Baked Potatoes with
Sour Cream
Marinated Tomatoes
Frozen Apricot Mousse*

———◆———

Apple-Ham Casserole*
Cheese-Broiled Asparagus*
Cucumber Salad
Corn Muffins
Maple Custard*

Scalloped Salmon
Tossed Green Salad with
Sesame-Seed Dressing
Cheese Toast
Apple Meringue Cake*

———◆———

Stuffed Celery*
Virginia Ham
Asparagus Soufflé*
Toasted Herbed Rolls
Corn Relish*
Cherry Pie*

Chicken-and-Sweetbread
Croquettes*
Braised Carrots and Celery
Coleslaw
Crisp Cornmeal Wafers
Scripture Cake*

———◆———

Spooned Codfish Cakes*
Scalloped Tomatoes
Carrot and Celery Sticks
Onion-Rye Bread
Honey Gingerbread*

Fresh Peach Cocktail*
Roast Loin of Pork
Pan-browned Potatoes
Green Beans, Mushrooms
Cucumbers with
Sour Cream Dressing
Basic Angel Food Cake*

———◆———

Broiled Halibut Steaks
with Pepper Butter*
Broccoli au Gratin
Boiled Potatoes
Pickled Beets
Apricot Upside-Down Cake*

Fisherman's Wharf Cioppino*
Lettuce Salad
French Bread
Almond Soufflé*

———◆———

Miss Mollie's Boiled Pot*
Mandarin Orange-
Watercress Salad
Baking Powder Biscuits
White Cake with
Double Frosting*

Topeka Fried Chicken*
Baked Acorn Squash
Cranberry Relish
Herb Biscuits
Creole Pralines*

———◆———

Boiled Leg of Mutton
with Caper Sauce*
Buttered Noodles
Artichoke Hearts Salad*
Rye Rolls
Ambrosia de Luxe*
Cookies

Roast Spring Chicken
Bread Dressing
Creamed Brussels Sprouts
Pickled Cherries*
Sweet-Potato Biscuits*
Telephone Pudding*

◆

Boston Baked Beans*
Grilled Frankfurters
Relishes
Boston Brown Bread*
Apricot and Banana Cup*

Scalloped Apples, Pork Chops,
and Sweet Potatoes*
Broccoli Vinaigrette
Sage Biscuits
Strawberry Sundae

◆

Barbecued Columbia
River Salmon*
Boiled New Potatoes with
Seasoned Butter
Asparagus and Mushrooms
in Cream*
Soft Rolls
Cranberry-Apple Crisp*

Korean Steak*
Green Peas with
Water Chestnuts
Pineapple Salad
Glazed Almond Cookies*

◆

Quail on Toast*
Artichoke Hearts Piquant
Vegetables in Aspic*
Kona Coffee Mousse*

Short Ribs with Vegetables*
Pickled Cucumbers
Potato-Flour Muffins
à la Marshall Field's*
Apple-Cider Raisin Pie*

◆

Chicken-Shrimp Gumbo Filé*
Rice
Buttered French Bread
Hearts of Celery
Pineapple Sherbet with
Strawberries

Roast Beef au Jus
Wild Rice Casserole*
French Fried Asparagus*
Marinated Tomatoes with
Watercress
Popovers
Apple Pie*

◆

Tamale Pie*
Shredded Lettuce Salad
Applesauce with Custard
Benne-Seed Cookies*

Barbecued Spareribs*
Baked Idaho Potatoes
Chinese Cabbage Slaw
Corn Bread Squares
Peach Slump*

◆

Stockyard Inn Beef-
Vegetable Soup*
Braised Rabbit*
Crisp Relishes
Hot Rolls
Sweet-Potato Pudding*

Cottage Cheese Appetizer*
Idaho Lamb Hash*
Artichoke Hearts Salad*
Pepper Biscuits
Dutch Apple Cake

◆

Fried Soft-Shell Crabs*
Herbed Summer Squash
Lyonnaise Potatoes
Marinated Green Beans
Lady Baltimore Cake*

Michigan Baked Beans*
Sausages
Apple-Herb Jelly*
Chicory-Cucumber Salad
Toasted Barbecue Buns
Lemon Ice with Grated
Orange Rind

◆

Biloxi Shrimp Stew*
Mixed Green Salad
Seeded Italian Bread
Lemon Velvet Pudding*

Cornish Game Hens
with Apples*
Glazed Sweet Potatoes
Green Beans with Celery
Endive-Watercress Salad
Corn Muffins
Old-Fashioned
Strawberry Shortcake

◆

Pot Roast with Apple Cider*
Whipped Potatoes
Asparagus and Carrots
Garlic Rolls
Apricot Strudel*

Corned Beef and Cabbage:
Nebraska Style*
Boiled Potatoes
Irish Soda Bread
Crisp Relishes
Baked Apple Dumplings*
Cheddar Cheese

◆

Deviled Crab Cakes*
Scalloped Celery
Carrot and Raisin Salad
Hot Buttered Biscuits
Hickory-Nut Cake*

Sooner-State Beans with
Spareribs*
Cole Slaw
Golden Cheese Spoon Bread*
Spiced Cantaloupe*

◆

Beefsteak and Oysters*
Toasted Rice*
Asparagus with Herb Butter*
Hot Onion Rolls
Flan Sol y Sombra*

Beef Picadillo*
Shredded Salad Greens
Quick Onion-Cheese Bread*
Orange Ice   Fruit Sauce

◆

Baked Fish in Blanket*
Indian Shuck Bread*
Tomato Wedges
Spread Apple Pie*

Baked Ham
Baked Lima Bean
and Pear Casserole*
Cucumber Salad
Hard Rolls
Fat Balls*

◆

Tatsuta-Age*
Gingered Pineapple
Bean Sprout Salad with
Water Chestnuts
Fried Cream*

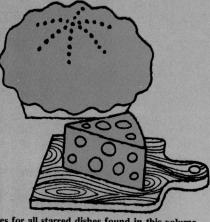

*Recipes for all starred dishes found in this volume.

GENERAL INFORMATION

The Ingredients and Measurements Used in Recipes

All recipes in this book have been tested in the Woman's Day Kitchens with standard American measuring cups (8 ounces = 16 tablespoons), measuring spoons (1 tablespoon = 3 teaspoons), and other standard kitchen equipment. All measurements are level. Liquids are measured in standard 8-ounce glass measuring cups, at eye level.

All sugar is granulated white sugar unless otherwise specified.

All flours, cake and all-purpose, are sifted before measuring unless otherwise specified. No self-rising flour is used.

All baking powder is double-acting baking powder.

All brown sugar is firmly packed when measured.

All confectioners' sugar is sifted before measuring.

All pepper is ground black pepper unless otherwise specified.

Fats and shortening are measured at room temperature, packed firmly into measuring cup and leveled with a straight knife. They are scraped out with a rubber spatula.

Salted butter or margarine, packed in ¼-pound sticks, is used unless otherwise specified. 1 stick = ½ cup = 8 tablespoons = ¼ pound.

1 tall can evaporated milk (14½ ounces) contains 1⅔ cups undiluted evaporated milk. Sweetened condensed milk is an entirely different product, and cannot be used interchangeably with evaporated milk.

⅓ to ½ teaspoon dried herbs can be substituted for each tablespoon fresh herbs. Crumble herbs before using to release flavor.

Before starting to cook or to bake, read the recipes carefully. Assemble all ingredients and equipment. Follow recipe exactly. Do not increase or decrease recipe unless you are a skilled enough cook to recognize what adjustments must be made as to ingredients, pan sizes, and/or cooking time.

Cooking Temperatures and Times

Cooking temperatures and times are approximate for meat. They depend not only on the weight and kind of meat, but also on its shape, temperature, and its bone and fat contents. A meat thermometer was used in testing.

Cooking times for meats are as recommended by the National Live Stock and Meat Board, 36 Wabash Avenue, Chicago, Illinois 60603.

Oven Temperatures

TEMPERATURES (Degree F.)	TERM
250 to 275	VERY SLOW
300 to 325	SLOW
350 to 375	MODERATE
400 to 425	HOT
450 to 475	VERY HOT
500 to 525	EXTREMELY HOT

Important—Preheat oven for 10 to 15 minutes before placing food in it. Many a cake has been spoiled by being placed in a barely heated oven. Baking times are based on the assumption that the oven is already at the stated temperature.

Check the oven temperature control frequently, especially if baking times vary from those given in recipes. (This can be done with a portable oven thermometer.) If a control is consistently off, call your public utility. They should be able to reset the oven temperature control.

Caloric Values

The caloric values, where mentioned, for each food are based on 100 grams, about 3½ ounces edible portion, as mentioned in Composition of Foods, Agriculture Handbook No. 8, Agricultural Service of the United States Department of Agriculture, Washington, D. C., revised December 1963.

COMPLETE RECIPE INDEX Volume 1–801 Recipes

ANISEED, Suggested Uses for 81
APPETIZERS
Almonds 89
Almonds, Salted 14
Almonds, Toasted 14
Antipasto Variato 82
Apple Appetizer 97
Apple Snacks 97
Canapé Butters
  Anchovy Butter 85
  Caper Butter 85
  Chili Butter 85
  Chive Butter 85
  Chutney Butter 85
  Curry Butter 85
  Egg Butter 86
  Garlic Butter 86
  Horseradish Butter 86
  Onion Butter 86
  Parmesan Butter 86
  Parsley Butter 86
  Pâté Butter 86
  Pickle Butter 86
  Sardine Butter 86
  Shrimp Butter 86
  Tarragon Butter 86
  Watercress Butter 86
Canapé Paste, Shrimp 67
Canapés, Anchovy 80
Canapés, Bahamian Tomato 86
Canapés, Crab 86
Canapés, Danish Beef 86
Canapés, Peanut-Onion 86
Canapés, Salami-Egg 86
Canapés, Savory 86
Caponatina 82
Caviar, Eggplant 90
Caviar, Red, In Cream 76
Caviar, Tomato 86
Celery, Stuffed 89
Cheese Appetizers 78
Cheese Canapés
  Blue Cheese Spread 86
  Camembert Cheese Spread 86
  Cottage-Cheese Spread 86
  Simple Cheese Spread 86
  Tiny Cheese Sandwiches 86
Chutney, Hot, and Bacon Fingers.. 86
Clam Bites 89
Cocktail, Diced-Cucumber 87
Cocktail, Fresh Peach 87
Cocktail, Watermelon 87
Cold Cuts, Cubed, with Tiered
  Fruit Salad 89
Dip, Avocado 130
Dip, Chili 87
Dip, Cream-Cheese and Clam 87
Dip, East Indian 87
Dip, Mustard, for Raw Vegetables. 87
Dip, Rémoulade, for Scallops or
  Shrimp 87
Dip, Two-Cheese 87
Frankfurter Rounds 86
Guacamole 130
Mushroom Beignets 89
Pork Pâté 90
Potatoes Mayonnaise 89
Rumaki 87
Sardine Rounds 86
Tomato Frost 37
Two-Cheese Logs 78
Walnut Spread 90
BEVERAGES
Barley Water 147
Eggnog 52
Fish House Cooler 32
Fizz, Apple-Cranberry 103
Nog, Grapefruit-Honey 24
Raspberry Shrub 75
Shake, Buttermilk 64
Wiener Eiskaffee (Viennese Iced
  Coffee) 123

BREADS, PANCAKES, AND DUMPLINGS
Cheese Bread, Toasted 145
Quick Breads
  Apple Bread, Autumn 100
  Banana-Nut Bread 139
  Bannocks, Drop 142
  Bannock, Trapper's Sweet 62
  Batter Bread, Virginia 75
  Beer Bread, French 149
  Biscuits, Bacon 134
  Biscuits, Buttermilk 69
  Biscuits, Cream 46
  Biscuits, Mammy's Sour-Milk .. 22
  Biscuits, Mormon, with Cream
    Gravy 74
  Biscuits, Sweet-Potato 61
  Brown Bread, Boston 47
  Corn Bread, Antebellum Spiced
    Nut 52
  Corn Cakes, Bacon, Egg and 134
  Corn Cakes, Lace-Edge 41
  Corn Dodgers 25
  Corn Mush, Grilled 55
  Doughnuts, Sour-Cream 66
  Dumplings 78
  Dumplings, Cornmeal 61
  Fried Bread 59
  Johnnycake 67
  Muffins, Potato-Flour, à la
    Marshall Field's 37
  Onion-Cheese Bread, Quick 79
  Orange-Nut Bread, Quick Allspice 11
  Pancake, Apple 100
  Pancakes, Liberal 39
  Ripe-Olive Bread, Visalia 26
  Shuck Bread, Indian 64
  Spoon Bread, Delaware 32
  Spoon Bread, Golden Cheese ... 65
  Squaw Bread, Fried 64
Yeast Breads
  Apple Kuchen 100
  Bagels 134
  Biscuits, Pike's Peak—Raised
    Potato 27
  Biscuits, Raised 34
  Bismarcks 63
  Cinnamon-Raisin Buns 56
  Coffee Ring, Almond-Filled 15
  Cracked Wheat Bread 40
  Doughnuts, Baked 53
  Doughnuts, Sourdough 54
  Election Cake 28
  Fat Balls 48
  Kolache, Prune 49
  Kugelhupf (Coffee Cake) 123
  Pancakes, Sourdough 23
  Rye Bread, Swedish 49
CAKES
Angel Food Cake, Basic 81
Boston Cream Pie 47
Chocolate Cake, Cheyenne 79
Cream Cheesecake with Cookie
  Crust 33
Dobostorte (Hungarian Seven-Layer
  Cake) 124
Fruitcake, Carolina 61
Gingerbread, Honey 53
Gingerbread, Old-Fashioned 45
Hickory-Nut Cake 37
Lady Baltimore Cake 46
Layer Cake, Banana-Filled Orange. 142
Lord Baltimore Cake 46
Maple-Syrup Cake, Buckeye 63
Pumpkin-Prune Cake 40
Scripture Cake 38
Sorghum Cake, Bluegrass 41
Strawberry Circle Cake 72
Upside-Down Cake, Apricot 108
Upside-Down Cake, Blueberry ... 57
White Cake with Double Frosting.. 55

CANDIES AND CONFECTIONS
Almond Brittle 16
Almonds, Burnt 13
Aplets 76
Figs Stuffed with Almonds 16
Halloween Apples on a Stick 102
Maple Sugar on Snow 74
Peach Leather 34
Peanut Brittle 75
Peanut Chews 75
Pralines, Creole 44
Saltwater Taffy 57
CASSEROLES
Anchovy and Potato Casserole ... 80
Apple-Frankfurter Casserole 97
Apple-Ham Casserole 97
Apples, Scalloped, Pork Chops,
  and Sweet Potatoes 102
Artichoke Hearts au Gratin 112
Barley Casserole 147
Beans with Breast of Lamb 158
Celery Gratin with Almonds 14
Egg Casserole, Hoosier 37
Fish Fillets au Gratin 119
Lima-Bean-and-Pear Casserole,
  Baked 76
Mutton, Tart 79
Pichelsteiner Fleisch (Pichel-
  steiner Casserole) 121
Pork, Applesauce and Kraut
  Casserole 63
Summer-Squash Casserole 63
Wheelspoke Casserole 52
Wild Rice Casserole 49
CEREALS, PASTA
Barley Pudding, Finnish 62
Cush 54
Hominy Grits with Cheese, Baked. 37
Noodles, Almond 14
Noodles, Alsatian 16
Pilaf 146
Rice, Green 39
Rice Pilaf with Almonds 14
Rice, Red 68
Rice, Toasted 73
Spaghetti with Garbanzo Sauce ...159
CHEESE
Cheese Board 89
Cheese Rabbit, Wisconsin 78
Liederkranz Appetizer Cheese Balls 62
Liptauer Cheese 90
Two-Cheese Molds and Mixed
  Fruit, Cornucopias of Cold Cuts
  with 89
Welsh Rabbit 10
COOKIES
Almond Cookies, Glazed 16
Almond Hearts, Nonsweet 15
Almond Macaroons 15
Almond Slices 74
Apple-Nut Bars 103
Apple Oatmeal Cookies 102
Apricot Crescents 109
Benne-Seed Cookies 68
Corn Flake-Coconut Macaroons .. 67
Filbert Squares, Oregon 65
Ischeler Torteletten (Almond
  Butter Cookies) 124
Molasses Cookies 77
Nusskipferln (Nut Crescents) 124
Porcupines 42
Snickerdoodles 29
Springerle 82
Sugar Squares, Newton 57
Wasps' Nests 78
DESSERTS
Cake-type
  Apple Cake, Old World 102
  Apply Pandowdy 101
  Baba au Rhum 131
  Baba au Rhum, Quick 132

Salzburger Nockerln (Dessert
Puffs) 123
Shortcake, Apple-Cranberry 101
Shortcake, Michigan 48
Torte, Almond 15
Frozen
Avocado Cream, Frozen 59
Baked Alaska 136
Ice Cream, Avocado 24
Ice Cream, Cherry 36
Ice Cream, Fresh Apricot
Ripple 106
Ice Cream, Iowa Farm 39
Ice, Pomegranate 24
Mousse, Apricot 74
Mousse, Frozen Apricot 108
Fruit
Ambrosia de Luxe 17
Ambrosia, Texas 73
Apple Betty 77
Apple Brown Betty 101
Apple Crisp 101
Apple Dumplings, Baked 96
Apple Fritters 101
Apple Fritters, Brandied 63
Apples, Baked 96
Apples, Baked, with Wine 102
Apples, Poached 101
Apples, Rosy Glazed Baked 102
Applesauce 1 (Chunky) 97
Applesauce 2 (Smooth) 97
Apricot and Banana Cup 107
Apricot Cream 108
Apricot Dessert, Jellied 109
Apricot Dessert, The Simplest ...108
Apricots, Stewed 107
Apricots with Kirsch 108
Avocado-Citrus Dessert 130
Banana Fritters 139
Bananas, Baked, with Honey 139
Blueberry Betty 45
Compote of Fresh Fruits with
Lemon Balm 138
Cranberry-Apple Crisp 65
Grapes, Thompson Seedless, in
Sour Cream 27
Melon, Gingered 27
Orange Slices, Spicy 11
Peach Slump 67
Persimmon Graham-Cracker
Dessert 38
Strawberry Cream 37
Meringue, Black Walnut 63
Puddings and Custards
Almond Custard, Thomas
Jefferson's 14
Bishop Whipple Pudding 50
Blancmange, Arrowroot 110
Bread Pudding, Raspberry-Jam . 23
Honey Custard, Baked 62
Flan Sol y Sombra (Sun and
Shadow Custard) 73
Fried Cream 69
Indian Pudding, Baked 47
Lemon Velvet Pudding 52
Maple Custard 56
Meringue Pudding, Banana 142
Ozark Pudding 25
Party Pudding 68
Persimmon Pudding 25
Rhubarb Pudding 28
Rice Pudding, Apricot 108
Sweet-Potato Pudding 22
Syllabub 68
Tapioca, Baked Apple (1) 60
Tapioca, Baked Apple (2) 102
Telephone Pudding 41
Refrigerator
Apricot Delight 108
Bavarian Cream, Almond 15
Bavarian Cream, Peach 32
Bavarian, Lemon 150

Cream, Avocado 130
Cream, Maple 74
Mousse, Kona Coffee 35
Refrigerator Cake, Apricot 109
Sherry Jelly 60
Soufflés
Almond Soufflé 15
Apricot Soufflé 108
DESSERT SAUCES
Apricot Glaze 109
Apricot Sauce 109
Brown Sugar Sauce 50
Kanari Milch (Canary's Milk) 123
DRESSINGS
Salads
Honey-Cream Salad Dressing ... 79
Snow Dressing 56
Thousand Island Dressing 60
Stuffings
Apple-Prune-Raisin Stuffing 100
Apple Stuffing, Savory 97
Giblet-Butternut Stuffing 74
Stuffing for Wild Goose 68
Wild-Rice Stuffing 62
EGGS
Bacon and Egg Skillet 133
Baked Eggs 32
Eggs Dropped in Cream 74
Eggs, Ranch Style 59
Kaiserschmarrn (The Emperor's
Omelet) 123
Omelet, Artichoke 112
Pickled Eggs and Red Beets 66
Poached Eggs alla Romana 57
Salmon-Stuffed Eggs 87
FISH
Albacore
Albacore Divan 8
Fresh Albacore Sauté Amandine. 8
Pickled Albacore 8
Alewives Baked with Lemon 10
Aspic, Fish 116
Baked in a Blanket, Fish 64
Bass
Poached Whole Bass 149
Stuffed Baked Bass 148
Cape Cod Turkey 47
Catfish, Fried, Home Style 25
Codfish Cakes, Spooned 47
Fish in Foil 146
Flounder Fillets, Broiled, with
Puffy Cheese Sauce 57
Freshwater Fish, Fried 37
Frogs' Legs à la Creole 41
Herring and Apples in Sour Cream. 87
Pickled Fish 49
Pompano
Broiled Pompano 32
Pompano en Papillote 41
Pudding, Norwegian Fish 49
Red Snapper, Gulf-Baked 22
Rockfish Muddle 61
Salmon
Baked Salmon 76
Barbecued Columbia River
Salmon 65
Lomi Lomi Salmon (Hawaiian
Salad) 34
Pirok (Salmon Pie) 23
Shad
Baked Shad with Oyster Stuffing.. 29
Broiled Connecticut River Shad.. 28
Norfolk Shad without Bones.....75
Smelts, Pan-Fried 78
Swordfish, Block Island Baked.... 67
Trout
Almonds and Cream, Trout with. 14
Baked Trout 54
Broiled Trout with Watercress
Butter 25
Campfire Trout 27

Walleyed Pike 78
FROSTINGS, ICINGS AND FILLINGS
Almond Filling 15
Almond Paste 15
Caramel Frosting 55
Chocolate Filling 124
Chocolate Frosting, Glossy 79
Confectioners' Sugar Frosting 15
Confectioners' Sugar Icing 50
Cream Filling 47
Fluffy Frosting 55
Fluffy White Frosting 46
Lemon-Orange Filling 15
Maple Icing 63
Prune Filling 49
GAME
Antelope, Roast Saddle of 82
Duck, Roast Wild 53
Game Mulligan 27
Goose, Wild 68
Hare, Maggi's Mad 29
Opossum, Roast 25
Quail on Toast 36
Quails, Braised 25
Rabbit, Braised 62
Rabbit, Smothered, and Onions... 52
Trapper's Game Stew 23
Venison, Marinated 23
Venison Mincemeat 76
Venison or Beef, Jerked 24
JELLIES, JAMS, AND PRESERVES
Apple Butter 97
Apple-Herb Jelly 103
Apple Jelly 97
Apricot-Pineapple Jam 109
Beach Plum Jam 150
Blueberries, Spiced 23
Chokeberry Jam, Wild 62
Prune Butter 76
Wild-Plum Jelly 40
MEATS
Beef
Beef Picadillo 72
Beefsteak and Oysters 72
Boeuf à la Mode 8
Boiled Dinner 28
Corned Beef and Cabbage:
Nebraska Style 54
Hamburgers with Apple Rings... 97
Hash, Red Flannel 56
Hollandsche Biefstuk (Dutch
Steak) 60
Kücherlkraut (Beef and
Sauerkraut) 121
Pickled Beef, Hot 52
Pot Roast, Bean 69
Pot Roast, Beef, with Vegetables. 55
Pot Roast with Apple Cider 77
Rib Roast of Beef on a Spit 54
Salisbury Steak, Charcoal-
Broiled 145
Short Ribs with Vegetables 38
Steak, Baked Sirloin 35
Steak Barbecue, Western 65
Steak, Grandmother's 73
Steak, Korean 35
Steak, Smothered 27
Steak, Tenderloin, with
Roquefort Spread 36
Swiss Steak, Spicy 11
Tamale Pie 59
Tenderloin, Broiled Whole 144
Combination
Bacon and Beef Succotash 133
Blind Rabbit 53
Koenigsberger Klops 62
Mexican Puchero 26
Pasties 48
Turkey and Beef Tenderloin 72
Lamb
Chops, Napa Valley Lamb 26
Curry, Apple-Lamb 97

Hash, Idaho Lamb 35
Lamb on Skewers 53
Leg of Lamb, Broiled Boned 146
Mutton, Boiled Leg of, with
  Caper Sauce 79
Roast Lamb, Kentucky 40
Shish Kebab 146
Pork
Bacon, Fried Apples with 45
Bacon-Kraut-Potato Skillet 133
Barbecued Pork Ribs 77
Chinese Sweet and Sour Pork ... 26
Chops, Curried Pork, Apricots
  with 107
Chops, Pork, Apple-Smothered .. 97
Chops, Roman Pork, Artichokes
  with 112
Choucroute Garnie (Garnished
  Sauerkraut) 16
Cubes of Cooked Pork 146
Ham, Baked Smithfield 75
Ham, Cranberry-Glazed 78
Ham or Shrimp à la King 8
Ham, Pan-Barbecued 68
Ham Rolls, Asparagus 113
Ham, Stuffed 50
Ham, Tennessee Baked 69
Ham with Mustard Crust 39
Hog and Hominy 69
Knackwurst in Ale 10
Pichola 24
Pork with Peas 34
Roast Crown of Pork, Florida
  Style 32
Roast Loin of Pork (1) 57
Roast Loin of Pork (2) 146
Schinkenfleckerln (Noodles with
  Ham) 122
Schinkenkraut (Ham and
  Sauerkraut) 122
Schnitz und Gnepp (1) 66
Schnitz und Gnepp (2) 103
Scrapple or Pannhaas 66
Scrapple, South Carolina 68
Selchfleisch (Smoked Butt) 122
Spareribs, Baked 61
Spareribs, Barbecued 25
Spareribs, Sooner-State Beans
  with 64
Variety
Geröstete Kalbsleber (Calf's
  Liver, Sautéed) 122
Liver Pudding 49
Sweetbread Croquettes, Chicken-
  and- 46
Tripe, Fried 56
Veal
Cordon Bleu 126
Kalbsgulasch (Veal Goulash) ...122
Parmesanschlegel (Leg of Veal
  with Cheese) 121
Piccata à la Kerzenstuberl 127
Pie, Veal Parsley, with
  Dumplings 78
Schnitzel à la Holstein 126
Schnitzel, Champignon 127
Schnitzel, Curry 127
Schnitzel Florentine 128
Schnitzel, Natur 126
Schnitzel, Paprika 127
Schnitzel, Pariser 126
Schnitzel Piccata 127
Schnitzel, Puszta 127
Schnitzel, Wiener 126

PICKLES, RELISHES, AND
GARNISHES
Angelica as a Garnish 81
Apples, Curried 97
Apples, Foil-Baked 146
Apricots, Broiled 107
Bananas, Baked, in Currant Jelly .139
Bananas, Baked, in Fresh Orange

Juice 139
Bananas, Fried 35
Beet and Cucumber Relish 90
Bread-and-Butter Pickles 74
Cabbage Pickle, Chopped- 23
Cantaloupe, Spiced 24
Ceci all' Olio (Chick-Peas in Olive
  Oil) 82
Cherries, Pickled 49
Chili Sauce 64
Chowchow, Pennsylvania Dutch .. 90
Chutney, West Indies Apple 102
Corn Relish 39
Cucumber-Onion Relish 90
Figs, 5-Day Pickled 59
Green Peppers, Pickled 82
Ketchup, Fruit 53
Ketchup, Green-Tomato 41
Mushrooms, Pickled Cooked 90
Olives, California Style 89
Olives, Garlic Ripe 89
Olives in Cheese 89
Peaches, Pickled 34
Potato Garnitures, Suggestions for
  Idaho Baked 35
Prune Plums, Pickled Idaho 36
Raw Vegetable Relish 34
Refrigerator Summer Relish 90
Tomato Appetizer 89

PIES, TARTS, AND PASTRIES
Apple
Apple Pie 96
Butter Pie, Apple- 79
Cream Pie, Apple 100
Deep-Dish Apple Pie 101
Dried-Apple Pie 103
Honey Apple Pie 56
Meringue Cake, Apple 101
Pam's Apple Pie with Cheese 28
Raisin Pie, Apple-Cider 39
Spread Apple Pie 75
Strudel, Apple 101
Turnover Apple Pie, New Hamp-
  shire 57
Upside-Down Apple Pie 102
Apricot
Cream-Cheese Tarts, Apricot ...106
Crumb Pie, Apricot 107
Prune Pie, Apricot 108
Strudel, Apricot 108
Avocado Lime Pie 130
Banana Cream Pie 139
Banbury Tarts 142
Carrot Pie 54
Cheese Tartlets 87
Cherry Pie 77
Cherry Pie, Chantilly 78
Huckleberry Pie, Wild 77
Peach Cream Almond Pie 65
Pecan
Arizona Pecan and Date Pie 24
Pecan Pie 34
Polynees (Swedish Almond Tarts) . 69
Rhubarb Pie 69
Sage-Honey Sour-Cream Pie 55
Shoofly Pie 66
Strawberry Chess Tarts 72

POULTRY
Chicken
Aspic, Chicken 116
Backhendl (Fried Chicken) 122
Charcoal-Broiled Chicken 146
Chicken Luau 34
Chicken Smothered in Oysters ... 67
Chicken with Hard Cider 37
Country Captain 33
Fried Chicken, Lemon- 29
Fried Chicken, Maryland 46
Fried Chicken, Topeka 39
Fried Chicken with Puffs and
  Gravy 22
Mousse, Chicken-Almond 14

Paprikahühner (Paprika
  Chicken) 122
Picnic Chicken 64
Picnic Dinner, Sand-Pail 73
Tatsuta-Age (Japanese Fried
  Chicken) 26
Cornish Game Hens with Apples . 57
Cornish Game Hens with
  Sauerkraut 52
Duck
Hausente als Wildente (Duck
  Cooked Like Wild Duck) 122
Jambalaya de Canard 44
Roast Long Island Duckling ... 60
Goose, Chinese Roast 81
Turkey
Barbecued Turkey 72
Roast Turkey with Savory Giblet-
  Butternut Stuffing 74

SALADS
Combination
Artichoke and Shrimp Salad 112
Avocado Crabmeat Salad à la
  Ritz 130
Avocados, Crabmeat Stuffed 130
Avocado Shrimp Boats, Puerto
  Rican 130
Caesar Salad 27
Eggs in Aspic à la Française.....117
July Day Salad 14
Maionese di Scampi e Cavol Fiori
  (Shrimp and Cauliflower Salad) 82
Waldorf Salad 60
Waldorf Salad, Jellied 100
Fruit
Apple-Bavarian Slaw 100
Apple Salad, Golden 77
Apple Salad, Party 100
Apricot-Cheese Salad 106
Apricot Salad, Stuffed 108
Banana and Cantaloupe Salad ...142
Cider Gelatin Salad 103
Fruit Salad Bowl 33
Guava Salads 33
Meat
Chicken-Avocado Salad 130
Chicken Salad, Almond- 14
Duck Salad, Alaska 23
Ham Salad 38
Tongue Ring, Jellied 117
Vegetable
Artichoke Halves 112
Artichoke Halves, Greek Style .112
Artichoke Hearts Piquant 112
Artichoke Hearts Salad 112
Asparagus Salad, Sesame 115
Aspic, Quick 116
Avocado Gelatin Salad 130
Bean and Cheese Salad 159
Bean Salad 79
Bean Salad, Cheyenne River.... 68
Bean Salad, Kidney- 159
Bean Salad, White and Red 159
Bean, Wax, and Onion Salad 157
Celery Salad, Oregon 65
Cucumber Mousse 36
Florida "Gaspachy" Salad 33
Gurkensalat (Cucumber Salad) ..123
Leek Salad 57
Lettuce or Spinach, Wilted 38
Lima-Bean Salad 146
Potato Salad with Bacon, Hot ...134
Spinach and Onion Salad 73
Tomato and Mushroom Salad ... 82
Tomato Aspic 119
Vegetables in Aspic 119
Virginia City Salad 56

SANDWICHES
Apple Sandwiches 102
Applesauce Frenchies 102
Denver Sandwiches 27
Peanut Butter and Bacon

Sandwich 134

SAUCES, GRAVIES, AND GLAZES
Aïoli 7
Allemande, Sauce 10
Amandine, Sauce 14
Asparagus Sauce 1: Hollandaise ..114
Asparagus Sauce 2: Hollandaise,
   Quick Blender 114
Asparagus Sauce 3: Polonaise ..114
Asparagus Sauce 4: Salsa Verde ..115
Bacon Sauce with Peas 134
Barbecue Sauce, Apricot 147
Barbecue Sauce, Greek 146
Barbecue Sauce, Orange 146
Barbecue Sauce, Savory Lemon ..146
Basic à la Grecque Recipe for
   Vegetables 7
Bordelaise, Sauce 144
Bread Syrup, Squaw 64
Butter, Pepper 64
Butter, Watercress 25
Caper Sauce 63
Cider Sauce for Meats 103
Gravy, Cream 74
Gravy, Raisin 39
Hawaiian Coconut Cream 35
Hot Sauce, Texas 146
Jelly Sauce 40
Onion Cream Sauce 41
Pesto Genovese 148
Shrimp Cocktail Sauce with
   Mustard 87
Sour-Cream Sauce, Apple- 96

SHELLFISH
Abalone Sauté 5
Clams, Fried, or Fannie Daddies.. 66
Crabs
   Custard, Crab 33
   Deviled Crab Cakes 29
   Dungeness Crab Louis 76
   Fried Soft-Shell Crabs 45
   Rémoulade, Crabmeat or Shrimp. 86
   Stuffed Crabs 50
Crayfish Sauté 73
Diamondback Terrapin 46
Lobster, Broiled 146
Oysters
   Antoine's Oysters Rockefeller ... 41
   Creamed Turkey and Oysters ... 47
   Fricassee, Oyster 45
   Pickled Oysters 28
   Steamed Oysters 60
Scallops, Scalloped 45
Shrimp
   Corn Pie, Shrimp and 67
   Curry, Banana-Shrimp 139
   Pilau St. Augustine, Shrimp 32

SOUPS AND STEWS
Almond Bouillon 75
Almond Soup 14
Cheddar Cheese Soup 60
Combination
   Booyaw 48
   Brunswick Stew 75
   Chicken-Shrimp Gumbo Filé ... 44
   Kentucky Burgoo 40
   Miss Mollie's Boiled Pot 61
   Okra Soup 22
   Pepper Pot Soup 65
Meat
   Beef-Vegetable Soup, Stockyard
      Inn 36
   Black Kettle Soup 40
   Meatball Soup 24
   Scotch Broth 147
   Sheepherder's Stew 55
   Sopa de Albondigas (Meatball
      Soup) 59
   Veal Stew with Almonds in Sour
      Cream 14

Seafood
   Abalone Chowder 5
   Bullhead or Catfish Soup 52
   Cioppino, Fisherman's Wharf .. 26
   Crab Soup, Martha Washington's. 75
   Crab Soup, Nutmeg State 28
   Lobster Stew, Wiscasset 45
   Maine Seafood Chowder 45
   Pine-Bark Stew 61
   Razor Clam Bisque 64
   She-Crab Soup, Charleston 67
   Shrimp Stew, Biloxi 50
   Whitefish Stew, Piquant 48
Vegetable
   Avocado Soup, Chilled 130
   Bean Soup, Different 54
   Bean Soup, Portuguese 158
   Bean Soup, Senate 157
   Bean Stew, Cowpuncher's 24
   Bean Stew, Western 158
   Cauliflower Soup, Cream of ... 55
   Corn Chowder, Iowa 38
   Gerstensuppe (Barley Soup) ...121
   Jungle Stew 79
   Lentil Soup 39
   Mormon Vegetable Stew 73
   Potato Soup, Aroostook County.. 44
   Rivvel Soup 66
   Salt-Pork Soup, Old-Time, with
      Dumplings 56

VEGETABLES
Acorn Squash
   Baked Acorn Squash Supreme ... 7
   Sausage-Stuffed Acorn Squash ... 7
   Steamed Acorn Squash 7
Artichokes, Two Simple Ways to
   Cook 112
Asparagus
   Asparagi all' Uovo 113
   Asparagus and Mushrooms
      in Cream 113
   Asparagus with Herb
      Butter 115
   Cheese-Broiled Asparagus 113
   French-Fried Asparagus 57
   Scalloped, Asparagus 114
   Soufflé, Asparagus 115
Bamboo Shoots, Sautéed 138
Beans
   Au Gratin, Beans 157
   Bacony Beans 132
   Baked Beans, Boston 47
   Baked Beans, Chutney 159
   Baked Beans, Michigan 48
   Baked Beans, New England ...159
   Baked Beans, Southern Style .. 158
   Baked Beans with Ham 158
   Black Beans and Rice 158
   Blackeye Beans, Southern Style .. 159
   Boiled Beans, Chuck Wagon .. 53
   Breton Beans 159
   Butter Beans with Pecans 69
   Creole Style, Beans 158
   Green Beans and Mushrooms ...154
   Green Beans with Tomatoes,
      Stewed 154
   Hoppin John 22
   Hot Bean Pot 59
   Mexican Re-fried Beans 59
   Ranch House Beans 73
   Red Beans and Rice 44
   Soybeans, Tomato-Cheese 158
   Succotash, Cranberry-Bean ... 159
   Succotash, Three-Bean 154
   Succotash, Two-Bean, with Pork
      Cubes 38
Bean Sprouts, Sautéed 159
Beets, Harvard 47
Cabbage
   Bacon and Cheese Sauce,
      Cabbage with 68

Paradeiskraut (Cabbage with
   Tomatoes) 122
Red Cabbage, Spicy Apples and..100
Carrots, Scalloped 54
Celery Fritters 73
Combination
   Apples, Onions, and Raisins,
      Sautéed 100
   Fiddleheads, Milkweed, and
      other Roadside Greens 45
   Kopfsalat mit Erbsen (Romaine
      Lettuce with Peas) 123
   Peas, Green, and New Potatoes
      with Cream 28
   Raw Vegetable Tray or Bowl 87
   Schlee 76
Corn
   Baked Corn 53
   Cakes, Green-Corn 67
   Fritters, Nebraska Corn 54
   Oysters, Corn 28
   Oysters, Idaho Corn 36
   Roast Corn 145
   Scalloped Corn 67
   Soufflé Pudding, Southern Corn-.. 22
   Squaw Corn 27
   Squaw Dish 61
Cucumber Slices 89
Endive Tempura 89
Hearts of Palm in Cream 32
Kale with Pork 48
Mushrooms
   Baked Mushrooms 77
   Marinated Mushrooms 89
   Mushrooms in Foil 144
Onions
   Baked Onions 36
   French-Fried Onion Rings 77
   Sweet Onions with Orégano ...145
Parsnip Fritters 68
Potatoes
   Filling, Berks County Potato 66
   Fried Potatoes, Raw 38
   G'röste' mit Rosmarin (Home-
      Fried Potatoes with Rosemary).123
Rutabaga Ring 49
Squash
   Pancakes, Squash 63
   Whole Glazed, Squash 62
Sweet Potatoes
   Allspice, Sweet Potatoes with ... 11
   Arizona Sweet Potatoes 24
   Candied Sweet Potatoes 50
   Sweet Potato Poi 35
   Sweet Potato Pone 33
Tomatoes
   Candied Tomatoes, Baked 22
   Fried Tomatoes, Hoosier,
      Creamy Gravy 37
   Spiced Whole Tomatoes, Hot ... 55
   Tomato Dish 46
Turnips
   Hashed Turnips 56
   Turnip Greens with Hog Jowl .. 69
   Turnip Greens with Raw
      Vegetable Relish 34

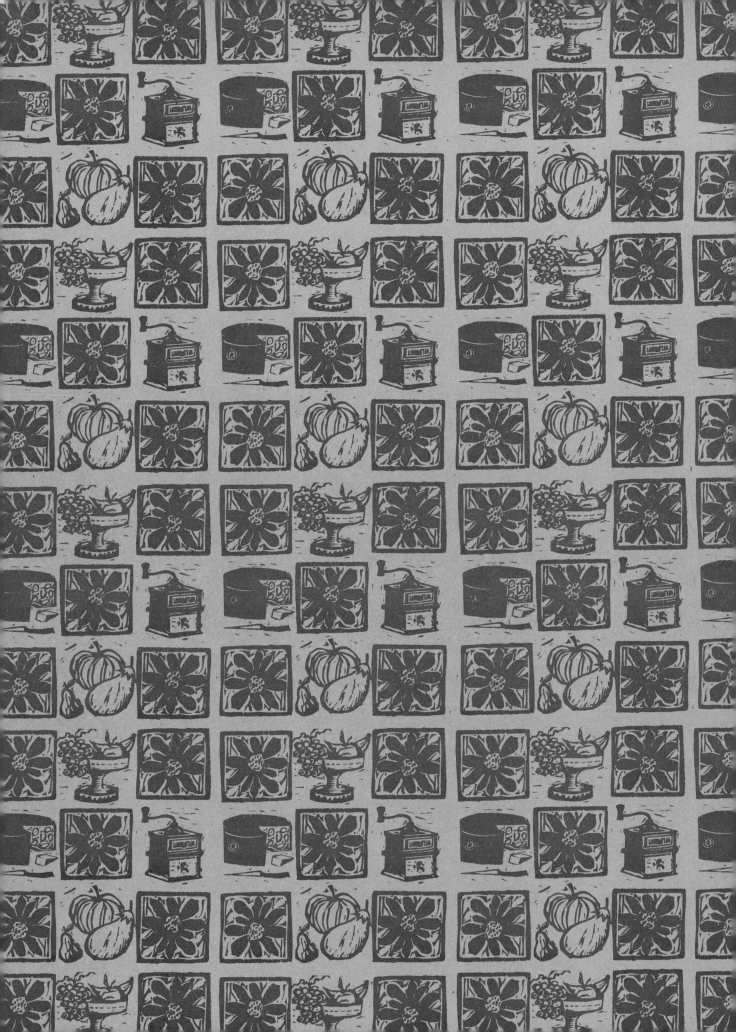